# Food, States, and Peasants

# About the Book and Editor

One of the most serious problems facing the Middle East and North Africa is the region's growing inability to feed its expanding population. Rapidly escalating demand has made the region highly dependent on food imports, and policy initiatives intended to increase domestic production have met with mixed success at best. The contributors to this volume examine the historical origins of state policies toward agriculture, recent policy changes and their effects on domestic supply, and the social and political implications of these shifts. Focusing on the region's largest agricultural economies, contributors analyze Turkey's strong performance as well as Egypt's weak response to its agricultural problems. Pricing, investment strategies, irrigation policies, and the impact of large-scale labor migration on agricultural sectors are discussed, and a common theme of the interplay between politics and economics runs throughout.

Alan Richards is associate professor of economics at the University of California, Santa Cruz. He is the author of *Egypt's Agricultural Development, 1800–1980* (Westview, 1981) and co-editor of *Migration, Mechanization, and the Agricultural Labor Market in Egypt* (Westview, 1983).

Sponsored by the Joint Committee
on the Near and Middle East
of the American Council of Learned Societies
and the Social Science Research Council

# Food, States, and Peasants

## Analyses of the Agrarian Question in the Middle East

Routledge
Taylor & Francis Group
NEW YORK AND LONDON

First published 1986 by Westview Press

Published in 2021 by Routledge
605 Third Avenue, New York, NY 10017
2 Park Square, Milton Park, Abingdon, Oxon OX14 4RN

*Routledge is an imprint of the Taylor & Francis Group, an informa business*



Library of Congress Cataloging-in-Publication Data
Food, states, and peasants.
(Westview special studies on the Middle East)
Includes index.
I. Agriculture and state–Near East–Addresses, essays, lectures. 2. Near East–Economic policy–Addresses, essays, lectures. I. Richards, Alan, 1946– . II. Series.
HD2056.S.Z8F66 1986 338.1'856 86-233
ISBN 0-8133-7117-1

ISBN 13: 978-0-3670-0576-4 (hbk)
ISBN 13: 978-0-3671-5563-6 (pbk)

For Piero Bronzi

# Contents

## Contents

# Tables and Figures

# Acknowledgments

This volume is based on papers presented at an international workshop sponsored by the Social Science Research Council (SSRC). and hosted by the International Fund for Agricultural Development (IFAD) in Rome during September, 1984. The themes of the workshop were the interaction of food problems, government policy, and social class formation; these issues are discussed in more detail in Chapter 1. The workshop focused on Turkey and Egypt with participation by specialists on the Maghreb, especially Tunisia, as well. Turkey is the principal "success story" of Middle Eastern agriculture; it is the only net grain exporter in the region, and its agricultural technology has undergone considerable change during the last generation. Further, state policy has generally aided and fostered this transformation. We hoped that consideration of the Turkish case might be instructive for those concerned with other countries. The inclusion of Egypt stems from that country's importance both as the largest Arab country and also as a nation with an extremely intensive agricultural production system, yet one which is increasingly incapable of feeding its own population. Since a similar situation, generally called the problem of "food security", is rampant throughout the region and is especially acute in North Africa, consideration of the country where this issue has advanced furthest seemed appropriate. The Egyptian government's policy of extracting resources from agriculture also makes an instructive contrast with the generally more supportive policies of Turkish governments.

The workshop was a somewhat unusual collaboration between an old, academically-oriented American institution and a new, practically-minded international development lending agency. The workshop organizers hoped that mutual benefits would accrue from bringing together analysts of Middle and Near Eastern agricultural problems who are based in universities with those who work in international development institutions. Although the perspectives of these two groups of specialists are too often perceived as conflicting, the workshop demonstrated the much greater degree of complementarity between them. The more theoretical, historical, and long-run perspectives of academic analysts help to provide a context for the daily problems which confront all those working in international agencies. At the same time, academics profit from the "reality therapy" afforded by close discussion of their theories with people with an intimate, immediate, first-hand knowledge of practical agricultural development problems. I would like to thank all of the workshop participants, and especially members of the IFAD staff, for their contributions to this dialogue.

IFAD was an especially appropriate host for our deliberations. The organization is committed to financing projects which are designed to promote the development of the small-farm sector in LDCs. Such an approach is eminently reasonable on grounds of static efficiency (small farmers usually produce more per unit land than do large farmers), economic growth (they constitute a huge potential domestic market for labor-intensive industrial products), and distributive equity (many of them are poor). The theoretical attractiveness of an "agricultural development-led strategy"[1] over alternative "import-substituting industrialization" approaches has been extensively argued for nearly two decades. Given current problems of the international economy, such a strategy is also more practical than the highly touted "export-led growth" strategy, especially for very poor countries.[2] Since the workshop focused on the interactions of farm distribution, state policy, and effects on the poor, IFAD was a logical choice of venue.

Further, IFAD is an institution borne of international cooperation, specifically, between the OECD and the OPEC nations. In its small way, the workshop was a microcosm of such cooperation, bringing together scholars from the Middle East, Western Europe, and the United States. For this reason, also, we are grateful to have had IFAD as our host. In particular, I would like to thank Mr. Abdelmuhsin Al-Sudeary, President of IFAD at the time of the workshop, Mr. Moise Mensah, Vice-President of IFAD, and Mr. Donald Brown, Vice-President of IFAD, for their encouragement and support. I would also like to thank the Joint Committee on the Near and Middle East of the SSRC/American Council of Learned Societies for funding the project. I am especially endebted to Dr. Nikiforos Diamandouros, of the SSRC staff, for his intellectual and practical assistance. I would also like to thank Alain de Janvry, who first suggested that I approach IFAD, not only for his practical assistance and encouragement, but also for his numerous acute interventions during the course of the workshop. We all benefited from his insights.

This volume is dedicated to Piero Bronzi, Technical Advisor at IFAD. Without his unflagging support, energy, and hard-work, the workshop would never have taken place at all. He combines an intimate personal knowledge of Mediterranean agriculture (as the son of a Tuscan farmer) and thorough professional training at the Universities of Bari and Illinois with a deep commitment to agricultural development. For nearly two decades, first at the Ford Foundation and now at IFAD, he has worked selflessly to ameliorate the living and working conditions of farmers and farm workers of the Near and Middle East and elsewhere in the Third World. By advocating, designing, supervising, and monitoring countless development projects aimed at such groups, he has made concrete contributions to agrarian development which are an inspiration to us

[1]As outlined, for example, by Irma Adelman: "Beyond Export-Led Growth", *World Development*, 9 (September, 1984).

[2]It is ironic that the increasing consensus among development specialists on the logic of agricultural development-led growth strategies, vigorously supported by IFAD and by its projects, has been accompanied by increasing financial niggardliness toward IFAD by the United States government.

all. The volume is dedicated to Piero as a modest recognition of his years of work on solving the problems which find analysis in this volume.

*Alan Richards*

# 1

# Introduction

*Alan Richards*

## THE ISSUES

The issues underlying the papers in this volume are both scholarly and practical. From an academic perspective, three intersecting issues stand out: 1) the choice of levels of analysis, 2) the dynamics of the differentiation of the peasantry, and 3) the role of state policy in that process and for agricultural development more generally. The first question is really an implicit one: How best to integrate analysis at the international, the national, and the local levels? Nearly all students of the rural Third World would agree that some comprehension of each level is essential for a grasp of the dynamics of agricultural development, but the relative weights given to each level vary considerably from one scholar to the next. Few doubt the necessity of detailed knowledge of local economic and political relations, but their conceptual and practical independence from national and transnational forces is highly contentious. The importance of national policy and its relations with both international and local forces implicitly inform all discussions of agricultural development, whether scholarly or practical. But how autonomous national economic policies in less developed countries are from transnational forces has been intensely debated for several decades. The impact of the international economic conjuncture on national governments' room for maneuver in constructing and implementing agricultural and industrial growth strategies is an especially salient question in the Middle East, where the problems of the largesse generated by a decade of oil wealth now suddenly give way to the problems of austerity during the "oil crunch". The contributors to this volume focus primarily on the national level, but many also include a local perspective, an international context, or both.

Second, all contributors to this volume investigate how agricultural development affects different social actors and the ways in which these actors in turn can shape that same process. That is, all offer analysis of the dynamics of the differentiation of the peasantry in the region: they constitute contributions to the debate on the "agrarian question" in the Middle East. Understanding the dynamics of interaction among large farms, on the one hand, and small farmers and farm laborers on the other is crucial for understanding the dynamics of agricultural output growth, of employment creation, of the distribution of income and of migration patterns. Such issues, in their turn, dominate debate on the political economy of food and agriculture in the region.

Third, all participants address the question of the role of state policy in shaping the processes of agricultural development and peasant differentiation and the implications of the problems created by those processes for state action. The impact of policy on agriculture is widely debated. At the risk of excessive generalization, workshop participants consider here two different "policy mixes", one designed primarily to extract a surplus from agriculture (Egypt) and one constructed to support agricultural incomes and, therefore, domestic demand for industrial products (Turkey). The impact of policies on different peasant groups or rural social classes receives considerable attention, and the extent to which such groups in turn mould state policy undergoes careful scrutiny. In particular, the often debated issues of the "autonomy of state policy" or of state actors looms large in several papers, and is implicitly treated (if in some cases to be rejected) in others.

The practical issues confronting Middle East agriculture and agricultural policy are straightforward--and stark. First, there is the overwhelming problem of "food security". One of the most serious problems facing the Middle East and North Africa is the region's growing inability to feed itself. The rising imbalance between consumption and domestic production constituted the Achilles heel of the oil boom of the 1970s. Rapidly escalating effective demand and sluggish domestic supply response have made the region the least food self-sufficient area of the world. Although there have been fears of politically motivated boycotts, the real problem has turned out to be economic: how to pay the enormous import bills? This trade problem is related to a second critical issue: how to finance the urban food subsidies which prevail in many countries of the region? Both are related to a final question: how to create sufficient employment for a rapidly growing labor force? This problem is especially acute in the cities, because of the "rural exodus". The combination of increased food dependency, faltering trade balances, inadequate job creation, and continual rural-to-urban migration creates strong political pressures on the states of the region. The trade-offs facing policy makers are often grim; practical development workers face the unenviable task of trying to promote growth with equity in an environment of growing austerity.

Merely stating these practical problems immediately raises the issue of the interpenetration of levels of analysis. A common perspective is an "internationalist" one, in which the policies and outcomes in Third

World countries are conceptualized as derivative of forces in the international political economy. Although there have been some useful recent additions to the study of the political economy of the Middle East which draw on the dependency approach or its cousin, the "world system's" framework,[1] the theoretical and empirical problems of these perspectives which assert the dominance of transnational forces have been repeatedly emphasized. In particular, the absence of a persuasive theory of social change, the lack of attention to unintended outcomes, the downplaying of forces specific to a nation or locality, and the rather mechanical approach to underdevelopment and class formation have come in for especially heavy criticism.[2] The evident difficulties and weaknesses of this cluster of theories have led to renewed attention to the national and local levels, an attention which, however, is now better informed by an understanding of the need to locate such developments in their international context.[3]

This recasting of the questions of how to approach complex problems of agrarian political economy seems especially appropriate for the Middle East and North Africa. There is little doubt that the agrarian question in the region has been dominated for the past ten years by the Oil Price Revolution, and now, by the apparent counter-revolution of drastically lower real oil prices. The escalation of demand for food, the sluggishness of domestic supply response, the ability to finance food imports, and the accelerating rural exodus have all been linked directly or indirectly to the oil boom. Such international forces have also, however, stimulated widely different responses by different social actors: by states, by large and small farmers, and by farm workers. The analyses in this volume focus on the national and local levels without ever losing sight of the critical importance of external factors, such as the availability of export revenues or migration outlets.

## THE DYNAMICS OF PEASANT DIFFERENTIATION IN THE MIDDLE EAST: POLARIZATION OR PEASANT SURVIVAL?

The second major scholarly issue raised in the volume is that of the differentiation of the peasantry. The vast literature on this world-wide topic may be divided into two broad arguments or "schools". On the one hand, there are those who believe that the process of agricultural development, of growth of output and of technological change, are fundamentally *polarizing*. This perspective may be traced back to the Marxist classics of Kautsky and Lenin.[4] The argument posits, first, a relatively undifferentiated pre-capitalist rural social structure. Second, as capitalism penetrates agriculture, the population divides into five classes: landlords, rich peasants, middle peasants, poor peasants, and landless workers. The origins of this schema were the direct empirical observations of the Russian and Chinese countryside by Lenin and Mao, respectively.[5] John Roemer has arrived at the same structure of classes by deductive logic, assuming only that actors maximize utility, that leisure is a normal good, and that land ownership alone differentiates peasants.

In essence, the concentration of land ownership (assumed to be exogenous) combined with the emergence of markets for outputs and labor (or credit) in a previously undifferentiated community will generate these five classes.[6]

Most importantly, however, adherents to the classical Marxist position on peasant differentiation hold that this five class structure is *unstable*; the continued development of capitalism in agriculture will generate *only two* major rural classes: a class of large, capitalist farmers on the one hand, and a class of landless agricultural wage-workers on the other. Defenders of this theory usually argue that such a result is a *long-run tendency*, the outcome of a protracted process of capitalist development. In earlier stages of development more characteristic of today's Third World, analysts working within this tradition typically employ the "five class scheme".

The stress throughout is on land ownership: peasants are fundamentally differentiated by their varying access to land. However, access to other inputs and the form of labor market participation (i.e., whether the family hires labor or family members hire themselves out to others) are also central variables in such analysis. The argument assumes that the peasantry is relatively undifferentiated before the rise of private property in land and the commercialization of farming. But once the peasants are "linked" to product and labor markets the five classes emerge, as some gain and others lose from the simultaneous processes of the consolidation of property rights and the expansion of economic opportunities. More empirical analyses try to take into account the extensive "interlinking" of markets in the rural Third World, in which, for example, a poor peasant's access to credit is tied to his willingness to work for a particular landlord at peak season.[7] Although such messy, intermediate cases are recognized, all analysts in this tradition argue that capitalist agrarian development tends to push most middle and poor peasants toward the bottom, while a few, lucky, relatively rich peasants will join the ranks of the agrarian capitalists or landlords. The mechanisms differ (default on loans, fragmentation through inheritance, outright seizure, distress sales of land, etc.), but the end result is held to be the same: polarization.

Examples of such a perspective abound in studies of the Middle East. For Egypt, perhaps the most prominent is the work of Mahmoud Abdel-Fadil.[8] Using data from the agricultural censuses of 1950 and 1960, he presented over ten years ago a detailed picture of the differentiation of the peasantry by land ownership, crop mix, and input use, especially of machinery and hired labor. As Aricanli notes (Chapter 2), discussions of the agrarian question in Turkey have been dominated by a similar perspective: the role of landlordism has attracted most attention. Similar work also exists on North African countries.[9]

Empirical evidence from many parts of the world suggests not only that in many cases the extent of differentiation has been exaggerated, but also that the "disappearance" of such intermediate groups as middle and poor peasants has been extremely protracted, at best. The second "school" on peasant differentiation is a loose collection of analysts going back at least to Chayanov[10] which argues the case for "peasant persistence". Researchers such as Lewin and Kingston-Mann have shown that Lenin's classical study of Russian agriculture, from which so many other analysts have drawn inspiration and a conceptual framework, greatly exaggerated the extent to which peasant differentiation had actually occurred there by the eve of World War I.[11] Indeed, the agricultures of even the most advanced capitalist countries fail to conform to the model of polarization. Wage-labor is not the norm in the agriculture of such nations; despite exceptions, as in some unmechanized fruit and vegetable production, highly mechanized farms employing largely family labor, not vast "factories in the field", are the norm. Similarly, in Turkey both Aricanli and Uner (Chapter 9) argue that small peasant farms continue to be the mode, while, as Adams stresses, in Egypt not only are small farms common (farms smaller than five *feddans*[12] cover more than one-half of Egypt's farm area), but also small and landless peasants are bound by vertical linkages of loans and jobs to their wealthier neighbors. Uner notes the same kind of vertical linkages in his "transitional" villages.

A major theme of many of the papers which treat the issues of peasant differentiation is that of the "survival strategies" of small peasants. The need for local level analysis is especially strong here; only by detailed empirical studies can we learn much about how poor rural people manage to survive. Small farmers and landless agricultural workers have been able to improve their situation during the past decade in two major ways: 1) by renting in land and cropping intensively (a "commercialization strategy"), and/or 2) by emigration (an "exit strategy").[13] In Egypt, for example, very small farmers produce the bulk of dairy and livestock products, whose demand is stimulated by growing incomes and whose supply is limited by government trade restrictions. By renting in small parcels of land and cropping them very intensively, they manage to obtain sufficient "food entitlements" and, in some cases, even some additional income.[14] Such a strategy also seems to have been available to small farmers in the better watered regions of Turkey.

However, such choices are not open to all small farmers: Adams (Chapter 6) presents evidence from Minya Governorate where government regulations thwart such activity; Radwan also stresses these difficulties. And, of course, such "commercialization" strategies are closed to most of the landless.[15] Only an increase in rural real wages and employment can help them. Their situation improved during the oil boom, as higher paying jobs appeared either in construction in the major cities or in the oil exporting countries. There is clear evidence of an increase in rural real wages throughout the region during the 1970s, implying both a considerable outflow of labor stimulated by the oil boom and an improved food entitlement position for those agricultural laborers remaining behind. At the same time, the responses in cropping systems, land yields, and (so far) the pattern of mechanization seem to have increased the demand for agricultural labor. The shift to fruit and especially vegetables has raised the demand for labor in many cases; the need to rely on increased land yields for production increases also implies considerable potential for raising the demand for agricultural labor.

Increased incomes from the "commercialization strategy" and (probably more important but poorly documented) the flow of remittances into rural areas from ex-peasants working abroad have stimulated considerable construction activity and service employment in some rural areas of the region. A nation-wide survey in Egypt has shown that most small peasant households now obtain a *majority* of their income from non-agricultural sources.[16] Uner documents similar processes--and their problems--in rural Turkey. Radwan's data indicate that the distribution of household expenditure became more equal in rural Egypt during the 1970s. Since land ownership was becoming less equal, improved employment opportunities (and perhaps gains from the "commercialization strategy") presumably explain this phenomenon of greater equity. A combination of the two survival strategies open to small farmers seems to have belied the "polarization" perspective and to have confirmed the "peasant persistence" viewpoint.

However, "the game is hardly over": there are reasons to doubt the long-run efficacy of either strategy, given the growth of population and the limitations on arable land inherent in regional geography. First, as Adams shows, some areas and many persons are left behind in this process; as Radwan stresses, having a family member who can migrate has become a new, critical variable in peasant differentiation. Second, private farmers are rapidly mechanizing their operations, usually with extensive governnment subsidies. Although there is no evidence that this pattern has yet reduced the demand for agricultural labor, there can be little doubt that eventually continued mechanization will have this effect. In Turkey, where mechanization has proceeded furthest, Uner argues that the demand for agricultural labor was reduced over a several decade period. Third and most importantly, the slackening of oil exporters' demand for unskilled labor will leave the remaining rural poor in a very difficult situation, as the supply of labor in rural areas grows more rapidly than in the last decade (when millions left the countryside), but the demand grows more slowly, due to past mechanization. Just as the emigration outlet for Turkish workers to Germany narrowed sharply in the 1970s, so too are openings for the emigration of rural Egyptians to the Gulf constricting now. The viability of the several survival strategies, and therefore, of peasant persistence, are being called into question by transnational forces.

The same processes are also inexplicable without considering the role of state action. In the first place, the distribution of assets, especially land, is the outcome of state action, as shown by Owen (Chapter 3) for Egypt for the periods both of "non-reform" before 1952 and of Nasser's reforms. Aricanli argues that the failure of large landlordism to emerge in Turkey can only be explained by positing and analyzing an independent state actor whose initiatives largely determined the outcome. Second, state policies toward agricultural production also affect peasant differentiation. Some policies, such as Egypt's protection of livestock products, contribute to peasant persistence, while others, such as generous subsidized credit schemes, stimulate polarization. Efforts to conceptualize this role of the state are treated in more detail below; here it is simply noted that it is impossible to understand the process of peasant differentiation without explicitly considering the role of state policy.

Why do we care about the process of the differentiation (or its absence) of the peasantry? Of course, one reason is a concern for peasant "entitlements" to food. But there are further economic and political reasons for such a focus. The economic issues arise on both the supply and the demand sides, while the political aspects include not only whether state policy towards the agricultural sector is determined independently of any rural social group, but also how the outcome of the development process in the countryside creates problems, such as migration to the cities, to which the state must respond.

One long standing position on the "agrarian question" holds that the differentiation of farmers and of farms into "large" and "small" impedes the growth of agricultural supply. Given the importance of increasing agricultural production to alleviate national and regional food dependency, the issue is vitally important in the region. We may distinguish several forms of the argument. An old tradition holds that large estates, are "inefficient remnants of feudalism". This viewpoint asserts that wealthy landlords were "unproductive", mere rent collectors and social drones, indulging in lavish display and conspicuous consumption, rather than investing in technological improvements. The existence of large estates, as in Egypt and Eastern Turkey, allegedly retarded technological change and reduced the responsiveness of the agrarian sector. Here, as elsewhere in debates on the political economy of development, much of the literature has come from Latin America, where such arguments undergirded the "structuralist" school of the 1950s and 1960s, which argued that the resulting unresponsiveness of the agricultural sector was largely responsible for inflation.[17]

Apart from the by now well-known difficulties of using terms like "feudalism" outside of their Western European (and perhaps Japanese) contexts, there are several problems with this argument. As Aricanli shows, successive Turkish governments continually combatted the emergence of large estates and of large landlordism. Consequently, the concentration of land ownership in most of Anatolia was considerably less pronounced there than in many areas of Latin America. In Egypt, by contrast, political exigencies spawned large estates and a highly skewed distribution of land ownership. But as Owen argues, the mere existence of gross inequalities of land ownership does not necessarily imply that Egyptian landlords were uninterested in improving their land or even in investing in industrial ventures; the historical record suggests otherwise.

It is true that, because of problems of supervising agricultural labor and because of the ecology of crop rotation in the Egyptian Delta, land and labor were combined in the so-called *ezbah* system, in which workers were paid by granting them a parcel of land on which to produce their own subsistence crops. However, as Owen and others have argued, this cannot be taken as evidence of inefficiency. *Given* the initial distribution of property rights, the concentation of land ownership, the difficulties of supervising agricultural labor, and the peculiarities of agricultural, as opposed to industrial, production, the resulting system seems "rational".[18] The case for the "inefficient, feudal landlord" seems weak.

However, this "Nth-Best efficiency" hardly implies that a skewed distribution of land ownership does not shape farm technology and crop choices. Nor does it mean that a redistribution of land might not have increased aggregate agricultural production, as well as enhanced social equity. There now exists something of a consensus that large and small farmers face different opportunity costs for different factors of production; consequently, differences in output mix and in input use are to be expected. The existence of such differences creates a *prima facie* case for inefficiency, since they imply some form of market failure.

This argument is most pronounced in the various forms of the theory of "dualism". Although more extreme earlier formulations obviously have little relevance to the Middle East, more recent, nuanced treatments seem worth considering. It is important to note, however, that the thrust of these arguments is *not* that large landlordism or inequality of land ownership impedes technological change or slows the supply response of the agricultural sector. Rather, the position is that the pattern of growth under these conditions is likely to be disequalizing and to do little to reduce mass poverty. Using Latin America, again, as the point of departure, economists of both the liberal (Johnston and Kilby) and the Marxist (de Janvry) persuasions argue that large landlords do indeed innovate and accumulate.[19] But the result is likely to be polarization, as argued in the Turkish case by Uner. The danger facing some Middle Eastern countries, perhaps especially those of the Maghreb, is that state responses to food deficits, which will naturally emphasize production above all, will contribute to the polarization of the rural population, to the rural exodus, and to the perpetuation of poverty of large numbers of people, as has occurred in countries like Brazil.

The real problem with the pattern of distribution of land ownership is not so much its consequences for agricultural supply and economic growth as its implications for the *kind* of growth, for the satisfaction of basic human needs, and for the resulting pattern of demand for industrial goods. This raises the issue of overall development strategy once again, and in particular, juxtaposes an "extractionist" policy towards agriculture with one which seeks to raise agrarian incomes to provide the source of demand for simple industrial goods. The discussion of this issue in the volume, which contrasts the Egyptian (extractivist) approach with the Turkish (supportive), tends to support those who advocate the latter.

The specific arguments offered here find support in both the orthodox and the Marxist literature on development. The concept of "articulation" or "linkages" is an old one in development theory of all types; recently the argument has been developed with particular relevance to Latin American agriculture by de Janvry, and more generally, by Adelman in her concept of "agricultural development-led industrialization".[20] For all of these analysts, the key is the development of a home market for simple industrial products. *If* the process can start with a relatively even distribution of assets, and *if* local industry produces such goods, then a "virtuous circle" of rising employment, rising incomes, rising demand for output, increasing output, and increasing demand for labor can be created. But a highly skewed distribution of land ownership and policies which discriminate against agriculture to the point of sharply lowering rural incomes will thwart such a development pattern.

This problem, rather than any problems with agricultural supply, may be the really baleful legacy of large landlordism of the Egyptian type, a legacy which the Nasserists only partially overturned.[21] By contrast, the better performance of both agriculture and industry in the Turkish case may be partly the result not only of the long campaign of the state against landlordism, but also of attempts to raise rural incomes through the various support policies enumerated by Somel (Chapter 4) and Kasnakoglu (Chapter 5). However, the benefits of such policies appear to be biased toward more prosperous farmers, just as is true in the U.S. for similar price-support benefits; the "demand creating" linkages are really more posited than demonstrated in the papers presented here. Clearly, we need more investigations of this theme in the region.

## STATE AUTONOMY AND THE RURAL MIDDLE EAST

Turning to the political impact of the process of the differentiation of the peasantry, we can again distinguish a range of hypotheses. A very general perspective on these problems is that we are analyzing the "dialectic of rulers and ruled", that is, the reciprocal, mutually transforming process of interaction of a differentiating rural population with state actors and their policies. A conventional perspective would be to focus on the impact of different rural social actors (or "classes", if one prefers) upon state policy. As Owen shows, before 1952 Egyptian large landlords exercised considerable political power on the national scale;

they induced the government to intervene in their favor in the cotton market, they thwarted any attempts at land reform, they blocked initiatives to tax them, and they stymied public investment in rural welfare. In short, a case can be made that when their perceived vital interests were at stake, the state acted as their instrument. The contrast with Turkey, where the Ottoman and Republican states long opposed the emergence of landlordism, is striking.

The example of the relative independence of various Turkish governments to pressures from rural elites should make us wary of adopting too simple an "instrumentalist" view of state action. Not only does the Marxist version of the "state as instrument of dominant classes" find relatively little support in the Turkish case, but as both Somel and Kasnakoglu note, naive pluralist views of state policy as responses to electoral volitions also appear quite dubious. As they demonstrate, changes in the level of government support for agriculture do not seem to be explained by voting shifts. Kasnakoglu rightly observes, however, that these results hardly mean that policy does not respond to political pressure; surely the preponderance of peasants in the Turkish electorate implies that whole-scale reversal of policies supportive of agriculture are infeasible options for any serious contender for power there.

An under-explored question is whether the generally favorable agricultural policies of Turkey are the result of the combination of electoral democracy with a peasant majority. Somel casts doubt on this happy interpretation, arguing that the "vision" or "image" of a future, industrialized Turkey in the minds of (autocratic, Ataturkist) policy makers played a larger role. This is plausible, but not proven, especially since the shift in policy in 1950 in favor of the peasantry is unexplained. The fact that the (highly authoritarian) Syrian regime has also strongly supported agriculture shows that democratic rule is not a necessary condition for rapid agricultural growth and development.[22]

This raises the thorny issue of establishing the *limits* of state autonomy. Most of us are prepared to admit that the state has some leeway in determining economic policy; few students of the Middle East would argue that governments there are simply "boards of directors of the upper classes". Not only can state actors launch initiatives, but they can also channel the process of peasant differentiation, whether by redistributing land, by extending credit to some farmers but not to others, or by taxing some farmers' crops more than others, to name only a few possible instruments. Yet it is clear that the successful exercise of state autonomy creates barriers for its further exercise. As Adams (and many others) notes, the land reforms of Nasser helped to consolidate the local power of the "second stratum" of the well-to-do peasantry. That same class, whose emergence over the past 150 years has been very much the outcome of state action, now constitutes an important barrier to additional policy initiatives, for example, to taxing agricultural land rather than crops. (See Alderman, Chapter 6). Of course, to say that rural social actors limit the actions of the state is quite different from arguing that they *control* the state; nevertheless, the ebb and flow of the relative autonomy of state policy toward agriculture from rural social classes requires continued investigation.

Of course, the state is also responding to problems thrown up by the process of agricultural development and the differentiation of the peasantry. In particular, it must respond to the problems of the rural exodus and to the issue of urban food entitlements. [23] One can indeed argue that this problem of food security increasingly dominates agricultural policy in the region. The extremely rapid rate of growth of demand for food, fueled by population growth and especially by the explosion of incomes due to the oil boom, has stimulated accelerating food imports, and, to some extent, a supply response, fostered in part by government subsidies. By international standards, Middle Eastern agricultural output has grown relatively repectably. According to the World Bank, the average annual rate of growth of agricultural output was 2.3%, 3.0% and 1.8% for low income, middle income, and industrialized market economies respectively during the decade 1970-1980.[24] Many Middle Eastern States (including Egypt and Turkey) have at least equalled this "international average" performance. But they have failed to match the growth of demand (with the notable exception of Turkey), have resorted increasingly to food imports, and have continued to subsidize urban consumption.

An important issue for investigation is how states' responses to this problem affect the differentiation of the peasantry. We may distinguish at least two broad classes of intervention, of policy levers which the state may use to increase agricultural production, and which also simultaneously shape the process of social differentiation among the peasantry: "price" and "technological" policies. Among the former would be included not merely formal government interventions in marketing networks but also taxation policy in general. The latter comprises largely attempts by the state to diffuse "new" technologies, both mechanical and biological/chemical.

Price policies have become something of the *bête noire* of agricultural development analysts. Led by scholars and analysts at the World Bank, many economists blame government policies which hold down the prices of agricultural goods, usually in order for the state to extract (or try to extract) an investable surplus for the slow growth of agricultural production.[25] In the Middle East and elsewhere, they argue that the removal of such "anti-agricultural" policies is a necessary (more extreme arguments hold it a sufficient) condition for agricultural growth. "Getting the prices right" has become a dogma of agricultural development.

At first glance, much of the material in this volume supports this position. In the crudest terms, the country which has offered prices above the world market price, Turkey, has the best agricultural output performance in the region, while countries which have repressed the price of major crops, such as Egypt, have done rather less well. At the same time, and without any desire to denigrate the importance of accurate signals of scarcity and of adequate incentives, it is easy to exaggerate the potential supply response which might result from a shift from a "low" to a "high" price policy for agriculture. Alderman notes that given the interdependencies and intricate crop rotations of Egypt, although the responsiveness of one crop (e.g., cotton) to a shift in its relative price may be substantial, the responsiveness of *agricultural output as a whole* to a reduction in the tax burden is likely to be much less striking. Other authors, as he notes, have obtained a similar result; the argument has been made generally by Raj Krishna.[26]

There are also some surprises in a country like Egypt awaiting those who believe that the problems of food dependency can be solved simply by "getting the prices right". Researchers at IFPRI have calculated that if all Egyptian farm prices moved to international levels, Egypt would actually grow *less* wheat than at present, simply because the country so obviously lacks a comparative advantage in this "land-using" crop.[27] Yet, of course, the core of the political problem of food subsidies in Egypt is the dependency on imported wheat and wheat flour.

It is also notable that price policies affect the process of peasant differentiation. Adams argues that in Egypt this occurs because 1) some crops are not taxed, and 2) small farmers are required to grow the taxed crops because of their need to follow a rotation which includes subsistence crops. By contrast, larger farmers can specialize in (untaxed) crops like fruits and vegetables. At least, this is the pattern which Adams discerns in Minya; a similar argument on a national scale was made by Abdel-Fadil. Some Tunisian evidence suggests that small farmers specialize in (taxed) durum wheat while larger farmers can specialize in (untaxed) bread wheats. A generalized form of the argument may be found in de Janvry, who traces the logic of differential price policy back to the absence of linkages between domestic demand and supply in the industrial sector. Wages, being merely a cost, are to be held down at all costs. Since basic cereals bulk large in workers' consumption, holding down these prices becomes a goal of government's "cheap food" policies.[28]

One should be wary of excessive generalization here, however. First, the Turkish evidence presented by contributors reveals relatively little differentiation of farms by crop mix, whether induced by government price policies or by different input prices. In general, crop mixes are quite similar within ecologically defined regions, regardless of farm size. Second, the evidence on Egypt at the national level is uncertain. In areas such as Sharkiyya Governorate, there is little evidence of significant differentiation of the peasantry by crop mix. Similarly, a national sample survey taken in 1977 also fails to support such hypotheses.[29] Finally, as mentioned above, one intervention by the

Egyptian government seems favorable to small farmers: the tariff on livestock products. Although this may benefit wealthier farmers also, in several regions of the country, and unlike in Adams' village in Minya, very small farmers (working farms smaller than one *feddan*) have been able to concentrate on *birsim* (Egyptian clover) and livestock production as a way of shoring up their incomes. In this case, government policy supported, rather than undermined, the survival strategies of very small farmers.

It is likely that technological policies and changes are at least as important both for increasing output and for their impact on the differentiation of the peasantry as are price policies. Of course, the two are intimately related: price policies contribute to the relative failure of attempts to diffuse higher yielding varieties of wheat in Egypt, an experience which contrasts sharply with Turkish success. In Egypt wheat-as-animal-feed is more profitable than wheat-as-food, in turn the result of price policies toward wheat and animal products. Adams presents a general indictment of the Egyptian state for its failure to transform agricultural technology there. He presents both detailed local evidence and some national comparisons which suggest that Egyptian agricultural productivity has stagnated. There is room for debate here: World Bank data indicate that Egyptian agricultural output grew at an annual rate of 3.0% from 1970 to 1982, not far behind Turkey's 3.2%, and that value added grew at 3.1% (compared to Turkey's 3.3%). These numbers are quite respectable by international standards. There can be little doubt, however, that Egypt is far from attaining the level of agricultural output of which its excellent agroecology is capable. [30]

The material on the Turkish case presented here indicates not only that farmers respond to incentives, but also that the Turkish state has offered a wide range of mechanisms designed to encourage farmers to adopt new technologies, with quite strong output results. But as both Somel and Uner stress, most of the benefits of the various price support and input subsidy schemes have accrued to the larger farmers.[31] Of course, all farmers gain from higher farm prices; however, in Turkey as in the United States, because the absolute benefits of price supports increase with the level of output, larger farmers reap most of the benefits of such policies. Similarly, as Adams notes, larger farmers have an easier time acquiring subsidized inputs than their smaller neighbors. Policies aimed at accelerating agricultural production appear to contribute to increasing inequality among farmers.

## THE POLITICAL ECONOMY OF FOOD SUBSIDIES

A final interrelation between state policy and rural social differentiation is to be found in the highly charged problem of food subsidies, and the related issue of the "food riots" which have shaken several countries. Several features of these systems and their problems stand out. First, throughout the region, basic urban consumption needs are guaranteed by the state. Any weakening of urban "food entitlements" is therefore transparently political and politicized. Second, these subsidies substantially augment poor people's consumption. In Egypt, for example, they provide fifteen to sixteen percent of the total income for the poorest twenty-five percent of the population.[32] Maintaining this guarantee is absolutely essential to the survival of the state, since any major cutback in subsidies will meet violent resistance. Owen argued in the workshop that guaranteeing consumption is part of a "bread and circuses" political strategy of many relatively unpopular regional governments toward their populations: unwilling or unable to offer meaningful political participation possibilities to their people, and (temporarily) awash in revenue, many states promoted consumption as a "diversion".

As is well known, cutting urban consumer subsidies has provoked wide-spread political unrest. Food or "IMF" riots have broken out at least seven times in the last eight years: Egypt in 1977 and again in 1984; Morocco in 1981 and again in 1984; the Sudan in 1981 and 1985; and Tunisia in 1984. Although hardly the cause of the overthrow of the Nimeiry regime, food subsidy cuts sparked the initial protests. Governments have usually retreated rapidly in the face of such protests; food prices remain very low to consumers, and the government deficit remains large.

Both Alderman and Seddon (Chapter 8) stress that the "food riots" are really "equity riots": they are protests against how the gains of the decade of the oil boom have been shared. As Seddon notes, governments have too often added insult to injury when cutting subsidies by pointing to (alleged) "waste" in food consumption habits. Stories of bread being fed to chickens or water buffaloes in Egypt are rampant, although Alderman and von Braun's very thorough survey, covering every Governorate, turned up no evidence to support such tales.[33] Stories of bread piling up in the Tunis rubbish dump are said to have convinced President Bourguiba to raise consumer prices there in early January, 1984. But, of course, poor people waste very little; they cannot afford such a luxury. Claims to the contrary simply show how far removed elite spokesmen are from the realities of the daily lives of those whom they claim to represent.

The poor may find such an allegation particularly insulting if the beneficiaries of oil-boom growth have been flaunting their wealth. This seems to be the case in Egypt, Tunisia, Morocco and, perhaps to a lesser extent, the Sudan. Poor residents of these countries apparently felt that those least able to afford it were being asked to shoulder the burden of austerity. In short, they found the cuts illegitimate. Given their dependence for food on a politically based entitlement, their behavior is understandable.

Such a perspective is reinforced when we recognize that there have been several instances of cuts in comsumption in the region which did not provoke riots. In Egypt under Nasser, per capita grain consumption fell from 115 kilograms per year in 1966 to seventy-two kilograms per year in 1969/70. Yet since these cuts were widely shared, and since the cause of the austerity was the popularly supported need to fight the Israelis to regain the Sinai, people accepted such hardships. More recently, Algeria raised consumer food prices by some thirty percent, again without protest. The long, bitter war of national liberation and the strong political institutions in that country may mean that most citizens perceive the state as relatively legitimate. *Infitah*[34] style growth has also been less marked in Algeria than in the other Maghreb countries. It is notable that the Algerians combined the announced cut in subsidies with a program to target them to the poor *and* to finance them by taxing luxury consumption. It is interesting to note that the Tunisians have begun to implement a similar policy after the riots of 1984.

Clearly, internationally-generated austerity threatens urban entitlements. Equally clearly, the urban poor in the Middle East and North Africa are unwilling to suffer alone. This highlights the fact that the problem of food subsidies is really primarily a macroeconomic and a political problem, rather than a micro or sectoral economic problem. The agricultural sector can ameliorate, but cannot solve, the food problems of the poor. The benefits of such programs are obvious: a guarantee of urban food entitlements and in many parts of the Middle East, political stability. It is then important to gauge the costs carefully. Some have argued that low prices for farmers follow necessarily and directly from maintaining low prices to consumers. Alderman debunks this argument, showing that there is no *direct* link between food subsidies and agricultural price policies: during the 1970s agricultural taxation declined while the subsidy bill soared. Consumer subsidies cannot be blamed, as so many have tried to do, for the slow growth of agricultural output in Egypt.

There are, however, important linkages between the subsidy programs and employment creation, via the macroeconomy. Egypt was able to improve farmers' incentives while simultaneously augmenting subsidies because the government could tap other sources of foreign exchange, such as oil exports, workers' remittances, and foreign aid. Similarly, Somel points out how American aid during the 1950s made it possible for Turkey to shift from taxing to subsidizing agriculture. In both cases, alternative funds for investment came from outside national boundaries. Not only are such funds unreliable, but as Scobie has shown, stabilizing consumption with subsidies implies that external shocks will have to be absorbed elsewhere in the economy.[35] In Egypt, investment seems to have been destabilized as a result of the government's policy of stabilizing food consumption. Such fluctuations might have adverse consequences for employment creation, although, as Radwan argues, public investment in Egypt has created relatively few jobs because of its capital-intensity Nevertheless, it is likely that the real opportunity cost of food subsidies should be sought here. As Alderman points out, such national opportunity costs are highly dependent on the international environment.

An alternative to responding to adverse shocks from the international economy by cutting subsidies would be to try to enhance the equity, efficiency, and total receipts of the taxation system. However, powerful internal social actors block adoption of such policies, leaving austerity as the only feasible alternative. The IMF invariably recommends subsidy cuts, rather than tax increases. Yet it has been estimated, for example, that Morocco could pay for its entire food subsidy bill simply by levying a tax of roughly nine percent on the income of the land of the large farmers in irrigated areas.[36] This may merely be a realistic assessment by the Fund of the nature of political economy of Morocco, however. Many, if not most, of the differences between Moroccan and Algerian policies can be traced to their different patterns of ownership of productive assets. Similarly, land taxes in Egypt are often recommended by economists, but they have been repeatedly thwarted by the political representatives of rich farmers.

We have come full circle: for an understanding of food riots we must look to the international level, while simultaneously analyzing the interaction of states and social classes in shaping policy choices. As Seddon makes clear, the Tunisian state provoked the "equity riots" fundamentally because of balance of payments pressures, but the actual choice of austerity and the manner of implementation revealed much about the distribution of political power in the country. Such balance of payments pressures appear to be a necessary cause of such upheavals, and they, in turn, are only explicable in terms of the insertion of the various national states into the international economy. It is possible that the Tunisian events, like the earlier ones in Cairo in 1977, are harbingers of things to come, given the linkages between agricultural development in all its aspects during the 1970s and the Oil Boom of that decade. We may be witnessing the "demise of a model" of agricultural development.

## CONCLUSION: THE RISE AND FALL OF A 'MODEL' OF AGRICULTURAL DEVELOPMENT?

The essence of the patterns of agrarian change in the region during the past decade may be summarized as follows. Very strong growth of domestic demand for food, stimulated by population increase and especially the rapid increase of incomes during the decade could not be met from local production because of natural and social constraints on domestic supply. Governments responded with increased imports and with programs of selective incentives for domestic producers. The ensuing "model" of agrarian change had the following elements: 1) abundant foreign exchange, directly or indirectly due to the oil price revolutions of 1973 and 1979; 2) outflows of labor from the major agricultural producers; 3) accelerating imports to feed the cities; 4) input subsidies and specialty crop promotion for the larger farmers; 5) migration and (some) increased commercialization for small farmers and the landless; 6) food subsidies for the urban population; and 7) some changes in the mode of finance of these subsidies, with a general tendency to take the funds from general tax revenues, now augmented by oil and aid, rather than to obtain the revenue by shifting the terms of trade against agriculture.

This model has come under considerable pressure during the 1980s. Since the key to the process was foreign exchange largesse, the decline in such revenues has forced many governments to move toward austerity. Morocco, Tunisia and Jordan have been forced to try to cut government spending and to promote exports. The North African countries face particular difficulties because the collapse of their export revenues from, e.g., phosphates, remittances from workers in France, or light industrial products has combined with increased debt burden due to high U.S. interest rates and with the devastating impact of a series of years of drought. They illustrate the "worse case" scenario from the food security point of view: declining foreign exchange *combined with* declining domestic production due to bad weather.[37] Even the wealthy Saudis have recently slashed price subsidies for wheat by over fifty percent.

The ensuing "political economy of austerity" has a number of implications for the food systems of the region. There is a renewed emphasis on export crops to increase foreign exchange; yet, the largest nearby market, the EC, is increasingly inaccessible with the accession of Greece, Spain, and Portugal to full membership. Government retrenchment seems to hit projects in rain-fed areas (where most non-Egyptian peasants in the region live) particularly hard. Understandably, planners mainly wish to increase urban food supply; this means promoting irrigation projects and helping the relatively well-to-do farmers.

In conclusion, the entitlements of both the urban and the rural poor are threatened by the current austerity in the region. The extent of this austerity varies across countries, and, of course, the unknown critical variable is the future trend of oil prices. With the exception of the Sudan, large-scale famine is probably not a threat. Nor is it likely that urban entitlements (food subsidies) will be withdrawn; resulting budgetary deficits may be covered by collecting "strategic rent". On the other hand, the process of social differentiation under the twin spurs of the food gap and responses to this gap are likely to continue the process of social differentiation in the countryside. Unless the Middle Eastern and North African countries can adopt "equitable growth" strategies, the situation of those at the bottom of the social scale, especially in the rural areas, is likely to remain rather grim. Continued analytical efforts such as those contributed here and persistent practical initiatives such as those of IFAD are likely to be even more important during the next decade than they were during the last.

## FOOTNOTES

[1] One of the principal thinkers of the dependency school, Samir Amin, is Egyptian, and his early work focused on the region. (e.g., *The Maghreb in the Modern World*. New York: Penguin, 1970). Subsequent landmarks which have been informed by these "internationalist" perspectives include Caglar Keyder, *The Definition of a Peripheral Economy: Turkey, 1921-1929*. Cambridge: Cambridge University Press, 1975, and most recently, Huri Islamoglu, ed.*The Ottoman Empire and the World System*. Cambridge: Cambridge University Press, 1986.

[2] The literature of critique and counter-critique of dependency and world-systems analysis is vast. A review of the debate appears in Alan Richards, *Development and Modes of Production in Marxist Economics: A Critical Evaluation*. London and Paris: Harcourt Academic Publishers, 1986, Chapter 4.

[3] On the ways in which international forces shape national social actors and state policies, see Peter Gourevitch, "The Second Image Reversed: The International Sources of Domestic Politics", *International Organization*, 32,4 (1978), pp. 44-67.

[4] Karl Kautsky, *Die Agrarfrage.*Berlin: Dietz Nachf. 1899; V.I.Lenin, *The Development of Capitalism in Russia* (Moscow: Progress Publishers, 1964; first published in 1904).

[5] Lenin, op.cit.; Mao Tse-Tung, "Analysis of Classes in Chinese Society", in *Selected Works of Mao Tse-Tung*. Beijing: Foreign Languages Press, 1971, 11-22. (First published in 1926).

[6] *A General Theory of Exploitation and Class*. Cambridge, Mass.: Harvard University Press, 1982.

[7] Much of the best work here comes from the Indian subcontinent. See, eg. Amit Bhaduri, *The Economic Structure of Backward Agriculture*. New York: Academic Press, 1983; Pranab K. Bardhan, *Land, Labor and Rural Poverty: Essays in Development Economics*. Delhi: Oxford University Press, 1984; and Meghnad Desai, et. al.., eds., *Agrarian Power and Agricultural Productivity in South Asia*. Berkeley: University of California Press, 1984.

[8] Mahmoud Abdel-Fadil, *Development, Income Distribution, and Social Change in Rural Egypt (1952-1970): A Study in the Political Economy of Agrarian Transition*. Cambridge: Cambridge University Press, 1975.

[9] For example, Karen Pfeiffer, *Agrarian Reform Under State Capitalism in Algeria*. Boulder, CO.: Westview Press, 1985.

[10] A.V. Chayanov, *The Theory of Peasant Economy*. Homewood, IL.: Irwin, 1966.

[11] M. Lewin, *Russian Peasants and Soviet Power: A Study of*

*Collectivization*. New York: W.W.Norton, 1968; Esther Kingston-Mann, *Lenin and the Problem of Marxist Peasant Revolution*. New York and London: Oxford University Press, 1985.

[12] One *feddan* is equal to 1.03 acres.

[13] Radwan (Chapter 10) notes an additional strategy: investment in human capital, especially, in acquisition of a degree which until recently guaranteed the holder a government job.

[14] The now standard concept of "entitlements" in analysis of food problems comes from Amartya Sen, *Poverty and Famines: An Essay on Entitlement and Deprivation*. Oxford: The Clarendon Press, 1981. On the Egyptian case, see the essays in Alan Richards and Philip L. Martin, *Migration, Mechanization, and Agricultural Labor Markets in Egypt*. Boulder, CO. and Cairo: Westview Press and the American University in Cairo Press, 1982.

[15] Some of them may be able to pursue such a strategy if they can rent land, as is common throughout Egypt.

[16] Samir Radwan and Eddy Lee, *Agrarian Change in Egypt: An Anatomy of Rural Poverty*. London: Croom Helm, 1986.

[17] The original argument appeared in Osvaldo Sunkel, "Inflation in Chile: An Unorthodox Approach," *International Economic Papers*, 10 (1960), pp. 107-131.

[18] Very similar systems to that in Egypt prevailed in other parts of the world where landownership rights were concentrated in the hands of market-oriented landlords, such as Prussia and Chile. A comparative analysis may be found in Alan Richards, "The Political Economy of *Gutswirtschaft*: A Comparative Analysis of East Elbian Germany, Egypt, and Chile", *Comparative Studies in Society and History*, 21,4 (October, 1979), 483-518. For a recent formalization of these arguments, see M. Eswaran and A. Kotwal, "A Theory of Two-Tier Labour Markets in Agrarian Economies", *American Economic Review*, 75, 1 (March, 1985), pp. 162-177.

[19] Bruce Johnston and Peter Kilby, *Agriculture and Structural Transformation: Economic Strategies in Late-Developing Countries*. Oxford: Oxford University Press, 1975, and Alain de Janvry, *The Agrarian Question and Reformism in Latin America*. Baltimore and London: Johns Hopkins University Press, 1981.

[20] Irma Adelman, "Beyond Export-Led Growth", *World Development*, 12, 9 (September, 1984), pp. 937-949.

[21] See John Waterbury *The Egypt of Nasser and Sadat: The Political Economy of Two Regimes* (Princeton: Princeton University Press, 1983) on the failure to develop such linkages.

[22] Syrian agricultural output grew ten percent per year from 1970 to 1982. World Bank, *World Development Report, 1984*. New York: Oxford

University Press, 1984.

[23] Indeed, some believe that the entire process of rural change in the region is now dominated by this emigration. After reading the workshop prospectus, the late Paul Pascon told the author, "This interaction of state policy and rural social differentiation would have been a fine topic for investigation ten years ago. But now, at least in Morocco, everything has been overwhelmed by drought and emigration!"

[24] The World Bank, *World Development Report, 1983.* New York: Oxford University Press, 1983.

[25] See, e.g., World Bank, *World Development Report, 1982.* New York: Oxford University Press, 1982.

[26] Raj Krishna, "Some Aspects of Agricultural Growth, Price Policy, and Equity in Developing Countries",*Food Research Institute Studies*, 18, 3 (1982), pp. 1-34.

[27] Joachim von Braun and Hartwig de Haen, *The Effects of Food Price and Subsidy Policies on Egyptian Agriculture.* Washington, D.C.: IFPRI Research Report No. 42, (November, 1983).

[28] de Janvry, op.cit.

[29] See the essays in Richards and Martin op.cit., and Luis Crouch, Gamal Siam, and Osman Gad, "A Descriptive Analysis of Egyptian Agrarian Structure". University of California, Berkeley, Department of Agricultural and Natural Resource Economics, mimeo (December, 1982).

[30] See the analyses presented in E.T. York, et. al. *Egypt: Strategies for Accelerating Agricultural Development.* Cairo and Washington, D.C.: Ministry of Agriculture of the Arab Republic of Egypt and the U.S. Agency for International Development in cooperation with the U.S. Department of Agriculture, 1982.

[31] The same thing has been noted in the Maghreb. See, among many others, *Morocco: Economic and Social Development Report: A World Bank Country Study*, Washington, D.C.: The World Bank, October 1981; Anne M. Findlay, "The Moroccan Economy in the 1970s", in Richard Lawless and Allan Findlay, eds. *North Africa: Contemporary Politics and Economic Development.* New York: St. Martin's Press, 1984, pp. 191-216. See also *Rapport de la mission speciale de la programmation au Maroc*, Rome: IFAD, December, 1982.

[32] Harold Alderman and Joachim von Braun, *The Effects of the Egyptian Food Ration and Subsidy System on Income Distribution and Consumption.* Washington, D.C.: International Food Policy Research Institute Research Report No. 45 (July, 1984).

[33] Alderman and von Braun, op.cit.

[34] "Opening up" in Arabic; usually used to refer to partial liberalization of import trade in the 1970s, a process which stimulated the growth of a class of "nouveaux riches".

[35] Grant Scobie, *Food Subsidies: Their Impact on Foreign Exchange and Trade in Egypt*. Washington, D.C.: IFPRI Research Report No.40, 1983.

[36] Samir Radwan, personal communication.

[37] The link of Moroccan and Tunisian currencies to the French franc combined with the precipitous rise in the dollar/franc exchange rate to raise the costs of food imports (denominated in dollars) even further. More recently, good weather and record harvests have brought some respite to Magrebian farmers and states, but few believe that the exceptional crops of 1985 will be repeated.

# 2

# Agrarian Relations in Turkey: A Historical Sketch

*Tosun Aricanli*

## INTRODUCTION

The fundamental features of Turkish agrarian structure are as follows: The basic unit of production in the agricultural sector in Turkey is the small, peasant-owned family farm. Large landownership is limited both in quantity and also in total cultivated area.[1] In terms of geographic distribution, the average size of property is smaller in more fertile regions, while the largest landholdings are more common in backward and less fertile areas. Family labor is by far the most fundamental element in the composition of the rural labor force. Few landless agricultural laborers can be found. High seasonal demand for agricultural workers in industrial crops, and regional complementarity in cycles of cultivation explain the presence of rural wage workers better than landlessness. The source of rural wage workers, at the times of peak labor demand is mostly smaller peasant-cultivators from the same locality and own-cultivators from cereal growing regions who migrate for seasonal work.

The most important peak-labor demand occurs in the weeding and harvesting of cotton grown on the coastal plains of southern and southwestern Anatolia. Each cotton growing region has a source of seasonal labor originating from the dry-farming regions of inner Anatolia. During peak-labor demand, dryland grain cultivators are usually free from agricultural activities on their own farms, and therefore can complement the local labor in cotton regions.

Inequality of wealth and income in Turkish agriculture is not generally due to monopolisation of landownership by a few. Discrepancies in income among *cultivators* need to be explained in terms of holding size and soil fertility among small to medium peasants themselves. Further inequality due to non-agricultural economic activities such as commerce and transportation is, of course, a separate issue.

## THE DISCREPANCY BETWEEN THE AGRARIAN REALITY AND ITS PERCEPTION

The agrarian picture presented above is a result of statistical and social science investigation conducted during the past two decades. These findings conflict with the framework common to most previous studies on Turkish agriculture[2] which held that widespread landlordism defined the social structure in the Agrarian Sector.

This perspective evolved out of certain perceptions of Turkish society. First, agriculture - the "traditional" sector - was seen as the site of backwardness as opposed to the modern, urban, "industrial" sector. At a time of limited urbanisation, with "model" cases of large and orderly state-industrial-enterprises, and in the absence of widespread urban poverty, the picture of rural-urban dichotomy was striking. The intelligentsia equipped with social theories of modernization and duality and with a great faith in technology blamed the country's backwardness on an allegedly stagnant agriculture.

Second, a "power", emerging to a great extent from the provinces, challenged the "modernizing" state in free elections of 1950 and began dominating the government. These provincial power-brokers could "manage" the votes of the rural population despite the seeming contradiction between their interests and those of poor peasants. Domination of peasants by local notables had been a well-known fact throughout Ottoman history.

What did this "domination" mean? Historically, the "strongmen" acted as intermediaries between the State and peasantry in extracting surplus. Domination was achieved either by license from the State or through imposing oneself on the administration of a region by virtue of local military power. Domination meant different things to the parties involved. From the viewpoint of peasantry, it was a form of a claim over the surplus. From the perspective of the State, if the "notable" was licensed, domination was the extension of the authority of the State; if he was not licensed, it was a form of "rebellion" according to the State, and implied a larger share of the surplus for the "notable". In the latter case, domination could also be interpreted by the government as oppression of the peasantry by rebellious elements. Domination came from *outside* the productive organisation of the peasant community, and was defined over the process of appropriation and distribution of surplus with no reference to property.[3] Such "purely political" access to resources (and the resulting "domination") must be distinguished from access (and domination) through legally sanctioned ownership of resources.

The power-brokers of the 1950s were frequently mistaken for landlords, and peasants for their subjects. The conceptual error was the reduction of the general phenomenon of domination into a specific form, i.e. property. Domination was definitely present in some form of political and social patronage although it was declining. In the *day-to-day* activities of the rural population, domination by the local notables had been hardly challenged by another category of authority - such as the State.

These two commonly accepted notions--domination and landed property--were used to paint a picture of "feudal" agrarian relations. Resulting backwardness was diagnosed to be due to concentration of "landed property," or "landlordism".

Given such views, when the first survey data on landholdings were analysed and interpreted by Korkut Boratav, the new notion of widespread small-peasant agriculture was not readily accepted despite the overwhelming evidence.[4]

While a gradual decline in the domination of peasants by local notables can be traced in recent history, there is no earlier data to compare with information on landholdings in the 1960s. Established notions of political domination in rural life are quite at odds with the evidence on the distribution of agricultural property. Could the present picture have developed as a reversal of a process of landlord domination and of a concentration of landholdings?

Observing the 150 year history of agrarian relations, one can detect conditions favorable to the monopolisation of property,[5] but no events marking a reversal of a trend. If such a major reversal took place, it would have been marked by a distinct period of open conflict over "property" relations, yet we do not observe such phenomena. There has been no major opposition, no large activity of legal land transfer, no notable occupation of "landlords'" land. It is evident that large landed *property* did not get established, despite the presence of domination.

It was not the "domination," but its assumed medium, "property" (or "title" to land), that was misperceived by the intelligentsia. The question needs to be reformulated: why could the locally dominant power in Anatolia not convert their provincial authority into landed *property*, especially at a period when the peasantry was weak and a basis for conflict between the two parties was absent?

## THE "STATE" AS AN EXPLANATORY VARIABLE IN THE EVOLUTION OF AGRARIAN RELATIONS

This "puzzle" is caused by the common (implicit) assumption that potential conflict on the issue of "property" in agricultural land would take place between peasant and landlord. In that case, the nature of conflict would be over the ownership of productive resources. However, there did exist another conflict between the Ottoman (and later Turkish) State and provincial powers on the "flow" of agricultural revenue and growth of "autonomous" provincial power. The nature of this conflict was "political" and "territorial."[6] In the process of undermining the growth of competing local power bases in provinces, the state disrupted the basis of potential "property" in land and its concentration. Simultaneously, the

State encouraged accumulation in urban areas and in industry to establish a client group (bourgeoisie) for itself; the State transformed the nature and basis of domination in society. Small peasant property emerged as a byproduct of this transformation. Conflict between the State and local notables over the division of surplus, and the exercise of independent political power kept local domination under control and ended up in peasant property. Attempts to apply the "Western Model" of conflict between landlords and peasantry, on the other hand, lead to an internally inconsistent analysis, or conclusions that cannot be supported by facts.

## IMPLICATIONS OF THE AGRARIAN POLICY OF THE TURKISH STATE FOR THE AGRICULTURAL WORK FORCE

As a result of the establishment of small-scale peasant production, the development of a large agricultural wage labor force has been inhibited. Because the peasantry primarily rely on family labor, the rural landless poor need to migrate in search of urban employment. At the same time, due to the high costs of supervising large numbers of agricultural workers in the agrarian setting of Turkey, expansion of agricultural activities into large capitalist enterprises under unified management has not been viable. Therefore, successful accumulation in agricultural production also led rich farmers to enter commerce or industrial production, resulting in further migration from the top of the scale of income distribution. This process left medium and small peasant farms as the most widespread kind of Turkish agricultural enterprise. This fact explains the absence of institutions (such as sharecropping)[7] to generate and preserve an agricultural labor force in the farming sector.

## PRODUCTION, DISTRIBUTION, PROPERTY AND POLITICAL AUTHORITY: INDIGENOUS VS. ASSUMED PROCESSES

As is true for the development literature in general, contemporary social science research on Turkey usually draws on European and Latin American experience to construct models. In this task the same "western" processes and variables are assumed to exist also in Turkey, the two most common being:

(1) Primacy of relations at the productive level in explaining social and economic change,

(2) Private property in agricultural land; presupposing clear cut, indisputable "titles" as a basis for "claims" on a part of the agricultural surplus.

In the Turkish case, however, the alleged primacy of relations in the productive sphere is undermined by distributive considerations involving the State. Such considerations indicate the relevance of political "autonomy" or "independence" of the state which is directly related to distributive process.[8] Approaching the same issue from a different angel, Mubeccel Kiray argues that there was almost no differentiation of control or status within the agricultural commonities while a great deal of control was exercised from the outside.[9] Again, the social dynamic is located in the sphere of interaction between forces outside the production process, i.e. between local powers and the State.

The argument, in short, is that the contemporary agrarian picture in Turkey is the outcome of the Ottoman-Turkish State's policy to contain and eliminate competing local powers (and to maintain the flow of revenues). Furthermore the institution of private property in agricultural land developed during the period of transformation up to the 1950s. Thus property will be observed in the context of its historical evolution rather than as a strictly legal concept. The remainder of this paper will trace this historical evolution, while emphasizing the differences between the Ottoman experience and the "western model."

## PROPERTY AND USUFRUCT IN ARABLE LAND

In the Ottoman system "property" in arable land did not exist in the contemporary sense. The modern "institution" of property emerged after the foundation of the Republic in 1923. However, other forms of "access" to revenues (surplus) from land existed for privileged individuals.

The traditional legitimate form of "access" was the State's allocation of specific revenues from designated regions to individuals in lieu of salaries since the initial period of Ottoman expansion in the fifteenth century. These allocations were for a specific time period and were not transferable, resembling a "prebendal" system. Furthermore, allocations were made in value terms, and particularly did not establish any legal connection between the recipient and the land or the producers. Later in the seventeenth and eighteenth centuries, tax farming increasingly replaced the above system. Again, privileged position within the hierarchy of the State determined the identity of recipients of tax farms. And again, the tax farm did not establish a link between the person and *land*. It was the farming of *revenue* for a specific duration.

For the totality of privileged or dominant elements in Ottoman society the State *distributed* revenues. The State had to maintain the flow of revenues for distribution to its "members." From the viewpoint of privileged individuals one way of securing a more favorable allocation for themselves was through maintaining (military and political) control at the source of surplus, thus keeping more than their "rightful" share of revenues; thus placing themselves as a threat against the interests of the totality of dominant elements, the State, and the redistributive system. To maintain the flow of revenues, it was the State's function to break solidified control at the source - agricultural production being by far the most important and most conducive to private control.

Throughout its history the Ottoman State successfully challenged, and broke ever re-emerging private control on revenue. As a result of this systemic struggle, territorial control by local military magnates did not turn into legitimate and inviolable large "property." It remained an infringement on the State's rights on the land, and functioned only as a temporary means to divert revenues. Such "property" could at best be *de facto*, never *de jure*, and it surfaced as intermittent episodes rather than a continuous institution.

To maintain the flow of agricultural revenues, the State had to preserve viable forms of agricultural production, that is, peasant cultivation. It was protected from nomadic and transhumant activities by restricting nomadic migrations into agricultural regions. During periods of provincial "autonomy" under rebellious governors, there were instances of conversion of arable land into pastures in pursuit of higher private returns.[10] This also was a topic of major concern in the preservation of revenue sources.

Under these systemic forces, and as a result of the success of the Ottoman State in preserving its redistributive function, the rights (and duties) of the peasantry survived. During the first two decades of the nineteenth century control of the autonomous power brokers (known as the Lords of the Valley) were broken, and the authority of the central government was reestablished. Both legally and in practice, the fundamental,*inviolable* right to cultivation for subsistence (private use) remained the *usufruct* of peasantry. Large property neither received comparable legal status nor the sanction of the State. In terms of legitimacy, continuity, and inviolability peasant family's form of access to land resembles the "western" notion of "property" more than any other alternative forms.

## NEW AGRICULTURAL POLICIES IN THE NINETEENTH CENTURY

The dichotomy between the developments in commerce and agriculture in the Ottoman territories during the nineteenth century is striking. Commerce and industry, and "classes" involved in those activities, were slipping under the control of the Great Powers, and Ottoman policy in these fields seemed to be in great disarray. By contrast, despite mounting pressures from the West, the government stubbornly protected its own control over agricultural resources. Agricultural surplus was the largest source of revenue, and moreover, unlike commerce, it was maintained through direct control of the channels of appropriation. It was due to the extraordinary importance of agricultural surplus in Ottoman finances that the Ottoman state had to protect its control over agrarian relations persistently despite its utter weakness against the Western Powers.

Europeans put substantial pressure on the government to open agriculture to European settlers and "*proteges*." Already in the 1840s there were some foreign farmers in Turkey who had special arrangements on tilling the land[11] In government circles there were high expectations of Europeans settling in the Turkish plains. However, it had to be on Ottoman terms. Later in the century Ali Pasha, a prominent Ottoman statesman, wrote: "Just as the European immigrants became Americans in America here they will be Ottomans. Are not many of our European civil servants more Ottoman than ourselves?"[12] However, the British sought extraterritorial rights for settlers. They wanted their own police, administration, and judicial system to have authority over colonists and local laborers.[13] The development of the role of foreigners in Turkish agriculture is taken up below.

While the law granting the right of landholding to foreigners was in the making, new and effective policies were being applied on the agrarian sector on several fronts. In 1856 a decree (Hatt-i Humayun) confirmed the guarantees of the 1839 decree and promised laws for transfer of land to foreigners. The new decree read:

> As the laws regulating the purchase, sale and disposal of real "property" are common to all the subjects of my Empire, it shall be lawful for foreigners to possess landed property in my dominions, conforming themselves to the laws and police regulations, and bearing the same charges as the native inhabitants, and after arrangements have been made with Foreign Powers.[14]

In 1858, a new land code was issued which very much eased the sale of the "right of possession," mortgage, and the inheritance of peasants' lands. It did not, however, contain any articles on foreign holdings. Although the ownership (servitude) of the state lands remained in the hands of the public treasury (beytulmal), this law was a development towards making all arable land in the Empire the property of the peasantry. Two points suggest that the new law was not intended as an empty formalism: first, the large agricultural holdings tied to pious foundations were treated as state property after 1836. Second, some articles of the land code were quite precise: for example, article 8 read:

> The whole of the lands of a town or a village cannot be granted *en bloc* to the whole of the inhabitants nor by choice to one, two, or three of them. Different pieces of land are given to each inhabitant, and title deeds (Tapu sened) showing their possession...are delivered to them.[15]

And article 88 read:

> The person employed as a Tapu official in a Kaza [Township] cannot during the time of his employment take over vacant land (Mahlule), or land which becomes the right of Tapu, nor can he hand it over to his children, brother, sister, father, mother, wife, servant, slave and dependents....[16]

There were obstacles to the easy transfer of the possession of land: not only was the sale or mortgage hard to carry out, but only the son of a deceased could inherit the possession without a fee.[17] The land code, by easing the transfer to a daughter or wife as well as to more distant relatives, attempted to coax cultivators into maintaining agricultural output. Moreover, the establishment of more effective rights of usufruct might have been considered a contribution toward creating an incentive to cultivate land more effectively.[18] These were all important steps directed to rationalisation of relations on land.

Furthermore, if repeated promises of the imperial decrees on the fair treatment of the peasants are considered, a democratisation of the system of landholdings appears to have been taking place.[19] Despite the contention of authors such as Karpat on the effect of the code on "property",[20] the land code did not include any articles establishing property on agricultural land. *All* titles of usufruct were revokable upon failure of the possessor to cultivate land for three consecutive years and in order to resume farming he had to pay a fine.[21]

It is remarkable that in a period of foreign domination of the legal system leading to wholesale adoption of European codes elsewhere in the political economy, the land code stands as a purely Ottoman enactment. This is indicative of the fundamental interest of the government in preserving its own control of agricultural revenues. Since the interest of the government was essentially to improve agricultural production and revenue, the State sought not only to secure the usufruct of peasants in settled ares, but also to find alternative ways to increase cultivation of vacant land.

Both before and during the nineteenth century the Anatolian countryside was underpopulated;[22] great expanses of unutilized agricultural land existed. Almost any traveler going through Anatolia mentions vast untilled areas. The tiller, not the soil, was the scarce factor, and in these conditions ownership of land would not make much of a difference from the viewpoint of the landlord, unless the control over the product of the laborer also was given to him.[23]

In the face of the low population density, one great source of agricultural labor was the nomad. A campaign was started for the settlement of the nomadic population in the plains, chiefly in Cukurove in the second part of the nineteenth century.[24] Nomads traditionally had been somewhat more privileged than sedentary people. They also somehow managed to slip away from the hands of the tax gatherer, and were definitely more prosperous than the peasantry.

In 1866 a military force known as the "improvement division" (Firka-i Islahiye) landed in Iskenderun in southeastern Turkey with the task of pacification and settlement of the Turcoman tribes in Cukurova.[25] The official reason for the campaign was to pacify the nomadic tribes so as to provide prospective soldiers for the army.[26]

The government troops were not always successful. But whatever the outcome of the specific military operation may have been, the result was the same: the defeated chief (or his kinsman) were put in charge of the territory that the tribe was settled on and the tribesmen turned out to be his peasants and "sharecroppers."[27]

Some nomads fared better than others. For example, thousands of households of the Nogay tribe who migrated from Russia after the Crimean War, leaving all their cattle behind, were settled in Cukurova; however only forty to fifty households remain today. The others appear to have moved or perished due to the change in climate and lifestyle.[28]

In relation to this method of settlement of vacant lands article 130 of the land code is rather revealing:

> ...if it is not possible to bring back that village to its original state by bringing fresh agriculturists to live there, and conferring on them the land separately, the land can be given in lots to one, two or three persons in order to make that village into a Chiftlik [Ciftlik: landed estate].[29]

In exchange for settling his men, a tribal leader could get the possession and the title of usufruct to large tracts of land. Some of the large landed property today originated from similar articles in the land code. However this article did not give property rights to the settlers - it was usufruct, but could be large. Land had to be continuously cultivated to keep the title, and if the documents could be produced to prove legal possession, the land could be considered private property by the middle of the 20th century.

In this way a new method of domination was opened through the auspices of the State. This method was available to those beyond the direct control of the central power, as in eastern Anatolia. However, it should be noted that it was not a grant of an arbitrary area to prominent local powers. Area of land on which a title could be obtained was restricted by the size of non-agricultural population that could be transformed into an agricultural and therefore taxable work force.

It is evident that settlement of Cukurova was achieved in the second part of the nineteenth century by forcing a transformation of the nomadic economy. It is also evident that all the tribal leaders in Anatolia did not feel the necessity of using the government's sanction in registering land in their own names. Fast growth of economic activity and high rates of settlement in Cukurova, however, must have induced the men of power in that region to get the title of prime agricultural land which was fast becoming a scarce factor.[30] Today, this region represents one of the highest concentrations of large landholdings in Turkey.

The settlement policy inevitably led to a new wave of monopolisation of land and solidification of claims on potential and actual sources of revenue. In the eyes of foreign observers such claims were "landed property," though in the Ottoman system there still was no legitimate or social basis of private property on land. The new solidifications went unchallenged until the 1930s.[31]

During the nineteenth century the Ottoman government also started thinking in terms of supporting agricultural production through economic and technical incentives. British influence in this enterprise was quite strong. There were efforts to introduce American cotton and to improve seeds and agricultural production in general.[32] In 1862 rather "modern" incentives were created for cotton producers:

(1) Cotton producers would be given vacant state lands without any charge for the transfer of possession.

(2) No taxes would be collected from such lands for five years.

(3) The best quality of cotton exported would pay no more taxes than the worst quality.

(4) All machinery used in cotton production and processing could be imported without any import duties.

(5) The State would provide free cotton seed and information to those who sought it.[33]

Such efforts were not always successful. However, it represented a genuine and sustained attempt to upgrade the major and purely Ottoman revenue bases in agriculture. An agricultural bank was in the making, and even abolishing the tithe was discussed.[34] Such activities to improve Ottoman agriculture stand in marked contrast with government lassitude and inactivity in the industrial and commercial sectors.[35] Mounting foreign debt and shrinking revenue sources, however, increased the tax burden on agricultural producers and caused continuing abuse by tax farmers leading to old forms of "solidification" of claims in the collection process.[36]

## ABORTIVE FOREIGN COLONIZATION: NATIONAL AGRICULTURE

With the monopolization of commercial activities by foreigners, privatisation of possible revenue sources in this field was curtailed for the Ottoman elite. Therefore, agriculture was the only remaining source for the State and indigenous private claims alike, and therefore that source was jealously defended against foreign encroachment.

Negotiations on the issue of foreign landholdings extended over eleven years; under mounting pressure a law granting foreigners the rights of possession of agricultural land was promulgated in 1867. The outcome was remarkable. For some it was a "sweeping readjustment": of the capitulations by the Ottoman State, for it gave this right to the foreigners:

> contingent on the consent [that they] become completely subject to Ottoman jurisdiction and law in all that concerned ownership of real property.[37]

The refusal of the Ottoman State to give in totally on the land issue is indicative of the vigorous interest in preserving the "property" of the State. It also accentuates the existence of extreme polarisation in the control of the sectors of Ottoman economy. This polarisation existed not only on the level of economic and exploitative activity of different nationalities but also within the exclusive power that separate legal bodies--the Ottoman State and the consular offices of European powers--had on these different spheres of economic activity.

Within the Ottoman sphere of influence, the State conducted two contradictory policies. It encouraged settlement to increase agricultural production, and therefore left large lands under the control of local powers. At the same time, by holding to the principle of State property, it preserved its traditional stand against local landed power. But now there were two different landed powers developing. One flourished under the protection and support of the State, and the other preserved the old attitude of non-cooperation, either as nomads in areas where government authority could not penetrate, or as tax collectors and local chiefs privatizing part of the revenue.

Attempts at European colonization brought most of those diverse groups under the protection of the State which tried to contain foreign infringement on the revenue base. However, foreign purchase of rights of usufruct from some local notables established a basis of symbiosis between those two groups.

Between 1857 and 1892, although British acquisitions in Anatolia exceeded 200,000 hectares of agricultural land, the prospects for foreigners were not very encouraging.[38] In 1872, Sir P. Francis reported:

> ...the prevailing mode of taxation, the absence of security for property, and in some places, for life, the want of roads, the deficiency of markets, and in fact, the lack of all requisite conditions of prosperity, must prove hostile to the success of the native farmer, but infinitely more so to that of the foreign immigrant.[39]

At the same time, American cotton could not be adapted to local conditions, and the end of the American Civil War reduced the impetus to expand cultivation in Turkey.

Perhaps the most important factor was that extracting an agricultural surplus in Anatolia depended more on controlling the peasantry than on owning land. Foreigners had neither the access to labor of settling nomadic chiefs, nor the powers of coercion of usurping tax collectors. They had to face extremely high labor costs in the face of low productivity. Daily wages were as high as two shillings for male workers primarily due to the scarcity of population and the availability of land for family farms.[40] The foreigners with their capital investments and an absence of "adequate" labor supply faced problems similar to those which Wakefield observed earlier in the U.S.[41] In Anatolia, the situation for colonizers was much worse, for the central authority backed the competing indigenous system. Colonizers could not create their own labor supply at desired wage rates and in adequate quantities. Consequently colonization failed and a foreign dominated capitalist sector could not survive in Anatolia.[42]

## FOREIGN DEBT, RAILROADS, AND EUROPEAN FINANCIAL CONTROL: PROLOGUE TO FOREIGN CLAIMS ON THE AGRICULTURAL SURPLUS

Although foreign settlement in Anatolia could not succeed, in the contest to control the agricultural surplus, the Ottoman state was also a loser. The Ottoman government started borrowing from European bankers in 1854. Financial transactions increased rapidly, and finally when the Ottoman default arrived in 1875, its shock "was even felt within the Vatican."[43] The Ottomans resisted foreign political domination of their finances for six years. The first constitutional monarchy was established in 1876 partly to demonstrate to European powers that the Ottomans could put their house in order without foreign interference. But it did not impress the Powers. Finally in 1881 after disastrous wars and embarrassing defeats, Istanbul was forced to concede the right to take over part of Ottoman finances to a private foreign administration made up of representatives of bondholders. This body was known as the Public Debt Administration (PDA), and its purpose was to supervise the payment of the "consolidated debt". The PDA became the most powerful public agency in the land. In 1910 about five thousand people were working for the agency.[44]

In 1881, PDA controlled the salt monopolies, the stamp taxes, the silk tithes, the fishing taxes around Istanbul, the beverage taxes, the tobacco monopolies, to mention only the most important.[45] But things did not stop there. Before long the Administration controlled most of the revenues shown as securities for the loans. For example, the Administration controlled the revenues that were allocated as the "kilometric guarantees" for the railroads, the construction of which accelerated after the 1880's.[46]

For some of the railroads the Ottoman government agreed to make up a guaranteed amount per kilometer of railroad that was constructed if the gross receipts from the operation of the railroads could not match that amount.[47] As securities for the kilometric guarantees, the government usually allocated specific taxes in regions along the routes of the railway. The PDA was made responsible for the collection and administration of such taxes. Furthermore such taxes, once allocated to the Administration, could not be changed to the detriment of the bondholders. By 1908, in addition to the revenues ceded to the Administration in 1881, the Public Debt collected the best revenues of the regions through which the railroads passed.[48]

What the foreign powers could not achieve through direct colonization, they attained through the financial system. This time control was not over the process of production--as it would have been under colonization--but over the already created surplus. The representatives of the Western nations were there materially to replace the Ottoman state on the well-established and much criticized mode of appropriation of surplus--the Ottoman tax system.

These developments had a very important impact on the Ottoman power structure. While in the period 1881-1908 over thirty percent of the revenues were used towards the payment of foreign debt, about a quarter of the revenue was collected by the PDA.[49] And a greater part of the Administration's revenue sources were taxes on the agricultural population--previously the undisputed area of influence of the locally powerful.

In 1878 in his report of Sultan Abdulhamid II, the British Ambassador, Sir Henry Austen Layard, mentioned among other things the low percentage of the actual levies that the government received as a result of tax farming. He suggested the employment of foreign personnel for the correction and development of Ottoman finances.[50] Soon afterwards the PDA took over this function. Tax revenues increased not only through the more efficient method of transportation which widened the local market,[51] but also by a more efficient method of tax collection. Adam Block, the president of the Debt Council, noted that

> the increase in Revenue [was not]...due only to fresh taxation... But the increase [was] due chiefly to improved methods of collection, and secondly, in certain districts, to the economic progress taking place in the country...[52]

Through its employees, who were considered state officials, the Administration could interfere easily in the collection of taxes even when it did not directly collect them.[53]

The PDA had been working to affect agricultural production through the introduction of improved methods, seeds, education, and even new crops.[54] The impact of such activity on tax yields must have been considerable. However, to a large degree, the increased yield of the taxes could have been achieved only through the elimination of some "middlemen." In other words, a large part of the increased yield was essentially the stuff which was formerly the subject of the extortions of the locally powerful.

In the current literature there does not, however, exist any mention of such a problem, let alone any systematic investigation of it. "Mortgaging the country to the foreigners" is a cliche that is frequently used, but it hardly refers to the above problem, at least in the context contemporary writers use the term.[55] However, in the 1920's, William Cumberland, an economist, wrote on this issue. He hinted at the problem of distribution of income that the financial management of the Administration had given rise to, without, however, going into the effects on social relations. Here is how he stated the problem:

> Can it be reasonably supposed that a per capita indebtedness of

> approximately L. T. 5.75 ($25.30) involving interest charges of about L. T. 0.20 ($0.90) is literally to be styled "insupportable"? Were it not for the fact that these payments for the most part went out of the country and thus necessitated an equal transfer of wealth from Turkish subjects to foreigners rather than a mere redistribution of wealth within the Empire, the debt would hardly have attracted attention.[56]

Cumberland's suggestion is to transform the debt into a general charge against general revenues as was the practice elsewhere. But the PDA would not have adopted such a solution, since the yields along railway lines were so much higher due to density of agricultural operations caused by easy communications.

Benefits accruing to peasants as a result of the operations of the PDA were substantial, according to Donald Blaisdell. "Peasants were assured a fair price for their grain, and could depend on the auctions being held at favorable moments."[57] Hypothetically at least this argument is sound since sharing the local tax collector's income with the peasantry could have established good working relations for the Administration.

What happened to the dominant elements who lived off the revenue? Those who had claims on the production of the peasantry can be grouped into three categories, each relating to land differently, or each commanding a different level of economic and political power. These are: a) the landlord, b) powerful non-owners, in other words, a big bureaucrat, or local potentate--someone not directly employed by the state, but having close ties with it, and c) small bureaucrats--employed by the State in much more insignificant jobs as policemen or clerks.

The first group, harbingers of a new class, (having begun to establish its right to the surplus of their land through ownership relations) was the group least affected by the operations of the Public Debt Administration. But those landlords, who were also the tax farmers of their region, must have been adversely affected because of the Administration's attempts to increase the yield of taxes.

The second group ought to have suffered greatly by losing the ability to purchase local tax-farming contracts on favorable terms. However, members of this group, upon being denied their "traditional" claim on the surplus, could have attempted to reestablish their claim through the utilization of their accumulated wealth either by establishing themselves as landlords or by controlling the trade in agricultural produce.

The small bureaucrats--the third group--must have been hardest hit because they lost their petty claims and could not make them up through alternative methods due to the lack of accumulated wealth. But still they could have turned to land ownership and commerce--as did the big bureaucrats. It is likely that petty officials were less successful at this, however.

The activities of the Public Debt Administration and the construction of railroads should have at least catalyzed the commercialization of agriculture. This would have resulted from their impact on the social relations between the ruling class and peasants and the effect of improved communications. Direct interference of the ruling class into the productive activities of the peasantry had already begun in the late nineteenth century. There is, however, a major qualitative difference between voluntary and non-voluntary shift of roles in the relations of production. In the non-voluntary case it involves a loss of income in the form of "extortions." Of course, an immediate and full repair of the loss through a change of roles is far from likely and with it comes the animosity towards the Administration and the State. In the voluntary case--where the landlord begins to turn into a capitalist farmer himself rather than as a result of being forced out of his previous role--even a symbiotic relationship with the new revenue collectors may be hypothesized due to the "rationality" of the new method of taxation. A similar argument can be made for those who undertook commercial activities voluntarily and involuntarily.

The end of the nineteenth century was a period of growing dissent and effective organization against the State. The organized movement was, however, taking place within the State. Nationalist sentiment was developing, especially among the lower cadres. The government was highly centralized. Not only was the bureaucracy pushed aside, its members suffered salary cuts in addition to frequent and extended delays in payment. The State had lost control over its own finances and was using the rivalry among the European powers to preserve its integrity. The gradual surrender to European demands could only take place at the expense of a part of the ruling class itself.

There are indications that there were strong local reactions to the activities of PDA, and that the attitude of the central government during the Young Turk period was supported in the provinces on this basis. The hypothesis that the impact of PDA on local power configurations created an impetus for centralisation and nationalistic sentiment needs to be scrutinized further.

## DEVELOPMENT OF OPPOSITION TO THE CENTER AND THE YOUNG TURKS

The Young Turk movement developed and gained strength on the grounds described in the last section. The distributive mechanism was not working for the power structure any more. According to the Young Turks, the State was in the hands of traitors collaborating with the foreigners. Their object was to make the State representative and competent. The common belief was as follows: if they could demonstrate to the European powers that the State structure could be modernized, and if they could show that they could put "their house in order," then the Great Powers would not interfere in the internal affairs of the Ottoman State any longer.

Eventually, after the turn of the century, the Young Turks took power and tried to present themselves to "Europe" as a civilized, Western, competent cadre sharing the same values as the Europeans. The British were not impressed. The PDA and other foreign domination in internal affairs continued, and the Young Turk reaction started assuming an anti-British flavor.

In the period of Young Turk domination, another approach to economic policy began developing. It can be summarized as follows: "Europe's power was based on its bourgeoisie. Ottomans had no bourgeoisie upon which to build the power of the State, since all commercial classes of remarkable strength were European proteges or subjects. Therefore the Ottomans had to develop their own to be successful and powerful."

With both of the sources of surplus under foreign control, this was an attempt to expand and diversify sources. After 1910, the Ottoman State's efforts concentrated on commercial and industrial development at an increasing rate. This approach would have also served the issue of removing power bases embedded in agricultural production by inducing the transfer of their activities into urban-based enterprises. Thereby common causes of internal cycles of distribution and political domination would also be eradicated.

## MAJOR TYPES OF LAND TENURE AND POSSIBLE FORMS OF DOMINATION IN EARLY 20TH CENTURY

There are no reliable data on land relations at the turn of the century. The foregoing account provides more information about the dynamics than non-comparable and highly aggregated information. For example, according to Table 1, there seems to be a relatively higher concentration of the smallest category of holdings in more backward and less fertile areas, while the cutoff point for large holdings is set so low that dominance structure cannot be inferred meaningfully.[58]

The definition of "holdings" is also fuzzy. If it refers to titles of "usufruct," then political dominance and concentration in the privatization of surplus is totally missed. Therefore, information on all the major forms of the Ottoman method of approriation and claims would be lost. Furthermore, from the rate of registration of early land holdings by peasants in the 1940's and early '50's, it is evident that titles were not established in vast areas by smaller peasants. This would lead to a bias in larger titles.

If "holdings" refer to the size of operations, again figures would miss "domination" and yield a more egalitarian distribution of farm operations by peasants in relations resembling sharecropping. Unless such information is complemented by the size and structure of tax farms and the identity of tax farmers, it cannot be effectively used to infer the nature of social relations.

To replace such deficiency in data, at least a rough estimate about the character of land tenure in Turkey at the turn of the century is necessary. Such a task cannot definitely be done at the micro level without an in-depth historical investigation. However, based on the developments of the 19th century, and the nature of settlements in Turkey today, it is possible to identify possible trends in land-holding structures at the turn of the century on a regional basis. Major geographic divisions would be adequate for this purpose.

1) The East and Southeast

These were the regions where the State's authority had not been able to penetrate until well into the 1940's. Social organization had been primarily "tribal." Cultivation was primarily for subsistence and the major economic activity was animal husbandry on a transhumant basis. Settlement and monopolization of land on the basis of the 1858 land code did not apply, for local power had been quite strong. Because the dominance of local powers was undisputed and solidified claims were strong, the "legal" basis for land holdings did not need to develop. Communications were poor and the local economy was far from the initial stages of integration with the "national" economy. Low taxation of animal husbandry further contributed to the semi-autonomous, tributary nature of this region. This is the area of highest concentration of landholdings today. However, the raw figures on landholding size need to be adjusted for the infertility of soil and the high percentage of fallow, in order to make the figures comparable with those from more fertile regions.[59]

2) Cukurova

As mentioned above, this fertile region was the prime target for settlement policies and consequently a transformation of the population occurred and large holdings emerged. Access to surplus was more on the basis of the reorganisation of production (i.e. development of capitalist relations) than on political control of revenue flows.[60]

3) The South, excluding Cukurova

The fertile plains of this region were summer pastures of small transhumant organizations (*Yoruk*). Settlement of this region increased only after the 1030's. Being poor in communications, the main route to the surplus of existing agricultural activities was through the political domination of local notables.

4) The West

Communications in this region developed rapidly during the period of railroad construction. The region contained extensive undeveloped plains and a considerable transhumant population. This area was the major source of industrial export crops. Being subject to stronger central authority (relative to previous regions), settlement did not require as much concession to local and transhumant power bases in terms of granting large areas of land for usufruct. However, production-based domination must still have been substantial due to the high level of commercialization of the region. This area was also a major recipient of migrant Muslims from the Balkans who were given individual family farms, essentially by the Government of the Republic.

5) The Northwest (Marmara and Thrace)

This region has been the most developed, due to its proximity to Istanbul. Communications were excellent, by Ottoman and Turkish standards. Control of large tracts of land was only possible under the State's sanction for its prominent members. Claiming semi-autonomous regions based on local power was least likely, and large landholdings could hardly be developed through tax-farming and similar authority.

6) The North (Black Sea)

This thin strip of agricultural land was populated by subsistence farmers and small-scale growers of industrial crops. Being an old settlement, creating large landholdings through transforming transhumant population was infeasible. Yet control of revenue through local power must have been possible.

7) Central Anatolia

Poor communications left this area underpopulated. There were scattered transhumant groups without strong political leadership. Construction of the Baghdad railway contributed significantly to settlement and agricultural activity at the end of the 19th century. Agricultural activities flourished by leaps and bounds only after the widespread introduction of tractors in the mid-twentieth century. This region was also a great recipient of migrants, especially in the Eskisehir area, again with family farms granted by the government, breaking possibilities of concentrated landholdings. At the turn of the century both the government and the railroad company actively participated in settling immigrating peasants from the Balkans and Crimea in the Beysehir region with the purpose of expanding agricultural production and revenues.[61] Being a sparsely populated, low fertility region, concentrated land control through political power was unlikely and the absence of tribal organization contributed to the same result.

Activities of the PDA were mostly concentrated in areas of good communications, as the Northwest and the West. In those regions, the PDA must have left its mark of breaking up of solidification of claims by the notables who could obtain tax farms. This could also apply to parts of central Anatolia. Thus "enterprise" and settlement were the only routes of control.

In terms of claims on land through settlement of population, the period was most important, for after the Republic, the government did not support the practice of giving large titles to landed powers for settlement, at last after the 1930's.

Thus we are left with three possible routes to the control of large areas of agricultural land: a) through illegitimate control of revenue--

challenged by the PDA in certain regions, b) throught the legitimate approach of promising to improve vacant land, mostly applicable in the 19th century, and c) through semi-autonomous control based on local power, as in the East.

## EARLY YEARS OF THE REPUBLIC: NO LAND POLICY, CHANGING REVENUE STRUCTURE

The power base of the Ankara government was the local notables of Anatolia. The war of independence was fought with resources obtained from and channeled by them. They had direct access to surplus in the hinterland.

Soon after the Republic, all revenues under the control of the PDA were seized, and a year later the tithe contributing 22% to the government's total revenue in 1924 and 63% to the revenue from direct taxes was abolished.[62] The tithe and its collection had been much abused. Relieving the farmer of this burden was the nominal reason behind the decision. The revenue loss was to be made up by alternative taxes, but the plans did not work. The net effect was relieving "agriculture"--the primary economic activity in the country--of the burden.

There was yet another symbolic and fundamental aspect of this act. By relieving agriculture of taxation, government claims on agricultural activities and cultivated lands were also effectively terminated. Distribution in those spheres could no longer be done through a redistribution of revenues. Logically, the target of distributive activity had to be either land or agricultural prices or both. Who benefited from the abolition of the tithe? There is no doubt that abolition was a gift to those large landholders holding a title to land, who were informed of government activities and were aware of their interests. They also had the power and the capacity to ask for their rights. With the peasantry, however, the answer is more complicated.

For the peasantry in proximity to the central government's authority, benefits cannot be doubted. But for those who were under the control of local powers who also arranged tax collection and its delivery with the central government, it must have been a different story. Extraction of surplus in those regions was a matter of fact and the central authority did not matter much. Also, in a period of sustained increase in population and settlement, the absence of the State's claims on any part of the land must have left those regions under the control of local powers. The timing, the abruptness, and the nature of the first parliament, and its prospective effects, suggest that the abolition was a gift, or a payment of dues, to local notables by the Republican government.

In any case, *de facto* control of the source of surplus was in the hands of the notables. Ideologically, the most criticized practice of the PDA had to be reversed and the State had to return the control of the "nation's property back to the "people."

However, this policy created its own contradictions. Ceding control of agriculture, or the State's claims on it, allowed the emergence of a power base independent of the State. The bureaucracy and the military were dominated by an urbanized centrist section of the ruling class, who sought recentralization and the building of a nation-state. Centrifugal tendencies based on local powers could not be permitted. The Eastern region with its disarticulation from the rest of the society with a possibility of Kurdish rebellion was a major source of concern. Every effort was made to dislocate their leaders. Similar developments could not be allowed to take place in the rest of Anatolia.

The same old Ottoman concern regarding "semi-autonomous" regions and landed power was widespread among the Republican bureaucracy although there was no longer any contest about direct revenues. However, by ceding control of direct revenues, the State did not release its claim to potentials of agricultural production; land policy and agricultural prices remained major concerns of the government.

Within a very short period of time a direct confrontation developed between the government and vested power bases in rural Anatolia. The attitude of high-ranking bureaucrats toward landholders is most revealing.[63] "Rebellious elements," "monopolization of landholdings" and "exploitation of peasantry" were common terms used by the intelligentsia. Fearing destabilizing action from rural areas, there were legislative, military, and political actions to eliminate or incorporate those elements. Incorporation of dislocated local power was possible through urbanization and commercial and industrial activity. The State opposed concentrations of power and wealth in agriculture but not in urban enterprises.

## REPUBLICAN OBSERVATIONS ON LANDED PROPERTY IN THE 1930'S AND THEIR INTERPRETATION

Against this background there emerged a new "notion" of landed property after the late 1920's. The figures that were circulating often reflected the bureaucracy's sentiments rather than the facts. For example, Hamid Sadi's figures implied that 33,000 units of large landholders owned eight million hectares.[64] 1934 government statistics showed, on the other hand, that the total cultivated area in Turkey was less than seven million hectares (See Table 7). Hamid Sadi, however, claimed that the eight million comprised thirty-five percent of the cultivated area. Other available figures also seem to be grossly biased towards showing a high concentration of property.[65] There were figures showing a distributional structure more or less similar to the situation today, but again they were understood to reflect a high distributional bias towards large property.[66]

The complementary side of the problem is the issue of landlessness. The bureaucracy frequently mentioned it, and it has been cited in most studies on agrarian change. For example, Tezel reports that in 1927 seventeen percent of all rural families were landless, and argues that most of them could not possibly be involved in non-agricultural activities. The conclusion is that those households provided agricultural labor for large holdings, implying that the monopolization of property leads to this result.[67] However, considering the underpopulation in Anatolia in the 1930's and the possibilities of expanding the agricultural area (tables 7 and 8), the existence of a landless peasantry is better explained by the *domination* of the agricultural population than by the concentration of *property*.

It seems that observers of Turkish agrarian relations took the domination of local notables in their surplus extracting activities to mean "titles" to land or "property" held by local powerholders. Had the State cooperated with the notables in their spoils, large property might have developed, but the State was far from following such a course. Then, what could be the basis of assuming large agricultural property?

## THE CIVIL CODE OF 1926 AND THE PRINCIPLE OF PROPERTY: PROBLEMS IN THE LEGALISTIC APPROACH

Investigation of the emergence of the phenomenon of property in land in Turkey tends to be legalistic. Studies concerned with the issue have been preoccupied with the identification of a specific incident or law which is assumed to establish private property on public lands. Even some social scientists choose to fall back upon a simple legalistic explanation.[68] An alternative approach, investigating the *process* of development of property, is not common. But the legalistic approach cannot provide an adequate answer to the problem.

Today the Civil Code is the legal basis of all issues relating to immovable property. Going backwards from this fact, some lawyers argue that the source of establishing property in land needs to be sought in this code. This thesis, however, led to a fifty-year old inconclusive debate.[69] The proponents of this view claim that it is the promulgation of the Civil Code of 1926 that established *de jure* private property on land. This argument is based on an "interpretation" of the "essence" of articles in the Civil Code relating to immovable property. Yet, it is not clear from the letter of the law (which is binding) that the articles on immovable property "contain" the State lands (i.e. *Miri.*)

Opponents of this view make three main points. First, the 1858 Land Code had never been annulled. Second, legally if a law is not annulled, the alternative method through which it loses its validity is through falling into "conflict" with a new law. The 1858 Land Code and the 1926 Civil Code do not embody any "conflict," rather they cover different ground. Therefore the Land Code is still in effect. Third, the 1858 Land Code was amended after the promulgation of the Civil Code proving that the Civil Code did not replace the Land Code.[70]

The opposition view is extremely clear and strong except that, for all practical purposes, there does now exist *inviolable* property in land in practice. Now that its claims on surplus have been abandoned, the State no longer has any basis for claiming peasant property (i.e., on grounds of noncultivation.)

On the other hand, the fact that today there exists private property in land, in practice and in understanding, does not make the first argument valid. Contemporary private property plus the opposition view show that it was *not* the legislation that made property possible.

Furthermore, the Civil Code cannot specify the rightful owner of land in the absence of titles and varying claims. Therefore, taking the concept of *private property* from the Civil Code and observation of *domination* in agricultural production does *not* establish the existence of *large property on land*. The connection remains to be established, and that could not be accomplished.

Thus, both sides of the legalistic debate are in error due to the implicit assumption that property on agricultural land can be explained on legalistic grounds. That leaves the alternative approach--the "process"--as a more fruitful route of investigation.

## STATE ACTION BETWEEN THE 1930'S AND THE 1950'S

Coercive action to dislocate local powers in the Eastern region[71] and to settle the transhumant population in the South was resumed in the 1930's. Together with this, a clear stand against large landholdings (which were principally in the form of *claims* on large tracts of land by virtue of local power) was taken by the government by raising the issue of land reform. It was clear that in the new settlement policy tribal leaders would not be given special privileges.

The land reform act took more than a decade to take shape. The maximum possible size of property was initially set at 50 hectares; eventually it went up to 500. Sanctions against absentee landlords could not be enacted. In general the act was watered down but the principle was there. Eventually it did not get applied vigorously, but in the course of its development, it became clear that the act was being written as a guideline to be adopted by land owners rather than for strict enforcement. The state did not seem to have the necessary support to enforce the letter of such a law. In the late 1940's, those parliamentary opponents of the legislation, some of whom were also large landholders, resigned from the party and joined the newly emerging opposition.[72]

In 1945, the "law to endow land to farmers" was passed. By 1947, this law was in operation. "Land distribution commissions" were set up to distribute titles to "landless" peasantry by surveying each village in Turkey.

During this process, the terminology used for land to be distributed to the peasantry was "property."

## PEASANT "PROPERTY" FROM THE 1930's TO THE 1950's

The following is a general picture of new settlements and of non-title holding farmers in Turkey.[73]

Some of the peasantry in the 1930's and 1940's had old titles of usufruct left over from the Ottoman period. But they seem to have comprised a minority. In the South, East, and even in the West, peasants could not document their titles. Until the 1950's, the concept of "property" of land was not common among the peasantry. If they were free from domination, they cultivated the land and "property" was not an issue. If local domination was strong, a portion of the crop was paid to the landlord as in a sharecropping contract, although the landlord may not have had title to the land.

The transhumant population paid dues to local authorities for cultivating in their winter camps. Settling transhumants undertook cultivation under the supervision of their leaders and paid a share to them, and could be evicted from the plots that they reclaimed at the will of their leaders.

Newly settling tribal leaders in this period lacked the government support which the settlers in Cukurova enjoyed in the second part of the 19th century. Also, in regions where local control was strong, the resident notables did not feel the need of government sanction in "titles." Therefore, the dominant power did not have the institutional means to continue their control of the peasantry. With the beginning of debates on land reform, notables and leaders sensitive to the attitude of the State must have felt the pressure developing, and started liquidating their control.

Thus, in the 1930's, initial "property" acquisition started appearing among non-title-holding peasants. This period also witnessed the emergence of new claims of large holdings. However, they did not as successfully materialize in property as did smaller peasant claims. The process progressed at an increasing rate. By the 1950's, from the viewpoint of the peasantry, the land was definitely something to be "owned."

This happened in several ways:

1) In the early 1930's, some of the old established powers started selling land to the peasantry. Such sales did not involve a transfer of title. It was done on the basis of an oral contract, and on rare occasions a handwritten document was issued by the seller. Such land transfers intensified in the 1940's with the progress in parliamentary debates on the land reform act. Even in the early 1950's, similar land transfers were taking place. Sellers were indiscriminately large "landlords" transferring their wealth into urban property and business.

2) In the late 1940's and early 1950's, there was a widespread movement among the peasantry and some other larger claimants to establish titles on land by taking their cases to court and proving twenty years

of continuous "usufruct" by providing two witnesses. The underlying motive in doing this was the availability of agricultural credit in the late 1940's, which could only be obtained by producing title to agricultural land as a collateral. The land for which titles were so sought were either purchased land or land on which cultivation had taken place. The main effect of distribution of credit and establishment of titles was building the notion of property in land.

The rapid rate of population growth and the decreasing availability of accessible land also contributed to the development of the concept of "property."[74]

3) Widespread action of land distribution commissions covered most of the unsurveyed territory between 1947 and 1960 and continued at a slower pace thereafter. What the commissions did was first to survey the land within village boundaries and to establish all existing titles. Then *de facto* usufruct was investigated by consulting with the villagers. Consequently, titled land and established usufructory "rights" were subtracted from all available cultivated land and were divided among the "landless" equally. This was the final and definitive measure eliminating the claims of local leaders on peasants' surplus. During 1940's and 1950's the area of arable land increased very rapidly. This took place at the expense of pastures. At the same time the settlement of the transhumant population continued. Therefore, the dramatic increase in the cultivated area in Turkey needs to be evaluated in conjunction with the remarkable transformation in the nature of productive activities and populations.[75]

For those peasants who purchased "public lands" from their rural "masters," the action of the "land distribution commissions" legitimized the transaction which originally had no legal basis.

The process of land distribution by the commissions did not always lead to an equitable outcome especially between villages. Distribution applied only to village lands and village residents. For example, those transhumant populations who were not settled in the plains but chose to continue their activities of animal husbandry and camel transportation ended up getting small and infertile plots due to their geographic locations. However, the "subject" population in the malarial plains seem to have fared better by the 1950's.

The story of a peasant receiving the "title" to a piece of land on which he used to be a sharecropper is common in areas where local notables still continue their agricultural activities. This story also applies to those "capitalist farmers" who attempted to enclose further land in the Republican period.

It is also common that tribal leaders employing their tribesmen as agricultural laborers after settlement received discretionary distributions from the government. But what they received does not seem to reach thousands of hectares as was assumed in the early Republic.

Successful monopolisation of landholdings by the privileged was not the rule even in those areas where concentration of ownership is highest today. In order to be able to assess the developments in the emergence of property on arable land realistically, successful cases of landlordism need to be evaluated together with the instances of failure. Recent observations show that failures are at least as common as the success stories.[76]

From the foregoing discussion, three interrelated factors emerge that explain the speedy erosion of seemingly large concentrations of 1930's. First, population pressure on arable land was not felt until 1950's. This eased the pressure on land. It was not a scarce factor and a scramble for land did not materialize before measures were implemented against monopolisation. In the same vein, activities of land distribution commissions helped to spread peasant property thereby diffusing already established larger concentrations. Second, because large claims on "property" were late to appear--i.e. it became a major issue in 1930's--there was practically no chance to establish or justify those claims on tradition, institutions, etc. Third, the State did not support the process of monopolisation of landholdings in principle. In the final analysis the State action in breaking down large claims was successful.

Paradoxically, those who argue the success of concentration of large landownership before 1950 blame this either on the complicity or the ineffectiveness of the government.[77] It is true that those who successfully consolidated their power and claims on land earlier in the century either defied the State or used their power and influence in the political system to establish their claims. Every government that came to power during the Republic has been able to obtain the support of some local powerbrokers. While the resulting political favoritism managed to extend the period of dominance of the supporters of the government, the principle of breaking local power was applied to the opponents. This had the interesting effect of erosion of landholdings with every change in government.

Influential power-brokers who attempted to retain their domination and keep control over the land suffered heavy losses. Bolukbasi of Kirsehir and Nigde provinces is a good example. He was a prominent political figure and the leader of his own political party. In mid-1950's, under the rule of Democrat party--frequently identified as a party of landowners--he had to give up thousands of hectares of his property in a lengthy process of prosecution to erode his dominance.

With so many examples of "expropriation" of landlords by an unfriendly government, local power-brokers were persuaded to divest. Today it is still possible to observe contrasting pictures in the agrarian scene. In eastern Anatolia, the government's impotence in land disputes occasionally surfaces. While in other regions those who were sometimes evaluated as oppressive "feudal lords" a few decades ago frequently now own only a small fraction of what they used to control.

The key to the paradox is to separate the *de facto* favoritism of *political power* from the consistent policy of the *State* to break local domination. A general picture emerges from this discussion: Whenever large domination is broken in some fashion, due to the stand taken by the State on the land issue, a unidirectional development emerges. It is not possible to observe cyclical reconsolidation of landholdings with changes in political power. The process yields an irreversible development towards more widespread peasant property in Turkish agriculture.

## CHANGING RELATIONS BETWEEN LOCAL POWER AND THE STATE

Those local notables who followed the guidelines set by the State and pulled out from agricultural production received high level support from the government. However, the support given to them cannot be interpreted as support of their domination of the peasantry as is frequently done. Symbiotic relations between the State and commercial classes with a rural origin are applicable to those who have eventually severed their ties to agricultural production. In the process of divestment, the notables continued with commercial activities in their rural base. For example, with the development of a highway network in Anatolia in the 1950's, transportation was controlled by those people who were turning into urban commercial classes. Thus, the divesting rural rich were turning into the commercial and industrial bourgeoisie that the State had been trying to create since the late Ottoman times.

The contrast between the divesting and non-divesting notables is quite striking. Government policy of breaking the power of eastern notables has not been as successful. In certain localities local "landlords" still maintain their influence and "defy" state authority. After the military coup of 1960, a group of landlords was transported to the Western region in internal exile.

## THE ROLE OF THE STATE RE-EMPHASIZED: THE WESTERN MODEL VERSUS THE TURKISH REALITY

After the 1950's, agricultural output grew impressively. In the same period, with the influx of foreign aid and the injection of technology, methods of agricultural production changed drastically. Again in the same period, rural-urban migration reached a high level.

Observing all those factors, social investigation in the field was directed toward the changing structure in agriculture. Fueled by the 1930's rhetoric about large landed property in the rural sector, the argument that developed identified landlessness (inferred from migration), large landed property, and technology as the main factors underlying the major transformation in social structure. However, due to the limited nature of large property on land, such a view could not be supported with facts.

From the foregoing account, we see that the social structure in Turkish agriculture had already taken its shape by the 1950's. Domination had been inhibited and peasant agriculture began to take root. The urban exodus had been taking place from peasant agriculture. Those who entered the migrant flow were the prospective agricultural workers of large holdings which did not exist to the degree that it was estimated.

"The tractor" was identified as the tool of the landlord driving the peasantry away. Today it is well incorporated into peasant agriculture. It did decrease the demand for agricultural labor, but primarily the demand of the middle peasantry rather than that of the landlord. However, considering the dramatic expansion in cultivated area in the decade following the World War II, it is worth considering whether without the introduction of the tractor rural employment could have reached the levels that it did in 1950's. In order to be able to construct a sound analytical model of agricultural transformation in Turkey the indigenous factors that differentiate the Turkish case from others need to be treated explicitly.

It is very difficult indeed to superimpose the "Western Model" onto Turkish agrarian history. There was no basis for large landed "property" in the Ottoman past that would have been able to define social interaction in the agrarian sphere. Consequently landed property did not develop as an institution.

It was the "civilizing" influence that came from the West early in the nineteenth century that brought the concept of private property. For the European observers in general, a social structure could not be explained without the categories of nobility and property. So, they applied those concepts in their attempt to understand the workings of the Ottoman society.

It is no surprise that the beginnings of this Eurocentric approach in explaining the Ottoman structure is almost contemporaneous with the Permanent Settlement in Bengal where the Zamindar was identified as nobility and his domain as his private property. In the Ottoman case, there was a consensus among European observers, that the growth of nobility was inhibited by the despotic state. But the notion of private property survived, if not as a fact, at least as a policy towards implanting "civilisation" in the Ottoman social structure. Interestingly, during the unceasing reform movements of the nineteenth century, the Westernising Turkish elite adopted this notion and interpreted power struggles in Turkey in terms of alien concepts.

Against this backdrop of the alien notion of property in land, there are three aspects of Turkish reality that explain the emergence of widespread peasant property. First is the nature of the agrarian social structure which is summarized by transhumance and migrations. It is hard to define a static agrarian structure in Anatolia during the past 150 years. Communities, crops, and production methods have experienced major changes. The source of agricultural surplus to supply Istanbul with food in the Ottoman period had been Wallachia and Egypt, primarily due to the ease of access through sea routes. Comparatively, Anatolia was of minor interest in terms of "exportable" surplus. The development and expansion of agricultural production in Anatolia began when Wallachia and Egypt slipped out of the control of the Ottoman government in the nineteenth century. The expansion of cereal and cash crop production meant the transformation of transhumant population which was to be the major source of the emergent peasant population. Thus, the agrarian structure of Anatolia in the past century cannot be cast in terms of peasants, landlords, and arable land, but rather in terms of a transhumant economy, animal husbandry, and a "tribal" structure.

Another major source of agricultural work force was the migration of Muslims into Anatolia from the Balkans as a consequence of national liberation movements. This phenomenon changed the outlook of the entire countryside. Both of these aspects of the composition of agricultural population and its transformation cast serious doubt on using the concepts of peasantry and landlords as universal categories. An influx of overwhelming numbers of new population into a productive structure, itself in a state of fast transformation, calls for the redefinition of agrarian relations instead of making assumptions about it. Therefore, twentieth century developments in Turkey need to be analysed with an emphasis on seeking discontinuities in agrarian relations such as the settlement and resettlement policies.

The second feature is the nature of the process of establishment of domination or the method of appropriation of surplus. As much as landed "property" is an alien concept in the Ottoman system, "claims" of revenue is a household term with overwhelming continuity. Struggles in the political and military arena have taken place over the "shares" of surplus rather than over "property." To concentrate on issues relating to property and to ignore the process of division of surplus is an error of identification, making an explanatory variable out of a non-existing category. It is necessary to concentrate on the nature of conflict--appropriation of surplus--in order to be able to define the social interaction effectively in the nineteenth century. With the abolition of the tithe in 1925 the process that defined this interaction also came to an end, and the conflict took more of a political nature concentrating mainly on the "power relations" between the center and the periphery. Here again we see the discontinuity at a different level of socio-economic organization highlighting the Republican period as the beginning of a new era of social interaction.

The third and the most crucial element in Turkish history, that makes the former aspects of social interaction operative is the State and its independence (or autonomy) in social structure. The continuity through all the periods of Ottoman and Turkish history is maintained by it. In the absence of any "class" that can be identified as dominant in the Ottoman system, the "State" appears as the only institution around which other social and economic relations rise and fall.

In order to draw a complete picture of the agrarian transformation, the function of the State and its relation to rural power structure need to be incorporated into the analysis. The State was never out of the picture, and its relation to the rural power structure did not change in essence despite the major discontinuities mentioned above. Although its dominant position in the social and economic interaction remained, its policies toward commerce, industry and agriculture have changed drastically since the Ottoman period. It is the elimination of the State from the picture that permits unacceptable variables such as "property" and "landlords" to find their way into the analysis. Therefore the State needs to be incorporated into the conceptual framework as an independent and explicit actor.

## FOOTNOTES

* I wrote the original draft of this article while visiting the Institute of International Studies at Berkeley during 1984-85. I would like to thank the Director of the Institute Carl Rosberg, and also J. Dasgupta and Alain deJanvry of the Development Studies Program who provided me with the opportunity.

Feroz Ahmad, Isenbike Aricanli, Herbert Gintis, Fatma Isikdag, Emine Kiray, Mubeccel Kiray, Roger Owen and Alan Richards read the draft and made suggestions. I am grateful for their comments.

[1] See Tables 1-6.

[2] For a review of the debate on "feudal" structures in Turkish agriculture, see David Seddon and Ronnie Margulies, "The Politics of the Agrarian question in Turkey: Review of a Debate," *Journal of Social Studies*, No. 19, (January 1983), pp. 1-44. Also see Korkut Boratav, "Turkiye Tariminin 1960' Lardaki Yapisi ile Ilgili Bazi Gozlemler" *SBF Dergisi*, Vol. 27, No. 3, Sept. 1972, pp. 771-814. For the statistical village studies conducted between 1963 and 1969, and for the Agricultural Census of 1970, see Mine Cinar and Oya Silier, *Turkiye Tarminda Isletmeler Arasi Farklilasma* (Istanbul: Bogazici Universitesi Yayinlari, 1979), pp. 4 ff.

[3] For a theoretical discussion of domination and its relation to exploitation and class see Samuel Bowles and Herbert Gintis, *Democracy and Capitalism: Property, Community, and the Contradictions of Modern Social Theory* (New York: Basic Books, 1986) especially Chapter 4 "Structure: Mosaic of Domination". For different forms of domination and patronage in a particular context in modern Turkey see Mubeccel B. Kiray "Changing Patterns of Patronage: A Study in Structural Change" in Cigdem Kagitcibasi (ed) *Sex Roles, Family and Community in Turkey* (Bloomington: Indiana University Turkish Studies, 1982) pp. 269-293. Also see Mubeccel B. Kiray and Jan Hinderink "Interdependencies Between Agroeconomic Development and Social Change: A Comparative Study Conducted in the Cukurova Region of Southern Turkey" *The Journal of Development Studies* Vol. 4, No. 4, July 1968, pp. 497-528, and Jan Hinderink and Mubeccel B. Kiray, *Social Stratification as an Obstacle to Development: a Study of Four Turkish Villages* (New York: Preager 1970), for an argument that "landlordism" has not been a determining factor in the socio-economic transformation of the region studied. It should be noted that the locations the last two works focus upon are the places where concentration of land holdings have been the highest among the *fertile* regions in Turkey.

[4] Sedden and Margulis, (1983). It is still common to explain the domination that existed in rural areas in terms of property relations. For a contemporary example from journalism see Kemal Sulker, "Yakilip

Yikilisinin 40. Yilinda Tan Olayi" *Gunumuzde Kitaplar* No. 24 December 1985 pp. 9-15. Ellen Kay Trimberger *Revolution From Above: Military Bureaucrats and Development in Japan, Turkey, Egypt, and Peru* (New Brunswick: Transaction Books, 1978) is an excellent example towards the development of a theory of the State outside the Capitalist model. Here the "relative autonomy" of the State is emphasized, and its pivotal role in social change is analysed. In her argument, the independence of the bureaucracy from "landlords" and other social categories is emphasized. In reviewing Trimberger's book James Petras "Revolution From Above" (Review Arhzlo) *Contemporary Sociology* Sept 1950 Vol 9 No 5. pp. 717-713 assumes a social structure that Trimberger argues does not exist and utilizes the concepts of "property" and "landlord" to define the power base of the State.

[5] For example, the 1858 land code and the abolition of the tithe in 1925. Also see Yahya Sezai Tezel *Cumhuriyet Doneminin Iktisadi Tarihi* (*1923-1950*) (Ankara: Yurt Yayinlari, 1982) pp. 306-378. Historically there had been special forms of "property" on land used for the settlement of non-agricultural population, but those forms did not gain status sufficient to affect and define agrarian relations.

[6] Here "territory" needs to be differentiated from "property". Consider the following scenario, representative of eighteenth and early nineteenth century power relations in the Ottoman context: A rebellious notable could establish his domination over a "territory" by controlling the penetration of central authority to that region, and thereby could claim a greater share of the surplus than the State would willingly yield. Under such circumstance, one could identify borders within which the notable's domination is supreme. It may appear that the territory "belonged" to the notable or that it was his "property". However it must be emphasized that in this context the contestation is again over the surplus. The "borders" are *instrumental* in keeping the central authority from determining its share of the *surplus*, and does not result in a contestation over *property rights*. (As a matter of fact, contestation over property rights has always taken place through an appeal to the legitimate authority--the state).

Control of territories by notables, which was continuously and systematically challenged by the State, did not imply "property rights" because historically, contestation over property did not take this form, and the attributes of the concept of property, namely inviolability and mutual agreement, did not exist. That is, the sanction of the legitimate authority which would manifest itself in the form of a "title" did not exist. Moreover, one cannot detect any social or legal developments that could lead towards the emergence of large landed property.

Domination by notables in Ottoman history can be explained by distance and poor communications, rather than by the presence of property relations. Such domination was more common in remote areas where the central authority could not reach, and least likely in close proximity to the central authority.

[7] See table 9 on the practice of sharecropping. Note that practice of sharecropping-out is more common among the smaller plots.

[8] The issue of the "relative autonomy" of the State is directly related to the question of the primacy of the distributive process in social relations. The fundamental question is whether the state can be defined as an agent of (or in terms of) one of the actors (or classes) which have a direct access to surplus. The fact that in the Ottoman context it is impossible to define the State in terms of other social categories establishes its "autonomy" or "independence."

[9] Hinderink and Kiray (1970), pp. 226.

[10] The scale of production under a single operational unit could be expanded much further with animal husbandry. At the same time, it was not as easily taxed in practice. Moreover, tax rates on animal husbandry were much lower. All these factors created an incentive to turn arable land into pasture when individual control was established in remote regions. The State wanted to keep tax yields high, to control the sources of taxation, and to fight monopolization of local control. Consequently, it sought to protect the existing state of agricultural production and tried to control the expansion of the transhumance or nomadism. Thus there was a direct relation between the two goals of the State: 1) preservation of the existing productive forces and 2) redistribution of the wealth that it produced with least opposition from local monopolization.

This suggests a contribution by the Ottoman State to agricultural development. Although agricultural production under Ottoman rule did not exhibit progress, its protection against the inhibiting forces of nomadism was a positive contribution under the existing social and economic circumstances.

[11] See for example Charles MacFarlane, *Turkey and Its Destiny*, Vol. 1 (London: John Murray, 1850), pp. 126, 148-155.

[12] An extract of Ali Pasa's will appears in Cemil Meric, *Umrandan Uygarliga* (Istanbul: Otuken, 1974), pp. 29-37. For the complete text, see Engin Deniz Akarli, *Belgelerle Tanzimat: Osmanli Sadrazamlarindan Ali ve Fuad Pasalarin Siyasi Vasiyyetnameleri*, (Istanbul: Bogazici Universitesi Yaginlar, 1978)

[13] MacFarlane, (1850), Vol. II, pp. 171-177.

[14] F.E. Bailey, *British Policy and the Turkish Reform Movement* (Cambridge, Mass.: Harvard University Press, 1947), pp. 290-291.

[15] *The Ottoman Land Code*, F. Ongley, translator (London: William Clowes and Sons, 1892), pp. 8.

[16] *Ibid*., pp. 45-46.

[17] See O. L. Barkan, "Turkiyede Toprak Meselesinin Tarihi Esaslari," *Ulku*, Vol. XI, No. 61, (1938), pp. 55.

[18] O. L. Barkan, "Turk Toprak Hukuku Tarihinde Tanzimat ve 1274 (1858) Tarihli Arazi Kanunnamesi," *Tanzimat I* (Ankara: Maarif Vekaleti, 1940), pp. 401-402.

[19] *Ibid.*, passim.

[20] Kemal Karpat, "The Land Regime, Social Structure, and Modernization in the Ottoman Empire," in *Beginnings of Modernization in the Middle East*, Eds., W. R. Polk and R. L. Chambers (Chicago: Chicago University Press, 1968), pp. 69-90. Karpat sees the land code as a turning point in the emergence of private property although he states that the law did establish the basis of usufruct and no more. For a brief discussion of the goals of the 1858 Land Code see Charles Issawi, *The Economic History of Turkey, 1800-1914* (Chicago: The University of Chicago Press, 1980) pp. 202. Also see Doreen Warriner "The Real Meaning of the Ottoman Land Code" in Charles Issawi, *Economic History of the Middle East 1800-1914*, (Chicago: The University of Chicago Press, 1966) pp. 73.

[21] Barkan, (1940), pp. 410.

[22] A set of population figures from diverse sources for 19th century Anatolia is given in U. Nalbantoglu, "Osmanli, Toplumunda Trim Teknolojisi Arti-Urun ve Kent Ekonomisi," *Turkiye Iktisat Tarihi Semineri, 1973*, (Ankara: n.p., 1975) pp. 56.

[23] For an explanation of the existence of serfdom through the relative scarcity of labor, see Evsey D. Domar, "The Causes of Slavery or Serfdom: A Hypothesis," *Journal of Economic History*, Vol. 30, No. 1, 1970, pp. 18-32. See also Maurice Dobb, *Studies in the Development of Capitalism* (New York: International Publishers, 1947), pp. 33-82.

[24] For examples of the same process in other regions, see A. Jawaideh, "Midhat Pasha and the Land System of Lower Iraq" in *St. Antony's Papers*, No. 16, Albert Horani (ed.), (London: Chatto and Windus, 1963), pp. 115-135.

[25] Bernard Lewis, *The Emergence of Modern Turkey*, 2nd ed. (London: Oxford University Press, 1961), pp. 451. See also the memoranda of one of the officials involved in the operations of the division: Cevdet Pasa, *Tezakir 21-39* [Vol. III] (Ankara: TTK, 1963), pp. 107-212.

[26] Cevdet, (1963), pp. 107.

[27] See Wolfram Eberhard, "Nomads and Farmers in South Eastern Turkey," in *Settlement and Social Change in Asia, Collected Papers*, Vol. I (Hong King: Hong Kong university Press, 1967), pp. 286, 289.

[28] Eberhard, "Types of Settlement in Southeastern Turkey," *Collected Papers*, pp. 300; Cevdet, (1963), pp. 124.

[29] *Ottoman Land Code*, pp. 68. For a statement of the meaning of Ciftlik, see Bruce W. McGowan, "The study of Land and Agriculture in the Ottoman Provinces Within the Context of an Expanding World Economy in the 17th and 18th Centuries," *International Journal of Turkish*

*Studies,*, Vol. 2, 1981, pp. 57-63.

[30] See Hinderink and Kiray (1970), and also Nur Yalman "On Land Disputes in Eastern Turkey" *Research in Economic Anthropology* Vol 2, 1979, pp. 269-302, for illustrations of contemporary (after 1920's) claims to large property on land which do not have any basis on either nineteenth century titles of usufruct, or continuity of cultivation. It is evident that modern claims result from post-Republic (1923) power relations.

[31] See S. Pamuk, "Osmanli Tariminda Uretim Iliskileri (1840-1913)," *Toplum ve Bilim*, No. 17, Spring 1982, pp. 3-50, on European assessments of land holdings in Turkey. Western observers in the nineteenth century treated control of large agricultural operations as private property, and the author accepts this approach without further scrutiny. Newly consolidated lands did not necessarily continue under the same hereditary management. After World War I new claims on the lands vacated during the war due to dislocation of ethnic groups appeared. Although it is possible to detect an increase in the claims on land starting from the middle of the nineteenth century, it is noteworthy that continuity of those claims by the same families were much less common. Thus, much of the twentieth century phenomena seem to be new, based on changing power relations and the increasing commercialization of agricultural production.

[32] MacFarlane, (1850), Vol. I, pp. 59-62. O. Kurmus, *Emperyalizmin Turkiyeye Girisi* (Istanbul: Bilim, 1974), pp. 81.

[33] *Turk Ziraat Tarihine bir Bakis* (Istanbul: n.p., 1938), pp. 178-179. See also Kurmus (1974), pp. 82-83.

[34] See fn. 12 above.

[35] See for example Donald Quataert, "Ottoman Reform and Agriculture in Anatolia, 1876-1908," unpublished Ph.D. dissertation, University of California at Los Angeles, 1973.

[36] See Donald Blaisdell, *European Financial Control in the Ottoman Empire* (New York: Columbia University Press, 1929); A. du Velay, *Turkiye Maliye Tarihi*, translated from French (Ankara: Maliye Bakanligi, 1978); Roger Owen, *The Middle East in the World Economy, 1800-1914* (London: Methuen, 1981), pp. 189-199.

[37] P.M. Bown, *Foreigners in Turkey* (Princeton: Princeton University Press, 1914), pp. 42.

[38] Kurmus, (1974), pp. 105-106.

[39] Great Britain: *Parliamentary Papers*, 1872, Vol 62. *Further Reports*, 1872), pp. 369-370.

[40] Kurmus, (1974), pp. 109-110.

[41] Edward Gibbon Wakefield, *England and America* (2 vols.; London, Richard Bentley, 1833). For a critical evaluation of Wakefield's work, see Karl Marx, *Capital*, Vol. I (Hammondsworth: Penguin, 1976), pp. 937-40.

[42] See Kurmus, (1974), pp. 100-110

[43] Blaisdell, (1929), pp. 40.

[44] *Ibid.*, pp. 90-107.

[45] *Ibid.*; Own, (1981), pp. 191-199.

[46] See M.K. Chapman, *Great Britain and the Bagdad Railway*, Smith College Studies in History, Vol. XXXI, Northampton, Mass., 1948; E. M. Earle, *Turkey, the Great Powers and the Bagdad Railway* (New York: Macmillan, 1973); Blaisdell, (1929).

[47] Earle, (1973), pp. 21-32, 76-77, 90.

[48] Herbert Feis, *Europe: The World's Banker, 1870-1914* (New Haven: Yale University Press, 1930), pp. 333.

[49] Engin Deniz Akarli, "Economic Problems of Abdulhamid II's Reign (1876-1909)," paper presented at the Conference on Economy, Society and Polity in the Magreb and Turkey, of the SSRC, Istanbul, May 1975, P. 70.

[50] M. Aktepe, "Osmanli Imparatorlugunun Islahi Hakkinda Ingiltere Elcisi Layard'in II. Abdulhamidie verdigi Rapor," *Belgelerle Turk Tarihi Dergisi*, Vol. IV, No. 22 (1969), pp. 18.

[51] Blaisdell, (1929), pp. 175-178.

[52] In R. G. Landen, *Emergence of the Modern Middle East* (New York: Van Nostrand Reinhold, 1970). pp. 172.

[53] *Ibid.*, pp. 169; Blaisdell, (1929), pp. 7.

[54] On silkworm production, du Velay, *Maliye Tarihi*, pp. 322-325, and Issawi, (1980), pp. 253-258.

[55] Chapter IV of Earle's *Bagdad Railway* is titled "The Sultan Mortgages His Empire."

[56] W. W. Cumberland, "The Public Treasury," *Modern Turkey* E. G. Mears (ed) (New York: Macmillan, 1974), pp. 401, 404-405.

[57] Blaisdell, (1929), pp. 7.

[58] Five hectares is an area that could be cultivated by a peasant family with a pair of oxen.

[59] See footnote 1 and Yalman (1979).

[60] See Hinderink and Kiray (1970), on the discontinuity in that process.

[61] Issawi, (1980), pp. 229-231.

[62] Blaisdell, (1929), pp. 199; C. Keyder, *The Definition of a Peripheral Economy: Turkey 1923-1929* (Cambridge: Cambridge University Press, 1981), pp. 33.

[63] For example, Cemal Bardakci, *Andolu Isyanlari* (Istanbul: Riza Koskun, 1940); also from the same author, *Devsirmeler'le Sigintilar'dan ve*

*Mutegallibe'den Neler Cektik*? (Bolu: n.p., 1947), especially pp. 161-247.

[64] Hamid Sadi, *Iktisadi Turkiye* (Istanbul: Yuksek Iktasat ve Ticaret Mektebi Yayini, 1932), pp. 62, cited in Tezel, *Iktisadi Tarih*, pp. 332.

[65] *Ibid.*, pp. 332-333.

[66] *Ibid.*; Keyder, *Peripheral*, pp. 13.

[67] Tezel, *Iktisadi Tarih*, pp. 335-336.

[68] For an example see Keyder, (1981): "In 1926 the new civil law reinforced the legality of private property by replacing the Ottoman categories, which varied between usufruct right and *de facto* ownership, with *de jure* private ownership" (p. 27).

[69] Halil Cin, *Osmanli Toprak Duzeni ve Bu Duzenin Bozulmasi* (Ankara: Kultur Bakanligi, 1978), pp. 478-497. Although Cin favors the argument that the Civil Code established the basis of private property on agricultural land, the evidence that he provides fails to support his thesis.

[70] Another important aspect of the 1858 Land Code is that it has been used to check the validity of claims on land on the basis of usufructory rights. For example, since the 1950's, titles on what was proven to be wastelands and swamps--i.e. uncultivable land--at the date of issue of the titles were annulled on the basis of the Land Code. (I owe the information of the practice of 1858 Land Code to Mr. Hakki Yasar of the Court of Appeals in Ankara.)

[71] Tezel, (1982), pp. 346-347,, cites Code No. 2510, dated June, 1934.

[72] *Ibid.*, pp. 341-357.

[73] Some of the observations on the following pages were made during the fieldwork of a research project funded by MEAwards in Cairo to investigate the "Paths of Rural Transformation in Turkey." Co-participants in the project were Bahattin Aksit, Huricihan Islamoglu, Caglar Keyder and Ayse Kudat.

I would also like to thank Mr. Hakki Yasar of the *7. Hukuk Dairesi* of the Court of Appeals in Ankara for discussion on the practice of the Land Code of 1858 since 1940. (Time of interview May 17, 1984)

[74] See the population figures in Table 8. Fast increase in the agricultural population between 1935-55 and its dramatic slowdown in the subsequent period is especially noteworthy.

[75] See Table 7.

[76] Yalman (1979), and Hinderink and Kiray (1970).

[77] Tezel, (1982).

TABLE 1: SIZE DISTRIBUTION OF AGRICULTURAL LANDHOLDINGS IN VARIOUS PROVINCES OF TURKEY IN 1909/10 (percentages)

| | Under 1 Hectare | 1-5 Hectares | Over 5 Hectares |
|---|---|---|---|
| Diyarbakir | 17 | 36 | 47 |
| Aydin | 18 | 36 | 46 |
| Bitlis | 21 | 41 | 38 |
| Konya | 23 | 46 | 31 |
| Ankara | 13 | 58 | 29 |
| Harput | 27 | 45 | 28 |
| Van | 36 | 37 | 27 |
| Bursa | 15 | 60 | 25 |
| Sivas | 32 | 46 | 22 |
| Trabzon | 38 | 46 | 16 |
| Erzurum | 45 | 40 | 15 |
| Kastamonu | 28 | 58 | 14 |
| Izmir | 67 | 33 | |
| Biga | 21 | 49 | 30 |

Source: E.F. Nickoley, "Agriculture," in Eliot Grinnel Mears (ed.) *Modern Turkey* (New York: McMillan) 1924. Table reproduced in Roger Owen *Middle East in the World Economy 1800-1914* (London: Methuen, 1981), p. 207.

TABLE 2: PERCENT OF LAND* OPERATED BY EACH TENTH OF FARM FAMILIES (1950)

| Percent of all rural farm families | Percent of all land operated |
|---|---|
| lowest 10% | |
| | 1.8 |
| 2nd lowest 10% | |
| 3rd " | 2.1 |
| 4th " | 3.2 |
| 5th " | 4.5 |
| 6th " | 5.7 |
| 7th " | 7.5 |
| 8th " | 10.1 |
| 9th " | 15.3 |
| highest 10% | 49.8 |

Source: 1950 *Census of Agriculture*, Table 8 in Eva Hirsch, *Poverty and Plenty on the Turkish Farm* (New York: Columbia University Press, 1970).

**Total amount of land* operated = 19,452 hectares**

**Total number of rural farm families = 2,527,800**

*** Includes fallow (approx. 6 million hectares)**

TABLE 3: DISTRIBUTION OF AGRICULTURAL OPERATIONS ACCORDING TO SIZE GROUPS (1970)

| Size Group of Holdings |  | Average Size of Cultivated Land | (1) As a % of all Cultivated Land | Number of Operational Units | (4) As a % of all Operational Units |
|---|---|---|---|---|---|
| (1) |  | (2) | (3) | (4) | (5) |
| I | Less than 2 hectares | 0.9 | 8.1 | 1,350,584 | 44.1 |
| II | 2.1 - 5 hectares | 3 | 18.7 | 877,764 | 28.7 |
| III | 5.1 - 10 hectares | 7 | 22..0 | 479,391 | 15.7 |
| IV | 10.1 - 20 hectares | 13 | 21.5 | 239,245 | 7.8 |
| V | 20.1 - 50 hectares | 27 | 17.9 | 95,536 | 3.1 |
| VI | Over 50 hectares | 101 | 11.9 | 17,478 | .6 |

Sources: (for Tables 3-6): 1970 Agricultural Census in Mine Cinar and Oya Silier, _Turkiye Tariminda Isletmeler Arasi Farklilasma_. (Istanbul: Bogazici Universitesi Yayinlari) 1979, pp. 50, 182-186, 334-335.

DIE, _Statistical Yearbook 1975_, Ankara 1976, pp. 16, 22.

Average income per hectare: 3126 TL*

* Exact date unknown (mid 1970s)

TABLE 4: DISTRIBUTION OF AGRICULTURAL OPERATIONS ACCORDING TO SIZE GROUPS: SOUTH EASTERN REGION (1970) (LOW FERTILITY RAINFED FARMING)

| | Size Group of Holdings (1) | Average Size of Cultivated Land (2) | (1) As a % of all Cultivated Land (3) | Number of Operational Units (4) | (4) As a % of all Operational Units (5) |
|---|---|---|---|---|---|
| I | Less than 2 hectares | 0.7 | 3.1 | 87,595 | 38.7 |
| II | 2.1 - 5 hectares | 3 | 7.0 | 46,163 | 20.4 |
| III | 5.1 - 10 hectares | 7 | 12.3 | 37,138 | 16.4 |
| IV | 10.1 - 20 hectares | 13 | 20.2 | 32,267 | 14.2 |
| V | 20.1 - 50 hectares | 28 | 23.7 | 17,748 | 7.8 |
| VI | Over 50 hectares | 123 | 33.6 | 5,626 | 2.5 |
| Note: | (50.1 - 100 hectares | 67 | 15.6 | 4,778 | 2.1) |

Percentage of fallow 42% (Minimum* 27%, Maximum* 48%)

Average income per hectare 1600 TL**

South Eastern Region contains 7.4% of all operational units and 14.0% of all cultivated land in Turkey.

Yearly Rainfall: 384-756 mm

Altitude: 650-1755 m

* Minimum and maximum figures are averages of provinces in the region. (9 provinces in total)

** Average includes five provinces of the North Eastern Region. Exact date for this figure unknown (mid-1970s).

TABLE 5: DISTRIBUTION OF AGRICULTURAL OPERATIONS ACCORDING TO SIZE GROUPS: MEDITERRANEAN REGION (1970) (HIGH FERTILITY WIDESPREAD IRRIGATION)

| Size Group of Holdings (1) | Average Size of Cultivated Land (2) | (1) As a % of all Cultivated Land (3) | Number of Operational Units (4) | (4) As a % of all Operational Units (5) |
|---|---|---|---|---|
| I Less than 2 hectares | 0.9 | 8.7 | 135,366 | 47.8 |
| II 2.1 - 5 hectares | 3 | 19.0 | 80,613 | 28.5 |
| III 5.1 - 10 hectares | 7 | 21.0 | 39,872 | 14.1 |
| IV 10.1 - 20 hectares | 13 | 18.6 | 18,006 | 6.4 |
| V 20.1 - 50 hectares | 27 | 14.9 | 6,927 | 2.4 |
| VI Over 50 hectares | 103 | 17.5 | 2,169 | 0.8 |

Percentage of fallow 19% (Minimum* 5%, Maximum* 35%)

Average income per hectare:** 4581 TL

Mediterranean Region contains 9.2% of all operational units and 8.6% of all cultivated land in Turkey.

Yearly Rainfall: 558-1173 mm (region incudes Gazaiantep and Maras)

Altitude: 3-855 m

* Minimum and maximum figures are averages of provinces in the region. (6 provinces in total)

** Exact date for this figure unknown (mid-1970s).

TABLE 6: DISTRIBUTION OF AGRICULTURAL OPERATIONS ACCORDING TO SIZE GROUPS: MARMARA REGION (1970) (HIGH FERTILITY TEMPERATE ZONE-IRRIGATION)

| Size Group of Holdings (1) | | Average Size of Cultivated Land (2) | (1) As a % of all Cultivated Land (3) | Number of Operational Units (4) | (4) As a % of all Operational Units (5) |
|---|---|---|---|---|---|
| I | Less than 2 hectares | 0.9 | 6.5 | 90,480 | 33.3 |
| II | 2.1 - 5 hectares | 3 | 22.8 | 95,631 | 35.1 |
| III | 5.1 - 10 hectares | 7 | 29.1 | 57,430 | 21.1 |
| IV | 10.1 - 20 hectares | 13 | 21.2 | 21,764 | 8.0 |
| V | 20.1 - 50 hectares | 27 | 12.3 | 5,960 | 2.2 |
| VI | Over 50 hectares | 136 | 8.1 | 804 | 0.3 |

Percentage of fallow 17% (Minimum* 11%, Maximum* 23%)

Average income per hectare 3690 TL**

Marmara Region contains 8.8% of all operational units and 9.1% of all cultivated land in Turkey.

Yearly Rainfall: 590-713 mm

Altitude: 4-100 m

* Minimum and maximum figures are averages of provinces in the region. (7 provinces in total)

** Average includes nine provinces of the Agean Region. Exact date for this figure unknown (mid-1970s).

## TABLE 7: TOTAL AREA SOWN AND FALLOW (000 HECTARES)

| | Sown | Fallow |
|---|---|---|
| 1934 | 6,883 | 4,000 |
| 1944 | 8,087 | 4,814 |
| 1954 | 13,208 | 6,408 |
| 1964 | 15,367 | 8,476 |
| 1974 | 16,121 | 8,506 |

Sources: Istatistik Umum Mudurlugu, *Statistical Yearbook 1942-1945* (Ankara: 1946) p. 219.

DIE, *Statistical Yearbook 1975* (Ankara: 1976) p. 164.

## TABLE 8: ECONOMICALLY ACTIVE POPULATION ('000)

| | Total | Economically Active (2) | In Agriculture including Animal Husbandry (3) | 2 as a % of 3 |
|---|---|---|---|---|
| 1935 | 16,157 | (7,921)* | (6,480)* | (82)* |
| 1945 | 18,790 | 7,626 | 5,810 | 76 |
| 1955 | 24,065 | 12,205 | 9,446 | 77 |
| 1960 | 27,755 | 12,993 | 9,737 | 74 |
| 1965 | 31,391 | 13,558 | 9,750 | 72 |
| 1970 | 35,605 | 14,051 | 9,218 | 66 |

Sources: *Statistical Yearbook 1942-45*, p. 103.
*Statistical Yearbook 1951*, p. 106.
*Statistical Yearbook 1975*, p. 165.

* Definition is not exactly comparable to rest of the series.

TABLE 9A: AGRICULTURAL HOLDINGS BY LAND TENURE AND SIZE (1963 CENSUS OF AGRICULTURE SAMPLE SURVEY RESULTS)

| Agricultural Holdings | Land Tenure | | | | | | | | |
|---|---|---|---|---|---|---|---|---|---|
| | Number and area of holdings | | | Land cultivated by owner | | | Land rented from others | | |
| | Number | Size hectares Estimate | Size hectares Upper Limit | Number | Size hectares Estimate | Size hectares Upper Limit | Number | Size hectares Estimate | Size hectares Upper Limit |
| Holdings with and without ownership . . . . . . | 3 514 476 | 17 142 777 | - | 3 069 921 | 16 968 119 | - | 293 518 | 713 058 | - |
| Holdings without ownership . . . . . . | 308 899 | - | - | - | - | - | - | - | - |
| Small holdings totally rented to others on share basis partnership, etc. . . | 104 347 | - | - | 104 347 | 531 905 | 1 089 | 10 600 | 33 181 | |
| Large holdings totally rented to others on share basis partnership, etc. . . | 283 | - | - | 275 | 76 139 | 135 033 | 1 | 810 | 810 |
| Holdings by hectare groups: | | | | | | | | | |
| 0.1 - 0.5 | 398 866 | 114 385 | 131 375 | 373 743 | 474 909 | 621 071 | 14 843 | 5 482 | 9 020 |
| 0.6 - 1.0 | 375 329 | 317 324 | 405 880 | 360 161 | 523 028 | 661 547 | 20 294 | 9 100 | 13 784 |
| 1.1 - 2.0 | 494 623 | 744 767 | 798 270 | 471 885 | 814 371 | 887 233 | 42 718 | 27 994 | 39 229 |
| 2.1 - 3.0 | 349 096 | 869 763 | 946 042 | 336 551 | 850 087 | 942 503 | 28 378 | 34 743 | 48 754 |
| 3.1 - 4.0 | 291 121 | 1 024 284 | 1 491 427 | 281 385 | 1 002 465 | 1 114 125 | 26 156 | 32 333 | 43 004 |
| 4.1 - 5.0 | 223 253 | 1 008 863 | 1 146 244 | 214 593 | 967 974 | 1 109 358 | 27 286 | 37 653 | 47 073 |
| 5.1 - 10.0 | 561 732 | 3 995 311 | 4 274 753 | 536 570 | 3 546 951 | 3 751 923 | 71 929 | 152 664 | 221 931 |
| 10.1 - 20.0 | 291 693 | 3 973 076 | 4 500 393 | 280 104 | 3 546 351 | 4 166 613 | 43 045 | 185 739 | 300 767 |
| 20.1 - 50.0 | 99 785 | 2 842 127 | 3 589 428 | 94 296 | 2 533 225 | 3 237 164 | 14 738 | 133 426 | 226 851 |
| 50.1 - 99.9 | 11 029 | 755 158 | 1 342 909 | 11 566 | 662 165 | 1 142 071 | 2 166 | 26 663 | 62 407 |
| 100.0 - 250.0 | 2 851 | 369 923 | 844 930 | 2 894 | 353 914 | 792 047 | 731 | 11 558 | 24 251 |
| 250.1 - 499.9 | 981 | 313 742 | 787 725 | 973 | 315 987 | 773 609 | 48 | 4 051 | 77 957 |
| 500.0 + | 491 | 405 811 | 513 072 | 482 | 370 379 | 444 209 | 82 | 38 125 | 5 354 |
| State Establishments and farms . . . . . | 97 | 408 443 | 408 443 | 96 | 398 209 | 398 209 | 14 | 2 117 | 2 117 |

(continued next page)

TABLE 9B: AGRICULTURAL HOLDINGS BY LAND TENURE AND SIZE (1963 CENSUS OF AGRICULTURE SAMPLE SURVEY RESULTS)

| Land Tenure | | | | | | | | | |
|---|---|---|---|---|---|---|---|---|---|
| Land operated on a share or on a partnership basis | | | Land operated on other bases | | | Land rented to others on a share or on partnership basis | | | |
| | Size hectares | | | Size hectares | | | Size hectares | | |
| Number | Estimate | Upper Limit | Number | Estimate | Upper Limit | Number | Estimate | Upper Limit | Agricultural holdings |
| 521 176 | 1 532 312 | - | 115 703 | 224 015 | - | 566 896 | 2 294 727 | - | Holdings with and without ownership |
| - | - | - | - | - | - | - | - | - | Holdings without ownership |
| - | - | - | 536 | 536 | 1 916 | 104 347 | 543 101 | 711 198 | Small holdings totally rented to others on share basis, partnership, etc. |
| 1 | 50 | 50 | 6 | 1 751 | 5 733 | 283 | 78 750 | 205 535 | Large holdings totally rented to others on share basis, partnership, etc. |
| | | | | | | | | | Holdings by hectare groups |
| 16 372 | 4 106 | 6 159 | 7 559 | 2 241 | 4 387 | 97 180 | 372 353 | 763 472 | 0.1 - 0.5 |
| 31 516 | 14 458 | 18 300 | 8 452 | 4 697 | 12 770 | 45 440 | 233 959 | 308 425 | 0.6 - 1.0 |
| 64 051 | 52 062 | 64 037 | 15 757 | 12 126 | 20 462 | 66 978 | 161 786 | 192 230 | 1.1 - 2.0 |
| 63 522 | 74 115 | 94 430 | 14 895 | 10 068 | 15 011 | 51 801 | 99 250 | 145 533 | 2.1 - 3.0 |
| 60 143 | 86 314 | 109 620 | 4 358 | 6 211 | 14 482 | 37 319 | 103 033 | 176 144 | 3.1 - 4.0 |
| 48 562 | 89 588 | 134 959 | 7 577 | 9 790 | 25 992 | 28 110 | 98 142 | 152 723 | 4.1 - 5.0 |
| 138 604 | 403 326 | 1 258 203 | 30 996 | 55 705 | 93 573 | 71 774 | 163 335 | 252 721 | 5.1 - 10.0 |
| 71 841 | 367 055 | 750 830 | 16 777 | 47 250 | 68 413 | 40 186 | 173 319 | 318 867 | 10.1 - 20.0 |
| 23 857 | 250 448 | 442 048 | 9 875 | 42 280 | 85 954 | 17 900 | 117 252 | 284 163 | 20.1 - 50.0 |
| 3 831 | 112 541 | 281 795 | 1 077 | 15 367 | 54 753 | 4 475 | 61 578 | 161 026 | 50.1 - 99.9 |
| 746 | 49 831 | 279 317 | 11 | 432 | 1 040 | 859 | 45 812 | 119 895 | 100.0 - 250.0 |
| 65 | 7 961 | 12 892 | 9 | 1 334 | 2 192 | 129 | 15 591 | 25 146 | 250.1 - 499.9 |
| 65 | 20 457 | 40 620 | 11 | 5 938 | 8 684 | 109 | 29 283 | 43 236 | 500.0 + |
| - | - | - | 9 | 8 289 | 8 289 | 6 | 172 | 172 | State establishments and farms |

Source: DIE, Statistical Yearbook, 1975, pp. 180-1.

# 3

# Large Landowners, Agricultural Progress and the State in Egypt, 1800–1970: An Overview with Many Questions

*Roger Owen*

## INTRODUCTION

**'L'Egypte est un pays de grand propriété mais de petits exploitants.'[1]**

**The main outlines of Egypt's agricultural progress from 1800 to the 1960s are well known. They include a rapid extension of the cultivated area from some 3,200,000 to about 5,000,000 *feddans* in the 19th century and a somewhat slower growth to around 5,900,000 *feddans* by 1960. (Table 1)[2] This was accompanied by an even larger expansion in the area of land subject to perennial irrigation which could be put under two or more crops a year, from about 500,000 *feddans* at the end of Muhammad Ali's reign in 1849 to some 85 percent of the cultivated area in 1959.[3] The result was a considerable rise in production and income due to the increase in the cropped area, to bigger yields and to the introduction of higher-value crops, particularly long-staple cotton. Thus, according to Hansen and Wattleworth's index, total agricultural output almost doubled between 1895/99 and the early 1960s. (Table 2)[4] Finally, all observers have noted that, for most of the 20th century, production has failed to keep up with the increase in population, leading to an almost continuous fall in output per head, and that progress has often been interrupted by a short-term lack of investment in the drains necessary to prevent the salination of Egypt's intensively-watered fields and in the purchase of chemical fertilisers.[5]**

**Economists and economic historians have also called attention to another central feature of Egypt's agricultural system and that is the extreme inequality of land-holdings. This began anew in the 19th century as a result of the deliberate creation of large estates by Muhammad Ali and his successors and of the ability of village notables to use their positions within the local administration to amass considerable holdings of land their own right.[6] As a result, by the beginning of the 20th century, over 40 percent of the land was held in 12-13,000 properties of 50**

*feddans* and over (which in Egypt are conventionally classified as 'large') while the remainder was divided up into some 140,000 medium units of 5-50 *feddans* and nearly a million small parcels of 5 *feddans* or less. Fifty years later, at the time of the first Land Reform legislation in 1952, the situation had only been modified to the extent that, while the number of large properties had remained more or less steady, the host of smallholders had now multiplied to well over 2,500,000. (Table 3)

But it is one thing to call attention to the co-existence of large estates and tiny holdings, quite another to determine its influence - for good or ill - on Egypt's agricultural development. Sadly, however, the vast majority of writers have not attempted to argue their case by detailed analysis but have simply asserted that inequality was bad, with the aid of one or more extremely simplistic arguments. Thus, as a rule they have gone no further than to insist that the role of the large landowners was a pernicious one: (a) because they used their political power to obtain more than their fair share of government support while paying less than their fair share of taxes, (b) because they were largely absentee and managed their estates badly or (c) because the mere existence of their estates made any attempt to improve the position of the small owners almost impossible.[7] What has also been characteristic of the way in which such arguments have been used is that they have generally been deployed to make a political rather than an economic point, with the general aim of encouraging the state to use its power to change the situation in one way or another or of blaming it, retrospectively, for not having done enough in the past. This is understandable, given the central role which the state has always played in Egypt's agricultural life. But it has generally tended to lead writers to see agriculture as constituting a set of problems to be solved rather than a set of relationships to be examined for their own sake.

In this essay I want to insist that the historical connection between the pattern of landholding and the development of Egypt's agricultural sector is a good deal more complicated than the nature of the usual discussion would suggest. And in what follows I would like to take another look at these same arguments in an effort to try to discover just how much explanatory power they really have. This procedure will have the additional advantage of raising a number of important, but as yet unanswered, questions about Egypt's agricultural history while, at the same time, paving the way for some concluding remarks about the impact of the Land Reform of 1952, one of the major aims of which was to destroy the power of the large landowners for good.[8]

## THE POLITICAL POWER OF THE LARGE LANDOWNERS

The political and economic advantages of owning a large Egyptian estate have still to be fully catalogued.[9] They began with the control of the land itself and with the fight (institutionalised in 1885) to establish an ezba containing sometimes hundreds of peasants who were housed and given a small plot of land in exchange for their labour service.[10] This at once created a community of people, totally dominated by the landlord, which also acted as an important focus for economic activity, whether as a market for goods and services or as a source of credit, within the whole district. To this might be added the additional power and influence which went with the fact that the owner or members of his family would almost inevitably occupy several important posts within the local and provincial administration, from that of Umda (or "mayor") up. Finally, most of the estate owners were able to play an increasingly important role in national politics, first simply by virtue of the fact that Egypt's rulers relied on them to maintain order in the rural areas and to help in the execution of certain necessary tasks like taxation and conscription, then, from the late 1970s onwards, by their majority in all of the representative assemblies which were established in Cairo by the Khedive Ismail and by the British, culminating in the overwhelming influence which they were able to exercise during the period of Parliament and parties from 1923 to 1952, whether through their domination of the Senate, their place among the leadership of the main political groups or simply as the class which controlled the largest section of the voting population in the popular elections of the time.[11] Thus right up to the Land Reform of 1952 it is possible to talk of the Egyptian countryside as being dominated by some 2,000 estate holders, including many members of the Royal Family, and of a densely populated province like Sharkiya being controlled by no more than a hundred or so wealthy families.[12] Among the many ways in which the landowners used their political power to their own advantage, three seem to be of particular importance. The first concerns the fact that for most of the period until the reforms of 1949 they were able to ensure that they paid a very much smaller share of land tax than their rural wealth should really have warranted. To begin with this was a function of their relationship with the country's rulers which allowed them to have much of their land classified as '*ushr*' rather than '*kharaj*' and thus to pay taxes at a very much lower rate than the rest of the land owning population. Thus, in the 1870s and 1880s the *ushr* was fixed at only must over a quarter of the *kharaj*, while many estate owners followed the example of the Khedive Ismail and paid no tax at all.[13] Much the same relationship was reestablished under the British, causing Lord Cromer and his fellow administrators, first to postpone any reform of the existing inequitable system of taxation for over a decade after 1882, then to make sure that they obtained the cooperation of the large landowners by declaring that the purpose of the new system was not to increase the total amount of tax to be raised but simply to undertake a redistribution of the overall burden so that it connected more closely with the value and fertility of the land.[14] While the abolition of the distinction between *ushr* and *kharaj* now meant that some estate owners were forced to pay at a higher rate per *feddan* once the new schedules were introduced in the first decade of the 20th century, the fact that the tax was now related directly to the rental value of the land as assessed in 1895 (a year of unusually low rents due to the agricultural depression) and that the assessors fixed a relatively low maximum of LE1.64 per *feddan* meant that, as rental values increased, estate owners paid an increasingly smaller and smaller fraction of their income in tax. (Table 4) Thus, while the initial burden was fixed at 28.64 percent of the rental value in the 1890s it had fallen to only a tenth or a twelfth of this in some provinces in the mid-1920s and was still no more than 15.73 percent when rents were depressed in the mid-1930s.[15]

Large estate owners were also able to benefit from the fact that the British period assessment was fixed to last for thirty years and that they were well placed to influence the next reassessment which took place in 1935-7.[16] Once again the government was particularly anxious to ensure the cooperation of the families which controlled the Egyptian countryside and attempted to allay any fears they might have had about an increase in their tax burden by declaring at the outset that (a) the new rates would be fixed at no more than sixteen percent of the rental value and (b) the old maximum of LE1.64 per *feddan* would be retained.[17] This last proviso was in spite of the fact that there were a number of fertile provinces in which rental values were generally so high that almost all the land would otherwise have paid at much more than the maximum rate.[18]

A final example of landowner pressure can be found in the report by the Briton Andrew Holden, who supervised the last re-assessment of the monarchical period in 1946-8. In spite of the fact that there was, by now, considerable lobbying by both industrial interests and social reformers to force large estate owners to make a more substantial contribution to national revenues, the government not only fixed the general rate at 14 percent of the rental value but also decided that, as rents had reached an inflated level during the war, the new rates should be levied on only half of the assessed rental value for 1945/6.[19] The only concession to the reformers was that the old maximum of LE1.64 should go. And it was this reform which, since the new rates were introduced in 1949, allowed the amount collected in tax to rise from the sum of LE5,500,000 at which it had remained for over three-quarters of a century to LE17,900,000 in 1951. Holden also writes of the pressures exerted by the large landowners who dominated the Finance Committee of the Senate to make sure that individual assessments were made public and so open to challenge and of the haphazard practices of the Reassessment Appeals Committee which, in some cases, changed the new rates without making a personal inspection of the land as laid down in the official regulations - thus raising the possibility of political interference by the rich and powerful.[20] As figures in Table 4 plainly show, agriculture's tax contribution fell sharply between 1895 and 1946-8, whether expressed in terms of its share of government revenues or as a proportion of the average rental of Egypt's land or of the total value of the cotton harvest.

A second area in which the large landowners exercised important political power was in their ability to protect their own interests when their income seemed at risk from falling commodity prices in the early 1920s and again in the 1930s. On both occasions the question of cotton was of particular importance. Thus, in the early 1920s, the large landowners, using the instrument of the newly-founded Egyptian Agricultural Syndicate, pressed successfully for an official restriction on the amount of land which could be planted with cotton (in force between 1921/2 and 1922/3) on the mistaken assumption that a smaller Egyptian harvest would force up the international price.[21] They also encouraged the government to purchase and store part of the cotton crop in 1921 (and again in 1926 and 1929) as well as to intervene directly in the spot market between 1921 and 1923 - both costly ways of preventing prices from sliding further.[22]

Much the same tactics were also tried during the first part of the much more dangerous crisis which began in 1930. Once again, there were restrictions on cotton acreage between 1931 and 1933 before wiser councils prevailed and cultivators were allowed to grow as much as they liked.[23] And in 1930 the government also spent LE2,200,000 out of its total reserves of LE40,000,000 in cotton purchases designed to keep up the price.[24] However, on this occasion, the major government effort to help the large landowners was directed towards preventing a collapse of the land market as a result of a general failure to keep up payments on loans borrowed from the major mortgage banks. According to one estimate, some 30 percent of the big estates were heavily mortgaged at this time.[25] Here the government acted directly to persuade the Mortgage Companies to reduce their interest rates in 1933 and again in 1935 and 1936 in exchange for financial support.[26]

Two other initiatives taken by the government of Aziz Sidqi (1930-33) ought also to be mentioned. The first is the decision to support local cereal prices by placing a higher and higher tariff on imported flour in 1932 and 1934; the second the creation of a protected market for locally produced Egyptian sugar as a result of the state's financial rescue of the Societe Generale des Sucreries et de la Raffinerie D'Egypte in February 1931. As both initiatives were clearly in the interest of Egypt's cultivators, and as both had the immediate result of raising the price of two basic necessities above that of foreign imports, there is some justice in Issawi's remark that the former at least represented a triumph for the landowners over urban interests for whom protection meant dearer food.[27] However, it is not clear that this was how it was generally perceived at the time, particularly as the Sidqi government and its supporters were anxious to go out of their way to persuade estate owners that agriculture and industry could develop in harmony together using agricultural capital to finance the factories needed to process Egypt's own raw materials at home.[28] On the other hand, whenever the Sidqi government was faced with an obvious conflict between agrarian and industrial interests - as when it failed to respond to the industrialists' pressure to lift the 1916 ban on imported cotton even though Egypt's own cotton was too valuable and of too high a quality to be used efficiently in the production of coarse woven goods which were the main stay of the local market - it inevitably tended to support the former over the latter.[29]

The political power of the landowners was also much in evidence in one other important area - their successful attempts to preempt any effort by the state to assist the small owners by providing them with either extra land or access to cheap credit. In my opinion this is one of the most serious charges against them and I will return to it in some detail in Section 3. For the time being I will try to spell out some of the implications of the discussion so far. From what has just been argued, it is clear that Egypt's large landowners enjoyed considerable success in influencing certain types of government policy towards the agricultural sector. But to demonstrate that this success was harmful to Egypt's economic progress it would have to be shown that it was at the expense of the smaller cultivators or that the money saved in taxes was all consumed rather than reinvested in the sector itself or used to provide capital for new industry. On the basis of present evidence, both cases are difficult to make. In so far as the large estate owners were successful in keeping taxes low or the price of cotton high this must certainly have been to the benefit of everyone who owned land. As for the question of whether agricultural profits were all spent unproductively - or simply wasted in what some writers have called the 'bottomless sink of land purchase' - the work of Radwan on capital investment and of Davis and others on the Bank Misr would seem to demonstrate that many of the largest landowners were quite prepared to spend money on machines and fertilisers and small irrigation works, as well as providing most of the initial capital of the Bank itself and for the Bank's new industrial enterprises in the 1930s.[30] The level of private savings may not have been high by modern standards.[31] But this is not the same as to suggest that it was usually near zero. According to Hansen's research, the level of public savings was also low before 1914, and it may be that there would have been more investment if tax revenues were higher -- but this is a big if given the British-controlled government's belated recognition of the need for increased expenditure on public works, notably the improvement of the drainage system.[32] Finally, in the interwar period, there is no evidence that the successful programme of improving the whole irrigation system required larger public funds than were than available.[33] At the very least, the case is not proven.

## THE MANAGEMENT OF THE LARGE ESTATES

A second common criticism of Egypt's large landowners is that they managed their estates badly and were more concerned with making huge profits through rack-renting their unfortunate tenants than by farming the land directly themselves. Here the key work used by the critics is 'absenteeism', a notion which first came in to vogue at least as early as the 1920s and was used consistantly by their opponents until it came to provide major justification of the Land Reform of 1952.[34] Efforts have also sometimes been made to give this notion some statistical reality by asserting that 70 percent of the large owners lived permanently away from their estates. However, as I will try to argue, the notion of 'absenteeism' is very misleading, while there is good reason to suppose that the figure of 70 percent is also very suspect, appearing first as an attempt by the British Inspector, Edwards, to estimate the number of absentees in Buhaira province in the early 1920s, only to be generalized by him for the whole of Egypt in an official report which was then copied by many subsequent writers.[35] The main point is that, in an Egyptian context, where distances between Cairo and most of the provinces are so small, and where many estates were owned and managed by families rather than individuals, the place of residence of the proprietors is of no great importance. Those who lived in Cairo could appoint either a member of their family or an agent (wakil) or supervisor (nazir) to manage things in their absence.[36] And it was a relatively easy matter to come to live on the ezba for several months each year (particularly in the early summer for the wheat harvest and the late summer for the cotton harvest) when management needed to be exercised at first hand.[37]

In these circumstances a more important distinction is between the various types of large estates, on the one had, and between the different methods of exploiting them, on the other. As already noted, the area held in estates of fifty *feddans* and over remained fairly steady in the 20th century declining by only some 400,000 *feddans* from a high of nearly 2,500,000 *feddans* in 1906 to a low of just over 2,000,000 *feddans* in 1952. However, it is also important to point out that the large estates in this category were owned by a variety of different types of people and organizations and subject to a number of different kinds of legal status. A breakdown of some of these different types is given in Tables 5a and 5b. According to these figures, the easiest sub-group to identify among the large estate-holders was the foreigners, who owned a quarter of all such estates in 1919 and 10 percent of them in 1949. Of these owners the majority were individuals (most of them permanent residents in Egypt) and the rest foreign-owned companies engaged either in reclaiming land for sale or in some other type of transaction involving the buying and selling of estates. Another group of owners consisted of members of the Royal Family, all of whom it may be argued, owned estates well in excess of 50 *feddans*.[38] Finally, by the 1920s, more than 10 percent of Egypt's cultivated area had been converted into *Waqf* property, the greater proportion as *waqf ahli* (a family *waqf* in which the income was assigned to specific persons) and a lesser amount as *waqf khairi* where the proceeds were dedicated to some religious or charitable purpose.[39] As far as the management of these lands were concerned, it would seem that in 1952 it was divided more or less half and half between Ministry of Waqfs (160,000 *feddans*), the Royal Waqf Office controlled by the King (120-130,000 *feddans*) and the Coptic Community, on the one hand and a large number of individual or institutional *nazirs* (or supervisors) on the other.[40] Unfortunately it is not possible to tell what proportion of *waqf* properties existed as large estates. But it would seem reasonable to suppose that both the Ministry and the Royal Waqf Office would have tried to manage their lands as a single holding.

If the foregoing argument is correct, then just before the Revolution, about two thirds of Egypt's large estates were owned by native Egyptians while the rest were controlled by the King and his family, by foreigners (both individuals and companies), by Egyptian and companies and by the two major Waqf administrations. It is important to note, however, that these proportions would have been different in the inter-war years, with more land being held by foreigners and less by the Royal Family. The years of the 1930s Depression also witnessed yet another category of land management consisting of estates which had either been sequestrated for non-payment of debts and were being held before re-sale or which were being looked after on a temporary basis by a mortgage company until the owner had accumulated enough money to reclaim them.[41] Once again, there are no exact figures either for the amount of land managed in this way or of the proportion of it which consisted of large estates.

The next question to ask is how were the estates in these various categories actually exploited and in what size of units? As far as those in individual or family ownership are concerned (whether by Egyptians or foreigners) the key to the answer probably lies in the institution of the ezba which, at least in theory, gave the owners the option of running the family estates as a single unit, obtaining all the economies of scale to be derived from the bulk purchase of inputs (including technical and managerial expertise) but also allowing the possibility of subdividing the land itself into a variety of smaller units each subject to a different form of arrangement with tenants and workers. Support for this hypothesis comes from the fact that, by the late 1920s, there were nearly 17,000 officially recognized ezbas, or more than enough for each of the estates over 50 *feddans*.[42]

Evidence from the turn of the century suggests that there were then three possible types of exploitation. At one extreme there was the estate of Riaz Pasha who farmed all his 530 *feddans* himself with the exception of perhaps 100 *feddans* which he leased to his 100 service tenants in exchange for their labour service.[43] At the other extreme there was the estate of E. Zervudachi, almost all of which was leased except for the central farm buildings and an experimental field which were used to assist the tenants to improve their yields.[44] Finally, there was the mixed pattern of exploitation employed on the Manzaloui ezba in which the owner place 200 of his 600 *feddans* under cotton for himself and leased the remainder.[45] Other pieces of more impressionistic evidence would suggest that the Manzaloui mix was the most characteristic form of exploitation down to the Revolution, but that the balance between direct exploitation and leasing and type of leases used may well have changed over time. For what it is worth, the conventional wisdom seems to be that there was a movement towards leasing more and more of the estates for cash in the late 1890s and early 1900s and again in the 1940s, while Richards has found some evidence to suggest that there was a counter move towards greater direct exploitation by the owner in the 1920s.[46] Unfortunately the official statistics for the amount of land farmed directly or leased in 1929 and 1939 are of little help as they do not seem to have taken account of the widespread practice of renting plots to tenants for less than a year. And without reliable figures it is not feasible to begin to explain the rationale behind the changes which may have taken place in the estate owners' management decisions.

The one study which does throw some light on the situation on the large estates is that conducted by the Paris-based Groupe d'Études de l'Islam established by Centre d'Études de Politique Etrangère in the mid-1930s. Their researches suggest that, at this period, only a small portion of the large estate was farmed directly but that, contrary to many of the critics of the landowners, the latter paid considerable attention to their properties, in the interests both of preserving the fertility of the soil and of their own profits. The major method of leasing was that of *fermage* by which the rent was paid in cash or kind. Under this system, plots of land were let for periods of months with the tenant compelled to follow a fixed pattern of rotation. This usually involved the cultivation of cotton which had to be taken directly to the owner's warehouse after the harvest and then sold on the tenant's behalf as a way of making sure that the rent was paid. General supervision was exercised by the owner's agent who looked after the irrigation and drainage system, while the owner himself might appear at harvest time to satisfy himself that his rules about the harvesting, sorting and sale of crops were properly observed.[47] As for payment in kind, the researches of the Groupe d'Etudes d'Islam suggest that this was only used for a short period in the early 1930s in an effort to compensate for the general uncertainty about the future price of cotton (on which fixed rents were based), but that this had come to an end by 1937 with the return of more stable market conditions.[48] On this last point, it is interesting to note that at least one Egyptian official, Ahmed Abdel-Wahab was so convinced that the practice of changing the terms of leases annually with relation to a fluctuating price of cotton was responsible for driving up rents that he had put forward a plan for trying to stablize cotton prices just before Egypt was hit by the worst effects of the

World Depression in 1930.[49]

The methods by which other types of large estates were exploited are even more difficult to evaluate. Practices on *waqf* properties were regularly attacked from at least the late 1920s when Prince Mohammed Aly described them all as 'badly managed'.[50] Saab repeats the same accusation for the early 1950s when he suggests that 'trustees, whether private persons or individuals delegated by the Ministry of Waqfs, took little interest in improving anything but their own profit' and that the Ministry's own estates were sub-leased by intermediaries.[51] However, it would seem reasonable to assume that, in reality, the situation was very much more mixed than this, with some of the *waqfs* being well-administered by members of founder's family (as the law attempted to ensure) and with the Royal Waqfs probably being subject to good agricultural practice as well.[52] Two last types of estates were those being brought into cultivation by a land improvement company and those managed on a temporary basis by a mortgage company while the owner tried to sort out his debts. In each case, according to the Groupe d'Études d'Islam, the usual system was to sub-let the fields for two or three years at a time via intermediaries with little restriction in the way they were farmed except, perhaps, compulsory adherence to a three year cotton rotation designed to protect the fertility of the soil.[53] On the basis of this kind of evidence it may be that many of the ill-effects often ascribed to owner absenteeism could well have been much more common on certain types of company-managed estates than on those owned by private individuals or families. Nevertheless, with so little hard evidence, it would seem hazardous to generalize about the efficiency of all the large estates and the way in which they were administered. Perhaps for this reason, opinions vary enormously, from Mabro's assertion that the large properties were 'generally well-managed' to their whole scale condemnation by their critics.[54] It is also quite characteristic of the literature that a contemporary observer like Saab can easily contradict himself, writing in one place that the 'frequent practice of leasing to intermediaries' was one of the 'most obnoxious forms of absentee land ownership', and in another that approximately 85 percent of the estates subject to redistribution in 1952 were 'highly productive at the time of requisitioning'.[55] Perhaps the answer to the conundrum lies in the fact that the ezba system of combining large-scale ownership with intensely supervised, small-scale cultivation by tenants was at once an efficient method of exploiting Egypt's agricultural resources in terms of productivity and the cause of great rural poverty, social waste and general distress. But without more research and better statistics it is impossible to prove this for sure.

## THE LARGE ESTATES AND THEIR SMALLER NEIGHBOURS

One way in which the landlords clearly used their economic and political power was to block, or to divert, government efforts to improve the conditions both of their own tenants and those of the rural small-holders in general. An important example concerns the repeated efforts to release peasants from the clutches of local usurers by providing them with regular access to cheap credit. However, as has been demonstrated in India and in many number of other Third World Countries, efforts to target particular groups of cultivators are administratively very difficult, and in Egypt successive governments ran into all the well-known problems involved in developing simple procedures which small cultivators could understand which did not involve them having to pledge their precious land (or their animals and tools) as security. As elsewhere, there was also the usual tendency for the commercial banks which the government used as its agents in the matter to lend more and more of their money to medium, or even large, landowners whose security was so much better than that of their peasant neighbours. This was very much the story of the Agricultural Bank established in 1898 which in the first decade after it began operation in 1903 lent only LE2,800,000 in what were called 'A' loans (short-term, unsecured and repaid with the land tax) as against LE15,700,000 in 'B' Loans (five years with a mortgage on the land), almost all of which must have gone to owners of considerably more than five *feddans*.[56] It was much the same with the Agricultural Credit Bank established by the Sidqi government in 1931.[57] However, on top of all the usual problems associated with trying to create mechanisms for reaching small cultivators, there is also evidence of pressure from large landowners to get the banks to alter their regulations so as to allow more money to be directed their way. One example of this is the manner in which the Agricultural Bank was persuaded to raise the minimum loan which it was able to grant from LE500 in 1905.[58] A similar process occurred in the 1930s with the Agricultural Credit Bank being pressured to raise the maximum size of properties for which cash loans could legally be granted from 30 *feddans* in 1931 to 90 *feddans* in 1933 and 200 *feddans* in 1937 - by which time, as Eshag and Kamal remark, 99.9 percent of Egypt's landowners were eligible for its services.[59] But perhaps the most significant example of the way in which the large estate owners were able to re-direct government efforts to provide small-holders with credit was their practice of creating 'tame' cooperative societies from among their own tenants and other dependent persons through which they obtained low interest loans for the Agricultural Credit Bank, either for their own use for re-lending, at a profit, to those who worked for them.[60] Government money could also be obtained directly in a similar manner as Andrew Holden discovered when he was sent by the Prime Minister, Sidqi, to Asyut province to investigate the case of a local estate owner, Mohammad Mahfouz Pasha, who had simply submitted names of a large number of his alleged tenants to the local *mudiriya* office, on whose behalf he had received LE400 in credit which he had simply put into his own pocket. The final outcome of Holden's investigations is also significant: in spite of the fact that Mahfouz Pasha was convicted of misappropriation and that he was a political enemy of Sidqi's he was still important and influential enough to avoid serving any of his sentence in prison.[61]

But certainly the most important demonstration of landowner political power was the way in which they and their political representatives were able to defeat every single measure designed either to place a ceiling on land purchases by large owners or to regulate relations between them and their tenants and wage workers before 1952. Criticism of the role of the large estate owners in the rural economy can be found at least as early as the 1920s. Initially this tended to focus on the role of these estates in limiting the amount of land available to the small peasants and thus of encouraging the fragmentation of plots and of the payment of excessive rents.[62] But by the time of World War II there were also voices arguing that a general redistribution of land was necessary in the interests of raising rural incomes so as to provide a wider market for Egypt's industrial products.[63] But it was not until 1944 that a Senator, Muhammad Khattab, attempted to introduce a bill limiting the amount of land which could be bought in any one lot to 50 *feddans*.[64] The rationale behind this initiative was probably the same as that set out a few years later in Mirrit Ghali's 'Policy for Tomorrow' in which he argued that the large estates would naturally become smaller and more fragmented as a result of the Muslim law of inheritance unless the large owners were constantly able to buy more land as a compensation.[65] But, whatever the case, Khattab's proposal was attacked so fiercely from all sides that not only did it make no headway in the Senate but the man himself was quickly dropped as a candidate in his party, the Saadists, as an embarrassment.[66] Other initiatives to limit the power of the landowners, such as the recommendation by the Finance Committee for the Chamber of Deputies that the land tax be made somewhat progressive by levying higher rates on estates over 100 *feddans*, or the attempt by Sayed Marei and a few friends to introduce a bill regulating rents in 1948, also received so little support that they were not even put to the vote.[67] Meanwhile, the only clear proposal by a political group for an actual limit on the size of agricultural properties came from the Egyptian Socialist Party (former Misr Fatat) in their programme for 1951.[68] And it was this concept which had a great deal of influence on the thinking behind the Land Reform law introduced by the Free Officer regime after the Revolution in September 1952.

## THE LAND REFORM OF 1952 AND SOME OF ITS CONSEQUENCES

As is well known, the set of proposals enshrined in the Egyptian Land Reform Law included initiatives in several different directions. The first involved a general limitation of ownership to 200 *feddans* per individual, with another 100 *feddan*s which could be transferred to the owner's own immediate family, the excess to be expropriated and redistributed to peasant cultivators in small plots of up to five *feddans*.[69] Initially a grace period was given to those with excess land to allow them to sell it on their own behalf. By the time it was brought to an end in September 1953, 150,000 *feddans* had been disposed of in this way. To begin with members of the Royal Family were also subject to the same regulations as every other large owner. However, as the result of a new law in November 1953 their land (some 180,000 *feddans* in all) was confiscated in its entirety. Finally, waqf ahli land was reclassified as ordinary private property and returned to its current beneficiaries, subject to the general limit of 200 *feddans* per individual. As a result of all these measures, some 460,000 *feddans* had been expropriated by 1959.[70] However, there is reason to suppose that this figure should have been nearly 50,000 *feddans* more if there had been no 'cheating' and if the law had been properly applied in every case.[71]

The land expropriated from the large estates formed the major part of the amount divided up and redistributed to small cultivators. (Table 6) To this should be added some 150,000 *feddans* of waqf kairi transferred from the Ministry of Waqfs to the Ministry of Agrarian Reform in 1957 and some 135,000 *feddans* of state land surrendered by the State Domains Administration. Given the fact that the process of expropriation, transfer and redistribution took some time, the rate at which the new owners actually came into possession of their plots was quite slow and by 1961 only some 326,000 *feddans* had been processed, making an average distribution of about 36,000 *feddans* a year. (Table 6) More land was then made available as a result of the 2nd Reform Law of 1961 which reduced the ceiling on individual holdings to 100 *feddans* - soon changed to 100 *feddans* per *family* in 1962. This led to the expropriation of another 215,000 *feddans* of excess land, augmented by another 200,000 *feddans* which came from the sequestration of property belonging to political enemies of the regime and other sources. Of this, 370,000 *feddans* was redistributed between 1962 and 1966, to bring the total amount of land which passed into new ownership to 696,000 *feddans* - just under nine percent of Egypt's cultivated area. (Table 6)

The second aspect of the 1952 Reform Law was that those who received the land were forced to join the cooperatives which were established in all the major Land Reform areas. The co-ops provided inputs of credit and fertilizers, organized the cultivation of all the redistributed land as a single unit with uniform pattern of rotation and then marketed the produce on behalf of its members. As Mabro and others have noted, this system reproduced many of the features of the old ezba - with its combination of economies of scale with small-plot cultivation - to which might be added a high degree of onerous supervision by men who, at least in the early years, had often been employed as a *nazir* by the land's previous owner.[72] Even when the co-operatives were more firmly under the control of agricultural engineers sent from Cairo, they still provided a vehicle for those large and medium owners who lived in the district to continue their domination of the local economy. Nevertheless, the establishment of the co-operatives did allow the introduction of measures designed to make the cultivation of the land more efficient - for example, the division of the total area into several large blocks each planted with a single crop - and it was this, as well as the general improvement in the health and welfare of the peasant cultivators, which must have been largely responsible for the increase in output reported in some Land Reform areas.[73] In 1963 the system of supervised co-operatives was extended to cover 87 percent of Egypt's cultivated land. And, once again, it is clear that the co-ops tended to be dominated by the large and medium owners of the district in spite of the fact that there were some official efforts to use the presence of small peasants on the village committees of the Arab Socialist Union to act as a counter-balance.[74] Just as important, the experiment with supervised co-operatives was soon overtaken by the economic recession following the total defeat in the 1967 war, and their role still remains to be properly evaluated.

Finally, it is important to remember that there were two basic features of the 1952 legislation which affected agrarian relations throughout Egypt and not just in the reform areas. One was the regulation fixing rents at seven times the land tax, a measure which, when properly observed, reduced the average pre-Revolutionary level by almost a half.[75] The other was the establishment of a minimum wage for agricultural labourers.

In conclusion I will turn to a consideration of a last unanswered question: what was the effect of the 1952 Reform on Egypt's agricultural progress? Two large and related problems immediately present themselves. The first is that the implementation of the 1952 law was followed by a period of uneven growth in agricultural output with stagnation between 1952 and 1956, a period of rapid increase 1957-60, a catastrophic fall in 1961 due to a particularly bad cotton harvest and then another period of slower advance 1962-67.[76]

The second is that there is a marked lack of detailed research which would allow the two processes to be properly related. Many writers try to make the link directly, but it is not that simple.[77] Even a quick glance at the official figures should be enough to demonstrate that neither the redistribution of land nor the establishment of the new co-operatives could have had much to do with a general growth in output. As Table 6 indicates, the process of redistribution was too slow and affected too small a proportion of Egypt's cultivated land to be able to have had the influence which is sometimes suggested. It may also be the case that much of the land actually expropriated was sufficiently well-farmed before 1952 as to allow very little opportunity for any great improvement in productivity. In these circumstances it would seem more reasonable to look for factors which affected the agricultural sector as a whole in the post-Reform years. As it happens there is no shortage of candidates, including a large increase in investment (according to Radwan the total supply of chemical fertilizers increased by 126 percent between 1952 and 1967 and the value of agricultural machinery by 97 percent), the greater intensity of land use made possible by the provision of extra water and by the extension of the areas planted with rice and maize and the general rise in the welfare of the peasant population made possible by their extra income and the growth in public money spent on providing the villages with electricity, piped water, schools and health clinics.[78]

Having said all this, however, it may well be that the Land Reform itself shares at least some of the responsibility for this improvement. One way to make the connection would be by way of the large increase in private investment in agriculture in the 1950s. This, it could well be argued, was partly a function of the fact that the remaining large estates of 50 *feddans* and over (which in 1967 still consisted of 1,750,000 *feddans* or 30 percent of the cultivated area) may well have been more compact and better managed after 1952, with owners who were prepared to spend money on them again once the threat of expropriation seemed to have been lifted. Given the many advantages they still continued to enjoy by way of their ownership of the best land, their ability to manipulate the local Administration and so on, they would have had to be very perverse not to try to make the cost of the new situation in which they found themselves.[79] As for capital, it may well be that they were able to use some of the quite large funds which were distributed in inflated dividends to shareholders by Egyptian companies fearful of nationalization.[80] Meanwhile, where the smaller cultivators were concerned, another source of funds was the money they retained once they were saved from the necessity of paying crippling rents. Finally, when it comes to the increase in public investment, particularly in rural welfare, it could be argued that this too required the prior destruction of some of the political power of the large owners who, prior to 1952, had acted as a barrier to much needed social legislation.

## CONCLUSION

In the light of the foregoing discussion only one conclusion is possible: the study of Egypt's agricultural history still raises many more questions than it answers. This is partly the function of the general lack of statistical sources, particularly those which would allow a detailed examination of the methods of exploitation and the efficiency of different sizes of holdings in the country's various agricultural regions. It is also a reflection of the fact that, from the 1920s, if not before, questions relating to the unequal distribution of landownership have been answered with more attention to politics than to economics. In the light of some of the few studies which are available it would not seem possible to agree with those who have argued that the large estates were rack-rented by absentee (and thus uncaring) landlords or that large units were, by definition, inefficient. Nevertheless, it is equally possible to argue that many of the advantages enjoyed by the large estate holders were obtained at the expense of Egypt's small proprietors and landless peasants and that the only way to assist the latter to become more productive was for the state to find ways of reaching them directly, without landowner intervention.

Given the great lack of data, it is equally unsurprising that the case for and against land reform could only be made in the most general terms without reference to the efficiency of any actual system. And it also follows that there is no way of testing the efficacy of the actual Reform package which was finally introduced in 1952. On the face of it it would seem that the law itself represented a reasonably good compromise between political, social and economic desiderata. At the very least it made some contribution to raising agricultural output while giving the new Revolutionary regime a breathing space within which to work out its strategy towards the sector as a whole and to experiment with a new type of institution, the supervised co-operative, before extending it to include most of rural Egypt in the 1960s. However, having set itself at the centre of the stage the state proved to be only partially effective in devising new policies for developing Egypt's agricultural resources. So to say the least, its record is very mixed. For all the money invested in raising output, almost as much was wasted on ill-advised reclamation projects such as in Tahir province. Like the British irrigation engineers before it, the regime proved to be better at providing the fields with extra water than at building the drains needed to take it away. And, perhaps most important of all, the Nasser period governments showed little willingness to address the vital question of how to develop the mix of crops which would make best use of the country's major assest - its rich and fertile land.

## FOOTNOTES

[1] Le Groupe d'Etudes de l'Islam, Centre d'Etudes de Politique Etrangère, Paris, *L'Egypte Independente* (Paris, 1938), pp. 281.

[2] The figure for the beginning of the 19th century is based on the sources cited by Dr. Afaf Lutfi al-Sayyid Marsot in her *Egypt in the Reign of Muhammad Ali* (Cambridge, 1984), pp. 152.

[3] Idem, pp. 156; B. Hansen and G. A. Marzouk, *Development and Economic Policy in the UAR (Egypt)* (Amsterdam, 1965), pp. 52n.

[4] B. Hansen and M. Wattleworth, 'Agricultural output and consumption of basic foods in Egypt, 1886/7-1967/8', *International Journal of Middle East Studies*, 9 (1978), pp. 457.

[5] For example, Hansen and Marzouk, *Development and Economic Policy*, pp. 46-49, A. Richards, *Egypt's Agricultural Development, 1800-1980: Technical and Social Change* (Boulder, Colo. 1981), pp.69-80, 142-4 etc.

[6] G. Baer, *A History of Landownership in Modern Egypt 1800-1950* (London etc. 1962), chpt. II; K. M. Cuno, "Egypt's wealthy peasantry, 1740-1820: A study of the region of al-Masura" in T. Khalidi, ed. *Land Tenure and Social Transformation in the Middle East* (Beirut, 1984), pp. 303-32.

[7] For example, G. S. Saab, *The Egyptian Agrarian Reform 1952-1962* (London, 1967), pp. 8-13; S. Radwan, *Agrarian Reform and Rural Poverty: Egypt, 1952-1975* (ILO, Geneva, 1977), pp. 6-9.

[8] On the purpose of the Land Reform see, Sayed Marei, *La réforme agraire en Égypte* (Cairo, 1957), chpt. III.

[9] There are a number of good books on the subject - for example Rauf Abbas Hamid, *al-Nizam al-ijtima*$^{c}$*i fi Misr fi zill al-milkiyat zira*$^{c}$*iya al-kabira 1837-1914* (The Social Order in Egypt under Large Agricultural Estates) (Cairo, 1973) but none which fully analyses the way in which estate ownership was transformed into economic and political power.

[10] On the early history of the ezba see R. Owen, 'The development of agricultural production in nineteenth century Egypt: capitalism of what type?' in A. L. Udovitch, ed. *The Islamic Near East, 700-1900: Studies in Economic and Social History* (Princeton, NJ, 1981), 521-46.

[11] For example, M. Deeb, *Party Politics in Egypt: The Wafd and its Rivals 1919-1939* (London, 1979), pp. 22-26, 182-3 etc.: A.L. Al-Sayyid Marsot, *Egypt's Liberal Experiment: 1922-1936* (Berkeley, 1977) pp. 14-18.

[12] R.L. Tignor, *State, Private Enterprise and Economic Change in Egypt, 1918-1952* (Princeton, 1984), pp. 10; Springborg, *Family Power and Politics in Egypt: Sayed Bey Marei - His Clan, Clients and Cohorts* (Philadelphia, 1982), pp. 90.

[13] For example, 'The report by Mr. Cave on the financial condition of Egypt' cited in E.R.J. Owen, *Cotton and the Egyptian Economy 1820-1914* (Oxford, 1969), pp. 145; Baer, *History of Landownership*,, pp. 31.

[14] R.L. Tignor, *Modernization and British Colonial Rule in Egypt 1882-1914* (Princeton, NJ, 1966), pp. 107-8.

[15] F.M. Edwards, 'Reports on Beheira Province, 1923-24', *Edwards Papers*, St. Antony's College Middle East Centre, Oxford; A. Holden, 'Report on land tax assessment', *Holden Papers*, St. Antony's College, Middle East Centre, Oxford.

[16] According to the original government statement that the first assessment was the last for 30 years, the next assessment should not have been implimented before 1942, the year at which the new rates were finally introduced into Minya and Bani-Suaif province: J.I. Craig, 'Les finances publiques de l'Egypte', *L'Egypte Contemporaine*, 118 (Jan. 1931), pp. 39. But it may be that the official ending of the Capitulations in 1937 allowed the government to ignore this ruling.

[17] Holden, 'Report on land tax assessment', pp. 17-18.

[18] Ibid., pp. 6-8.

[19] Ibid., pp. 18-19.

[20] Ibid., pp. 79-80.

[21] Deeb, *Party Politics in Egypt*, pp. 25; Davis, *Challenging Colonialism*, pp. 130. The view that restricting the size of the Egyptian harvest would raise prices was finally discredited for most economists in Egypt by G. Gresciani-Turroni's study 'Relations entre le récolte et le prix du coton égyptien', *L'Egypte Contemporaine*, 124 (Dec., 1930), pp. 633-89.

[22] Deeb, *Party Politics in Egypt*, pp. 25.

[23] Ibid., pp. 223, Tignor, *State, Private Enterprise and Economic Change* (pp. 114) is wrong to say that this policy only applied to 1931/2.

[24] Tignor, *State, Private Enterprise and Economic Change*, pp. 114-115.

[25] Deeb, *Party Politics in Egypt*, pp. 222.

[26] Tignor, *State, Private Enterprise and Economic Change*, pp. 119-21.

[27] C. Issawi, *Egypt at Mid-Century: An Economic Survey* (London, 1954), pp. 122-3.

[28] Tignor, *State, Private Enterprise and Economic Change*, pp. 110-111; H. Naus, 'L'industrie égyptienne', *L'Egypte Contemporaine*, 118 (Jan. 1931), pp. 13-14.

[29] A. Eman, *L'industrie du coton en Égypte: Étude d'economie politique* (Cairo, 1943), pp. 64-5.

[30] Davis, *Challenging Colonialism, pp. 108; S. Radwan, Capital Formation in Egyptian Industry and Agriculture 1882-1967* (London, 1974), pp. 131-4; Tignor, *State, Private Enterprise and Economic Change*, pp. 101-

03.

[31] Radwan (*Capital Formation*, pp. 235) estimates that Egypt's gross fixed capital formation at 10-15 percent for the years 1880-1914. But Professor Bent Hansen, in some unpublished calculations, believes that the savings ratio was perhaps only half this in the decade before the First World War.

[32] Richards, *Egypt's Agricultural Development*, pp.77-80.

[33] Egyptian governments managed to maintain a surplus of revenue over expenditure throughout the 1930s except for 1938/9 and 1939/40, *Annuaire Statistique 1939-40* (Cairo 1941), pp. 511.

[34] For example, Edward, Report on Beheira Province, 1923-4; S. Avigdor, 'L'Egypte agricole', *L'Egypte Contemporaine*, 118 (Jan., 1931), pp. 103.

[35] See, Edwards, "Report on Beheira Province, 1923-4; British report (1926) in Deeb, *Party Politics*, pp. 90, note 1 and Edwards, 'The Egyptian rural problem' (draft for article in the Contemporary Review, pp. 6, *Edwards Papers*).

[36] Springborg, *Family, Power and Politics*, pp. 58-9.

[37] *L'Egypte Independente*, pp. 290.

[38] Baer, *History of Landownership*, Appendix III.

[39] Ibid., pp. 151.

[40] Ibid., pp. 169-78

[41] Tignor, *State, Private Enterprise and Economic Change*, pp. 118-19; pp. 163-66.

[42] E. Minost, 'Essai sur le revenu agricole de l'Egypte', *L'Egypte Contemporaine* 123 (N0v.,) 1939), pp. 709.

[43] Y. Aghion and M. Roilay, "Excursions dans les grande domains - propriété S.E. Riaz Pacha', *Bulletin d'Union Syndicale des Agriculteurs d'Egypte*, I,5 (Aug., 1901), pp. 164-70.

[44] M. Poilay Bey, "Excursions dans les grands domains d'Egypte - Daira Draneth Pacha," *Bulletin d'Union syndicale des Agriculteurs d'Egypte*, I,2 (Aug., 1901), pp. 9-17.

[45] Information from the copy books of the Manzalawi estate in the possession of Professor Mahoud Manzalaoui who has kindly allowed me to use them. Further information about these estates can be found in Owen, "Development of agricultural production," pp. 529-30.

[46] Richards, *Egypt's Agricultural Development*, pp. 156-7.

[47] *L'Egypte Independente*, pp. 288-90.

[48] Ibid., pp. 291.

[49] Editor's review of "Note présenteé à SE le Ministre des Finances en

vue d'adoption par le gouvernement d'une politique cotonnière stable", *L'Egypte Contemporaine*, 124 (Dec., 1930), pp. 728-9.

[50] Avigdor, 'L'Egypte agricole', pp. 101.

[51] Saab, *Egyptian Agrarian Reform*, pp. 9-10.

[52] For example, Baer, *History of Landownership*, pp. 173-8.

[53] *L'Egypte Independente*, pp. 228.

[54] R. Mabro, *The Egyptian Economy 1952-1972* (Oxford, 1974), pp. 62.

[55] Saab, *Egyptian Agrarian Reform*, compare pp. 10 with pp. 109.

[56] J. Zannis, *Le Crédit Agricole en Égypte* (Paris, 1937), pp. 91.

[57] E. Eshag and M.A. Kamal, 'A note on the reform of the rural credit system in U.A.R. (Egypt)', *Bulletin of the Oxford University Institute of Economics and Statistics*, 29,2 (May, 1967), pp. 99-100.

[58] Ibid., pp. 99.

[59] Ibid., pp. 100.

[60] Idem.

[61] A. Holden, 'Witness in a criminal trial', *Holden Papers*.

[62] For example, Avigdor, 'L'Egypte agricole', pp. 99-100.

[63] For example, Mirrit Ghali Bey, 'Un programme de reforme agraire pour l'Egypte', *L'Egypte Contemporaine*, 236-237 (Jan.-Feb., 1947), pp. 6.

[64] Tariq al-Bishri, *Al-Haraka al-siyasiya fi Misr 1945-1952* (Cairo 1972), pp. 195. Baer (*History of Landownership*, pp. 202) asserts, wrongly, that the bill attempted to limit the size of land holdings to 50 *feddans*.

[65] Ghali, 'Programme de reforme agraire', pp. 13.

[66] Al-Bishri, *Al-Haraka al-siyasiya*, pp. 195.

[67] Ibid., pp. 194; Springborg, *Family, Power and Politics*, pp. 236.

[68] Ibid., pp. 390.

[69] Saab, *Egyptian Agrarian Reform*, chpts. II and III.

[70] Ibid., pp. 22.

[71] Radwan, *Agrarian Reform*, pp. 16.

[72] Mabro, *Egyptian Economy*, pp. 70-1.

[73] For example, Saab, *Egyptian Agrarian Reform*, pp. 109; Hansen and Marzouk, *Development and Economic Policy*, pp. 92n.

[74] L. Binder, *In a Moment of Enthusiasm: Political Power in the Second Stratum in Egypt* (Chicago, 1978), pp. 334; I. Harik, *The Political Mobilization of Peasants: A Study of an Egyptian Community* (Bloomington, 1974).

[75] Radwan, *Agrarian Reform*, pp. 28-9.

[76] Hansen and Wattleworth, 'Agricultural output', pp. 459.

[77] For example, S. Radwan and E. Lee, 'The State and Agrarian Change: A case study of Egypt, 1952-77' in D. Ghai, A.R. Khan, E. Lee and S. Radwan, eds. *Agrarian Systems and Development* (London, 1979), pp. 170.

[78] Radwan, *Capital Formation*, pp. 138.

[79] This is certainly how the Marei family viewed the situation: see Springborg, *Family, Power and Politics*, pp. 58-62.

[80] J. Ducruet, *Les capitaux européens au Proche-Orient* (Paris, 1964), pp. 318-27.

TABLE 1: EGYPT'S CULTIVATED AREA, CROPPED AREA, COTTON AREA AND AGRICULTURAL LABOUR FORCE 1897-1960

| | Cultivated area (million *feddans*) | Cropped area (million *feddans*) | Cotton area (million *feddans*) | Agricultural Labor Force (millions) |
|---|---|---|---|---|
| 1897 | 5.0 | 6.7 | 1.1 | - |
| 1907 | 5.4 | 7.7 | 1.6 | 2.40 |
| 1917 | 5.3 | 7.7 | 1.7 | 2.82 |
| 1927 | 5.5 | 8.7 | 1.5 | 3.50 |
| 1937 | 5.3 | 8.4 | 2.0 | 4.28 |
| 1947 | 5.7 | 9.2 | 1.3 | 4.22 |
| 1957 | 5.8 | 10.3 | 1.8 | - |
| 1960 | 5.9 | 10.4 | 1.9 | 4.40 |

Source: Egypt, Annuaire Statistique for various years (areas); B. Hansen and G.A. Marzouk, *Development and Economic Policy in the UAR (Egypt)* (Amsterdam, 1965), p. 61 (labor force)

TABLE 2: EGYPTIAN AGRICULTURAL OUTPUT AND AGRICULTURAL OUTPUT/CAPITA, 1895-9 to 1960-4 (1895-9=100)

| | Agricultural output | Output per capita of major field crops |
|---|---|---|
| 1895-9 | 100 | 100 |
| 1900-04 | 104 | 97 |
| 1905-09 | 106 | 93 |
| 1910-14 | 114 | 93 |
| 1915-19 | 107 | 79 |
| 1920-24 | 112 | 79 |
| 1925-29 | 131 | 88 |
| 1930-34 | 133 | 83 |
| 1935-39 | 152 | 87 |
| 1940-44 | 135 | 69 |
| 1945-49 | 149 | 68 |
| 1950-54 | 159 | 63 |
| 1955-59 | 177 | 60 |
| 1960-64 | 192 | 58 |

Sources: B. Hansen and Michael Wattleworth, "Agricultural output and consumption of basic foods in Egypt, 1886/7 - 1967/68," *International Journal of Middle East Studies*, 9 (1978), p. 457; and Michael Wattleworth and B. Hansen, "Report on the construction of agricultural indexes for Egypt, 1887-1968," mimeo (Institute of International Studies, University of California, Berkeley, 15 Sept. 1975)," Table XLV.

TABLE 3: THE DISTRIBUTION OF LANDOWNERSHIP 1900-1964

| | Large Properties (50 feddans and over) | | Medium Properties (5-50 feddans) | | Small Properties (under 5 feddans) | |
|---|---|---|---|---|---|---|
| | Number ,000 | Area ,000 feds | Number ,000 | Area ,000 feds | Number ,000 | Area ,000 feds |
| 1900 | 12 | 2,244 | 141 | 1,757 | 761 | 1,113 |
| 1906 | 13 | 2,476 | 134 | 1,662 | 1,084 | 1,293 |
| 1916 | 12 | 2,356 | 133 | 1,645 | 1,480 | 1,450 |
| 1936 | 12 | 2,254 | 146 | 1,747 | 2,242 | 1,837 |
| 1943 | 12 | 2,142 | 147 | 1,774 | 2,376 | 1,944 |
| 1952 | 12 | 2,042 | 148 | 1,817 | 2,642 | 2,122 |
| | | (Land Reform) | | | | |
| 1957 | 12 | 1,756 | 155 | 1,915 | 2,718 | 2,274 |
| 1961 | 11 | 930 | 171 | 1,982 | 2,919 | 3,172 |
| 1964 | 10 | 813 | 168 | 1,956 | 2,965 | 3,353 |

Source: Eprime Eshag and M.A. Kamal, "Agrarian reform in the United Arab Republic (Egypt), *Bulletin of the Oxford University Institute of Economics and Statistics*, 30, 2 (May 1968), p. 76.

TABLE 4: THE RELATIONSHIP BETWEEN LAND TAX AND RENTAL VALUE IN THE EVALUATIONS OF 1895, 1935-7 AND 1946-8 COMPARED WITH TOTAL LAND TAX,

| | 1895 | 1935-7 | 1939/40[a] | 1946-8 | 1949/50[a] |
|---|---|---|---|---|---|
| Land tax as % of rental value | 28.64 | 15.73 | 16.0 | 9.9[b] | 14.0 |
| Average rental value of all land (LE/*fed*.) | 3.36[c] | 5.715 | NA | 18.431 | NA |
| Total land tax (LE million) | 4.8 | 5.3 | 5.2 | 5.4 | 7.9 |
| Total Gov. Rev. (LE million) | 10.7 | NA | 39.4 | NA | 158.6 |
| Total value of cotton harvest (LE million) | 11.8 | NA | 28.3 | NA | 213.7 |

Source: (Land tax and rental value) Andrew Holden, "Report on land tax assessment 1946-1948," Andrew Holden Papers (St. Antony's College, Oxford): (Total land tax, revenue and value of cotton harvest), *Annuaire Statistique*

Notes: [a] Years in which new rates introduced. The 1895 rate was introduced province by province, between 1898 and 1907.

[b] This is the rate after the average rental values for the year 1945/6 were halved on the grounds that they were artificially high due to wartime conditions.

[c] Calculated by dividing total rental value of all lands (LE 16,356,000) by the size of the cultivated area for 1894/5.

TABLE 5A: THE PROPORTION OF EGYPTIAN LAND OWNED BY FOREIGNERS AND THE PROPORTION OF FOREIGN LAND HELD IN LARGE ESTATES, 1919-1949

| | Total foreign-owned land (feddans) | Foreign-owned land as % of total land | % of foreign-owned land held in large estates of 50 feddans+ |
|---|---|---|---|
| 1919 | 627,589 | 25.6 | 92.9 |
| 1929 | 489,741 | 19.6 | 93.0 |
| 1939 | 403,656 | 17.1 | 92.9 |
| 1949 | 233,013 | 10.2 | 90.9 |

Source: G. Baer, A History of Landownership in Modern Egypt, 1800-1950 (London, 1962), pp. 121, 230.

TABLE 5B: ESTIMATES OF LAND HELD AND ADMINISTERED IN VARIOUS CATEGORIES 1907-1953 (FEDS)

| | Waqfs | | | Royal Family | Land Co.s |
|---|---|---|---|---|---|
| | Min. of Waqfs | Royal Waqfs | Total | | |
| 1907 | | | | | 240,000 |
| 1914 | | | 350,000 | | |
| 1924 | | | | | 170,000 |
| 1925/6 | 172,830 | 52,000 | | | |
| 1927 | | | 611,203 | | |
| 1932 | | | | | 208,000 |
| 1940 | | | 662,700 | | 200,000 |
| 1941/2 | 151,586 | | | | |
| 1949 | 174,735 | | | | |
| 1950 | | | 587,122 | | |
| 1952 | | 120-130,000 | | 179,157 | |

Source: Baer, History of Landownership, passim.

TABLE 6: LAND REQUISITIONED UNDER THE TWO REFORM LAWS AND OTHER ACTS AND THE RATE AT WHICH IT WAS REDISTRIBUTED, 1952-1966

| Requisition | | Distribution* | |
|---|---|---|---|
| Source of land | Area ('000 *feddans*) | Year | Area ('000 *feddans*) |
| 1st Reform Law, 1952 | 434 | 1953 | 16 |
| | | 1954 | 65 |
| Waqfs khairi, 1957 | 110 | 1955 | 67 |
| | | 1956 | 36 |
| 2nd Reform Law, 1961 | 175 | 1957 | 42 |
| | | 1958 | 43 |
| Charitable Trust, 1962 | 38 | 1959 | 6 |
| | | 1960 | 23 |
| Sequestration decrees, 1962, 1964 | 69 | 1961 | 28 |
| | | 1962 | 106 |
| Alien's properties, 1963 | 48 | 1963 | 90 |
| | | 1964 | 122 |
| | | 1965 | 26 |
| | | 1966 | 26 |
| Total | 875 | | 696 |

Source: Eshag and Kamel, "Agrarian reform," p. 79.

Note: * Excludes distribution of some 180,000 *feddans* from Public Domains and reclaimed waste land.

# 4

# Agricultural Support Policies in Turkey, 1950–1980: An Overview

*Kutlu Somel*

## INTRODUCTION

This paper discusses the effects of agricultural policies with respect to price and income stability, output increases and technological developments, income distribution and inflation. The stance adopted in this discussion is contrary to the accepted and orthodox view that development requires that a surplus be extracted from a traditional agricultural sector. A synthesis is developed such that in agricultural policies the political influences are discounted and instead, economic motives are emphasized. The basic hypothesis that evolves from this discussion is that there were conscious agricultural policies in Turkey whereby resources were transferred to agriculture with the purpose of developing this sector as a viable market for consumption and production goods.

Agricultural support, encompassing price supports, input subsidies, credit policies, etc., is a pervasive phenomenon in Turkish agriculture. The topic is and has always been a controversial one. Hence it has caused a significant amount of scientific input and exchange in the literature. This literature is surveyed to review agricultural policies in Turkey to develop a hypothesis about their rationale. The period covered is 1950-1980. Subsequent to 1980, there have been major structural changes in policies involving liberalization of the economy, but it is too early to analyze their effects.

## MAJOR CATEGORIES OF AGRICULTURAL SUPPORT

Agricultural support policies are one aspect of the more comprehensive phenomenon of government intervention in the economy (Hill and Ingersent, 1977:169-196; Kazgan, 1977:501-566; Aktan, 1973; Pekin 1973a). They become manifest in three broad categories:

a. *Intervention in output and input markets.* This can take place through various forms, e.g., input subsidies, support prices, rationing of inputs, etc.

b. *Intervention in the credit markets.* This can be utilized to promote the ends in a and c but is also of paramount influence in one particular aspect. Because of the lag between the use of inputs and the realization of output in agriculture, credit is essential. Furthermore, governments, in extending organized credit to agriculture also try to replace the usurious unorganized credit markets and their adverse influences. Longer term credits, on the other hand, essentially influence investment.

c. *Research and extension activities in the development of agricultural technologies.* A particularly effective mode of intervention by governments in agriculture is the research and extension activities of government agencies in developing and transmitting agricultural technologies. The high costs and risks involved in such activities usually leave them within the domain of government support even though actual activities may take place in academic or other scientific environments. The supportive aspect of government research and extension activities in the development of technologies is a substantially neglected topic. (DPT, 1971 is a rare example that emphasizes this aspect).

Obviously, these three broad categories are not mutually exclusive; there is substantial overlap and interaction involved.

In Turkey, one observes all these manifestations of government intervention. For example, some inputs (e.g. fertilizers) are sold to the producers at prices considerably lower than cost and world prices. Through this medium, the promotion of technologies is also effectively supported. Other research and extension activities of government agencies are documented in Aruoba (1978), Mann (1978, 1977), Somel (1979c, 1977), Aresvik (1975) and USAID/Turkey (1969). Credit is extended widely to agriculture through the organized markets. However, the distribution of funds is biased towards larger farms and the smaller farms have to resort to unorganized credit markets, (T.C. Ziraat Bankasi, 1973; Koksal, 1971).

The intervention activity that receives the most attention in Turkey is agricultural support prices. The publicity that surrounds this activity is so overwhelming that invariably it is incorrectly and unjustly identified as the only mode of government intervention in agriculture in Turkey.

Since 1932, when wheat prices began to be supported, 24 agricultural commodities have come to be subjected to price supports. However, all commodities have not received price supports continuously and all price supports have not been equally effective (Donmezcelik, 1979:32; Ergun, 1978b:19-20; Bulmus, 1978:150). Price supports in Turkey essentially imply that government agencies will purchase all that is supplied to those agencies at the announced prices. In opium poppy, tea and sugar beets, the government agencies were the sole authorized purchasers. In tobacco, purchases for national consumption were handled by the State Monopoly while private purchases were made for export purposes only.

In 1976, support purchases totaled an amount equivalent to 6.36% of GNP and 23.67% of the gross agricultural product (Ergun, 1978b:155). However, the consequences of those purchases are considerably more than what is reflected by those figures. They exert a considerably wider influence not only on other activities in agriculture but also on social and economic life in Turkey as a whole (Aksoy, 1978; T.C. Merkez Bankasi, 1978; DPT, 1977, Akyuz, 1973).

A look at the chronological list of commodities that have received price supports gives the following impression:

a. Support activities prior to 1950 were confined primarily to cereals. In fact, all these policies towards the main cereals (i.e. excluding maize and rice) originated in the post-depression era between 1932-1938 (Aktan, 1955).

b. Three exceptions to these activities prior to 1950 are opium poppies, tobacco and tea. The intervention in poppies originally had a strong control motive. On the other hand, support for tobacco (the most important export item in value terms; Aktan, 1955:211) and tea (a newly developing product which was previously being imported) were probably responses to the effects of the Second World War on international trade.

c. In the period 1950-1960, the only commodity that was introduced into the price support schemes was sugar beets. However, it is well known that this period was characterized by extensive and intensive price support activities (Erguder, 1980).

d. In the post 1960 era, with minor exceptions, the commodities that were introduced into price support schemes were primarily export commodities. A most significant industrial crop, cotton, also came under price supports in 1966.

Hence, the focus on the post-1950 era is justified on the following grounds:

i. The price support activities in Turkey prior to 1950 had as their primary motive the elimination of adverse effects on the producers' incomes that were brought about initially with the Great Depression and later on by the Second World War (not so much the war, during which agricultural prices actually increased, but the post-war period. Aktan, 1955).

ii. The motives for price support activities after 1950 are qualitatively considerably different (as will be discussed throughout this paper) from those prior to 1950.

## AGRICULTURAL SUPPORT POLICIES; MOTIVES AND TARGETS-GENERAL

There is consensus about the justification for government intervention in agriculture. The most commonly stated reason that is claimed to necessitate this intervention is the risk and uncertainty involved in agricultural production that result in the instability of agricultural prices and incomes. This arises because,

a. The role of natural, climatological, biological and other environmental factors are considerable,

b. The effects of long gestation periods and periodicity of production are substantial,

c. Agricultural products are relatively more perishable,

d. Techniques of production are more rigid primarily because of the dependence on land as a factor of production (i.e. there is less flexibility in the reallocation of resources), and,

e. Demand for agricultural products is generally characterized by low price and income elasticities. (Bulmus, 1978:1-3, 146-148; Civi, 1977:4-6; Aktan, 1973:136-137; Aras, 1973:17-18; Keskiner, 1973:59-60; Pekin, 1973b: 145-148).

Other reasons that are given to justify government intervention are:

f. The relative difficulty of organization among large numbers of producers to protect their interests (Aras, 1973:18; Pekin, 1973b:148),

g. The tradition bound and inelastic behaviours of agricultural producers which increase their vulnerability (Aras, 1973:18; Pekin, 1973b:147) (Some researchers, e.g. Scott, 1977, would disagree with this),

h. The high costs of market information to small producers and the higher role of intermediaries in the determination of prices. (Bulmus, 1978:23; Aktan, 1955:31.)

Given these reasons that justify government intervention in agriculture, actual policies that are implemented are categorized under two general classes.

1. Price Policies. These include price supports, minimum prices, input subsidies, credit, etc.

2. Structural policies. Other non-price oriented policies such as policies to change land tenure, development of cooperatives, services to promote new technologies, etc. (Pekin, 1973b:148).

In Turkey most agricultural support policies are of the first kind, i.e. price policies. However, recently, technology oriented structural policies are also gaining significance[1].

There also appears to be substantial agreement over the targets for agricultural support policy. The most widely stated ones are:

a. To reduce price instability,

b. To reduce income instability,

c. To stimulate increases in output,

d. To influence the composition of output,

e. To change (or maintain) the distribution of income. (Bulmust, 1978:3; T.C. Merkez Bankasi, 1978:36; Aktan, 1973:38-39; Aras, 1973:29; Pekin, 1973b:152-164; DPT, 1971:4-6).

f. Another, less laudatory aspect of agricultural support policies has been indicated to be their use to achieve political ends (Aksoy, 1978; Erguder, 1980; DPT, 1977:27-28; Forker, 1971d:61).

g. In contradiction with the next point a rather futile target has been to prevent price increases (DPT, 1972:2),

h. Regardless of whether it is an openly declared target or not, a consistent result of price support activities appear to be the inflationary processes which they generate. (Aksoy, 1978; T.C. Merkez Bankasi, 1978:35-59; Akyuz, 1973:131-180).

An obvious implication of the multiplicity of targets is the problem of consistency in agricultural policies. The probability of finding a set of policy instruments that will achieve consistency among so many targets is quite low.

The inevitable consequence of agricultural support activities is that they prevent what would have taken place under normal circumstances. What would have taken place, for example, had market forces been allowed to determine prices, can only be conjectured. Such counterfactual conjectures, educated as they may be, would hardly be helpful in evaluating these agricultural policies. There is however, ample theoretical treatment of agricultural policies in this respect. (For example, cf., Bulmus, 1978:51-82; Hill and Ingersent, 1977:187-196).

What needs to be done is to evaluate the degree to which the targets of agricultural policy have been achieved. The following sections attempt to do this.

## PRICE INSTABILITY

Have agricultural support policies, especially support prices, increased price stability? The kind of stability that is emphasized in the literature is not the stabilization of seasonal variations in prices. It also is not the instability of price brought about by changes in demand with inelastic (or fixed) supply. The literature deals primarily with the variations in price from year to year. This obviously is a serious omission, because the first two causes of instability are no less serious than the last one. The various stock policies of government agencies do not appear to have the purpose of smoothing price fluctuations within the year. The large carryover stocks in some commodities as well as the losses involved in the spoilage of some stocks are indicative of the lack of a purposeful stock policy. (Forker, 1971b:7; T.C. Merkez Bankasi 1978, Vol. 2; DPT, 1977).

There are very few studies that have specifically looked into the level of stability that has been achieved in agricultural prices and still fewer that have asked whether such stability as has been achieved can be attributed to support policies. For example, Aresvik (1975:107), somehow reaches the conclusion that "... (p)rices have been subsidized; seasonal and yearly variations in price have been somewhat stabilized...", but there is nothing that he can offer as supportive evidence. Forker (1971d:61), who has done considerable work on price policy in Turkey, probably bases his claim that "the government is able to maintain... price stability..." on more solid ground. For example, he has estimated a linear trend for current wheat (farm) prices between 1950 and 1969 (Forker, 1971:19a) and has found the following relationship.

$$P = 14.15 + 4.31t, R2 = 0.9448, SEE = 6.297$$

with the average price for the period being 59.45 ks/kg, the coefficient of variability around the trend is only 10.6%.

Civi (1977:144-160) also estimates real price trend equations for cotton, tobacco, tea, sugar beets, wheat and hazelnuts and finds that between 1963 and 1974, while the real price of the first two commodities increased, the last four showed a real price decrease. However, Civi does not supplement these estimates with any statistical information that might give an idea about stability.

By themselves, these trend estimates do not give a clue as to whether stability can be attributed to support policies. Soral (1973), however, does provide an interesting contrast where the effects of support policies can be compared with cases where such policies are non-existent. Soral estimates (real) price elasticies of supply and demand for onions, potatoes and wheat from time series for the period 1951-1968. Using a cobweb model type analysis he concludes that in the first two commodities, which are not supported, there are tendencies toward instability: disturbances from equilibrium can result in widening price oscillations. For wheat, however, such disturbances result in dampening oscillations, indicating a stabilizing tendency. Soral attributes this to the beneficial effects of price supports. These results must be interpreted with caution, however, due to possible specification errors and autocorrelation.

A most meticulous study, not only from the point of analysis of price stability in agriculture, but for analyzing agricultural price policies as a whole is Gurkan (1979). He analyzes the effects of government support policies on a number of crops with respect to price and income stability. To analyze price instability, he (1979:233-259) looks at the prices of twenty agricultural commodities and calculates coefficients of variation (net of trend for the period 1951-1973) from national averages, for each commodity. He then classifies the commodities into three groups according to whether they are subject to strong, weak or no "government involvement." The analysis indicates that price stability increases with government involvement. However, the differences between weak and strong government involvement are not significant when current prices are used. When real prices are used, the only significant difference is between strong and no government involvement. Analysis of products sensitive to international market conditions indicate that this factor increases price instability significantly. Gurkan then uses analysis of variance with data for the same commodities at the provincial level. Using information from 30 provinces, he finds again that with current prices, price stability for wheat increases with government involvement. With data from 10 provinces and using real prices, the results are in the same direction for cotton. Hence, there appears to be substantial evidence to indicate that agricultural support activities enhance price stability.

## EFFECTS OF SUPPORT POLICIES ON AGRICULTURAL INCOMES

Support policies can influence changes in current and real agricultural incomes, the stability of those incomes, and the distribution of income. Only the first two effects are discussed in this section.

Few researchers have conducted specific studies that have tried to associate increases in agricultural incomes with support policies. The basic reason for this could be that most believe that agriculture in Turkey could not have survived without support policies, let alone have exhibited any increases in income. Hence, the income increasing effects of support policies are more or less taken for granted. Support purchases between 1970 and 1976 varied from 9.80% to 23.67% of the agricultural gross product (Ergun, 1978b:155). The commodities that were covered by support activities comprised a considerable part of agricultural production and hence were influenced by those activities. Therefore, such activities probably have had a very significant effect on whatever has happened to agricultural incomes.

Some relevant indices are presented in Table 1. There are differences in those indices that arise due to different methods of computation. However, there are generally increases in real per capita agricultural incomes according to Gurkan (1979), and Keyder (1970, 1976). (Gurkan's figures relate to total agricultural income. However, when the agricultural population growth rate is taken into consideration, his figures still imply an annual growth rate of over 3% in per capita income.) Furthermore, according to Keyder and Karayalcin and Arat (1975) a rural welfare index constructed as the product of the internal terms of trade (TOT) and the real per capita agricultural income index also shows welfare gains for the agricultural sector. However, one must notice the substantial fluctuations around the trend in Keyder's rural welfare index. The TOT also indicate that, even though there are periodic setbacks, developments are in general favourable to agriculture. According to the more detailed study by Varlier (1978a) the TOT have never but once (in 1959) been against agriculture. TOT is a more significant factor in the distribution of income between agricultural and the rest of the economy and this aspect of support policies will be dealt with later on. It can be concluded that indices that are pertinent in measuring the changes in agricultural real incomes uniformly imply an upward trend (Keyder, 1970:41-42).

On the question of income stability, the only study of record is by Gurkan (1979). In a manner similar to the treatment of price instability mentioned above, using dummy variables for strong, weak and no government involvement on the crops analyzed and regressing those variables on the coefficient of variation of gross income per hectare, Gurkan (1979:248-259) reaches the conclusion that support price policies have not been effective in reducing income instability. When the analysis is conducted with provincial figures there appears to be some effect of strong government involvement, but in real prices, government involvement has no effect in reducing income instability.

If one recalls that gross income is the product of price and quantity, these results by Gurkan imply that even though support activities have substantially reduced price variability, it has not had a significant effect on reducing output variability.

Kip (1973), supports this to a certain extent. He calculates coefficients of variation for deviations from the trend for the period 1948-1970. For barley, wheat, rye, olives and hazelnuts, the coefficient of variation for yield is greater than that of price. However, for potatoes, beans, corn, tobacco, cotton and sugar beets the situation is the reverse. The coefficient of variation of gross income is, of course, greater than that of both yield and price for all products.

Turkish agriculture is influenced by climatic variability. The instability of agricultural production can be attributed to this (Bulmus, 1978:157; Uras, 1973). Mann (1977:40) estimates the rough probability of moderately bad and bad weather years to be 37.5%. It has been a consistent part of the five year development plans to incorporate some statement about the effects of weather variability (DPT, 1963:151; 1976:302; 1973:210; 1979:337). It appears that there are limits to reducing the effects of variable weather, even with the recently accelerated changes in the use of modern inputs (PAK, 1974; 1979).

At low levels of production, instability is a serious problem. Price supports, even though achieving price stability, will be totally inadequate in assuring income stability. But, if incomes are fairly low to begin with due to low level of production, the instability of those incomes impart a high degree of risk to the livelihood of the rural populace (Scott, 1977).

Clearly, governments actively involved in agricultural support activities cannot ignore this problem. The solution lies in the fact that even though it is difficult to remove the effects of weather variability it is possible to increase production. In this manner the risks associated with low levels of production are eliminated. Weather variability and associated production instability might still remain. However, the instability does not involve the risk of starvation. Instability at a higher level of production can be counter-acted with appropriate stock policies.

## POLICIES ON AGRICULTURAL RESEARCH AND TECHNOLOGICAL CHANGE

One way to achieve increases in production is technological change. Turkish government agencies have been active in the research, development and extension activities involving the improvement of agricultural technologies.

The Turkish efforts at agricultural research and technological change have generally been successful in achieving their objectives. It currently is the only country in the Middle East that has achieved self-sufficiency in food production. Agricultural research is conducted in the Ministry of Agriculture, other ministries and in universities[2]. Agricultural research is confined to experiment stations with very little on-farm research under farmer conditions, but experiment stations are fairly diffused into the countryside. Research, in both the universities and the ministry is commodity and discipline oriented. For some critical commodities such as cotton, tobacco, citrus, etc., there are independent research organizations within the ministry[3]. Due to the crop discipline orientation in research and the lack of on-farm research, the social and economic component of agricultural research is fairly traditional and weak. Several examples of interdisciplinary on-farm research, such as the Wheat Project, have indicated the usefulness of this alternative research strategy.

An important aspect of the research structure is the fairly distinct separation of extension from research, except in a few externally funded projects such as the Wheat Project. Extension (which used to be known as the Directorate of Agricultural Affairs) is both part of the Ministry of Agriculture and local government administration. Hence, apart from the functions of communicating to the farmers the extension "messages" from the ministry, the extension officials have to supervise the distribution of inputs, authorization of credits, conducting censuses, etc. Such diverse duties result in a diffusion of effort, and combined with scarcity of resources in transportation and extension aids, result in the extension agents losing effectiveness. However, the farmers who recognize the value of information related to agricultural improvements are not unwilling to go to the extension agents or to bring them to their villages.

Agricultural research has produced successful results in crops but not in livestock. The lack of success in livestock can be attributed on the one hand to the relatively longer periods involved in such research and on the other hand to the structure of livestock production in Turkey. It takes place with local adapted breeds and under a low productivity-low management system that exploits common grazing grounds, the fallow, agricultural by-products and scavenging. Improved breeds for intensive livestock production may not have been profitable relative to this traditional system.

Recently, there have been significant improvements in poultry, egg and dairy production. As the limits of common pastures are reached, as fallow decreases, the increasing demand for meat and dairy products will induce an intensification of livestock production. However, the projected investment costs of such a shift in building up new stocks, buildings, etc. will be quite high.

In crops, a first surge in production came in the fifties with the introduction of tractors through the Marshall Plan. This resulted in an extension of cultivated land but could not produce sustained productivity increases. However, till the early sixties with PL480 surplus aid, the agricultural situation remained tolerable.

In the latter part of the sixties and the early part of the seventies the development of technologies related to irrigated and rainfed wheat made Turkey a showcase in this respect. The supply of purchased inputs, especially fertilizers, at subsidized prices by the various government agencies obviously provided substantial incentive and stimulus in the diffusion and adoption of these technologies. (Somel, 1979, 1977; Aktan, 1979; Aruoba, 1978; Mann, 1980, 1977; Demir, 1976). The success of these research activities can hence be ascribed partially to complementary support policies. However, there was not much planning involved in these policies. There was selective use of price supports to change relative prices to the advantage of the commodity being promoted.

As Mann (1977:37-44) indicates, even though wheat production has increased dramatically, so has the absolute magnitude of production variability due to weather. But it was possible now to get equally good yields under the worst weather conditions from improved technologies as under the best weather conditions from traditional technologies. Bulmust (1978:157) also estimates the role of natural conditions in yield variations for 1954-1963 and for 1964-1973. It appears that even though production as well as yields increased for the crops analyzed, the role of natural conditions in yield variability has increased for wheat, barley, rice and sugar beets and decreased for tobacco, cotton and sunflower seeds.

In Section 5, the source of income instability was identified as output instability because a substantial degree of price stability had been achieved through support policies. The solution to this has been intensive involvement by government agencies in research and extension activities for diffusing improved agricultural technologies. Through this, production has been increased to levels where the nature of the risks inherent in output instability have changed.

## CHANGES IN PRODUCTION AND COMPOSITION OF OUTPUT

It was indicated above that there were significant government policies to increase production through technological change. The purpose was pointed out to be the reduction of income instability. However, neither is this motive the sole reason for increasing output, nor is technological change the only policy instrument. There is an inherent need during the process of economic development for not only increases in agricultural production but also qualitative changes therein. This is reflected on the composition of the output too as export commodities and commodities with high income elasticities gain significance.

The most effective tool in stimulating production can be expected to be agricultural price policies. If support prices put a lower limit on agricultural prices, their success depends to a large extent on the price elasticity of supply. Many studies, with differing levels of sophistication have attempted to estimate supply elasticities[4].

In spite of the diversity of the approaches and the range in the findings, one can conclude that the supply of most of the significant crops such as wheat, tobacco, etc. are responsive to prices. The question is whether this price responsiveness of supply of agricultural commodities has been exploited in agricultural policies with the purpose of influencing the composition of the output. There is a lot of conjecture about some of the macroeconomically undesirable effects of changes in relative support prices. Some examples in this respect are related to wheat and sunflower seeds in Thrace, tea in the eastern Black Sea region, hazelnuts in the Black Sea region and wheat and cotton in the Cukurova region. In the first case, the relative profitability of wheat produced by relatively favourable support policies have replaced sunflower seeds with Bezostaya wheat in Thrace (World Bank, 1979, Vol. 2:39-40). For tea and hazelnuts, it is claimed that they have expanded into areas which ecologically do not have suitable and optimal characteristics (T.C. Merkez Bankasi, 1978; DPT, 1979:122). The introduction of high yielding varieties followed by favourable support policies have shifted land from cotton to wheat in the Cukurova region (USAID/Turkey, 1969). However, most of these are conjectures and not backed by solid evidence on causalities and magnitudes.

The intent, however, to use relative support prices and other policies have always been there for the purpose of altering the composition of output at least since the second five year plan (DPT, 1967:111,308; 1971:3,5; 1973; 1979:122; World Bank, 1979, Vol. 1:14). However, as stated in the last DPT reference, support policies have not been successful in this respect. The basic reason for this is the lack of a policy planning model. Recent efforts in this vein were the agricultural production planning proposal generating from within the Ministry of Agriculture (PAK, 1978) and the Turkish Agricultural Sector Model (TASM) of the World Bank, and in World Bank (1983). The progress of these activities will provide a rational and scientific basis for developing policies so that agricultural production can be planned in conformity with various objectives.

INCOME DISTRIBUTION

One of the most intensively analyzed aspects of support policies is their effects on the distribution of income. This problem has drawn interest from the point of the intersectoral distribution of income as well as the distribution of income within the agricultural sector. The latter aspect will be discussed in this section.

The distribution of income in agriculture exhibits a relatively higher degree of inequality according to most classifications. According to DPT (1976a:100,157,165) the following three results are characteristic of Turkey. First, the distribution of agricultural incomes is more equal than non-agricultural incomes even though there are intersecting sections of the Lorenz curves. Second, incomes of families whose head is working in the agricultural sector exhibit a higher degree of inequality as compared to the industrial or services sector. Third, the incomes of farmers exhibit a considerably higher degree of inequality as compared to other occupations. Again according to DPT (1976a:124,131) incomes within agriculture from plant production exhibit a higher degree of inequality than incomes from animal husbandry. Furthermore, in a rather particular classification of plant products, the three most significant groups exhibit a decreasing degree of equality as industrial products, cereals and cereals plus industrial products. However, the difference between the last two groups is probably not significant.

Initial analyzes of the impact of support policies from the distributional point of view have been related to credit policies. In the fifties the extension of credit for the purchase of tractors and other equipment as well as current expenditures was widespread. Koksal (1971:514-517), analyzing the period between 1950-1968, reaches the conclusion that a large majority of the farmers receive small amounts of credit at the expense of a minority who are getting an increasingly larger portion of credits. In 1973, the situation has not changed much (T.C. Ziraat Bankasi, 1973). According to this study by the Agricultural Bank, which is based on a survey, 8% of total farms which have land holdings greater than 20 hectares have received 61.3% of organized credit. In 1973, such farms comprised 4.7% of agricultural households and owned or operated 40% of the agricultural land (Varlier, 1978b:15). It is evident that such credit policies could not have been conducive to the promotion of equality in the distribution of income. Furthermore, the generally prevalent high delinquency rates on repayment essentially transform credits into direct transfers.

Another aspect of credit is that there are substantial financial economies of scale which bias related policies towards larger farms. The high information and fixed administration costs and the high collateral requirements cause a bias against small farmers (Somel, 1978; Mann,

1978:81).

A pathbreaking research that established the methodological base for several later studies was DPT (1969). In this study, using 1965 population data, and using productivities and costs for three grades of land for wheat, and farm size distributions from the village inventory studies of 1967 for part of the provinces in six regions of Turkey, the average quantity of wheat marketed was calculated for seven farm sizes. It was established that farms smaller than 2.5 hectares had deficits in wheat, i.e. they were net purchasers (DPT, 1969:20). At a price of around 0.8 TL/kg this implied a net expenditure of around 400 TL/annum for wheat per farm less than 2.5 hectares. In 1967, agricultural income per capita was around 2600 TL. As these farms would be considerably below this level, their wheat purchases would impose a substantial burden on their budgets. Farms larger than 2.5 hectares marketed an average of 6.7 tons/farm. The argument is that increases in the support price reflected on the market price of wheat. A 0.05 TL/kg increase in the price of wheat would imply an increased expenditure of around 25 TL/farm for those less than 2.5 hectares, whereas those larger would gain around 336 TL/farm. Hence, government support prices favour larger farms at the expense of smaller farms. The adverse distributive effects of this is clear.

The trap here is to consider this a static phenomenon. In other words, to claim that there will be a farm size below which farms will have a deficit in food grains and hence to conclude that support policies have undesirable distributional effects is not a satisfactory argument. As Mann (1980:234) has indicated, according to a study by Erkus (1976:758-759), in a sample of 330 farms from Central Anatolia, the average amount of wheat marketed by farms less than 2.5 hectares is equal to 8.95% of their output. For larger farms, the marketing ratio reaches to a maximum of 68.32%. In Varlier (1978b:21) it is indicated that according to the 1970 Agricultural Census, the marketing ratio for wheat is 7.23% for farms smaller than 2 hectares and increases as high as 76.18% for larger farms. As one can see, even if food grain deficiency is eliminated, the problem is not eliminated. Larger farms have larger outputs and get a larger share of the pie. Obviously support policies must have an effect in propagating the inequalities but the basic source of the problem is the inequality in the distribution of land ownership and farm size (Mann, 1978:82; Kazgan, 1977:511).

Using the same methodology DPT (1976b) looks at the effects of support policies on the producers of tea, sugar beets, cotton and hazelnuts. However, this study utilizes fixed costs and yields for all sizes of farms for the respective products. Furthermore, official prices are utilized in the valuation of the outputs. This appears to be necessary due to data limitations, but, it undeniably detracts from the explanatory power of the analysis, because, with all these assumptions, the distribution of benefits becomes proportional to land size. Again we arrive at the same conclusion that the basic problem is in the distribution of land. (If profits per decare are equal to price times yield minus costs per decare and if these three variables are assumed to be constant for all farms, then the distribution of total profits is proportional to land size.)

The implausibility of a scheme of differential pricing according to farm size points to the fact that, as long as there are inequalities in land distribution, the benefits of effective uniform support prices will be inequitably distributed. This fact appears to have been resigned to in DPT (1977, Vol. 1:3, 29 ff). It is argued there that in spite of all the problems of inequality support purchases must continue because it would cause a greater inequality to deprive 96.4% of the farmers, who have holdings less than 10 hectares, from the benefits of these purchases in order to prevent the 3.6% of the farmers who have more than 10 hectares from benefiting.

On the other hand, there is no reason why other policies could not have been used to achieve a more equitable distribution of benefits. In particular, technological developments and related research and extension activities could have been directed at the less privileged and smaller farms. However, a fairly universal characteristic of technological development policies aiming at accelerated increases in agricultural production has exhibited itself in Turkey too. Inevitably, such policies are either addressed to and/or are more compatible with the resource endowments of larger farms. Hence, they are the first to adopt and reap the substantial initial benefits of such policies (Griffin, 1979:46-94; Wharton, 1969; Falcon, 1970; Cleaver, 1972). Analyses by Demir (1976:16, 22, 24), Aruoba (1978:133) and particularly by Mann (1978) supply evidence for the case that technologies related to wheat production have been somewhat biased towards large farmers.

## AGRICULTURAL INVESTMENT

Several aspects of agricultural investment are touched upon in other sections, hence the discussion will be brief. Agricultural investment is defined to include expenditures in agricultural machinery, equipment and buildings, large and small scale irrigation facilities including drainage and land leveling, rural roads and electrification, changes in the quality and quantity of land and changes in the quality and quantity of livestock.

Data to observe expenditures on these items are not available in Turkey, particularly distinguishing private and public investment. Private investment is not negligible as the recent evolution of custom services would indicate. There is also a requirement of participation in some of the small scale irrigation projects conducted by TOPRAKSU. This agency usually provides engineering services whereas the farmers provide labour and other resources for building small reservoirs, land leveling, etc. Similar practices characterize the activities of YSE, the rural road and electrification agency.

However, these activities are small when compared to public investment in agriculture. The government has been heavily involved in infrastructural investments in large irrigation schemes, dams, drainage networks and land leveling as well as rural roads and electrification. There has been very little private involvement in these investments which are characterised by very high capital/output ratios and unit costs (World Bank, 1983:61,65).

There is a tendency to use agricultural credits (medium or long-term) as a proxy for private investment. This is quite unreliable for three reasons which will be discussed in the next section.

a. Repayment of credit has been continuously and habitually low,

b. Amnesties and consolidations have eliminated some of these bad debts, and

c. The credits were subsidized so that the real interest rates were negative.

Hence, while private investment in agriculture is not negligible, it is first hard to quantify and second, it would be small in proportion to public investment. Public investment in agriculture obviously involves a transfer of resources to agriculture.

THE INTERSECTORAL DISTRIBUTION OF INCOME, INFLATION AND POLITICS

The various calculations of the terms of trade (TOT) by several researchers, shown in Table 1, indicate that the long run developments, in spite of periodically adverse conditions, have been favourable to the agricultural sector.

The most significant phase of these policies can be crudely stated to be the fifties when the TOT increased from extremely adverse levels to almost parity. The sixties saw fluctuations hovering around parity and for most of the seventies, the trends were extremely favourable to agriculture and the TOT were well above parity for most of the years. As stated before, according to the more detailed calculations of Varlier (1978a), except for 1959, the TOT have always been favourable to agriculture since 1956.

If one compounds these developments with the increases in real per capita incomes in agriculture one can claim that there have been fairly continuous transfers of resources to agriculture (Bulmus, 1978:197). This has obviously resulted in increases in the purchasing power and welfare of the rural populace.

One approach to estimate part of the costs of support policies, viz. the costs of support prices has been propounded by Forker (1971d) and also used by Gurkan (1979:198-203). Funds for support purchases are essentially created by the Central Bank with intricate discounting procedures for the Treasury Guaranteed Bonds issued by the government purchasing agencies. Forker and Gurkan use the changes in the accumulated debts of the purchasing agencies to the Central Bank as the cost of intervention. This totaled 12674 million TL. between 1951 and 1973, which implied an average annual cost of 576 million TL.

There are several discussions on who bears these costs. As indicated before, and as Gurkan reiterates (1979:216), net purchasers of agricultural commodities, both urban and rural, paid. (However there were partial efforts to control the price of bread, confined mainly to municipalities.) On the other hand, the credits to the supporting agencies were usually defaulted at quite high rates. On certain occasions these accumulated debts were eliminated through various accounting procedures. For example, "... the claims of the (Central) Bank ... were transferred in 1961, with Act 154 to a special fund, entitled "Claims to be Liquidated." In this year, due to the apparent inability of (the Public Financial Sector) and (the Public Economic Sector) to repay their outstanding debts to the (Central Bank), TL 1597 million of the (Public Financial Sector's), TL 1389 million of the (State Economic Enterprises'), and TL 2008 million of the (Agricultural Policy Institution's) debts were transferred with the above act into this fund. In 1955, TL 550 million of the treasury guaranteed bonds of the Soils Product Office (SPO) was cancelled and TL 54 million was immediately settled between the treasury and the (Central) Bank. The remaining TL 496 million was transferred into a "Liquidation Fund" in the (Central) Bank, to be paid from the shares of the government and the (State Economic Enterprises) in the (Central Bank) profits. In 1961 about TL 265 million of this claim was outstanding and it was transferred together with the above claims into the funds. Hence, the total amount to be liquidated was TL 568 million. In return, the (Central Bank) acquired bonds issued by the treasury with 0.5% interest, to be repaid with equal 6-monthly installments over a period of 100 years. The present (1970) Balance Sheet of the (Central) Bank indicates that no such payment has yet been made, (Akyuz, 1973:136). The following figure can give an idea about the fate of these installments; between 1970-1975, the average rate of repayment of credit received by the various government agencies using public funds for support purchases was 49.16%, with the rate being the lowest in 1975 as 35.72% (T.C. Merkez Bankasi, 1978:41,44). By themselves, these are direct monetary transfers to the agricultural sector. Furthermore, these transfers have not arisen from a reallocation of credit funds from other borrowers nor have they been drawn from newly created resources. Instead, they have to large extent been created through increasing the money supply, mainly by printing money (T.C. Merkez Bankasi, 1978:37-52; Akyuz, 1973:132-180).

The paramount effect of these policies is inflation. Support policies can contribute to inflation through several ways. A number of studies have emphasized the direct effects of price increases through support prices on the various price indices. DPT (1969:59) indicates that the weight of bread alone in the cost of living indices in Ankara and Istanbul is around 12% and hence increases in wheat prices will cause significant increases in the cost of living. Elaborating and refining this approach DPT (1971:17-21) measures the effects of alternative price increases by

SPO for wheat, rye, barley and oats in the wholesale price and Ankara cost of living indices and their components. The results indicate that even at low levels of price changes the impact on price indices is not negligible. T.C. Merkez Bankasi (1978:52-59) also uses a similar approach but takes into consideration sixteen crops under support schemes. The direct effect of support price increases for those crops on the wholesale price index has been 17.73% for 1973-1974, and 2.62% and 2.46% respectively for the two consecutive years. The share of these contributions in the total increases in the index has been 59.10%, 26.38% and 15.66% for the three years.

These are the direct effects; there are two significant indirect effects of support prices on inflation. The first is the second wave of price increases caused by wage increases and price increases in industrial products for which some agricultural commodities are raw materials or inputs. Studies in this respect include Aksoy (1978:216-228) which first analyzes the effects on the changes in consumer prices within a pure cost pricing model for 1950-1975. In this model, Aksoy emphasizes the influence that agricultural prices exert on consumer prices through the prices of manufactured goods. In order to do this, he has to assume that agricultural prices are more politically determined and not sensitive to excess demand. This is a very rigid assumption and unfortunately various studies do not reconcile the problem. Aksoy, using a proxy variable for excess demand, finds it to be significant in determining agricultural prices. Due to the problems involved in having to use proxy variables for excess demand, the analysis is fraught with debate. Hence, taking it purely as an assumption: one can still get illuminating insights from Aksoy's results which indicate that, together, current and lagged agricultural prices have a considerable and significant impact on consumer prices. This effect, according to Aksoy, arises not only because a considerable part of the manufactured consumer goods sector (especially in the food sector) comprise industries that process agricultural products and raw materials. There is also an effort by the manufacturing sector to maintain its share in the intersectoral distribution of income.

In order to analyze these effects of agricultural prices, Aksoy also looks at a model involving the distribution of income. This model seeks to analyze the effects of changes in the TOT on intersectoral distribution and consumer prices. His argument is that when agricultural prices increase, the TOT deteriorate against the manufacturing sector and input costs also increase. When prices consequently increase in the manufacturing sector, this causes increases in consumer prices and, hence, also wages. All this causes a second round of increases in the prices of manufacturing goods.

To lend support to this argument, Aksoy finds that consumer prices are significantly and positively influenced by the changes in the TOT.

Hence, Aksoy gives the following description of the inflationary processes between 1950-1975 (1978:226-227): the government, in its efforts to alter the distribution of income for agriculture, increases the support prices. As this resource transfer cannot be financed from taxes, it is met by increasing the money supply. This causes price increases in the private manufacturing sector which in turn cause increases in consumer prices and hence wages. Increased input prices and wages in the State Economic Enterprises in the public manufacturing sector causes losses which are financed with means that increase the money supply too. Continued efforts to support agriculture require higher increases in support prices the following year.

This argument relates to the second indirect effect of support prices on inflation, viz. through increases in the money supply. Most of the funds for support purchases are derived from Central Bank credits which are widely claimed to be inflationary. Akyuz (1973:131-180) indicates that changes in money supply and the monetary base are caused to a large extent by the credits to the institutions for agricultural policy. According to T.C. Merkez Bankasi (1978, Vol. 1:50), the share of support purchases in the change in money supply varied between 0 and 103%, and averaged 39.5% between 1964-1975. However, Aksoy claims that this is more a correlation and does not imply causality. He indicates that according to his findings inflation and increases in money supply arise due to the reasons explained above. At the basis of all are government policies to change the distribution of income to the advantage of agriculture. A contrasting study is by Ulusan (1980) who interprets agricultural credits extended by the Central Bank as the sign of agricultural support efforts. In his model these appear not to have a significant direct effect on land sown. However, they do have an indirect effect on agricultural output and land sown through the capital stock (tractors are used as a proxy). Furthermore, there is significant neutral technological change in agricultural production. Ulusan finds neither political factors nor changes in the relative share of agricultural and non-agricultural incomes significant in influencing Central Bank credits to agriculture; the only significant factor is agricultural output. This Ulusan attributes to the need for larger purchases by government agencies when output is larger. As could have been predicted by Aksoy, Ulusan finds a close relationship between Central Bank credits and the money supply.

In the final analysis, in answering the problem of intersectoral distribution of income, Ulusan reaches the conclusion that what the state gives with one hand -- agricultural support -- is taken by the other -- inflation. The various TOT and rural real income and welfare indices are not in conformity with this result, and given those evident welfare gains it cannot be argued that inflation has taken all, if any, away from agriculture. Furthermore, contrary to Ulusan, Erguder (1980:188) does find that political factors are significant. "... (W)e found out that politically critical periods -- when party competition is intense -- play a significant role in the upward adjustment of the prices. What this conclusion tells us is that price supports induce cost-push through inflation..., which in turn -- when political competition is intense in the critical periods and there are pressures building in the agricultural sector due to cost push -- induces a fresh surge in support prices."

Dervis and Robinson (1980) also credit the agricultural support policies for the changes in TOT in favour of agriculture after 1968.

On the whole, there appears to be substantial evidence to indicate that support policies have been used commonly and primarily to achieve the explicit and implicit government goals of income transfers to agriculture. The non-agricultural sector, especially manufacturing, appear to respond to this with a lag (Aksoy, 1978) and are only beginning to organize fairly recently (Ulusan, 1980).

The question that needs to be answered then is why the government policies sought to transfer resources to agriculture. The first reason that comes to mind is, of course, the wide gap between per capita incomes between agriculture and non-agriculture. However, this is not the most prevalent answer that is found in the literature. The most common reason stated to be behind support policies is politics. This usually is emphasized in lay arguments, especially in the press and the motivation is usually given as the vast voting power of the rural population. In the literature two prominent proponents of the dominance of political motives is Erguder (1980) and Forker (1970, 1971d).

Erguder states that: "Whatever its merits and demerits, observers have been unanimous in identifying politics as responsible for the lack of economic rationality in the making of agricultural price support policy... The evidence analyzed in this paper points to the fact the income stability and thus the support of the grower rather than the crop is an important policy goal in Turkey... It is our conclusion that agricultural price-support policy has been viewed in the 1950s and the 1960s both by policy makers and agricultural producers as a tool providing income security -- rather than as a tool of allocative efficiency -- which, in turn, has led to its political importance" (Erguder, 1980:172, 190).

Forker emphatically states the importance of politics on several occasions: "... the system lends itself to political influence and thus decisions that may be more political than economic ... It is apparent that the motivating forces behind the intervention programs and the established price levels are both economic and political, but mostly political." (Forker, 1971d:61). This is a considerably milder stand as compared to an earlier one: "There is a naive assumption by many prominent persons that economic considerations dominate in setting agricultural prices. In practice, political considerations dominate." (Forker, 1970:2)[5].

In the next section, I will develop an alternative hypothesis emphasizing the dominance of economic motives in agricultural support policies, keeping in mind that income transfers to agriculture have been a salient goal of these policies.

## THE USE OF SUPPORT POLICIES TO DEVELOP THE AGRICULTURAL SECTOR AS A MARKET

In the fifties the most dominant theoretical discussion of development was based on the exploitation of a "surplus" wrenched out of agriculture. Lewis (1954), Nurkse (1953), Ranis and Fei (1961) and Nicholls (1963) are the well-known proponents of this stand. Agriculture was viewed simply as a self-sufficient sector that at the same time would be the supplier of surplus food, funds for capital formation, taxes and labour.

The focus was on industrialization and agriculture was expected to be the goose that laid the golden egg. However, in actual experience neither was industry able to develop an increasingly absorptive capacity nor was it possible to induce agriculture to generate and deliver a "surplus," in the broad interpretation of the term (Yotopoulos and Nugent, 1976:198-218). In was only in the sixties that the importance of the development of agriculture began to be acknowledged in the literature (Johnston and Mellor, 1961; Mellor, 1966).

Why, then, did the support policies in Turkey in the fifties aim at transferring resources to agriculture while accepted economic wisdom dictated diametrically opposite goals? To answer this question, it will be necessary to go back in history and come back to the fifties. Birtek and Keyder present an excellent discussion of the policies towards agriculture in Turkey between 1923-1950. The gist of their argument is that the policies were aimed, especially in the thirties, to the "middle farmer" in a manner more compatible with the theoretical frame of the Lewis school.

> "(During the thirties), (o)n the industrial front, the state sought to develop a domestic basis of capital accumulation by strengthening an interior bourgeoise. In agriculture, however, the alliance was formed with the newly marketised middle farmer. First, the middle farmer stratum was protected against the crisis and depression, and it was prepared as the producer of the necessary agricultural surplus in cereals while at the same time policies were created enabling the transfer of this surplus to the state for purposes of industrialization" (Birtek and Keyder, 1975:452).

The way this was done was by increasing the dependence of the middle farmer on the market with active price supports but later on by reversing the TOT against agriculture with high industrial prices, mostly decreed by the state (Birtek and Keyder, 1975:455-456).

So far, the Turkish experience was a couple of decades ahead of theory. However, the Second World War puts a dent in this development. Mobilization and forced procurements ended the affair between the state and the "middle farmer." The significance of the poorer farmers as potential political allies was recognized by a radical faction of the ruling

Republican People's Party. A land reform bill was promoted to distribute land to poor farmers. It passed but was ineffectual and eventually had more serious repercussions. In 1950, the Democratic Party took power. Its policy was not to make allies with poor farmers but to make poor farmers richer. (Pictures of Democratic Party leaders still adorn coffee-house walls in villages and the fifties are fondly remembered as when "The peasant's hand saw money for the first time.") The Democratic Party, headed by a landowner, in coalition with the import dependent "Istanbul" industrialists, was the principal actor in this change of policy. During the reign of the Democratic Party and its continuations, various price and other support policies were vigorously implemented with the purpose of transferring resources to agriculture. (This includes direct transfers as well as transfers through irrigation investment, research, land levelling activities, etc.)

Several birds were killed with one stone:

1. The welfare of the rural masses increased and hence they became faithful allies -- i.e. the political motive.

2. However, more important, a process was started whereby previously self-sufficient subsistence producers were gradually integrated into the market economy. They became consumers not only of consumer goods but also, and maybe more importantly, of capital goods like tractors, combines, etc.

Some analyses (T.C. Merkez Bankasi, 1978:37; DPT, 1977:33, Bulmus, 1978:197-198) criticize price support policies because they increase the incomes of the rural population which have a high propensity to consume. First of all, this is quite a reversal of the arguments of the fifties and sixties which claimed that peasants hoarded money and/or bought gold and did *not* have a high propensity to consume. Second, it also implies a low propensity to save. One then wonders whence the finances for the current capital stock in agriculture originated. Clearly, some came from credits, but some also came from savings. The implication is that, in the agricultural sector, the propensity to save and invest is probably higher than suspected.

3. Consequently, the industrial sector also got a strong stimulus for development, even with adversely developing terms of trade, and, maybe with the help of inflation, in meeting the needs of this new and developing agricultural market.

The Turkish experience is still a decade ahead of theoretical developments.

Obviously, the needs of the industrial sector for investment and working capital had to be satisfied. As is well known, the policy alternative chosen was to throw the industrial sector wide open to foreign investment. Hence, the industrial sector developed primarily by funds from abroad.

Thus the industrial sector, represented mainly by the "Istanbul" capitalists, received its principal stimuli for development through foreign investment. This foreign dependence brought with it a multitude of problems, but this is not the place for their discussion. One interesting aspect is the following: in this arrangement the main crises are brought about by the scarcity of foreign exchange. As long as foreign exchange reserves are sufficient, hard currency imports satisfy the needs of the industrial sector. Between 1963-1985 the agricultural sector contributed to the foreign exchange reserves by having a continuous and large trade surplus (including indirect imports of inputs for machinery, fertilizers and other chemicals) (Somel and Onur, 1979). However, the scarcity of foreign exchange reserves put a squeeze on the dependent industrial sector. Most industrial products become subject to increasing (usually black market) prices. The inflationary process through which the agricultural sector is supported adds fuel to the fire. The contradiction is that devaluations provide only temporary relief because of the limited export capacity of the economy. This is due to (a) the relatively weak position of the agricultural exports, (b) the reluctance of foreign-based industries to export to markets where the products would compete with exports from their own home industries, and (c) the limits to remittances of workers abroad.

In the seventies, another source of conflict was the development of the agriculturally-based nascent "Anatolian" industrialists. This group's interests were export oriented and conflicted with the "Istanbul" capitalists.

## CONCLUSION

As far as the purposes of this survey are concerned, the argument then is that there have been dominant economic motives behind support policies. At the root is the goal of developing agriculture as a viable market for consumer and more significantly, for producer goods. Short-term electoral considerations, emphasized by many researchers, were actually subservient to the realization of this long-term economic policy.

This aspect of support policies has received considerably less attention than it deserves. A lot of statistics, like the increases in the number of tractors, in the use of fertilizer, changes in the consumption patterns of the rural population, etc. are all looked at from different vantage points. Yet, I believe that the cumulative effects of support policies, which have the development of agriculture as a market as a goal, should get a considerable portion of the credit.

There are few studies that touch upon this aspect of support policies. Varlier (1978a:6) claims that the support policies of the early seventies were aimed at relieving the problems of low demand for industrial products. The mechanisms analyzed by Aksoy (1978), mentioned above, also lend support to our hypothesis. DPT (1977:3), states it very clearly: "With the increase of the purchasing power, through support purchases of the producers who constitute a large part of the population, there has been a corresponding increase in the expansion of the market for industrial products and an increase in commercial activities ..." (Translation by me, K.S.). Gurkan (1979) also analyzes the effects of government policy on market integration. He indicates that even though "... the effects of government policies on regional market integration is not uniform across different types of commodities ... (w)here the analysis is applied to a group of commodities with homogeneous characteristics, the average degree of market integration is significantly greater for those crops that are subject to strong government control than those that are not. Even where there is only weak government involvement, the results indicate that the degree of market integration is significantly greater in those where there is no government "involvement" (Gurkan, 1979:231). Galip (1977:11-12) also agrees with the importance of support price policies for the industrial bourgeoisie producing for the home market and discusses the contradictions involved in these policies.

All this points out to the weakness, if not the fallacy, of arguments which attribute support policies to non-economic motives. The significance of government intervention as a stimulus for agricultural development is now well recognized (Mellor, 1966:196-219; Wortman and Cummings, Jr., 1978:343-379). Turkey has lived this experience in a particular way where, paradoxically, income transfers to agriculture, however inequitable they were within agriculture, were used to stimulate in a very effective manner both agricultural and industrial development.

## FOOTNOTES

* Senior Economist, Farming Systems Program, the International Center for Agricultural Research in the Dry Areas (ICARDA), Aleppo, Syria. This paper was presented at the Workshop on the Food Problem and State Policy in the Middle East, organized by the Social Science Research Council (SSRC) and hosted by the International Fund for Agricultural Development (IFAD) in Rome, Italy, 17-18 September 1984. This paper utilizes extensively and reproduces material previously presented in Kutlu Somel (1979a), "Agricultural Support Policies in Turkey: A Survey of Literature" *METU Studies in Development*, 6:24/25, 275-323. Hence, this paper can be considered a revision and an update of the 1979 article.

[1] I do not believe that this is the place to hold a post mortem on the fate of mostly still-born land reform policies in Turkey, hence they will not be discussed (cf. Gorun and Somel, 1979, for references).

[2] Until 1980, several ministries operated in relation to rural areas and agriculture. They have now been combined into the Ministry of Agriculture, Forestry and Rural Affairs.

[3] Currently, the ministry, as well as research structure within the ministry, are going through a radical reorganization.

[4] A detailed discussion of these studies can be found in Somel (1979a). The principal studies reviewed were Bulmul (1978), Donmezcelik (1979), Ekmekcioglu and Kasnakoglu (1979), Gurkan (1979), Kazgan (1977), Kip (1973), Somel (1979b, 1977), Soral (1973), Unver (1976) and World Bank (1979).

[5] Erguder is a political scientist and Forker is an agricultural economist.

# REFERENCES


Aksoy, A. 1978. *Türkiye Imalat Sanayii Fiyat Davranişlari: Ekonometrik bir Çalişma,* (Basilmamiş Doçentlik Tezi), Ankara.

Akyuz, Y. 1973. "Money and Inflation in Turkey, 1950-1968," *Siyasal Bilgiler Fakultesi,* Yay. No. 361, Ankara.

Aktan, R. 1979. Türkiye'de Yüksek Verimli Buğday Türlerinin Yayilmasi, Türkiye Kalkinma Vakfi Yayini, Ankara.

Aktan, R. 1973. "Tarimsal Ürünlerde Destekleme," *Tarimsal Ürünlerde Riyat ve Destekleme Politikasi Semineri,* Izmir Ticaret Borsasi Yayinlari; 10, 129-143.

Aktan, R. 1955. "Türkiye'de Ziraat Mahšulleri Fiyatlari," Ankara Universitesi SBF Yayini 44-26, Ankara.

Aras, A. 1973. "Tarimda Üretici Geliri," *Tarimsal Ürünlerde Fiyat ve Destekleme Politikasi Semineri,* Izmir Ticaret Yayinlari; 10, 15-45.

Aresvik, O. 1975. *The Agricultural Development of Turkey,* New York: Praeger Publishers.

Aruoba, C. 1978. *Türk Tariminda Farkli Uretim Teknikleri ve Yenileşme,* (Basilmamis Doçentlik Tezi), Ankara.

Behrman, J.R. 1968. *Supply Response in Underdeveloped Agriculture: A Case Study of Four Major Annual Crops in Thailand, 1937-1963,* Amsterdam: North Holland Publishing Company.

Birtek, F. and Keyder, C. 1975. "Agriculture and the State: An Inquiry into Agricultural Differentiation and Political Alliance: The Case of Turkey," *Journal of Peasant Studies,* 2:4, 446-467.

Bulmus, I. 1978. *Tarimsal Fiyat Olusumuna Devlet Müdahalesi,* Ankara ITIA Yayini, 113, Ankara.

Cleaver, Jr., H. M. 1972. "The Contradictions of the Green Revolution," *Monthly Review*, June.

Civi, H. 1977. "Tarimsal Ürünlerde Taban Fiyatlari ve Türkiye'de Taban Fiyat Politikasi," Ataturk Universitesi Yayinlari; No. 485, Erzurum.

Demir, N. 1976. *The Adoption of New Bread Wheat Technology in Selected Regions of Turkey*, Mexico City: CIMMYT.

Dervis, K. and Robinson, S. 1980. "The Structure of Inequality in Turkey (1950-1973)," in Ozbudun and Ulusan (1980), 83-122.

Dhrymes, P. J. 1971. *Distributed Lags: Problems of Estimation and Formulation*, San Francisco: Holden-Day.

Dinç, H. 1978. *Tarimda Destek Fiyat Politikasi ve Ticarete Etkisi*, (Uzmanlik Tezi), Ankara: Devlet Planlama Teşkilati.

Dönmezçelik, U. 1979. *Türkiye'de Tarimsal Destekleme Fiyat Politikasinin Etkinliği*, Maliye Bakanligi Tekkik Kurulu Yayini; 1979-204, Ankara.

DPT 1979. (State Planning Organization) *Dördüncü Bes Yillik Kalkinma Plani, 1979-1983*, Ankara.

DPT 1977 (State Planning Organization) *Devlet Adina Yapilan Destekleme Alimlarini Inceleme ve Değerlendirme*, Yayin No. 1564, (In 2 Volumes).

DPT 1976a. (State Planning Organization) *Gelir Dagilimi 1973*, No. 1495, Ankara.

DPT 1976b. (State Planning Organization) Destekleme Politikasi *Uygulamasinin Çay*, Şeker Pancari, Pamuk, Findik Üreticileri Üzerindeki Etkileri, DPT: 1476, Ankara.

DPT 1974. (State Planning Organization) *1974-1975 Üretim Yili Buğday Destekleme Fiyati Hakkinda Not*, Ankara.

DPT 1973. (State Planning Organization) *Yeni Strateji ve Kalkinma Plani Üçüncü Bes Yil, 1973-1977*, Ankara.

DPT 1971. (State Planning Organization) *Tarimsal Destekleme Politikasinin Esaslari*, Özel Seri No. DPT:55, Ankara.

DPT 1969. (State Planning Organization) *Buğdayin Fiyatini Etkileyen Faktörlerde Son Yillarda Taban Fiyatin Değistirilmesini veya Aynen Korunmasini Gerektiren Gelişmeler*, Yayin No. DPT:820, Ankara.

DPT (State Planning Organization) *Kalkinma Plani Ikinci Bes Yil, 1968-1972*, Ankara.

DPT 1963. (State Planning Organization) *Kalkinma Plani Birinci Beş Yil, 1963-1967*, Ankara.

Ekmekcioğlu, Ç. and Kasnakoglu, H. 1979. "Supply Response in Turkish Agriculture-Preliminary Results on Wheat and Cotton, 1955-75," *ODTÜ Gelişme Dergisi*, 22/23; 113-143.

Ergüder, U. 1980. "Politics of Agricultural Price Policy in Turkey," in Özbudun and Ulusan (1980), 169-196.

Ergun, Y. 1978a. "Tarimsal Ürün Destekleme Alimlarinin Kirsal Kesimde Gelir Dagilimina Etkileri," *Maliye Tetkik Kurulu Araştirmalari*, No. 1978/197, 53-67.

Ergun, Y. 1978b. *Tarimsal Ürün Destekleme Alimlari*, Maliye Bakanligi Tetkik Kurulu Yayini: 194, Ankara.

Erkus, A. 1976. "Iç Anadolu Bölgesi Tarim Işletmelerinde Üretilen Buğdayin, Isletmede Kullanim ve Pazara Arzi Üzerine Bir Araştirma," Ankara Universitesi Ziraat Fakultesi Yilligi, 1975, Cilt 25, Fasikül 3; 751-764, Ankara.

Falcon, W. P. 1970. "The Green Revolution: Generations of Problems," *American Journal of Agricultural Economics*, 706.

Forker, O.D. 1971a. "Wheat Production in Turkey-Analysis of Trends and Variation in Yield, Area Sown and Production, the Source of Variation in Production and Income and Projection to 1975 and 1980," in *Agricultural Price Policy in Turkey*, Vol. 1.

Forker, O.D. 1971b. "Some Impressions on the Determination of Appropriate Purchase and Selling Prices for Wheat for Toprak Mahsulleri Ofisi," in *Agricultural Price Policy in Turkey*, Vol. 1.

Forker, O.D. 1971c. "Agricultural Price Policy in Turkey, I: An Evaluation and Some Recommendations," in *Agricultural Price Policy in Turkey*, Vol. 2.

Forker, O.D. 1971d. "Agricultural Price Policy in Turkey, II: A Description and Appraisal," in *Agricultural Price Policy in Turkey*, Vol. 2.

Forker, O.D. 1971e. "A Technique to Predict the Quantity of Wheat That Will be Purchased by Toprak Mahsulleri Ofisi," in *Agricultural Price Policy in Turkey*, Vol. 1.

Forker, O.D. 1970. "A Treatise on the Timing of the Agricultural Price Support Announcement," in *Agricultural Price Policy in Turkey*, Vol. 2.

Gorun, G. and Somel, K. 1979. *Bibliography of Economics of Agriculture in Turkey, 1960-1975*, ESA Working Paper No. 1, Middle East Technical University, Ankara.

Griffin, K. 1977. *The Political Economy of Agrarian Change*, London: Macmillan.

Gurkan, A. A. 1979. *Aspects of a Statistical Analysis of Some Selected Agricultural Price Policies in Turkey: 1950-1973*, Unpublished PhD Dissertation, School of Economic Studies, University of Leeds.

Hill, B. E. and Ingersent, K. A. 1977. *An Economic Analysis of Agriculture*, London: Heinnemann.

Johnson, B. F. and Mellor, J. W. 1961. "The Role of Agriculture in Economic Development," *American Economic Review*, 51, 566-593.

Karayalcin, M. and Arat, Z. 1975. "Kirsal Refah Endeksi 1968-1972," SPD:283, Ankara.

Kazgan, G. 1977. "Tarim ve Gelişme," Istanbul Üniversitesi Yayinlari; No. 2261, Iktisat Fakültesi No. 387, Istanbul.

Kazgan, G. 1976. "State Objectives, Agricultural Policy and Development," *Economies et Societes* (*Serie Developpement Economique et Agriculture*), Paris.

Keskiner, Y. 1973. "Tarimda Üretici Gelirini Azaltan Nedenler ve Bazi Çözüm Teklifleri," *Tarimsal Ürünlerde Fiyat ve Destekleme Politikasi Semineri*, Izmir Ticaret Borsasi Yayinlari; 10, 57-71.

Keyder, N. 1976. "Türkiye'de Tarimsal Reel Gelir ve Kirsal Refah Indeksi." *ODTÜ Gelisme Dergisi*, 12, 57-74.

Keyder, N. 1970. "Türkiye'de Tarimsal Reel Gelir ve Koylünün Refah Seviyesi," *ODTÜ Gelisme Dergisi*, 1, 33-59.

Kizilyalli, H. 1971. "Tarim Sektöru Planlamasi," Özel Seri No. DPT: 54-M: 3, Ankara.

Kip, E. 1972. "Bazi Tarimsal Ürünlerimizde Arz-Fiyat Ilişkileri," *Ziraat Ekonomisi Dergisi*, Cilt 3; 9, 70-80.

Kip, E. 1973. *Türkiye'de ve Kuzey Dogu Anadolu Tariminda Belirsizlik ve Ekonomik Etkileri*, Erzurum: Basilmamiş Doçentik Tezi.

Koksal, E. 1971. "Türkiye'de Tarimsal Kredi Sorunu," *ODTÜ Gelişme Dergisi*, 3, 499-529.

Lewis, W. A. 1954. "Economic Development with Unlimited Supplies of Labour," *Manchester School of Economic and Social Studies*, 22, 138-191.

Mann, C. K. 1980. "The Effects of Government Policy on Income Distribution, A Case Study of Wheat Production in Turkey Since World War II," In Ozbudun and Ulusan (1980), 197-246.

Mann, C. K. 1977. "The Impact of Technology on Wheat Production in Turkey," *METU Studies in Development*, 14, 30-49.

Mellor, J. W. 1970. *The Economics of Agricultural Development*, Ithaca: Cornell University.

Nerlove, M. 1958. *The Dynamics of Supply: Estimation of Farmers' Response to Price*, Baltimore: Johns Hopkins University Press.

Nicholls, W. H. 1969. An "Agricultural Surplus" as a Factor in Economic Development, *Journal of Political Economy*, 71:1-29.

Nurkse, R. 1953. *Problems of Capital Formation in Underdeveloped Countries*, New York: Oxford University Press.

Ozbudun, E. and Ulusan, A., eds. 1980. *The Political Economy of Income Distribution in Turkey*, New York: Holmes and Meier.

PAK 1978. (Ministry of Agriculture, General Directorate of Planning Research and Coordination) *Tarimsal Üretim Planlamasinin Kavrami ve Iş Plani*, Yayin No. 65, Ankara.

PAK 1974. (Ministry of Agriculture, General Directorate of Planning, Research and Coordination) *Tarimsal Girdiler ve Fiyatlar: 1960-1974*, No. 56, Ankara.

Pekin, T. 1975a. "Taban Fiyat Politikasinin Etkileri ve Ülkemizdeki Uygulamaya Iliskin Görüşler," *Ege Universitesi Iktisadi ve Ticari Bilimler Fakültesi Yayini*, Izmir.

Pekin, T. 1975b. "Türkiye'de Pamuk Ekonomisi ve Pamukta Devlet Mudahalesi," *Ege Universitesi Iktisadi ve Ticari Bilimler Fakültesi*: Yayin No. 64/51, Izmir.

Pekin, T. 1974. "Teşvik Tedbirleri Olarak Sübvansiyonlar ve Işletme Kararlari Üzerindeki Etkileri," *Ege Universitesi*, Izmir.

Pekin, T. 1973a. Türkiye'de Tarim Kesimine Verilen Sübvansiyonlar, *Ege Üniversitesi ITIA*, Izmir.

Pekin, T. 1973b. "Destekleme Alimlarinda Fiyat Tesbit Metotlari," *Tarimsal Ürünlerde Fiyatlar ve Destekleme Politikasi Semineri*, Izmir Ticaret Borsasi Yayinlari; 10, 143-175.

Ranis, G. and FEI, J. C. H. 1961. "A Theory of Economic Development," *American Economic Review*, 51, 533-565.

Scott, J.C. 1977. "The Moral Economy of the Peasant," Westford: Murray.

Somel, K. 1979a. "Agricultural Support Policies in Turkey: A Survey of Literature," *METU Studies in Development*, 6:24/25, 257-323.

Somel, K. 1979b. "Technological Change in Dryland Wheat Production in Turkey," *Food Research Institute Studies*, 17:1, 51-65.

Somel, K. 1979c. "Orta Anadolu'da Buğday Üretiminde Gelir-Girdi-Teknoloji Ilişkileri," *Türkiye'de Geliştirilmis Tohum ve Girdilerin Saglanmasi Seminerine Bildiri*, Ankara.

Somel, K. 1977. "Orta Anadolu'da Buğday Üretimindeki Teknolojik Gelişmelerin Ekonomik Değerlendirmesi," *ODTÜ Gelişme Dergisi*, 15; 70-109.

Somel, K. and Onur, T. 1979. "The International Trade Balance of the Agricultural Sector in Turkey," *ESA Working Paper No. 4*, Middle East Technical University, Ankara.

Soral, E. 1973. "Tarim Ürünlerinde Fiyat Teşekkülü ve Devlet Müdahalesi," *Eskişehir ITIA Dergisi*, 50. Yil Özel Sayisi, 146-176.

T.C. Merkez Bankasi. 1978. *Destekleme Alimlari*, Ankara (two Volumes).

T.C. Ziraat Bankasi. 1973. *1973 Türkiye Tarimsal Kredi Arastirmasi Anketi Soru Kagitlarindan Editing Yapilmadan Bulunan Agirliklar*, Ankara.

Ulusan, A. 1980. "Public Policy Towards Agriculture and Its Redistributive Implications," in Ozbudun and Ulusan (1980), 125-168.

Uras, N. 1971. *Tarim Sektöründe Üretim ve Verimlilik Ilişkileri*, Ankara: Devlet Planlama Teskilati.

USAID/Turkey 1969. *Spring Review, New Cereal Varieties: Wheat in Turkey*, March.

Unver, S. 1976. *Desteklenen Tarimsal Urün ve Girdi Fiyatlarinin Tespiti Metotlari ve Bu Metotlarin Türkiye'de Buğday Için Uygulamasi Uzerinde Bir Araştirma*, Ankara Universitesi Ziraat Fakultesi, Doktora Tezi, Ankara.

Varlier, O. 1978a. *Türkiye'de Ic Ticaret Hadleri*, yayin No. DPT:1632, Ankara.

Varlier, O. 1978b. Türkiye Tariminda Yapisal Değişme, Teknoloji ve Toprak Bölüşümu"', Yayin No. DPT:1636, Ankara.

Wharton, Jr., C.R. 1969. "The Green Revolution: Cornucopia or Pandora's Box," *Foreign Affairs*, 47; 3, 464-476.

World Bank 1983, *Turkey: Agricultural Development Alternatives for Growth with Exports*, Report No. 4204-TU, (in three Volumes).

World Bank 1979. *Turkey Agricultural Sector Survey*, Report No. 1684-TU, (in two Volumes).

Wortman, S. and Cummings, Jr., R. 1978. *To Feed this World, the Challenge and the Strategy*, Baltimore: John Hopkins University Press.

Yotopoulos, P.A. and Nugent, J. 1976. *Economics of Development: Empirical Investigations*, New York: Harper and Row.

TABLE 1: VARIOUS INDICES RELATED TO TURKISH AGRICULTURE

| Year | 1a | 1b | 1c | 2 | 3a | 3b | 3c | 4a | 4b | 4c | 4d | 4e | 5a | 5b | 5c | 5d | 5e |
|---|---|---|---|---|---|---|---|---|---|---|---|---|---|---|---|---|---|
| 1950 | | | | | 96 | 104.4 | 99.0 | 31.2 | 45.8 | 68.2 | 76.5 | 52.1 | 25.7 | 25.0 | 74.9 | 38.2 | 34.3 |
| 1951 | | | | | 104 | 104.0 | 101.0 | 32.5 | 45.9 | 70.9 | 90.5 | 64.1 | 27.8 | 30.4 | 77.4 | 47.1 | 35.9 |
| 1952 | | | | | 112 | 116.7 | 106.7 | 33.5 | 48.5 | 69.5 | 94.5 | 65.6 | 28.8 | 39.0 | 78.7 | 52.7 | 36.6 |
| 1953 | | | | | 119 | 119.0 | 111.2 | 34.4 | 48.9 | 70.3 | 101.4 | 71.3 | 31.2 | 28.3 | 84.1 | 61.2 | 37.1 |
| 1954 | | | | | 119 | 110.2 | 102.6 | 37.8 | 49.8 | 75.8 | 95.4 | 72.3 | 31.7 | 31.4 | 82.9 | 50.4 | 39.5 |
| 1955 | | | | | 135 | 108.9 | 104.7 | 40.8 | 54.0 | 75.6 | 101.1 | 76.4 | 35.1 | 35.5 | 77.0 | 52.9 | 45.6 |
| 1956 | 100.0 | 100.0 | 100.0 | | 150 | 110.3 | 103.5 | 47.4 | 54.3 | 87.3 | 91.7 | 80.0 | 38.8 | 40.1 | 77.4 | 55.7 | 50.1 |
| 1957 | 119.5 | 133.0 | 111.3 | | 200 | 122.0 | 120.5 | 61.4 | 64.1 | 95.8 | 92.4 | 88.5 | 51.7 | 44.9 | 95.4 | 73.2 | 54.2 |
| 1958 | 114.7 | 149.4 | 103.2 | | 215 | 103.4 | 109.1 | 68.2 | 78.7 | 86.6 | 90.8 | 78.6 | 56.8 | 58.6 | 87.2 | 73.1 | 64.3 |
| 1959 | 169.2 | 165.8 | 98.0 | | 242 | 85.2 | 96.4 | 74.8 | 94.3 | 79.3 | 94.5 | 74.9 | 62.6 | 70.0 | 76.7 | 64.5 | 81.6 |
| 1960 | 173.4 | 175.1 | 101.0 | | 254 | 89.4 | 98.5 | 77.7 | 93.9 | 82.7 | 96.9 | 80.1 | 66.4 | 70.5 | 79.1 | 67.7 | 83.9 |
| 1961 | 179.8 | 181.8 | 101.1 | | 265 | 96.0 | 98.5 | 84.2 | 91.5 | 92.0 | 90.0 | 92.9 | 69.1 | 67.8 | 80.4 | 65.8 | 85.9 |
| 1962 | 174.2 | 197.7 | 113.5 | | 304 | 95.0 | 104.1 | 94.1 | 94.6 | 95.5 | 94.6 | 94.1 | 78.4 | 82.0 | 93.1 | 79.1 | 84.2 |
| 1963 | 177.9 | 212.5 | 119.5 | | 319 | 97.3 | 103.6 | 100.0 | 100.0 | 100.0 | 100.0 | 100.0 | 82.6 | 86.2 | 95.1 | 88.6 | 86.9 |
| 1964 | 186.8 | 212.6 | 113.8 | 97.3 | 319 | 96.1 | 100.3 | 97.4 | 99.5 | 97.9 | 98.2 | 96.1 | 82.9 | 93.7 | 95.0 | 88.1 | 87.3 |
| 1965 | 187.5 | 222.2 | 118.5 | 101.4 | 327 | 92.9 | 98.2 | 101.2 | 104.2 | 97.1 | 93.3 | 90.6 | 84.7 | 106.3 | 95.3 | 84.7 | 88.9 |
| 1966 | 206.4 | 242.4 | 117.4 | 101.9 | 358 | 97.3 | 102.0 | 107.5 | 108.8 | 98.8 | 101.4 | 100.1 | 92.9 | 108.7 | 100.2 | 98.7 | 92.7 |
| 1967 | 208.2 | 252.0 | 121.0 | 100.4 | 377 | 94.7 | 100.5 | 110.0 | 112.9 | 97.4 | 100.7 | 98.1 | 97.6 | 119.4 | 100.3 | 98.5 | 97.3 |
| 1968 | 215.6 | 261.7 | 121.4 | 101.9 | 385 | 96.3 | 112.7 | 117.1 | 96.3 | 101.6 | 101.6 | 97.8 | 100.0 | 100.0 | 100.0 | 100.0 | 100.0 |
| 1969 | 227.0 | 280.8 | 123.7 | 105.7 | 408 | 100.0 | 88.7 | 122.5 | 122.0 | 100.4 | 102.0 | 102.4 | 100.2 | 105.3 | 93.7 | 100.3 | 106.9 |
| 1970 | 244.1 | 314.6 | 128.9 | 105.7 | 462 | 104.1 | 102.4 | 131.5 | 133.5 | 98.3 | 105.6 | 103.8 | 120.2 | 121.5 | 98.9 | 103.7 | 121.5 |
| 1971 | 284.9 | 375.0 | 131.6 | 107.0 | 527 | 97.6 | 98.3 | 141.8 | 154.6 | 91.7 | 119.1 | 109.2 | 137.7 | 130.2 | 93.2 | 110.1 | 147.7 |
| 1972 | 312.1 | 393.3 | 126.0 | 124.0 | 631 | 105.3 | 102.8 | 152.3 | 173.7 | 87.7 | 118.0 | 103.5 | 163.2 | 140.3 | 97.7 | 115.2 | 167.0 |
| 1973 | 403.2 | 529.1 | 131.2 | 130.9 | 865 | 122.2 | 118.2 | 213.0 | 211.9 | 100.5 | 105.6 | 106.1 | 228.2 | | 124.7 | 130.0 | 182.9 |
| 1974 | 568.2 | 741.9 | 130.5 | 125.7 | 1138 | 121.1 | 122.6 | 318.0 | 255.5 | 124.5 | 116.2 | 144.7 | | | | | |
| 1975 | 664.9 | 845.9 | 127.2 | 121.9 | 1327 | 126.1 | 123.6 | | | | | | | | | | |
| 1976 | 816.3 | 962.1 | 117.9 | 131.7 | 1531 | 134.8 | 125.6 | | | | | | | | | | |

NOTES TO TABLE 1

| | | |
|---|---|---|
| 1a. | prices paid by farmers, 1951=100, | Varlier, (1978a, 30). |
| 1b. | prices received by farmers, 1956=100, | Varlier, (1978a, 30). |
| 1c. | terms of trade (TOT); (1b/1a), | Varlier, (1978a, 30). |
| 2. | TOT based on the wholesale price indices of the Ministry of Commerce, | Varlier, (1978a, 29). |
| 3a. | implicit farming income deflators, 1948=100, | Varlier, (1978a, 7). |
| 3b. | TOT between agriculture and industry, derived from implicit GNP deflators, | Varlier, (1978a, 7). |
| 3c. | TOT between agriculture and nonagriculture from implicit GNP deflators. | Varlier, (1978, 8). |
| 4a. | price index of agricultural products, 1963=100; revised after 1968, | Keyder, (1970, 38; 1976, 63). |
| 4b. | village cost of living index, 163=100, revised after 1968, | Keyder, (1970, 38; 1976, b3). |
| 4c. | TOT (4a/4b), 1963=100; revised after 1968, | Keyder, (1970, 38; 1976, 63). |
| 4d. | agricultural real per capita income, 1963=100, | Keyder, (1970, 38; 1976, 63). |
| 4e. | rural welfare index (4c x 4d), 1963=100, revised after 1968, | Keyder, (1970, 38; 1976, 63). |
| 5a. | price index of agricultural and livestock products, 1968=100, | Gurkan, (1979, 209). |
| 5b. | price index of modern inputs, 1968=100, | Gurkan, (1979, 209). |
| 5c. | TOT 1968=100, | Gurkan, (1979, 209). |
| 5d. | index of real agricultural and livestock income. (5a/5e), 1968=100, | Gurkan, (1979, 209). |
| 5e. | cost of living index 1963=100, | Gurkan, (1979, 209). |

# 5

# Agricultural Price Support Policies in Turkey: An Empirical Investigation

*Haluk Kasnakoglu*

## INTRODUCTION

This paper examines agricultural support price policies in Turkey and studies their possible resource allocation effects. In the first parts of the paper, the extent and institutional aspects of support policies are reviewed and recent changes in emphasis and direction are summarized. In the following parts the consequences of such policies on price and income stability, income distribution between sectors and within agriculture, and inflation are reviewed. The impact of price support policies on relative prices and hence output composition are then addressed. Within this context the questions of viability of support prices as a policy tool, the nature of changes in relative support and market prices and their interactions are analyzed. Finally, additional evidence is provided on the debate concerning the motives behind support price policies.

## AN OVERVIEW

As in most developing economies, agriculture plays a crucial role in the economic development of Turkey. The agricultural sector contributed twenty percent of GDP and over fifty percent of employment of the labor force in 1983. Turkey's agriculture is highly diversified due to its variety of soils and agro-climatic conditions. It produces continental products (such as wheat, corn, barley, cotton, tobacco, sugarbeet, etc.) as well as Mediterranean products (such as fruits, nuts and vegetables), all of which share vast resources of land (about 25 million hectares of cultivated land) and labor (over 10 million in 1980). Furthermore, Turkey is one of the few countries in the world which has enjoyed self-sufficiency in foodstuffs. Since the 1940's agricultural sector has been the major source of exports. With the exception of a few years (bad crops or war years) Turkey has been a net exporter of cereals (such as wheat, rye, barley, millet), pulses (such as chickpea, dry beans, broad beans, lentils), industrial crops (such as cotton, tobacco), nuts (such as hazelnuts, pistachios), fresh and dried fruits (such as raisins, figs, citrus, apples), vegetables (such as tomatoes, potatoes, onions), oils and oilseeds (such as olive-oil, poppy, cotton, sesame, peanuts), and livestock products (such as live animals, wool, hides, meat).[1] In 1980, nearly 60 percent of the value of exports were agricultural and livestock products. While textiles, processed food and livestock products which are classified as industrial products in statistical tables are included, over 80 percent of total exports in 1980 were based on agriculture (Table 1).

## AGRICULTURAL SUPPORT POLICIES: THE EXTENT AND INSTITUTIONS OF INTERVENTION

The agricultural sector has been subjected to direct and indirect government intervention for a long period of time, starting with wheat in 1932 and followed by other cereals like barley, rye, oats and rice in the 1940's. Various instruments of agricultural policy such as output support prices, input subsidies, credits, quotas, tariffs, taxes, land distribution, investments in infrastructure, extension services, etc. have been employed to achieve various stated objectives such as income and price stability, stimulation of output and income, satisfaction of demand, improving balance of payments, etc.

Among important agricultural commodities only fresh fruits and vegetables do not enjoy price supports established and maintained by the government. Tables 2 and 3 illustrate the extent of government involvement in the output markets. Commodities which are under the government support purchase scheme constitute over 90 percent of the total value of agricultural production (ranging in number from 16-28), with over 25 percent of the total value being procured by the state, state economic enterprises or state financed and controlled agricultural sales or credit cooperatives. This is a fairly large ratio, especially when one considers both the ratios of non-marketed production to total production as shown in Table 3, and the percentage of marketed production (instead of total) purchased by government.

Five ministries and about 20 semi-autonomous agencies-state economic enterprises (SEE), state monopolies (TSM) and unions of sales and/or credit cooperatives (ASC) -- are directly involved in formulation and administering agricultural price policies.[2] The primary state or state controlled agencies involved in the procurement, marketing, and foreign trade of agricultural commodities, and their respective areas are summarized below in Table 4.

Support prices established annually by decree from the council of ministers are announced to farmers, usually late in the crop year. At these prices the various implementing agencies must purchase any quantities offered to them by the farmers. Price support activities of MFO and MIO are limited by the capacities of their own processing plants, and they are not required to buy beyond their capacities. For all major commodities (except for tea, sugarbeets and poppy for which the state is a monopoly buyer) farmers are free to sell to private buyers. Area quotas are established for tea, sugarbeets, poppy and tobacco. Otherwise, crop production decisions by farmers are unrestricted by the state.

With minor exceptions (such as tobacco and livestock products) support prices for the various crops are uniform nationwide. Cooperative members are paid a slightly higher price. Although a single price is announced for most commodities, price differentials are made at the time of procurement based on quality differences.

The picture is not too different in the case of input markets as illustrated in Table 5. Most of the inputs are either produced, distributed or priced by the government. Pesticides and insecticides are sold to farmers or custom applied by the General Directorate of Plant Protection and Quarantine (GDPPQ). Ninety-five percent of the chemical fertilizers used are sold by the Agricultural Supply Organization (ASO). This state economic enterprise also sells about fifteen percent of tractors and agricultural implements in the market. The activities of these organizations are supplemented by programs of product marketing agencies, which provide input purchase and resale at cost, credit in kind, or input grant aid to the farmers with whom they deal. Inputs such as water, credit, land improvement, seeds are also provided at subsidized prices or rates which are controlled by the council of ministers, through ceiling prices.[3]

The operations of the above agencies are basically financed through direct budget allocations from the Ministry of Finance. Purchases exceeding budgeted amounts and all purchases of sales cooperatives are financed by loans from the Agricultural Bank, or occasionally other banks or foreign sources. The losses sustained are absorbed by the agency or the Agricultural Bank and subsequently discounted to the Central Bank or covered by supplemental budget allocations.

## RECENT CHANGES IN POLICY

"In 1980 the Government embarked on a more outward-oriented development strategy which emphasized market forces rather than government direction and intervention. In the agricultural sector this new strategy meant an abrupt dismantling of the incentives system. There was a sharp reduction in input subsidies, particularly fertilizer, and in the number of production price supports with the remaining supports gradually converted to floor prices. The overall restraint on monetary policy forced a curtailment of agricultural credit, although interest rates remained negative in real terms."[4] In addition to reducing the levels of price support in real terms, the government also has begun to rationalize the financing of support prices by reducing the budgetary transfers to SEE's and TSM's and by introducing private banks as creditors both to the SEE's and SAC's thus easing the pressures on the Agricultural Bank.[5]

It is the stated objective of the government to eliminate all input and output subsidies gradually in the next two or three years and adopt farmgate price stabilization as the main objective instead of incentive pricing and income parity.

## PERFORMANCE OF SUPPORT POLICIES

While the objective and instrument priorities might have shown slight changes over time, depending on the social, economic and political circumstances facing the policy makers, government intervention in agriculture to date remains one of the major items in the policy makers' agenda. It is therefore important that the consequences of these policies on resource allocation, efficiency, income distribution, foreign trade, growth, stability and other ends, be studied properly.

Kutlu Somel carried out a very extensive review of the literature on the motives, targets and consequences of agricultural support policies in Turkey (see Chapter 4). I will therefore summarize his conclusions here and elaborate further on resource allocation effects of support policies in the following sections, based on some additional observations.[6]

| | |
|---|---|
| Price Stability: | "There appears to be substantial evidence to indicate that agricultural support activities enhance price stability." |
| Income Effect: | "Even though the terms of trade may be against agriculture, the changes in the terms of trade have usually been favourable to agriculture." |
| Income Stability: | "...support activities...has not had a significant effect on reducing output variability." The source of income instability has been identified as output instability, and a substantial degree of price stability has been achieved through support policies. |
| Income Distribution: | "The various calculations of the TOT by several researchers, indicate that long run developments, in spite of periodically adverse conditions, have been favourable to the agricultural sector." Within agriculture, on the other hand "obviously, support policies must have an effect in propagating the inequalities, but the basic source of the problem is the inequality in the distribution of land ownership and farm size" and the nonexistence of land size specific pricing policies. |
| Productivity and Output: | "There were significant government policies to increase production through technological change. Production has been increased to the levels, where the risks inherent in output instability has substantially changed character." |

The Burden: Although the inflationary effects of support policies as a result of the way they are financed through expanding the money supply, and through their impact on consumer prices and wages is granted, "there appears to be substantial evidence to indicate that support policies have been used commonly and primarily to achieve the explicit and implicit government goals of income transfers to agriculture."

## EFFECT OF PRICE SUPPORTS ON COMPOSITION OF OUTPUT

"The intent,...to use relative support prices and other policies have always been there for the purpose of altering the composition of output...However, as stated in the last DPT (State Planning Organization) reference, support policies have not been successful in this respect."[7] The question whether price support policies can be and have been effective in changing resource allocation requires the testing of the following four hypotheses:

a. The farmers are responsive to relative price changes.

b. The relative support prices have changed.

c. The support prices determine prices received by the farmers.

d. The relative prices received by the farmers have changed.

In this section, the above hypothesis will be addressed in reference to the findings of researchers as reported in the literature and in reference to new evidence which will be reported.

*Are the Turkish Farmers' Supply Responsive to Relative Prices?*

This hypothesis has probably received the most attention from students of Turkish agriculture. As one would also expect, the findings range from unresponsive, to responsive but negative, to responsive and positive supply.[8] I shall argue that the farmers in Turkey are responsive to relative prices, and that this response is sufficiently large to justify support price policies as a viable policy tool in influencing resource allocation. The argument is based on the findings of a research team in METU which recently completed a comprehensive analysis of agricultural policies in Turkey. Utilizing various supply response specifications ranging from naive expectations to rational expectations for major crops such as wheat, cotton, sunflower, tobacco, they have concluded that:

a. Turkish farmers seem to be responsive to changes in expected relative farmgate prices and expected relative yields.

b. The derived supply elasticities of expected relative prices and yields tend to be statistically significant, and positive. Nevertheless, important inter-crop and inter-regional variations were discovered both in signs and magnitudes of these elasticities.

Furthermore, the above research concludes the following with respect to the importance of model specifications, which explains why different researchers may have come up with different supply elasticities.

c. Model specification influences the values and significance of the estimated supply elasticities substantially.

d. Model specifications which do not account for regional and inter-crop dependencies may result in misleading conclusions.

That is why it is not surprising to find researchers concluding that farmers are not responsive to relative prices, and hence that support prices are not an effective tool for changing output composition, while given (almost always) the naive expectation specification inherent in their model specifications, all they are saying (or should be saying) is that farmers' expectations or adjustments are not "naive."[9]

*Did Relative Support Prices Change Over Time?*

There has been a misconception in the support policy literature, with respect to the changes in the structure of relative support prices over time. Many researchers and policy agencies accept that relative support prices have not changed in time, and hence that price support policies do not have an effect on resource allocation. Such conclusions are generally based on the partial correlation matrix between support prices for different crops and wheat parities of support prices. However, the basic problem with these has been the use of current support prices, rather than deflated ones. It is then no wonder that the partial correlation matrix is full of values over 0.95. In fact, any nominal variable, related or unrelated would have resulted in a similar matrix, given the rates of inflation observed in the economy over the years.[10] Tables 6 and 7 which show the deflated partial correlations and wheat parity prices present a different picture. Table 6 shows that, while the changes in the real relative support prices within cereals and to some extent within industrial crops, have been relatively small (but not negligible), the changes between them, and others have been significant (even in opposite directions as in the case of cotton). Table 7 supports the same argument. Relative support prices not only fluctuated widely throughout the years studies, but they had a long-run trend of moving in favor of industrial crops like cotton, tobacco and sugarbeets.

*How are Support Prices Related to Realized Producers' Prices?*

Having shown that the relative support prices had registered changes overtime, it remains to be shown to what extent market prices reflect such changes. Another misconception among researchers of agricultural support policies in Turkey concerns this point. It is generally accepted (again due mainly to the analysis of current prices, rather than deflated prices) without any question that support prices dominate the actual prices received by farmers. The evidence presented in Table 8 below, which relates real support prices to real prices received by the farmers does not fully support this argument.

Examining Table 8 one observes that the relationship between support prices and relative prices is not a simple one-to-one relationship. One observes that the correspondence between the two changes is closely related to the extent of government involvement in the procurement, but even then it is not a one-to-one mapping. There appears to be a functional free market or a credit market (as in hazelnuts) which regulates the prices received by the farmers, given the possible price leadership position played by the state. Therefore, while the evidence supplied here does not refute the existence of a relationship between support prices and market prices, it suggests that the interaction between the two is more complicated than it appears at casual observations.

*Did the Relative Prices Received by Farmers Change Over Time?*

As opposed to current relative farmgate prices (as given in Appendix V), not only one observes structural changes in real farmgate prices in the long-run but also non-symmetric changes in the short-run between different crops, as illustrated by Tables 9 and 10. Furthermore, the changes in realized relative prices are more dramatic, and have stronger signals for resource allocation, than the support prices. This suggests that, to the extent support prices have contributed to the changes in relative prices, they have also contributed to the output composition in Turkish agriculture, and cannot be readily dismissed.

Therefore, agricultural support price policies in Turkey, in addition to their short-run price, output and income effects, probably have resulted in long-run structural changes in the economy via resource allocation effects. The indirect effects of such changes and their welfare implications need to be studied carefully before reaching welfare conclusions.[11]

## THE MOTIVES BEHIND SUPPORT PRICES

A very controversial topic related to support prices in agriculture is the implicit motives behind them. On the one hand there are those who claim that the basic motive has been electoral; these outnumber those who claim that the economic motives dominated.[12] The first group basically argues that changes in support prices cannot be explained by economic variables and attempt to offer political variables, such as election years, changes in political power, non-elected government years as more powerful explanatory variables. The second group, on the other hand, argues that while electoral motives were non-existent, the main (admittedly partially political) motive was to transfer resources to agriculture and to integrate agriculture into the market economy.

The purpose of this section is not to elaborate on this debate (see Somel, this volume) but rather to contribute additional evidence on the explanatory power of political variables as approximated in the literature by the proponents of the first view.

Table 11 presents the regression results of the following models to test the significance of political proxies in explaining support price levels and changes:

Model 1: $Y_t \quad = a + bE + u_t$

Model 2: $\ln Y_t = a + bE + u_t$

Model 3: $Y_t \quad = a + bE + CN + u_t$

Model 4: $\ln Y_t = a + bE + CN + u_t$

where

Y = Real Support prices

E = Dummy variable with 1 for election years and 0 otherwise.

N = Dummy variable with 1 for non-elected administration periods and 0 otherwise.

t = 1946,...., 1984.

The results of the regression suggest that there is no statistically significant relationship, in any of the three crops studied, between levels of or changes in support prices and election years. These results suggest that in years with non-elected governments, real support prices and changes in real support prices were inversely affected. The two political proxies, in the 1946-1984 period can only explain six to twelve percent of the variation in support prices. This simple exercise certainly does not lead to the conclusion that political motives have not been important in shaping the price support policies, but it certainly suggests that, as with the response of farmers to prices, the effect of politics on support price cannot be expected to be explained with naive behavioral specifications.

## SOME CONCLUDING REMARKS

In this paper we have attempted to review the nature and institutional framework of Turkish agricultural price support policies. The viability of price support policies as a resource allocation policy tool was examined. It was argued that support prices were indeed a viable policy tool, but unfortunately are not fully exploited in this regard. It was also argued that the relative support prices have resulted in changes in the relative price structure in agriculture. Whether such changes in the relative price structure and the resulting resource allocation were in the direction of welfare improvements for the society remains to be studied. Finally, the question of the political vs. economic motives behind price supports were addressed. In the light of the simple analysis conducted, it is concluded that simplistic arguments of support prices as election tools should be rejected.

# FOOTNOTES

[1] Türkiye Iş Bankasi, A.S. "Economic Indicators of Turkey 1979-1983."

[2] Reduced to 3 ministries, as a result of the organizational reforms in 1984 which combined the Ministries of Finance and Customs and Monopoly, and Ministries of Agriculture, Forest and Village Affairs.

[3] The World Bank (1977), Vol. II.

[4] The World Bank (1983), Vol. I.

[5] *Ibid.*

[6] Quotations are from an earlier (1979) paper. (Somel, 1979).

[7] *Ibid.*

[8] See Somel (1979) for a review of supply response literature.

[9] See Bulmuş (1978), Forker (1968) and The World Bank (1977).

[10] See for example Bulmuş (1978) and Dönmezçelik (1979). Furthermore, the correlation matrix of support prices computed by Bulmuş and later borrowed by many like Dönmezçelik, not only employ current support prices and relative prices, but the prices they state as support prices on the table headings are actually farmgate prices.

[11] See Le-Si, Scandizzo, and Kasnakoglu (1983) for a modelling attempt to study the resource allocation effects of agricultural policies.

[12] See Ergüder (1970) and Forker (1971) for the first view and Somel (1979) for the second.

# REFERENCES


Aktan, R. 1973. Tarimsal Ürünlerde Destekleme, Semineri, Ismir Ticaret Borsasi Yayinlari: 10, 129-143.

Aresvik, O. 1975. *The Agricultural Development of Turkey*, New York: Praeger Publishers.

Baysan, T., H. Kasnakoglu, K. Somel and A. A. Gürkan. 1983. "Agricultural Policy Analysis," Final Report submitted to Rockefeller Foundation, December, Ankara.

Bulmuş, I. 1978. *Tarimsal Fiyat Oluşumuna Devlet Müdahalesi*, Ankara ITIA Yayini, 113, Ankara.

Dönmezçelik, U. 1979. *Türkiye de Tarimsal Destekleme Fiyat Politikasinin Etkinligi*, Maliye Bakanligi Tetkik Kurulu, Yayin No: 204, Ankara.

Ekmekçioglu, Ç. and H. Kasnakoglu. 1979. "Supply Response in Turkish Agriculture: Preliminary Results on Wheat and Cotton, 1955-1975," *METU Studies in Development*, 22/23, pp. 113-141.

Ergüder, U. 1978. "Politics of Agricultural Price Policy in Turkey," Paper prepared for the *Princeton-Turkey Distribution Project*, Istanbul.

Ergün, Y. 1978. *Tarimsal Ürün Destekleme Alimlari*, Maliyi Bakanligi Tetkik Kurulu, Yayin No: 194, Ankara.

Forker, O.D. 1968. "Effects and Strategies of Price Interventionism in Turkish Agriculture" Paper presented at the *Seminar on Fiscal Incentives to Promote Agricultural Development*, Istanbul.

Forker, O.D. 1971. "Agricultural Price Policy in Turkey," in *Agricultural Price Policy in Turkey*, Vol. I and II.

Gürkan, A.A. 1980. "An Application of the Polynomial Distributed Lag Model to Measuring Supply Responsiveness in Turkey: The Case of Wheat," *ESA Working Paper*, No. 16, June.

Imrohoroglu, S. and H. Kasnakoglu. 1979. "Supply Response in Turkish Agriculture: Further Results on Wheat and Cotton, 1968-1977," *METU Studies in Development, 26/25, pp. 327-339.*

Kasnakoglu, H. and A. Sayer. 1983. "Regional Supply Response in Turkish Agriculture: The Case of Sunflower," Ankara, (mimeo).

Le-Si, V., P.L. Scandizzo and H. Kasnakoglu. 1983. "Turkey: Agricultural Sector Model," The World Bank, *AGREP Division Working Paper*, No. 67, March.

Ministry of Agriculture. 1968. *Trends in Turkish Agriculture: Graphics and Statistics, 1938-66*, Pub. No. 31, Ankara.

Somel, K. 1979. "Agricultural Support Policies in Turkey: A Survey of Literature," *METU Studies in Development*, 24/25, pp. 275-325.

State Institute of Statistics. 1976. *Bitkisel Üretim Miktarli, Üretici Fiyatlari ve Girdiler, 1948-1974*, Ankara.

State Institute of Statistics. 1983. *Statistical Yearbook of Turkey, 1983*, Ankara.

Tüurkiyi Is Bankasi, A.S. 1983. *Economic Indicators of Turkey, 1973-1983*, Ankara.

Tütüncü, M.B. 1984. "Türkiyi de Destekleme Politikasinin Uygluamasi Hakkinda Not,' KFB/KKID-TKS, Ankara (mimeo).

The World Bank. 1977. *Turkey: Agricultural Sector Survey*, Report No. 1684 TU, Washington, D.C. (2 Vols.).

The World Bank. 1983. *Turkey: Agricultural Development Alternatives for Growth with Growth with Exports*, Report No. 4204 TU, Washington, D.C. (3 Vols.).

TABLE 1: COMMODITY COMPOSITION OF TURKISH EXPORTS (1980) (in million $)

| | | | | |
|---|---|---|---|---|
| Agriculture and Livestock | | | 1671.7 | (57.4%) |
| Cereals and Pulses | | 181.0 | | |
| Cereals | 80.0 | | | |
| Pulses | 101.0 | | | |
| Nuts, Fruits and Vegetables | | 753.9 | | |
| Hazelnuts | 394.8 | | | |
| Raisins | 130.3 | | | |
| Figs | 39.0 | | | |
| Citrus | 86.0 | | | |
| Vegetables | 35.0 | | | |
| Fruits & Others | 68.8 | | | |
| Industrial Crops | | 605.9 | | |
| Tobacco | 733.7 | | | |
| Cotton | 322.6 | | | |
| Others | 49.6 | | | |
| Livestock Products | | 180.2 | | |
| Live | 78.0 | | | |
| Meat | 23.0 | | | |
| Other | 7.2 | | | |
| Fishery Product | | 22.7 | | |
| Mining and Quarry Products | | | 191.0 | (6.6%) |
| Industrial Products | | | 1047.4 | (36.0%) |
| Food and Beverages | 190.2 | | | |
| Textiles | 439.8 | | | |
| Forestry Products | 8.1 | | | |
| Hides and Leather Products | 49.5 | | | |
| Others | 359.8 | | | |
| Total Exports | | | 2910.1 | (100.0%) |

Source: T. İş Banksi A.S. (1983).

TABLE 2: GOVERNMENT INVOLVEMENT IN THE PROCUREMENT AND MARKETING OF AGRICULTURAL PRODUCTS.

| Commodity | Beginning year of Support Purchases | Procure from Farmer | | | Domestic Sales | | | Further Process | | | Export/Import | | |
|---|---|---|---|---|---|---|---|---|---|---|---|---|---|
| | | SEE | ASC | Private | SEE | ASC | Private | SEE | ASC | Private | SEE | ASC | Private |
| Wheat | 1938 | X | - | X | X | - | X | X | - | X | X | - | - |
| Barley | 1940 | X | - | X | X | - | X | X | - | X | X | - | - |
| Rye | 1940 | X | - | X | X | - | X | X | - | X | X | - | - |
| Oats | 1940 | X | - | X | X | - | X | X | - | X | X | - | - |
| Rice | 1944, 1967 | X | - | X | X | - | X | - | - | X | X | - | - |
| Corn | 1940 | X | - | X | X | - | X | X | - | X | X | - | - |
| Chick Pea | 1979 | - | X | X | - | X | X | - | - | X | - | X | X |
| Lentil | 1979 | X | X | X | X | X | X | - | - | X | - | X | X |
| Tobacco | 1940, 1967 | X | - | X | X | - | - | X | - | X? | X | - | X |
| Sugar Beet | 1926 | X | - | - | X | - | - | X | - | X | X | - | - |
| Opium Gum | 1938, 1975 | X | - | - | X | - | - | X | - | - | X | - | - |
| Cotton | 1966 | X | X | X | X | X | X | X | X | X | X | X | X |
| Sunflower Oil | 1969 | - | X | X | - | X | X | - | X | X | - | X | X |
| Soybean | 1976 | - | X | X | - | X | X | - | X | X | - | X | X |
| Rapeseed | 1979 | - | X | X | - | X | X | - | X | X | - | X | X |
| Olive Oil | 1968 | - | X | X | - | X | X | - | X | X | - | X | X |
| Pistachio | 1968 | - | X | X | - | X | X | - | X | X | - | X | X |
| Hazelnut | 1962 | - | X | X | - | X | X | - | X | X | - | X | X |
| Dried Figs | 1962 | - | X | X | - | X | X | - | X | X | - | X | X |
| Raisins | 1962 | - | X | X | - | X | X | - | X | X | - | X | X |
| Tea | 1962 | X | - | - | X | - | - | X | - | - | X | - | - |
| Rose | 1976-80 | - | X | X | - | X | X | - | X | X | - | X | X |
| Fresh Cocoons | 1976-80 | - | X | X | - | X | X | X | X | X | - | X | X |
| Sheep | 1976 | X | - | X | X | - | X | X | - | X | X | - | X |
| Cattle | 1976 | X | - | X | X | - | X | X | - | X | X | - | X |
| Angora Wool | 1970 | X | X | X | X | X | X | X | X | X | X | X | X |
| Sheep Wool | 1979 | X | X | X | X | X | X | X | X | X | X | X | X |
| Milk | 1976 | X | X | X | X | X | X | X | X | X | X | X | X |

Sources: Aresvik (1975); World Bank (1983); Ergün 1978); Dönmezçelik (1979); Tütüncü (1986); Egilmez (1984).

Notes: SEE: State Economic Enterprise or Monopoly.
ASC: Agricultural Sales and/or Credit Cooperative

TABLE 3 SHARES OF SUPPORT PURCHASES IN AGRICULTURAL PRODUCTION

| Commodity | % of total production purchased by SEE or ASC | % of total production marketed | % of marketed production purchased by SEE or ASC |
|---|---|---|---|
| Wheat | 5-19 | 35 | 14-54 |
| Barley | 0.3-14 | 30 | 1-47 |
| Rye | 0.2-12 | 30 | 0.6-40 |
| Oats | 0.01-2 | 30* | 0.3-7 |
| Rice | 0.1-22 | 100 | 0.1-22 |
| Corn | 0.07-0.6 | 35 | 0.2-2 |
| Chick Pea | 10-15 | 40* | 25-38 |
| Lentil | 5-10 | 40* | 13-25 |
| Tobacco | 13-91 | 100 | 13-91 |
| Sugar Beet | 100 | 100 | 100 |
| Opium Gum | 62-89 | 90* | 69-99 |
| Cotton | 49-100 | 100 | 49-100 |
| Sunflower Oil | 1-56 | 100 | 1-56 |
| Soybean | 10 | 100 | 10 |
| Olive Oil | 0.01-0.6 | 90 | 0.01-0.7 |
| Pistachio | 1-25 | 90* | 1-28 |
| Hazelnut | 44-79 | 90 | 49-88 |
| Dried Figs | 8-10 | 80 | 10-13 |
| Raisins | 1-3 | 80* | 1-4 |
| Tea | 100 | 100 | 100 |
| Fresh Cocoons | 16-58 | 100* | 18-58 |
| Sheep | 6-35 | 50 | 12-70 |
| Cattle | 34-50 | 50 | 64-100 |
| Angora Wool | 0.3-14 | 80* | 0.4-18 |
| Sheep Wool | 5-10 | 80* | 6-13 |

Sources: Bulmuş (1978); Tütüncü (1984).

Notes: The percentages purchased by SEE or ASC show ranges between 1970-1983.

* Estimated by the author, based on similar commodities.

TABLE 4 AGENCIES OF OUTPUT SUPPORT

| Agency(ies) | Commodities |
|---|---|
| Soil Products Office (SPO) | Cereals, pulses and opium |
| Sugar Factories Co. (SFC) | Sugarbeet |
| Sales and/or Credit Cooperatives (SAC) | Cotton, figs, raisins, (one for each or group of commodities) hazelnuts, pistachios, olive oil, oil seeds, mohair and silk cocoons. |
| Turkish State Monopolies (TSM) | Tobacco and tea |
| Meat and Fish Organization (MFO) | Livestock, meats and fish |
| Milk Industry Organization(MIO) | Milk and milk products |

TABLE 5: GOVERNMENT INVOLVEMENT IN THE PRICING, MANUFACTURING AND DISTRIBUTION OF AGRICULTURAL INPUTS

| Input | Government Sets Selling Price | Production or Manufacture | | Distribution | | Imports | |
|---|---|---|---|---|---|---|---|
| | | Public | Private | Public | Private | Public | Private |
| Fertilizer | X | X | X | X | X | X | - |
| Certified Seeds | - | X | X | X | X | X | - |
| Pesticides | - | - | X | X | X | - | X |
| Tractors | X | X | X | X | X | X | X |
| Combines | X | - | - | X | X | - | X |
| Other Farm Mach. | - | - | X | X | X | - | X |
| Feeds | - | X | X | X | X | X | X |
| Fuel | X | - | - | X | X | X | - |
| Water | X | X | - | X | - | - | - |
| Improved Herds | - | X | X | X | X | X | X |

Sources: Aresvik (1975); The World Bank (1983).

Notes: All imports are subject to some degree of control, as they require licenses.

TABLE 6: PARTIAL CORRELATION MATRIX OF DEFLATED SUPPORT PRICES

| | Wheat | Barley | Rye | Oats | Cotton | Tobacco | Sugarbeet | Sunflower | Hazelnuts |
|---|---|---|---|---|---|---|---|---|---|
| Wheat | 1.00 | 0.85 | 0.92 | 0.73 | -0.05 | 0.53 | 0.47 | 0.61 | 0.65 |
| Barley | 0.85 | 1.00 | 0.86 | 0.73 | 0.32 | 0.69 | 0.56 | 0.67 | 0.46 |
| Rye | 0.92 | 0.86 | 1.00 | 0.78 | -0.06 | 0.47 | 0.43 | 0.61 | 0.58 |
| Oats | 0.72 | 0.73 | 0.78 | 1.00 | -- | -- | -- | -- | -- |
| Cotton | -0.05 | 0.32 | -0.06 | -- | 1.00 | 0.72 | 0.56 | 0.12 | -0.28 |
| Tobacco | 0.53 | 0.69 | 0.67 | -- | 0.72 | 1.00 | 0.73 | 0.49 | -0.02 |
| Sugarbeet | 0.47 | 0.56 | 0.43 | -- | 0.56 | 0.73 | 1.00 | 0.70 | 0.12 |
| Sunflower | 0.61 | 0.47 | 0.61 | -- | 0.12 | 0.49 | 0.70 | 1.00 | 0.12 |
| Hazelnuts | 0.45 | 0.46 | 0.58 | -- | 0.28 | -0.02 | 0.12 | 0.12 | 1.00 |

Sources: Appendix I

Notes: Support prices are deflated by the wholesale price index with 1979= 100. Also, since the support periods and data availability were not idenitical for all crops, the partial correlations are based on different numbers of observations for different crop pairs.

TABLE 7: DEFLATED SUPPORT PRICES RELATIVE TO WHEAT

| Year | BarleyW | RyeW | OatsW | CottonW | TobacoW | SugarW | TeaW | SunflW | HazelnW |
|---|---|---|---|---|---|---|---|---|---|
| 1938 | .71 | .71 | .47 | | | | | | |
| 1939 | .81 | .81 | .85 | | | | | | |
| 1940 | .75 | .75 | .8 | | | | | | |
| 1941 | 1 | 1.1 | .8 | | | | | | |
| 1942 | .7 | .74 | .7 | | | | | | |
| 1943 | .7 | .74 | .7 | | | | | | |
| 1944 | .68 | .73 | .59 | | | | | | |
| 1945 | .68 | .73 | .59 | | 8.2 | | | | |
| 1946 | .73 | .82 | .68 | | 10 | | | | |
| 1947 | .73 | .82 | .68 | | 8.5 | | | | |
| 1948 | .73 | .82 | .68 | | 8 | | | | |
| 1949 | .73 | .82 | .68 | | 8.6 | | | | |
| 1950 | .63 | .7 | .63 | | 7.4 | | | | |
| 1951 | .63 | .7 | .63 | | 7.4 | | | | |
| 1952 | .73 | .83 | .73 | | 8.6 | | | | |
| 1953 | .73 | .83 | .73 | | 8.4 | | | | |
| 1954 | .73 | .83 | .73 | | 9.2 | | | | |
| 1955 | .7 | .8 | .7 | | 7.9 | | | | |
| 1956 | .7 | .8 | .7 | | 11 | | | | |
| 1957 | .72 | .84 | .72 | | 9.7 | | | | |
| 1958 | .72 | .84 | .72 | | 8.3 | | | | |
| 1959 | .63 | .79 | .62 | | 12 | | | | |
| 1960 | .59 | .78 | .55 | | 16 | | | | |
| 1961 | .57 | .76 | .53 | | 12 | | | | |
| 1962 | .57 | .76 | .53 | | 11 | | | | |
| 1963 | .62 | .73 | .58 | 2.3 | 12 | .18 | | 1.9 | 6.7 |
| 1964 | .64 | .73 | .6 | 2.4 | 11 | .18 | | 2.1 | 6.4 |
| 1965 | .64 | .73 | .6 | 2.7 | 10 | .18 | | 2 | 6.8 |
| 1966 | .71 | .73 | .67 | 2.9 | 11 | .19 | | 2.1 | 6.8 |
| 1967 | .75 | .75 | .69 | 2.9 | 11 | .18 | | 1.9 | 7 |
| 1968 | .76 | .76 | .71 | 3.3 | 13 | .24 | 3.5 | 2.1 | 8.8 |
| 1969 | .78 | .73 | .71 | 3.3 | 11 | .19 | 3.2 | 1.9 | 8.3 |
| 1970 | .78 | .73 | .71 | 3.6 | 13 | .19 | 3.6 | 2.1 | 8.3 |
| 1971 | .79 | .75 | .73 | 5 | 19 | .25 | 3.5 | 2.1 | 8.1 |
| 1972 | .8 | .77 | .75 | 3.9 | 15 | .2 | 3 | 1.8 | 6.6 |
| 1973 | .75 | .71 | .71 | 3.4 | 17 | .21 | 3.2 | 2.4 | 6 |
| 1974 | .73 | .69 | .69 | 4 | 17 | .22 | 3.3 | 2.2 | 5.6 |
| 1975 | .69 | .66 | | 3.8 | 18 | .22 | 3.5 | 2.3 | 5.8 |
| 1976 | .84 | .78 | | 4.8 | 17 | .28 | 3.8 | 2.7 | 7.2 |
| 1977 | .78 | .92 | .73 | 4.9 | 12 | .27 | 2.8 | 3.1 | 8.8 |
| 1978 | .81 | .76 | .79 | 4.8 | 10 | .29 | 2.5 | 2.9 | 10 |
| 1979 | .68 | .64 | .52 | 3.1 | 9.2 | .2 | 2 | 2 | 6.2 |
| 1980 | .7 | .7 | .55 | 3.5 | 9.5 | .22 | 2.5 | 2.2 | 6.7 |
| 1981 | .78 | .64 | | 3.3 | 10 | .21 | 2.6 | 2.2 | 6.2 |
| 1982 | .82 | .84 | | | 8.5 | .17 | 2.2 | 2.1 | |

Source: Appendix 1.

TABLE 8: SIMPLE CORRELATIONS BETWEEN REAL SUPPORT AND FARMGATE PRICES

| Crop | $R^2$ |
|---|---|
| Wheat | 0.19 |
| Barley | 0.17 |
| Cotton | 0.78 |
| Tobacco | 0.83 |
| Sunflower | 0.37 |
| Hazelnuts | 0.72 |

TABLE 9: PARTIAL CORRELATION MATRIX OF REAL FARMGATE PRICES (1948-1982)

| | Wheat | Harley | Lentil | Potato | Tomato | Sunflr | Cotton | Tobaco | Apple | Hazeln | Livest |
|---|---|---|---|---|---|---|---|---|---|---|---|
| Row 1 | 1 | .714 | -.189 | -.399 | -.197 | .253 | .531 | .263 | -.405 | -.130 | -.053 |
| Row 2 | .714 | 1 | .097 | -.073 | .092 | .520 | .329 | .496 | .054 | -.039 | .292 |
| Row 3 | -.189 | .097 | 1 | .557 | .605 | .660 | -.297 | .062 | .569 | .025 | .094 |
| Row 4 | -.389 | -.073 | .557 | 1 | .542 | .148 | -.209 | -.001 | .754 | -.248 | .34 |
| Row 5 | -.197 | .092 | .605 | .543 | 1 | -.303 | .127 | .416 | .032 | .330 | |
| Row 6 | .253 | .520 | .660 | .148 | .424 | 1 | -.190 | .429 | .167 | .221 | .148 |
| Row 7 | .531 | .328 | -.297 | -.209 | -.323 | -.190 | 1 | .070 | -.025 | -.190 | -.020 |
| Row 8 | .263 | .496 | .062 | -.003 | .127 | .429 | .070 | 1 | .126 | .486 | .230 |
| Row 9 | -.405 | .054 | .569 | .754 | .416 | .167 | -.025 | .126 | 1 | -.045 | .365 |
| Row 10 | -.130 | -.039 | .025 | -.247 | .032 | .221 | -.180 | .486 | -.045 | 1 | -.329 |
| Row 11 | -.053 | .292 | .094 | .345 | .330 | .149 | -.030 | .230 | .365 | -.329 | 1 |

Source: Appendix 2.

TABLE 10: FARMGATE PRICES RELATIVE TO WHEAT PRICES

| Year | BarleyW | LentilW | PotatoW | TomatoW | SunflrW | CottonW | TobacoW | AppleW | HazelnW |
|---|---|---|---|---|---|---|---|---|---|
| 1938 | .7 | | | | | 7.9 | 10 | | 5.4 |
| 1939 | .64 | | | | | 8.6 | 11 | | 4.4 |
| 1940 | .66 | | | | | 9.5 | 9.4 | | 2.1 |
| 1941 | .65 | | | | | 8.2 | 13 | | 2.9 |
| 1942 | .71 | | | | | 3.3 | 6.8 | | 1.6 |
| 1943 | .79 | | | | | 1.9 | 3.3 | | .72 |
| 1944 | .7 | | | | | 5.1 | 8.7 | | 1.3 |
| 1945 | .7 | | | | | 5.2 | 9.1 | | 1.9 |
| 1946 | .65 | | | | | 5.9 | 12 | | 2.6 |
| 1947 | .61 | | | | | 6.4 | 8.4 | | 3.2 |
| 1948 | .57 | 1.2 | .82 | .56 | 1.1 | 6.4 | 8 | .82 | 1.9 |
| 1949 | .76 | 1.1 | .76 | .6 | 1.2 | 7.2 | 7.2 | .79 | 1.9 |
| 1950 | .62 | 1.2 | .56 | .6 | 1.1 | 12 | 7 | .78 | 4.2 |
| 1951 | .59 | 1 | .56 | .57 | .97 | 12 | 6.7 | .83 | 3.3 |
| 1952 | .61 | .96 | .63 | .66 | .93 | 10 | 7.7 | .93 | 3.3 |
| 1953 | .64 | .96 | .73 | .8 | .92 | 7.2 | 7.1 | .97 | 3.4 |
| 1954 | .66 | .96 | .78 | .79 | 1.2 | 8.9 | 8.8 | .65 | 4.2 |
| 1955 | .77 | 1 | .83 | .84 | 1.2 | 9.6 | 7.9 | 1.4 | 5.4 |
| 1956 | .8 | 1.5 | 1.2 | .97 | 1.6 | 11 | 9.3 | 1.3 | 6.4 |
| 1957 | .77 | 2.3 | 1.3 | .89 | 1.4 | 10 | 8.5 | 1.9 | 5.8 |
| 1958 | .72 | 2.5 | 1.2 | .9 | 2 | 11 | 12 | 1.9 | 6.7 |
| 1959 | .71 | 2.5 | .9 | .88 | 1.5 | 9.7 | 9.4 | 1.5 | 6.7 |
| 1960 | .81 | 2.4 | .83 | .9 | 1.7 | 10 | 9.8 | 1.7 | 6.7 |
| 1961 | .69 | 1.5 | .82 | .78 | 1.3 | 8.2 | 12 | 1.1 | 7 |
| 1962 | .68 | 1.3 | .71 | .82 | 1.3 | 7.7 | 16 | .94 | 7.4 |
| 1963 | .69 | 1.7 | .71 | .82 | 1.6 | 7.6 | 12 | .93 | 7.5 |
| 1964 | .68 | 1.7 | .73 | .81 | 1.6 | 7.5 | 11 | .95 | 7.2 |
| 1965 | .68 | 1.5 | .69 | .81 | 1.4 | 6.8 | 11 | .9 | 6.4 |
| 1966 | .73 | 1.5 | .69 | .84 | 1.9 | 6.7 | 11 | .91 | 6.8 |
| 1967 | .73 | 1.7 | .71 | .83 | 1.9 | 7.5 | 10 | .92 | 6.2 |
| 1968 | .76 | 1.7 | .73 | .86 | 1.9 | 7.1 | 11 | .97 | 6.6 |
| 1969 | .8 | 1.7 | .76 | .94 | 1.8 | 7 | 11 | 1.1 | 6.4 |
| 1970 | .67 | 1.5 | .69 | .75 | 1.6 | 6.7 | 7.5 | .85 | 5.6 |
| 1971 | .63 | 2.1 | .76 | 1 | 1.5 | 7.7 | 7.1 | .67 | 6.3 |
| 1972 | .57 | 2 | .79 | .87 | 1.5 | 6.9 | 6.3 | .7 | 5.2 |
| 1973 | .57 | 1.7 | .54 | .74 | 1.6 | 6 | 5.2 | .53 | 2.6 |
| 1974 | .68 | 2.5 | .71 | .75 | 1.7 | 7.7 | 7.3 | 1.1 | 4.2 |
| 1975 | .75 | 2.8 | .81 | .84 | 1.9 | 6.6 | 11 | 1.3 | 4.6 |
| 1976 | .77 | 2.8 | 1.1 | .86 | 2.1 | 8.8 | 13 | 1.4 | 5.2 |
| 1977 | .85 | 3.2 | 1.1 | 1.3 | 2.4 | 9.7 | 15 | 1.8 | 5.2 |
| 1978 | .94 | 3.9 | 1.8 | 1.9 | 2.3 | 8.6 | 13 | 2.5 | 5.8 |
| 1979 | .91 | 3.6 | 2 | 1.6 | 2.2 | 9.4 | 12 | 2.6 | 7.5 |
| 1980 | .78 | 3.9 | 1.6 | 1.6 | 1.7 | 8.5 | 7.4 | 1.9 | 7.6 |
| 1981 | .83 | 3.3 | 1.2 | 1.3 | 1.8 | 8 | 7.1 | 1.4 | 5.9 |
| 1982 | .77 | 3.1 | 1.1 | .87 | 1.9 | 7.9 | 8.1 | 1.6 | 6 |

Source: Appendix 2.

TABLE 11: EFFECTS OF POLITICAL VARIABLES ON SUPPORT PRICES

| | | Estimated Coefficients | | | |
|---|---|---|---|---|---|
| Crop | Model | Intercept | E | N | $R^2$ |
| Wheat | 1 | 7.59<br>(32.46) | 0.06<br>(0.09) | -- | 0.0002 |
| Barley | 1 | 5.36<br>(45.89) | 0.06<br>(0.23) | -- | 0.0015 |
| Tobacco | 1 | 83.61<br>(17.78) | 3.80<br>(0.40) | -- | 0.0042 |
| Wheat | 2 | 2.01<br>(62.72) | 0.01<br>(0.15) | -- | 0.0006 |
| Barley | 2 | 1.67<br>(75.19) | 0.12<br>(0.27) | -- | 0.0021 |
| Tobacco | 2 | 4.39<br>(86.96) | 0.05<br>(0.68) | -- | 0.0065 |
| Wheat | 3 | 7.79<br>(31.22) | -0.05<br>(-0.11) | -0.97<br>(1.89) | 0.0930 |
| Barley | 3 | 5.46<br>(44.50) | 0.006<br>(0.02) | -0.54<br>(-2.15) | 0.1180 |
| Tobacco | 3 | 86.83<br>(16.99) | 2.31<br>(0.24) | -15.53<br>(-1.48) | 0.0630 |
| Wheat | 4 | 2.04<br>(59.49) | -0.002<br>(-0.04) | -0.13<br>(-1.86) | 0.0905 |
| Barley | 4 | 1.69<br>(72.45) | 0.002<br>(0.06) | -0.10<br>(-2.18) | 0.1210 |
| Tobacco | 4 | 4.42<br>(79.20) | 0.03<br>(0.33) | -0.18<br>(-1.59) | 0.0735 |

Source: Appendix 1.

Notes: Numbers in parentheses are t ratios.

APPENDIX 1: SUPPORT PRICES AT CURRENT PRICES (TL/kg.) (PART ONE)

| Year | Wheat | Barley | Rye | Oats | Cotton | Tobaco | Sugar | Tea | Sunflr | Hazeln |
|---|---|---|---|---|---|---|---|---|---|---|
| 1938 | .05 | | | | - | - | | - | - | - |
| 1939 | .05 | | | | - | - | | - | - | - |
| 1940 | .085 | .06 | .06 | .04 | - | | | - | - | - |
| 1941 | .135 | .11 | .11 | .115 | - | | | - | - | - |
| 1942 | .2 | .15 | .15 | .16 | - | | | - | - | - |
| 1943 | .2 | .2 | .21 | .16 | - | | | - | - | - |
| 1944 | .27 | .19 | .2 | .19 | - | | | - | - | - |
| 1945 | .27 | .19 | .2 | .19 | - | | | - | - | - |
| 1946 | .22 | .15 | .16 | .13 | - | | | - | - | - |
| 1947 | .22 | .15 | .16 | .13 | - | 1.81 | | - | - | - |
| 1948 | .22 | .16 | .18 | .15 | - | 2.2 | | - | - | - |
| 1949 | .22 | .16 | .18 | .15 | - | 1.88 | | - | - | - |
| 1950 | .22 | .16 | .18 | .15 | - | 1.77 | | - | - | - |
| 1951 | .22 | .16 | .18 | .15 | - | 1.9 | | - | - | - |
| 1952 | .3 | .19 | .21 | .19 | - | 2.23 | | - | - | - |
| 1953 | .3 | .19 | .21 | .19 | - | 2.23 | | - | - | - |
| 1954 | .3 | .22 | .25 | .22 | - | 2.58 | | - | - | - |
| 1955 | .3 | .22 | .25 | .22 | - | 2.53 | | - | - | - |
| 1956 | .3 | .22 | .25 | .22 | - | 2.77 | | - | - | - |
| 1957 | .4 | .28 | .32 | .28 | - | 3.14 | | - | - | - |
| 1958 | .4 | .28 | .32 | .28 | - | 4.54 | | - | - | - |
| 1959 | .5 | .36 | .42 | .36 | - | 4.85 | | - | - | - |
| 1960 | .5 | .36 | .42 | .36 | - | 4.14 | | - | - | - |
| 1961 | .63 | .4 | .5 | .39 | - | 7.46 | | - | - | - |
| 1962 | .73 | .43 | .57 | .4 | - | 11.8 | | - | - | - |
| 1963 | .75 | .43 | .57 | .4 | - | 9 | | | - | |
| 1964 | .75 | .43 | .57 | .4 | - | 8.07 | | | - | |
| 1965 | .78 | .48 | .57 | .45 | 1.83 | 8.97 | .14 | | 1.49 | 5.25 |
| 1966 | .78 | .5 | .57 | .47 | 1.87 | 8.22 | .14 | | 1.6 | 5 |
| 1967 | .78 | .5 | .57 | .47 | 2.11 | 8.08 | .14 | | 1.58 | 5.3 |
| 1968 | .78 | .55 | .57 | .52 | 2.25 | 8.55 | .15 | | 1.6 | 5.29 |
| 1969 | .8 | .6 | .6 | .55 | 2.35 | 8.86 | .14 | | 1.55 | 5.58 |
| 1970 | .65 | .65 | .65 | .6 | 2.8 | 11.4 | .2 | 3.01 | 1.8 | 7.5 |
| 1971 | 1.03 | .9 | .75 | .73 | 3.4 | 11.7 | .2 | 3.34 | 2 | 8.5 |
| 1972 | 1.03 | .8 | .75 | .73 | 3.75 | 13.2 | .2 | 3.67 | 2.2 | 8.5 |
| 1973 | 1.2 | .95 | .9 | .88 | 6 | 23.2 | .3 | 4.17 | 2.5 | 9.7 |
| 1974 | 2.05 | 1.65 | 1.58 | 1.54 | 8 | 31.3 | .4 | 6.25 | 3.75 | 13.5 |
| 1975 | 2.34 | 1.76 | 1.67 | 1.66 | 8 | 39.1 | .5 | 7.5 | 5.5 | 14 |
| 1976 | 2.58 | 1.88 | 1.77 | 1.77 | 10.3 | 43.6 | .58 | 8.5 | 5.75 | 14.5 |
| 1977 | 2.86 | 1.98 | 1.9 | | 11 | 50.1 | .62 | 10 | 6.5 | 16.5 |
| 1978 | 3.2 | 2.69 | 2.48 | | 15.5 | 55.8 | .9 | 12 | 8.5 | 23 |
| 1979 | 5.1 | 4 | 4.7 | 3.7 | 24.8 | 61.5 | 1.39 | 14.5 | 16 | 45 |
| 1980 | 10.5 | 8.5 | 8 | 8.25 | 50 | 109 | 3 | 25.9 | 30 | 110 |
| 1981 | 20.2 | 13.7 | 13 | 10.4 | 62.5 | 185 | 4 | 41 | 4 | 125 |
| 1982 | 22.3 | 15.6 | 15.5 | 12.3 | 77 | 211 | 5 | 55 | 50 | 150 |
| 1983 | 28.2 | 22 | 18 | | 93.3 | 282 | 6 | 72.5 | 61 | 175 |
| 1984 | 45.2 | 37 | 38 | | | 385 | 7.85 | 101 | 95 | |

APPENDIX 1: DEFLATED SUPPORT PRICES (TL/kg.) (PART TWO)

| Year | Wheat | Barley | Rye | Oats | Cotton | Tobaco | Sugar | Tea | Sunfl | Hazeln |
|---|---|---|---|---|---|---|---|---|---|---|
| 1938 | 8.32 | | | | | | | | | |
| 1939 | 7.92 | | | | | | | | | |
| 1940 | 10.9 | 7.68 | 5.12 | | | | | | | |
| 1941 | 12.5 | 10.2 | 10.2 | 10.6 | | | | | | |
| 1942 | 9.64 | 7.23 | 7.23 | 7.71 | | | | | | |
| 1943 | 5.54 | 5.54 | 5.82 | 4.43 | | | | | | |
| 1944 | 9.76 | 6.87 | 7.23 | 6.87 | | | | | | |
| 1945 | 9.98 | 7.02 | 7.39 | 7.02 | | | | | | |
| 1946 | 8.41 | 5.73 | 6.12 | 4.97 | | | | | | |
| 1947 | 8.32 | 5.67 | 6.05 | 4.91 | | 68.4 | | | | |
| 1948 | 7.78 | 5.66 | 6.37 | 5.31 | | 77.8 | | | | |
| 1949 | 7.17 | 5.22 | 5.87 | 4.89 | | 61.3 | | | | |
| 1950 | 7.95 | 5.78 | 6.51 | 5.42 | | 64 | | | | |
| 1951 | 7.54 | 5.49 | 6.17 | 5.14 | | 65.1 | | | | |
| 1952 | 10.2 | 6.45 | 7.13 | 6.45 | | 75.7 | | | | |
| 1953 | 9.88 | 6.26 | 6.92 | 6.26 | | 73.4 | | | | |
| 1954 | 8.99 | 6.59 | 7.49 | 6.59 | | 77.3 | | | | |
| 1955 | 8.32 | 6.1 | 6.93 | 6.1 | | 70.1 | | | | |
| 1956 | 7.13 | 5.23 | 5.94 | 5.23 | | 65.8 | | | | |
| 1957 | 8.01 | 5.61 | 6.41 | 5.61 | | 62.9 | | | | |
| 1958 | 6.97 | 4.88 | 5.57 | 4.88 | | 79.1 | | | | |
| 1959 | 7.29 | 5.25 | 6.13 | 5.25 | | 70.8 | | | | |
| 1960 | 6.9 | 4.97 | 5.8 | 4.97 | | 57.1 | | | | |
| 1961 | 8.48 | 5.39 | 6.73 | 5.25 | | 100 | | | | |
| 1962 | 9.3 | 5.48 | 7.26 | 5.1 | 150 | | | | | |
| 1963 | 9.17 | 5.26 | 6.97 | 4.89 | | 110 | | | | |
| 1964 | 9.24 | 5.3 | 7.02 | 4.93 | | 99.4 | | | | |
| 1965 | 8.88 | 5.47 | 6.49 | 5.13 | 20.8 | 102 | 1.59 | | 17 | 59.8 |
| 1966 | 8.48 | 5.43 | 6.2 | 5.11 | 20.3 | 89.3 | 1.52 | | 17.4 | 54.3 |
| 1967 | 7.89 | 5.05 | 5.76 | 4.75 | 21.3 | 81.7 | 1.42 | | 16 | 53.6 |
| 1968 | 7.65 | 5.4 | 5.59 | 5.1 | 22.1 | 83.9 | 1.47 | | 15.7 | 51.9 |
| 1969 | 7.21 | 5.41 | 5.41 | 4.96 | 21.2 | 79.9 | 1.26 | | 14 | 50.3 |
| 1970 | 7.18 | 5.49 | 5.49 | 5.06 | 23.6 | 95.8 | 1.69 | 25.4 | 15.2 | 63.3 |
| 1971 | 7.5 | 5.82 | 5.46 | 5.31 | 24.7 | 85 | 1.46 | 243. | 14.6 | 61.9 |
| 1972 | 6.36 | 4.94 | 4.63 | 4.5 | 23.1 | 81.5 | 1.23 | 22.6 | 13.6 | 52.5 |
| 1973 | 5.9 | 4.67 | 4.43 | 4.33 | 29.5 | 114 | 1.48 | 20.5 | 12.3 | 47.7 |
| 1974 | 7.88 | 6.34 | 6.08 | 5.92 | 30.8 | 120 | 1.54 | 24 | 14.4 | 51.9 |
| 1975 | 8.39 | 6.31 | 5.99 | 5.95 | 28.7 | 140 | 1.79 | 26.9 | 19.7 | 50.2 |
| 1976 | 8 | 5.83 | 5.49 | 5.49 | 31.8 | 135 | 1.8 | 26.4 | 17.8 | 45 |
| 1977 | 7.15 | 4.95 | 4.75 | | 27.4 | 125 | 1.55 | 25 | 16.3 | 41.3 |
| 1978 | 5.25 | 4.41 | 4.07 | | 25.4 | 91.5 | 1.48 | 19.7 | 13.9 | 37.7 |
| 1979 | 5.1 | 4 | 4.7 | 3.7 | 24.8 | 61.5 | 1.39 | 14.5 | 16 | 45 |
| 1980 | 5.07 | 4.1 | 3.86 | 3.98 | 24.1 | 52.6 | 1.45 | 12.5 | 14.5 | 53.1 |
| 1981 | 7.11 | 4.82 | 4.59 | 3.67 | 22.1 | 65.3 | 1.41 | 14.5 | 14.1 | 44.1 |
| 1982 | 6.27 | 4.39 | 4.37 | 3.47 | 21.7 | 59.4 | 1.41 | 15.5 | 14.1 | 42.3 |
| 1983 | 6.07 | 4.74 | 3.88 | | 20.1 | 60.8 | 1.29 | 15.6 | 13.2 | 37.7 |
| 1984 | 6.72 | 5.5 | 5.65 | | | 57.2 | 1.17 | 15 | 14.1 | |

Sources: See sources to Appendix 2. Also, Ministry of Agriculture (1968), Turkiye IS Bankasi A.S. (1984), SIS (1983).

Notes: The support prices are deflated by the wholesale price index, where 1979=100, (-) means no support price announced.

APPENDIX 2: CURRENT FARMGATE PRICES (TL/kg.) (PART ONE)

| Year | Wheat | Barley | Lentil | Potato | Tomato | Sunflr | Cotton | Tobaco | Apple | Hazeln | Lives |
|---|---|---|---|---|---|---|---|---|---|---|---|
| 1938 | .043 | .03 | | | | | | .34 | .44 | .23 | .2 |
| 1939 | .044 | .028 | | | | | | .38 | .47 | .2 | .2 |
| 1940 | .059 | .039 | | | | | | .56 | .56 | .12 | .23 |
| 1941 | .085 | .055 | | | | | | .69 | 1.1 | .25 | .32 |
| 1942 | .26 | .18 | | | | | | .84 | 1.7 | .4 | .61 |
| 1943 | .56 | .45 | | | | | | 1.1 | 1.9 | .41 | .81 |
| 1944 | .25 | .18 | | | | | | 1.3 | 2.2 | .32 | .91 |
| 1945 | .25 | .17 | | | | | | 1.3 | 2.2 | .47 | .96 |
| 1946 | .21 | .14 | | | | | | 1.2 | 2.4 | .55 | .94 |
| 1947 | .22 | .13 | | | | | | 1.4 | 1.8 | .71 | .97 |
| 1948 | .28 | .16 | .33 | .23 | .15 | .32 | 1.8 | 2.2 | .23 | .51 | 1 |
| 1949 | .27 | .2 | .3 | .2 | .16 | .31 | 1.9 | 1.9 | .21 | .5 | 1.1 |
| 1950 | .26 | .16 | .3 | .15 | .16 | .29 | 3 | 1.8 | .2 | 1.1 | .94 |
| 1951 | .27 | .16 | .27 | .15 | .16 | .26 | 3.3 | 1.8 | .23 | .9 | .87 |
| 1952 | .28 | .17 | .27 | .18 | .19 | .26 | 2.8 | 2.2 | .26 | .94 | .96 |
| 1953 | .3 | .19 | .28 | .22 | .24 | .27 | 2.1 | 2.1 | .29 | 1 | 1 |
| 1954 | .3 | .2 | .29 | .23 | .23 | .35 | 2.6 | 2.6 | .2 | 1.2 | 1.2 |
| 1955 | .3 | .23 | .3 | .25 | .25 | .37 | 2.8 | 2.4 | .43 | 1.6 | 1.3 |
| 1956 | .29 | .24 | .45 | .35 | .29 | .48 | 3.2 | 2.7 | .38 | 1.9 | 1.3 |
| 1957 | .39 | .3 | .87 | .5 | .34 | .55 | 3.9 | 3.3 | .71 | 2.2 | 1.5 |
| 1958 | .39 | .28 | .99 | .49 | .36 | .77 | 4.1 | 4.5 | .74 | 2.6 | 1.7 |
| 1959 | .48 | .34 | 1.2 | .43 | .42 | .73 | 4.7 | 4.5 | .7 | 3.2 | 2.1 |
| 1960 | .48 | .39 | 1.1 | .4 | .43 | .81 | 4.9 | 4.7 | .84 | 3.2 | 2.5 |
| 1961 | .63 | .43 | .97 | .51 | .49 | .84 | 5.2 | 7.5 | .68 | 4.4 | 2.4 |
| 1962 | .68 | .46 | .87 | .48 | .56 | .86 | 5.2 | 11 | .64 | 5 | 2.3 |
| 1963 | .7 | .48 | 1.2 | .5 | .58 | 1.1 | 5.4 | 8.1 | .66 | 5.2 | 2.5 |
| 1964 | .7 | .48 | 1.2 | .51 | .57 | 1.1 | 5.2 | 7.6 | .67 | .5 | 2.5 |
| 1965 | .76 | .52 | 1.1 | .53 | .62 | 1.1 | 5.2 | 8.5 | .68 | 4.9 | 2.8 |
| 1966 | .77 | .56 | 1.2 | .53 | .65 | 1.5 | 5.1 | 8.1 | .7 | 5.2 | 3 |
| 1967 | .77 | .56 | 1.3 | .55 | .64 | 1.5 | 5.8 | 7.9 | .71 | 4.8 | 3.5 |
| 1968 | .78 | .59 | 1.3 | .57 | .67 | 1.5 | 5.5 | 8.4 | .75 | 5.1 | 3.3 |
| 1969 | .8 | .65 | 1.4 | .61 | .75 | 1.4 | 5.6 | 8.7 | .85 | 5.1 | 3.5 |
| 1970 | 1 | .67 | 1.5 | .7 | .76 | 1.6 | 6.8 | 7.6 | .86 | 5.6 | 3.8 |
| 1971 | 1.1 | .7 | 2.3 | .84 | 1.1 | 1.7 | 8.5 | 7.8 | .74 | 6.9 | 4.3 |
| 1972 | 1.3 | .75 | 2.7 | 1.1 | 1.2 | 2 | 9.2 | 8.4 | .93 | 6.9 | 4.7 |
| 1973 | 2.4 | 1.4 | 4 | 1.3 | 1.8 | 3.8 | 12 | 12 | 1.3 | 6.2 | 6.1 |
| 1974 | 2.8 | 1.9 | 7 | 2 | 2.1 | 4.6 | 21 | 20 | 3.1 | 12 | 8.1 |
| 1975 | 2.8 | 2.1 | 7.6 | 2.2 | 2.3 | 5.2 | 18 | 30 | 3.5 | 13 | 11 |
| 1976 | 2.7 | 2.1 | 7.7 | 3.1 | 2.4 | 5.8 | 24 | 36 | 3.9 | 14 | 11 |
| 1977 | 3 | 2.5 | 9.6 | 3.4 | 3.9 | 7.1 | 28 | 45 | 5.3 | 15 | 14 |
| 1978 | 3.6 | 3.4 | 14 | 6.4 | 7 | 8.2 | 31 | 48 | 9 | 21 | 24 |
| 1979 | 5.3 | 4.8 | 19 | 10 | 8.3 | 12 | 50 | 61 | 14 | 39 | 37 |
| 1980 | 11 | 8.4 | 42 | 17 | 17 | 19 | 92 | 80 | 21 | 82 | 66 |
| 1981 | 19 | 15 | 61 | 23 | 23 | 33 | 148 | 132 | 27 | 109 | 81 |
| 1982 | 23 | 18 | 71 | 25 | 20 | 43 | 184 | 190 | 36 | 139 | 105 |

APPENDIX 2: DEFLATED FARMGATE PRICES (TL/kg.) (PART TWO)

| Year | Wheat | Barley | Lentil | Potato | Tomato | Sunflr | Cotton | Tobaco | Apple | Hazeln | Lives |
|---|---|---|---|---|---|---|---|---|---|---|---|
| 1938 | 7.2 | 5 | | | | | 57 | 73 | 0 | 39 | 33 |
| 1939 | 7 | 4.4 | | | | | 60 | 74 | 0 | 31 | 32 |
| 1940 | 7.5 | 5 | | | | | 71 | 71 | 0 | 16 | 29 |
| 1941 | 7.9 | 5.1 | | | | | 64 | 101 | 0 | 23 | 30 |
| 1942 | 12 | 8.8 | | | | | 41 | 83 | 0 | 19 | 29 |
| 1943 | 16 | 12 | | | | | 29 | 52 | 0 | 11 | 22 |
| 1944 | 9.1 | 6.3 | | | | | 47 | 79 | 0 | 12 | 33 |
| 1945 | 9.1 | 6.4 | | | | | 47 | 83 | 0 | 17 | 35 |
| 1946 | 8 | 5.2 | | | | | 48 | 93 | 0 | 21 | 36 |
| 1947 | 8.2 | 5 | | | | | 53 | 69 | 0 | 27 | 37 |
| 1948 | 9.7 | 5.6 | 12 | 8 | 5.4 | 11 | 63 | 78 | 8 | 18 | 36 |
| 1949 | 8.7 | 6.6 | 9.8 | 6.6 | 5.2 | 10 | 63 | 62 | 6.8 | 16 | 35 |
| 1950 | 9.4 | 5.8 | 11 | 5.2 | 5.6 | 10 | 110 | 66 | 7.3 | 39 | 34 |
| 1951 | 9.3 | 5.5 | 11 | 5.2 | 5.6 | 10 | 110 | 66 | 7.3 | 39 | 34 |
| 1952 | 9.6 | 5.9 | 9.2 | 6.1 | 6.3 | 8.9 | 97 | 74 | 8.9 | 32 | 33 |
| 1953 | 9.7 | 6.2 | 9.4 | 7.1 | 7.7 | 9 | 70 | 69 | 9.4 | 33 | 34 |
| 1954 | 8.9 | 5.9 | 8.6 | 7 | 7 | 10 | 79 | 79 | 5.8 | 37 | 36 |
| 1955 | 8.2 | 6.3 | 8.3 | 6.8 | 6.9 | 10 | 79 | 65 | 12 | 44 | 36 |
| 1956 | 7 | 5.6 | 11 | 8.2 | 6.8 | 11 | 75 | 65 | 8.9 | 45 | 31 |
| 1957 | 7.7 | 5.9 | 17 | 10 | 6.9 | 11 | 78 | 66 | 14 | 44 | 30 |
| 1958 | 6.8 | 4.9 | 17 | 8.5 | 6.2 | 13 | 72 | 79 | 13 | 46 | 30 |
| 1959 | 7 | 5 | 18 | 6.3 | 6.2 | 11 | 68 | 66 | 10 | 47 | 30 |
| 1960 | 8.4 | 5.8 | 13 | 6.9 | 6.6 | 11 | 70 | 101 | 9.2 | 59 | 32 |
| 1961 | 8.4 | 5.8 | 13 | 6.9 | 6.6 | 11 | 70 | 101 | 9.2 | 59 | 32 |
| 1962 | 8.7 | 5.9 | 11 | 6.1 | 7.1 | 11 | 67 | 137 | 8.2 | 64 | 30 |
| 1963 | 8.6 | 5.9 | 15 | 6.1 | 7 | 14 | 65 | 99 | 8 | 64 | 30 |
| 1964 | 8.6 | 5.9 | 15 | 6.3 | 7 | 14 | 64 | 93 | 8.2 | 62 | 31 |
| 1965 | 8.7 | 5.9 | 13 | 6 | 7.1 | 12 | 59 | 97 | 7.8 | 56 | 32 |
| 1966 | 8.3 | 6.1 | 13 | 5.8 | 7 | 16 | 56 | 88 | 7.6 | 56 | 33 |
| 1967 | 7.8 | 5.7 | 13 | 5.6 | 6.5 | 15 | 58 | 80 | 7.2 | 49 | 35 |
| 1968 | 7.6 | 5.8 | 13 | 5.6 | 6.5 | 15 | 58 | 80 | 7.2 | 49 | 35 |
| 1969 | 7.2 | 5.8 | 12 | 5.5 | 6.8 | 13 | 50 | 79 | 7.7 | 46 | 32 |
| 1970 | 8.5 | 5.7 | 13 | 5.9 | 6.4 | 13 | 57 | 64 | 7.2 | 47 | 32 |
| 1971 | 8 | 5.1 | 17 | 6.1 | 8 | 12 | 62 | 57 | 5.3 | 50 | 31 |
| 1972 | 8.2 | 4.6 | 17 | 6.5 | 7.1 | 12 | 57 | 52 | 5.7 | 43 | 29 |
| 1973 | 12 | 6.7 | 20 | 6.4 | 8.7 | 18 | 71 | 61 | 6.3 | 31 | 30 |
| 1974 | 11 | 7.2 | 27 | 7.5 | 8 | 18 | 82 | 77 | 12 | 45 | 31 |
| 1975 | 9.9 | 7.4 | 27 | 8 | 8.2 | 19 | 65 | 107 | 13 | 46 | 39 |
| 1976 | 8.5 | 6.5 | 24 | 9.7 | 7.4 | 18 | 75 | 112 | 12 | 44 | 35 |
| 1977 | 7.4 | 6.3 | 24 | 8.4 | 9.8 | 18 | 71 | 113 | 13 | 39 | 36 |
| 1978 | 5.9 | 5.5 | 23 | 10 | 12 | 13 | 51 | 79 | 15 | 34 | 40 |
| 1979 | 5.3 | 4.8 | 19 | 10 | 8.3 | 12 | 50 | 61 | 14 | 39 | 37 |
| 1980 | 5.2 | 4.1 | 20 | 8.2 | 8.2 | 9.1 | 45 | 38 | 10 | 39 | 32 |
| 1981 | 6.5 | 5.4 | 22 | 8.1 | 8.2 | 12 | 52 | 47 | 9.5 | 39 | 29 |
| 1982 | 6.6 | 5 | 20 | 7 | 5.7 | 12 | 52 | 54 | 10 | 39 | 30 |

Sources: Aktan(1973), Ersuder (1978), Ersun (1979), Donmezelik (1979), World Bank (1977), 1983), Forker (1968), Tutuncu (1984), SIS (1976, 1983).

Notes: The farmgate prices are deflated by a wholesale price index, where 1979=100 (see also sources to Appendix 1).

APPENDIX 3: CORRELATION MATRIX OF DETRENDED QUANTITIES (PART ONE)

| | Wheat | Barley | Lentil | Potato | Tomato | Sunflr | Cotton |
|---|---|---|---|---|---|---|---|
| Row 1 | 1 | .88297 | .63636 | .91898 | .88543 | .73755 | .68716 |
| Row 2 | .88297 | 1 | .70106 | .79512 | .76415 | .49553 | .49699 |
| Row 3 | .63636 | .70106 | 1 | .56034 | .67287 | .42279 | .29427 |
| Row 4 | .91888 | .79512 | .56034 | 1 | .90674 | .77666 | .8037 |
| Row 5 | .88543 | .76415 | .67287 | .90674 | 1 | .82222 | .63452 |
| Row 6 | .73755 | .49553 | .42279 | .77666 | .82222 | 1 | .74335 |
| Row 7 | .68716 | .44699 | .29427 | .8037 | .63452 | .74335 | 1 |
| Row 8 | .71945 | .49447 | .35777 | .7264 | .65815 | .59776 | .62263 |
| Row 9 | .80034 | .61639 | .66228 | .78374 | .84177 | .82941 | .70805 |
| Row 10 | .63416 | .36738 | .30401 | .66471 | .65828 | .66474 | .62388 |
| Row 11 | .5814 | .63958 | .68168 | .62935 | .59894 | .4407 | .51334 |
| Row 12 | .85908 | .76095 | .59177 | .92123 | .88456 | .72534 | .69938 |
| Row 13 | .72592 | .73591 | .60796 | .8409 | .7536 | .54191 | .64442 |
| Row 14 | .832294 | .74634 | .43808 | .91548 | .7801 | .60685 | .74493 |

(PART TWO)

| | Tobaco | Apple | Hazeln | SMuttn | SWool | Beef | CWMilk |
|---|---|---|---|---|---|---|---|
| Row 1 | .71945 | .80034 | .63416 | .5814 | .85908 | .72592 | .83294 |
| Row 2 | .49447 | .61639 | .36738 | .63958 | .76095 | .73591 | .74634 |
| Row 3 | .35777 | .66228 | .30401 | .68168 | .59177 | .60796 | .43808 |
| Row 4 | .7264 | .78374 | .66471 | .62935 | .92123 | .8409 | .91548 |
| Row 5 | .65815 | .84177 | .65828 | .59884 | .88456 | .7536 | .7801 |
| Row 6 | .59776 | .82941 | .66474 | .4407 | .72534 | .54191 | .60685 |
| Row 7 | .62263 | .70805 | .62388 | .51334 | .69938 | .64442 | .74493 |
| Row 8 | 1 | .54006 | .52661 | .31293 | .59785 | .4236 | .63079 |
| Row 9 | .54006 | 1 | .69086 | .53566 | .82274 | .66208 | .70582 |
| Row 10 | .52261 | .69086 | 1 | .40528 | .6232 | .51405 | .57784 |
| Row 11 | .31293 | .53566 | .40528 | 1 | .61503 | .7206 | .54059 |
| Row 12 | .59785 | .82274 | .6232 | .61503 | 1 | .81621 | .8952 |
| Row 13 | .4236 | .66208 | .51405 | .7206 | .81621 | 1 | .78503 |
| Row 14 | .63079 | .70582 | .57784 | .54059 | .8952 | .78503 | 1 |

Source: SIS (1976), 1983), Ministry of Agriculture (1968)

APPENDIX 4: PARTIAL CORRELATION

| | Wheat | Barley | lentil | Potato | Tomato | Sunflr | Cotton | Tobaco | Apple | Hazeln | Livest |
|---|---|---|---|---|---|---|---|---|---|---|---|
| Wheat | 1 | .99808 | .9944 | .97863 | .96257 | .99771 | .99837 | .98414 | .98782 | .99303 | .986 |
| Barley | .98808 | 1 | .99621 | .98503 | .97204 | .99777 | .99837 | .98544 | .98682 | .99269 | .98808 |
| Lentil | .9944 | .99621 | 1 | .99336 | .98362 | .99288 | .99744 | .98042 | .99244 | .99724 | .49549 |
| Potato | .97963 | .98503 | .99336 | 1 | .99249 | .99017 | .98655 | .97089 | .94359 | .99062 | .9958 |
| Tomato | .96257 | .97204 | .98362 | .99249 | 1 | .96174 | .97086 | .94791 | .97546 | .9753 | .98137 |
| Sunflr | .99771 | .99777 | .99289 | .98017 | .96174 | 1 | .99801 | .99309 | .09934 | .99065 | .98773 |
| Cotton | .99537 | .99937 | .99744 | .98655 | .97086 | .99801 | 1 | .98732 | .99072 | .99607 | .99197 |
| Tobaco | .98414 | .98544 | .98042 | .87089 | .94791 | .99309 | .98732 | 1 | .88613 | .97845 | .98152 |
| Apple | .93382 | .98682 | .99244 | .99358 | .97546 | .98834 | .99072 | .98613 | 1 | .99268 | .99954 |
| Hazeln | .99303 | .99269 | .99724 | .99062 | .9733 | .98065 | .99607 | .97949 | .99268 | 1 | .99603 |
| Livest | .996 | .98808 | .99524 | .9959 | .98137 | .98773 | .99197 | .98152 | .99854 | .99603 | 1 |

Source: Appendix 2.

# 6

# Taxation, Control, and Agrarian Transition in Rural Egypt: A Local-Level View

*Richard Adams*

## INTRODUCTION

This essay examines the process of agrarian transition in Egypt since 1952. Two specific themes guide and inform the essay: the impact of Egyptian state policy on national agricultural development and the effect of such policy on the differentiation of the peasantry in one particular rural locale. These two themes complement one another. Over the years, the Egyptian state policy of "controlling" agriculture in order to extract a transferable surplus out of agriculture has set the course of agrarian change in Egypt. This government policy has not only helped to precipitate the current crisis in Egyptian agricultural production, but it has also affected the process of the internal differentiation of the peasantry.

The primary focus of this essay is on the process of agrarian transition in one specific rural Egyptian locale: *markaz* (district) El Diblah[1] in Minya Governorate in Upper Egypt. To date, precious little attention has been paid to analyzing the impact of national policy on the character of local-level relations in Egypt. This unfortunate lacuna has fostered a rather misleading view of the dynamics of agricultural development and peasant differentiation at the village level.

In the developing world the operation of socio-economic forces tends to differentiate the peasantry into three broad landowning groups[2] -- the rich, middle and poor peasantry. Yet in Egypt this process of differentiation has not led to the appearance of any full-blown social "classes," as envisioned by Marx, Lenin and others. According to Lenin (1956), the differentiation of the peasantry leads to the creation of two "new types" of rural inhabitants: the rural bourgeoisie and the rural proletariat. However, in *markaz* El-Diblah such horizontally-based social classes are only conspicuous by their absence. In this area the differentiation of the peasantry has instead taken place within the context of the more traditional vertical ties linking patrons with clients. In *markaz* El-Diblah, as well as in other rural Egyptian locales, many poor peasants are still quite dependent on the traditional patronage services provided by a handful of rich peasants.

The balance of this essay is divided as follows. Section 2 presents a broad overview of the Egyptian policy of controlling agriculture in order to extract a transferable surplus out of the rural sector. The following section (Section 3) analyzes the impact of this policy on the process of peasant differentiation in *markaz* El-Diblah. The final section (Section 4) summarizes the results of the study.

## EGYPTIAN STATE POLICY TOWARD AGRICULTURE

Since 1952 the Egyptian state has attempted to control agriculture in order to tax peasant producers. At the outset such a policy of taxing agriculture was perhaps inevitable given the fact that agriculture was the only sector of Egyptian society capable of generating a surplus. Yet over the years the Egyptian state has expended precious little effort to upgrade peasant production in order to increase the available amount of agricultural surplus. By and large, state agricultural institutions have failed to provide the resources and expertise needed to qualitatively transform the technological character of peasant production at the farm level.

It is possible to gain a fuller understanding of the Egyptian strategy of agricultural development by examining three elements of this strategy: (a) land reform; (b) agricultural cooperatives; and (c) state investment in agriculture.

### *Land Reform*

Egyptian land reform can be regarded as a classic expression of the state's desire to control agriculture. Land reform in Egypt was pursued mainly as a means of eliminating the large landowning class (i.e., access to over 100 *feddans*)[3] that had been allied with the pre-1952 regime. In practice, land reform involved the expropriation of the large landed elite, with the state itself assuming the role of the displaced landlords. In Egypt land reform was coupled with a variety of measures -- such as the creation of agricultural cooperatives and village banks -- designed to allow the state to assume control of agricultural production. Yet as will become clearer below, these measures were never coupled with any *concerted* state effort aimed at technologically transforming agricultural productivity. Since 1952 the Egyptian state has made no serious effort to provide the type of agricultural infrastructure -- research and extension services -- or technological inputs -- high-yield seeds and appropriate machinery -- designed to transform the productivity of Egyptian peasants.

While Egyptian land reform did not have a major impact upon peasant productivity, it did have two important effects on the process of differentiation among the peasantry. First, land reform helped consolidate (and protect) the status of the large number of tenants in the Egyptian country-side.[4] As a result of land reform, ceilings were placed on land rents and renters were given security of tenure. The usufruct that the Egyptian renter now enjoys over his land is almost complete; when the tenant dies, the owner is obligated by law to rent the land to his male heirs.[5]

Second, by removing the largest landowners from the countryside, Egyptian land reform facilitated the emergence of a new rural elite. Composed in the main of rich peasants owning over ten *feddans* of land, members of this new rural elite may not be as wealthy as their pre-1952 predecessors. Yet by virtue of the patronage ties they maintain with poorer peasants, members of this new rural elite have come to dominate local-level social and political relations.

### *Agricultural Cooperatives*

Created by the post-1952 regime, agricultural cooperatives in Egypt are responsible for providing peasant farmers with their basic agricultural inputs: seeds, fertilizer, and pesticide.[6] The cooperatives collect payment on these inputs by deducting from the imputed value of those cash crops -- principally cotton and rice -- which farmers are required to market through cooperative channels. By controlling the flow of inputs and outputs to farmers, the agricultural cooperatives in Egypt represent a clever mechanism for taxing the surplus produced by peasant farmers.

The cooperatives exercise their taxation powers in the following manner. Each agricultural cooperative in Egypt divides the land under its jurisdiction into two or three rotational blocs. In theory, each bloc is then assigned a different crop according to season, with all farmers having land within that bloc being required to grow the assigned crop, or risk being penalized. In practice, however, farmers have recently been permitted to substitute for the assigned rotational crop with one notable exception: cotton. Since it represents Egypt's main export crop,[7] most farmers are forced to grow cotton according to the assigned rotational cycles. Since 1965 all cotton grown in Egypt has been marketed through the cooperatives. This has enabled the state to tax the farmers indirectly by purchasing cotton at one set of prices and then selling it on the world market at much higher prices. Allowing for handling, ginning and transportation costs, the government during the period 1965-76 paid the Egyptian farmers only about 60 percent of the export price for cotton.[8]

It is important to realize that such price manipulation on cotton and other crops (e.g., rice, sugar cane, onions) has resulted in a substantial net flow of resources out of agriculture. As Table 1 indicates, transfers to the Egyptian government on one single crop -- cotton -- have been sufficient to cover the full costs of *all* direct and indirect subsidies extended to agricultural producers. While they include the subsidies extended on all crops, the figures in Table 1 make no mention of the large transfers to the state on such crops as rice and sugar cane. Unfortunately, cotton is the only crop for which the national accounts list explicit transfers from agriculture to the national treasury.

*State Investment in Agriculture*

Since 1952 the Egyptian policy of controlling agriculture in order to tax it has not been coupled with any type of concerted public investment program in agriculture. This is unfortunate, inasmuch as in many developing countries increased public investment in agriculture represents the primary means of developing and disseminating the type of new technological inputs that are needed to boost production.

In Egypt the share of total fixed public investment in agriculture (including irrigation and drainage) has declined steadily from twenty-four percent in the mid-1960s (when work on the Aswan Dam was at its peak) to about eight percent in 1978 (Ikram, 1980: 43). According to more recent development plans, the share of public investment in agriculture declined to only 3.5 percent during the period 1975-80 (Sayigh, 1982: 116).

The Egyptian government's relative neglect of agriculture means that services such as agricultural research, extension, and cooperative organization have all been virtually starved of allocations. This has had a deleterious impact on agricultural productivity. A good case in point here is provided by the low adoption rate of high-yielding variety (HYV) seeds in Egyptian agriculture. Over the years little research attention has been paid to the problem of adopting HYVs to meet the various needs of Egyptian farmers. The response of the latter has been to consciously avoid this new productive input. Thus, in 1982 less than one percent of the total rice area in Egypt was planted in HYV varieties, compared to forty-eight percent for India and eighty percent for the Philippines. The situation is somewhat better for wheat. In the case of wheat, fifty-two percent of total plantings in Egypt in 1982 were with HYVs, compared to seventy-six percent for India and eighty-four percent for Pakistan (Dalrymple, forthcoming).

*The Agricultural Crisis in Egypt*

Egypt's attempt to control agricultural development has produced a crisis in agriculture. The roots of this crisis lie in the interaction of food and population dynamics in Egypt. Between 1948-52 and 1978-82 the cropped area in Egypt increased by less than fifteen percent, while the total Egyptian population more than doubled. Coaxing higher yields out of a limited land base in order to feed a rapidly expanding population is thus the basic conundrum that Egyptian agriculture faces.

Over the years Egyptian agriculture has largely failed to meet this challenge. Since 1952 per capita food production in Egypt has declined by ten percent.[9] Part of the problem here lies in Egypt's disappointing rate of yield productivity growth in agriculture. While Egyptian crop yields may be high by world standards,[10] in recent years the rate of growth of Egyptian yields has faltered. Table 2 compares the rate of yield growth for the principal field crops in Egypt with those of the average of thirty-six other developing countries. Cotton is included in the calculations here because it is Egypt's leading export crop. The data show that between 1948-52 and 1963-67 the Egyptian rate of growth in output per hectare for three of the five crops -- wheat, maize, and sorghum -- exceeded that of the average of the thirty-six developing countries. However, after 1963-67 Egypt's rate of yield growth for all the crops -- except cotton -- declined significantly. Between 1963-67 and 1978-82 the thirty-six developing countries averaged a much higher rate of yield growth for all crops -- except cotton -- than Egypt.

Egypt's yield productivity problems have forced it to become increasingly dependent on food imports to feed its burgeoning population. Egypt now imports approximately seventy-five percent of its wheat, twenty-seven percent of its maize, and twenty-seven percent of its red meat (USDA, 1983). If its presently favorable foreign exchange situation were to ever deteriorate,[11] Egypt's agricultural crisis could become a very real food crisis.

## THE IMPACT OF EGYPTIAN POLICY ON LOCAL-LEVEL RELATIONS: THE CASE OF MARKAZ (DISTRICT) EL-DIBLAH

Having outlined the main elements of the Egyptian attempt to control agriculture in order to tax it, it becomes necessary to examine the impact of this policy on one specific rural locale.

*Markaz* (district) El-Diblah is a small administrative area located along the Nile River some three hundred kilometers south of Cairo. Because of its distance from Cairo and other major urban areas, *markaz* El-Diblah is still predominately rural in character. The bulk of its 155,000 inhabitants are peasants, who live scattered amongst some thirty villages. Depending on the size of their landholdings, these peasants grow such crops as cotton, sugar cane, wheat, maize and *berseem* (Egyptian clover). They tend these crops by largely labor-intensive means: the *fa's* (hoe), the *tunbur* (Archimedean screw), and the animal-driven *baladi* plow. Perhaps because of its remoteness from urban markets and capital, most land preparation, weeding, watering, and harvesting tasks in the *markaz* are *not* mechanized.[12] Some threshing is done mechanically, using tractor-powered drum threshers, but it is not unusual to see animal-driven *naurajs* (threshing sleds) performing the same task.

In *markaz* El-Diblah landownership represents the basis of wealth. Although it is not the only income-generating asset in the area, land is clearly one of the most important.[13] It is therefore possible to examine the stratification of the main agrarian groups in *markaz* El-Diblah on the basis of landownership.

In *markaz* El-Diblah, as in other rural Egyptian locales, the poorest peasants are generally the landless. According to the data in Table 3, the pool of landless peasants in *markaz* El-Diblah is quite large: about forty percent of the total *male* agricultural work force lacks land access. This figure is substantially higher than that estimated for Egypt as a whole (24 percent).[14]

The high incidence of landlessness in *markaz* El-Diblah is basically a reflection of heavy population pressure on a very limited cultivable land base. Because it was not the scene of large landownership prior to 1952, *markaz* El-Diblah did not benefit much from land reform. In the area immediately surrounding the main village of El-Diblah, less than two percent of the land was redistributed to about two percent of the peasantry. As a result, Table 3 indicates that fully sixty-four percent of the total *male* agricultural work force in *markaz* El-Diblah is either landless or near-landless (i.e., access to less than one *feddan*).

Table 4 present data on the main land owning groups in *markaz* El-Diblah: the near-landless; the small peasantry (i.e., access from three to ten *feddans*); and the rich peasantry (i.e., over ten *feddans*). It is interesting to note here the numerical predominance of the near-landless and small peasantry. In *markaz* El-Diblah -- and in Egypt as a whole -- approximately eighty percent of the landholdings are less than three *feddans* in size. In the modern Egyptian countryside the cumulative processes of population pressure on land and Islamic patterns of inheritance[15] mean that anyone owning over ten *feddans* of land must be considered "wealthy."

In order to see how the differentiation of the peasantry has proceeded in *markaz* El-Diblah, it is useful to study the survival strategies of each group of the peasantry. Such an examination can analyze each group of the peasantry in terms of three factors: impact of state policy, pattern of labor use, and type of crop mix. Close attention to these factors will help illuminate the micro-level processes of agrarian transition and peasant differentiation in *markaz* El-Diblah.

*Landless Peasantry*

The various post-1952 Egyptian initiatives in the rural sector have had only a marginal impact on the nearly forty percent of the *male* agricultural work force in *markaz* El-Diblah that is landless. To be sure, most of these peasants have benefitted greatly from state efforts to build new schools, hospitals, and health clinics. Yet in the all-important agricultural sphere of rural life, these landless peasants have not fared as well. None of the landless in *markaz* El-Diblah have benefitted from land reform or from state attempts to supply subsidized agricultural inputs (seeds, fertilizers, pesticides) to farmers.

In order to survive, the landless in *markaz* El-Diblah are forced to sell their labor power. In a relatively remote area like El-Diblah, where off-farm employment opportunities are quite limited, most of the landless find work planting, weeding, and harvesting agricultural crops.

The fact that most of the landless work in agriculture means that they have become the indirect beneficiaries of recent changes in government policy. Since the early 1970s the Egyptian government has been actively encouraging Egyptians to seek work abroad. According to official government sources, by 1980 an estimated one million Egyptians were working abroad, principally in the oil-rich states of Saudi Arabia, Iraq and Kuwait.

In 1980 about 260 people (i.e., 5.4 percent of the total *male* labor force) in the village of El-Diblah were working abroad. The overwhelming majority of these migrant workers from El-Diblah were young males less than thirty years of age. Landless (and near-landless) peasants may constitute up to 40 percent of the total migrant force from the village of El-Diblah.

In El-Diblah the flow of workers abroad has helped precipitate a sharp rise in agricultural wages which has benefitted the landless. For example, *real* agricultural wages in the *markaz* increased twenty-five percent between 1973 and 1979. In 1979 landless agricultural workers in El-Diblah, able and willing to work whenever the need arose, could earn about LE 146 (U.S. $209) per year.[16] This annual income figure was slightly higher than the annual *per capita* poverty line figure for 1979 -- LE 11.9.

In *markaz* El-Diblah most landless peasants work on farms over five *feddans* in size. This phenomenon points to an important socio-economic characteristic of the area, namely, the dependence of the poor on the patronage services provided by the rich. Unable to provide for themselves, most landless peasants in the *markaz* are forced to rely on the patronage services -- agricultural labor, consumer and emergency loans -- provided by others. However, local-level government institutions provide few agricultural work opportunities, and extend credit only to landowners. At the same time, government bureaucrats attached to these institutions are too poor to provide such patronage services themselves.[17] Poor and landless peasants in *markaz* El-Diblah are therefore forced to depend on the patronage services provided by a handful of rich peasants (i.e., access to over ten *feddans*).

Such patronage services are not provided *gratis*. In return for the work and credit opportunities they extend to poor peasants, rich peasants expect -- and receive -- the support of their clients in all important local matters. This provides the best explanation for the dominant position of the rich peasantry in village-level institutions like the agricultural cooperatives, village banks and village councils.[18] Poor and landless peasants serving on these institutions are usually quite willing to support the hand of the rich peasant patron that keeps them alive.

Since 1952 the Egyptian state has made no serious attempt to replace or supplant the powers of the new class of rich peasant patrons that has emerged in *markaz* El-Diblah. This is unfortunate, since the process of transforming peasant agriculture is largely a story of how to reach and capture the poor and landless peasantry. At the local level the productive capacity of poor landowners must be increased through the supply of modern technological inputs: high-yield seeds, fertilizer and appropriate machinery. At the same time the dependence of landless peasants on wealthier village elements must be terminated through the state-sponsored creation of new agricultural and non-agricultural opportunities at the local level. As Johnston and Kilby (1975) have shown, nowhere in the world has sustained agricultural development occurred without the state using the supply of new technological inputs to increase the productivity and the incomes of the poor and landless peasantry.

*Near-landless Peasantry (i.e., access to less than one feddan)*

The large number of near-landless peasants in *markaz* El-Diblah -- about 24 percent of the total *male* agricultural work force -- have benefitted only peripherally from the recent state initiatives in agriculture. In some instances, near-landless peasants in the *markaz* may have benefitted from government attempts to limit land rents and to supply subsidized agricultural inputs to farmers. Yet it is unlikely that such government changes have had a major welfare (or productive) impact on near-landless peasants in the area, since their landholdings are so miniscule to begin with.

Near-landless peasants are generally forced to follow a survival strategy similar to that of landless peasants: that of selling their labor power to wealthier peasants. Such peasants may well spend one or two days a week tending to their own tiny plot of land, and the rest of the time working for someone else.

Yet since they do own land, near-landless peasants can resort to one additional survival strategy. They are able to raise large animals, such as water buffalo and cattle. In *markaz* El-Diblah perhaps forty percent of the near-landless peasantry owns large animals, usually by means of a *shirka* (partnership) with a wealthier relative. *Shirkas* are quite common throughout rural Egypt and are generally formed around lactating animals, especially the water buffalo cow. Typically a wealthier urban person will purchase a young buffalo cow for his poorer rural relative. The latter will then feed and raise the animal until it bears a calf, whereupon the owner and peasant will divide the selling price of the calf.

In return for raising the water buffalo to maturity, the near-landless peasant is able to use the animal's milk for his own purposes. Each year a properly-fed water buffalo will produce between eight hundred and one thousand kilograms of milk.[19] Although a near-landless peasant will sell some of this milk on the open market, he will generally keep most of it to make cheese, fat and butter for his household.[20]

While livestock raising has traditionally been an important aspect of the survival techniques of the near-landless peasantry in El-Diblah, in recent years the attractiveness of this strategy has been bolstered by state policy. Since the early 1970s domestic meat and milk production in Egypt have been heavily protected, with domestic prices frequently running on the order of two or three times those of comparable international prices.[21]

According to some sources (Cuddihy, 1980: 105), such pricing policies should encourage poor Egyptian peasants to expand their livestock production and to devote more land to fodder (*berseem*) production. However, within *markaz* El-Diblah the ability of near-landless (and small) peasants to respond to such price incentives appears to be quite limited. While data on animal ownership are not available, fragmentary evidence shows that while the price of *berseem* (Egyptian clover) in *markaz* El-Diblah doubled between 1975 and 1980, the amount of land planted in this crop declined by 0.5 percent.[22]

*Small Peasants (i.e., access to between one and three feddans)*

Small peasants in *markaz* El-Diblah -- accounting for some 24 percent of the total *male* agricultural work force -- have felt most of the benefit and detriment of the recent state initiatives in agriculture. Much of the benefit here has come from the state-run agricultural cooperatives. From the cooperatives in the *markaz* small peasants can now draw state-subsidized agricultural inputs: seeds, fertilizers, and pesticides.

Through the cooperatives small peasants can also draw loans from the newly-created (1978) village bank system. This system extends credit against farmers' accounts at an average rate of interest of six to eight percent per annum. This is a significant improvement over the usurious rates of interest charged in the past by village moneylenders.

Yet at the same time it is the small peasantry that has come to bear the burden of the government's policy of controlling agriculture in order to tax it. Anxious to grow enough food to feed themselves and their animals, small peasants in El-Diblah plant three basic crops: maize in the summer, and wheat and *berseem* in the winter. When they are forced by the government, they also grow cotton in alternate summers. As we have seen, cotton is presently a heavily-taxed crop. In recent years the government buying price for the variety of middle-staple length cotton grown in *markaz* El-Diblah has been so low that most rich farmers have refused to grow it. Instead, these rich farmers have received government permission to plant more profitable, tax-free crops, like sugar cane and grapes. Because of their year-long growing cycles, such crops cannot be alternated with other food and fodder crops. Small peasants in El-Diblah cannot therefore afford to grow sugar cane and grapes, since they generally have to grow the crops they eat. Small peasants in the area thus have little choice but to follow the government-mandated cotton-wheat-*berseem*-maize rotational cycle.

The fact that small peasants in *markaz* El-Diblah are essentially locked into cotton production means that present state taxation policies are largely regressive in nature. Small peasants who are least able to *bear* any type of taxation are currently forced to bear the brunt of the state's taxation policies on cotton and other traditional crops. Such taxation greatly limits the small peasantry's ability to invest in the type of new technological inputs -- high-yield seeds, fertilizer, mechanical inputs -- needed to stimulate qualitative changes in their land and labor productivity.

As a result of state pricing policies, two parallel subsectors have emerged in agriculture in *markaz* El-Diblah. The first subsector focuses on the production of certain "unconventional crops": sugar cane, grapes, and vegetables. Members of this subsector possess full access to input subsidies provided by the government without, in many cases, bearing the burden of any government taxation.[23] In general, only rich farmers can enjoy the large profits associated with membership in this subsector; in 1979 farmers in El-Diblah could gross approximately LE 210 (U.S. $300) per *feddan* on sugar cane an LE 400 (U.S. $572) on grapes. The second subsector in *markaz* El-Diblah focuses on the production of the principal government-marketed crop: cotton. Members of this subsector, who include most small and near-landless peasants, are forced to settle on the relatively low returns associated with cotton, wheat, and maize. In 1979 farmers in El-Diblah could expect to gross only LE 52 (U.S. $74) per *feddan* on cotton and LE 85 (U.S. $122) on maize. Although these low returns are at least partially offset by the large returns currently associated with *berseem*, it is important to note that in *markaz* El-Diblah virtually all farmers -- rich and poor --- grow *berseem* to feed their animals.

*Middle and Rich Peasants (i.e., access to over three feddans)*

The small number of middle and rich peasants in *markaz* El-Diblah -- twelve percent of the total *male* agricultural work force -- have felt the most immediate benefit of the post-1952 state initiatives in agriculture. Not only have they been able to draw subsidized agricultural inputs without, in many cases, bearing the burden of taxation, but they have also benefitted greatly from the impact of Egyptian land reform. In fact, the twin forces of Egyptian land reform and Islamic patterns of inheritance have elevated middle and rich peasants to a position of socio-economic predominance in the *markaz*. Prior to 1952 three medium-large landowners (i.e., access to between 250 or 450 *feddans*) dominated local affairs in the main village of El-Diblah. Anxious to avoid the impact of land reform, these three landowners resorted to the well-known ploy of "deeding" their land over to trusted poor peasant clients. The land would then appear in official records as belonging to someone else, even though the original landowner would still retain full control over it.

This procedure started a process of estate fragmentation in El-Diblah. The "deeding" of land over to ostensibly trustworthy clients often encouraged the latter to seize the land for themselves. Moreover, as time passed and two of the three original large landowners died, their estates were divided up among Cairo-based heirs. These heirs usually placed their land in the control of local *wakils* (managers). The latter also tended to "help themselves" to the charges placed under their control, using one strategem or another to register the land under their names.

As a result of such forces, power in the village of El-Diblah has devolved from the hands of the three original medium-large landowners to a group of approximately twenty rich peasants (i.e., access to over ten *feddans*). Since only two or three of these rich peasants own over fifty *feddans* of land, they are nowhere as wealthy as their pre-1952 predecessors. This means that an important shift in the character of patron-client relations has occurred in the village of El-Diblah. Prior to 1952 large landowners owning over one hundred *feddans* of land were able to provide the type of patronage services -- agricultural work opportunities, consumer and emergency loans -- necessary to support poor peasants on a *permanent* basis. Now, however, the much-diminished resources of rich peasants in El-Diblah means that they can only provide such patronage services on a *temporary* basis. In order to survive, poor peasants seeking work and credit must now circulate between two or three rich peasant patrons.

While they may not be as dominant as their predecessors, rich peasants still wield considerable power at the local level in El-Diblah. These powers are largely a reflection of the complementary work requirements and needs of the rich and poor peasantry. In El-Diblah rich peasants tend to grow those crops -- especially grapes and vegetables -- that require a maximum of labor input. At the same time, because of the emphasis they place on the education of their children, these rich peasants tend to deploy a minimum of family labor in the field. Thus, at peak planting and harvesting times rich peasants are always in need of temporary agricultural workers. These workers are paid by the day, not by the month, and often approach their rich peasant employer for other patronage services -- credit, emergency loans -- to be repaid on the basis of future work.

By providing such patronage services rich peasants are able directly or indirectly to dominate decision-making in *markaz* El-Diblah. For example, by securing the election of their clients to the boards of the local agricultural cooperatives, rich peasants are able to gain permission to take their land out of the mandatory cotton rotation. Through similar means they are also able to enjoy favored access to the inputs -- especially fertilizer and mechanized inputs -- supplied by these cooperatives. In the words of one peasant in El-Diblah, "it is a well-known fact here that only the *'umda'* (village headman) and certain other rich farmers control the cooperative and the (local village) council. No one else around here had the connections within these (institutions) to make them work for them."

## CONCLUSION

After the revolution of 1952 the Egyptian state assumed direct control of agriculture with its land reform policy and system of agricultural cooperatives. With the curtailment of private entrepreneurship in the countryside, it was absolutely essential for the state to also assume the role of leading rural entrepreneur. At the national level it was necessary for the state to supervise the development of those new technological inputs -- high-yield seeds, fertilizer, and appropriate machinery -- needed to raise agricultural productivity. At the local level it was necessary for the state to create a group of dedicated bureaucrats to disseminate the elements of these new technologies to peasant farmers.

Yet as we have seen, since 1952 such developments have by and large failed to take place in Egyptian agriculture. At the national level the state's attempt to control agriculture in order to tax it has produced a considerable net flow of resources out of agriculture. Over the years the state's reluctance to reinvest a "fair share" of its agricultural earnings back into the development and dissemination of new technological inputs in agriculture has frustrated public efforts to stimulate peasant productivity. At the same time, individual peasant producers in Egypt have generally lacked both the technical know-how and the financial resources needed to qualitatively improve their own means of production.

The lack of qualitative change in the basic factors of agricultural production in Egypt serves to explain the relatively slow pace of agrarian transition in the rural area examined here: *markaz* El-Diblah. On the one hand, it may be objected that El-Diblah's relative remoteness from major urban markets has retarded the process of agricultural and economic development in this area. Yet while *markaz* El-Diblah is certainly not typical of those Egyptian rural areas lying in and round Cairo,[24] it does seem broadly representative of many village areas in Upper Egypt. In these areas the absence of the type of agricultural and non-agricultural employment opportunities that are created by technological change in agriculture[25] means that many poor peasants are still incapable of satisfying their daily economic needs. If they do not go to work abroad, these landless and near-landless peasants are forced to depend on the patronage services provided by a small number of rich peasants. It is therefore these rich peasant patrons who continue to dominate social and economic life in places like *markaz* El-Diblah.

While they may effectively control their own local village domains, the rich peasants in *markaz* El-Diblah can hardly be held up as a rich capitalist class, as posited by Lenin and others. Rich peasants in El-Diblah may be relatively "land wealthy," but they employ few permanent laborers and they have not yet undertaken significant commercial pursuits outside of the *markaz*. To the extent that a rich capitalist class does exist in Egypt, it is to be found in major metropolitan centers like Cairo or Alexandria, and *not* in remote rural areas like El-Diblah. At the same time, the poor peasantry in El-Diblah hardly constitutes a proletarian class, since it lacks the type of horizontal interdependence that is necessary for class formation. In *markaz* El-Diblah poor peasants are far more dependent for their day-to-day survival on the rich peasantry than they are on members of their own socio-economic group.

In this respect, it is interesting to speculate on the future character of agrarian transition in *markaz* El-Diblah. In the long term, the powers of the rich peasantry seem threatened by the twin horns of population growth and Islamic patterns of inheritance. A twenty *feddan* plot of land that is divided equally among four or five siblings will not confer much socio-economic power upon its recipients. Similarly, the powers of the rich peasantry seem threatened by the small, but growing, number of peasants seeking work abroad. Poor peasants returning from a three or four year work stint in Saudi Arabia or Kuwait may well possess the means to set themselves up as rich patrons. Although the price of land continues to escalate in El-Diblah,[26] and the ability of returning workers to convert their windfall incomes into land power still remains to be seen, such a scenario cannot be easily dismissed.

Those peasants who have not chosen to go to work abroad, however, seem to face far more limited prospects. Without the creation of new non-agricultural work opportunities in the area, landless peasants in El-Diblah will probably continue to remain dependent upon the landed elite for their survival. Near-landless peasants, however, may be able to reduce their dependence on such elite by branching more into dairy and livestock production. While few near-landless peasants are likely to become wealthy by employing this strategy, they may well find the means to at least pass their land onto their progeny. In view of the unfavorable population-to-land dynamics in *markaz* El-Diblah, this would represent no mean achievement.

# FOOTNOTES

[1] El-Diblah is a pseudonym, as are the names of all *markazs* (districts) and villages in this study. The names of governorates are real.

[2] In Egypt, as well as other developing countries, landownership is not the only element of peasant differentiation. As noted below, livestock, machinery and the receipt of remittances from abroad also serve to differentiate the rural population.

[3] One *feddan* equals 1.04 acres or 0.42 hectares. Although Law 50 (1969) lowered the limit on individual landownership to fifty *feddans*, it is not clear whether this law was ever implemented. See, for example, Harik (1979: 35).

[4] According to Marei (1969: 50), changes in tenancy regulations affected about forty-eight percent of the total land area in Egypt.

[5] Since such Egyptian tenancy regulations apply only to written rental contracts, landowners now typically refuse to extend a tenant a written contract. Most land that is leased out now is rented on an oral basis, for a crop or two at a time.

[6] Through the agricultural cooperatives peasant farmers can also secure loans to plant cotton, sugar cane and fruit from the newly-created (1978) village bank system.

[7] During the period 1978-80 cotton and cotton textile exports accounted for between thirteen and twenty-six percent of the total annual value of Egyptian commodity exports (Scobie, 1981: 15).

[8] The level of indirect taxation on cotton reported here is drawn from Cuddihy (1980: 125). Cuddihy's analysis for cotton and other Egyptian export crops covers the period 1965-76. In a more recent study covering the period 1965-80, Braun and de Haen (1983) found that the levels of indirect taxation on these crops have declined somewhat in recent years. However, we prefer to base our analysis here on Cuddihy's study, since his work still provides the most detailed examination of yearly fluctuations in nominal protection coefficients for the various Egyptian export crops.

[9] Between 1948-52 and 1978-82 food production in Egypt dropped from 205.4 kilograms per capita per annum to 185.7 kilograms.

[10] While high by world standards, Egyptian yields are almost one hundred percent under irrigation. If only *irrigated* yields between countries were compared, Egyptian yields would be relatively low, considering the excellent soil, sunshine and water inputs existing in Egyptian agriculture. When all these factors are taken into consideration, Egyptian yields still show much room for improvement (York et.al., 1982: 89).

[11] In the late 1970s Egypt's foreign exchange situation suddenly

blossomed as a result of receipts from oil exports, worker remittances and Suez Canal and tourist earnings. Yet as Richards (1982b) and Bruton (1983) rightly note, since all of these revenue sources are unstable, Egypt's foreign exchange situation could change at any time.

[12] In certain rural areas adjoining Cairo and other metropolitan centers, mechanization of agricultural tasks has proceeded more rapidly. For example, in Sharqiyya Governorate cow-driven *baladi* plows are now quite rare.

[13] Data from a consumer budget survey undertaken by the ILO in Egypt in 1977 show that while only fifty percent of total rural income is derived from agriculture, "land is (still) the dominant asset (in rural portfolios) and that the incidence of ownership increases sharply with income group" (Hansen and Radwan, 1982: 104-106).

[14] The actual percentage of the landless in the Egyptian agricultural population is unknown and is calculated as a residual. Other recent estimates of the incidence of landlessness among the Egyptian agricultural population have ranged from twenty percent (Hansen and Radwan, 1982) to thirty-eight percent (World Bank, 1975).

[15] Under Islamic law, land is divided equally between all male heirs, with females theoretically receiving equal half-shares.

[16] According to village sources, agricultural workers in *markaz* El-Diblah could work about 190 days a year. About 130 of these days would come during two seasonal peaks: one in April to June, and the second in September and October. While daily wages paid during these peak periods are much higher than normal, on the average agricultural workers in El-Diblah in 1979 could expect to receive about LE 0.77 (U.S. $1.10) per day.

[17] In *markaz* El-Diblah, as in the Egyptian countryside as a whole, bureaucratic salaries are so low -- averaging between LE 20 and LE 50 (U.S. $28 and $71) per month -- that most government bureaucrats are simply not in an economic position to hire workers or extend credit.

[18] For more on this point, see Waterbury (1983) and Adams (1985).

[19] The fat content of water buffalo milk is usually fifty to sixty percent higher than that of cow's milk. As a result of the low amount of animal protein in their diets, rural Egyptians generally need to derive more of their fat and protein from milk and milk-related products, such as cheese.

[20] Data from the 1977 Egyptian Farm Management Survey show that near-landless peasants consume almost eighty percent of the cheese they produce and close to one hundred percent of their butter.

[21] According to Ikram (1980: 194), in recent years prices of imported beef in Egypt have been on the order of LE 0.50 (U.S. $0.72) a kilogram c.i.f., whereas the actual domestic selling price has been about LE 1.60 (U.S. $2.29) per kilogram for approximately the same grades.

[22] Between 1975 and 1980 the areas of land planted in *berseem* in *markaz* El-Diblah decreased from 3,250 *feddans* to 3,100. During the same period of time the amount of land planted in *berseem* in rural Egypt as a whole declined from 2,800,000 *feddans* to 2,711,000 (USAID, 1984).

[23] The incomes of rich farmers growing sugar cane are taxed because they sell their cane to government-owned mills. However, rich farmers growing grapes and vegetables sell their produce on the open market, and thus evade the impact of all government taxation.

[24] For more information on the dynamics of economic change in areas adjacent to Cairo, see Fakhouri (1972) and Richards, Martin and Nagaar (1983).

[25] Research in other developing countries shows that technological change in agriculture helps create new agricultural and non-agricultural employment opportunities in the countryside. See, for example, Mellor (1976) and Hazell and Roell (1983).

[26] According to informants, in 1975 the price of a *feddan* of land in the village of El-Diblah averaged LE 800 to LE 1,000 (U.S. $1,140 to $1,430). In 1980 the price of that land averaged LE 1,800 to LE 2,000 (U.S. $2,570 to $2,860).

# REFERENCES

Adams, Richard. 1985. "Development and Structural Change in Rural Egypt, 1952 to 1982," *World Development*, Vol. 13, No. 6.

______________. 1986a. "Bureaucrats, Peasants and the Dominant Coalition: An Egyptian Case Study," *Journal of Development Studies*, Vol. 22, No. 2.

______________. 1986b. *Development and Social Change in Rural Egypt*. Syracuse, N.Y.: Syracuse University Press.

Braun, Joachim von and de Haen, Hartwig. 1983. *The Effects of Food Price and Subsidy Policies on Egyptian Agriculture*. Research Report 41. Washington, D.C.: International Food Policy Research Institute.

Bruton, Henry. 1983. "Egypt's Development in the Seventies," *Economic Development and Cultural Change*, Vol. 31, No. 4.

Cuddihy, William. 1980. *Agricultural Price Management in Egypt*. World Bank Staff Working Paper No. 388, Washington, D.C.

Dalrymple, Dana. Forthcoming. "Development and Spread of High-yielding Varieties of Wheat and Rice in the Third World." Seventh edition forthcoming. Washington, D.C.: United States Agency for International Development.

Fadil, Mahmoud Abdel. 1975. *Development, Income Distribution and Social Change in Rural Egypt, 1952-1970*. Cambridge: Cambridge University Press.

Fakhouri, Hani. 1972. *Kafr-el-Elow: An Egyptian Village in Transition*. New York: Holt, Rinehart and Winston.

FAO (Food and Agriculture Organization of the United Nations). *Production Yearbook*, various issues. Rome.

Hansen, Bent and Radwan, Samir. 1982. *Employment Opportunities and Equity in Egypt: Egypt in the 1980s*. Geneva: International Labor Office.

Harik, Iliya. 1979. *Distribution of Land, Employment and Income in Rural Egypt.* Rural Development Committee, Cornell University, Ithaca, N.Y.

Hazell, Peter and Roell, Ailsa. 1983. *Rural Growth Linkages: Household Expenditure Patterns in Malaysia and Nigeria.* Research Report 41. Washington, D.C.: International Food Policy Research Institute.

Ikram, Khalid. 1980. *Egypt: Economic Management in a Period of Transition.* Baltimore: Johns Hopkins University Press.

ILO (International Labour Office). *Yearbook of Labour Statistics.* Geneva.

Johnston, Bruce and Kilby, Peter. 1975. *Agricultural and Structural Transformation: Economic Strategies in Late-Developing Countries.* London: Oxford University Press.

Lehmann, David. 1982. "After Chayanov and Lenin: New Paths of Agrarian Capitalism," *Journal of Development Economics*, Vol. 11, No. 2.

Lenin, V. I. 1956. *The Development of Capitalism in Russia.* Moscow: Foreign Languages Publishing House.

Marei, Sayid. 1969. "UAR: Overturning the Pyramid." *CERES-FAO Review*, Vol. 2, No. 6.

Mellor, John. 1976. *The New Economics of Growth: A Strategy for India and the Developing World.* Ithaca: Cornell University Press.

Radwan, Samir. 1977. *Agrarian Reform and Rural Poverty in Egypt, 1952-1975.* Geneva: International Labour Office.

Richards, Alan. 1982a *Egypt's Agricultural Development, 1800-1980: Technical and Social Change.* Boulder, CO: Westview Press.

______________. 1982b. "Peasant Differentiation and Politics in Contemporary Egypt." *Peasant Studies*, Vol. 9, No. 3.

______________, Martin, Philip and Nagaar, Rifaat. 1983. "Labor Shortages in Egyptian Agriculture." In *Migration, Mechanization, and Agricultural Labor Markets in Egypt*, eds. A. Richards and P. Martin. Boulder, CO and Cairo: Westview Press and the American University in Cairo Press.

Sayigh, Yusif. 1982. *The Arab Economy: Past Performance and Future Prospects*. New York: Oxford University.

Scobie, Grant. 1981. *Government Policy and Food Imports: The Case of Wheat in Egypt*. Research Report 29. Washington, D.C.: International Food Policy Research Institute.

USAID (United States Agency for International Development). 1984. "Egypt: FY 1986 Country Development Strategy Statement. Annex C: Agricultural Sector Strategy." Cairo.

USDA (United States Department of Agriculture). 1983. *Egypt: Annual Agricultural Situation Report - 1982*. Cairo: United States Embassy.

______________. 1984. *World Cotton Statistics, 1947-83*. Foreign Agricultural Circular. Washington, D.C.

Waterbury, John. 1983. *The Egypt of Nasser and Sadat: The Political Economy of Two Regimes*. Princeton: Princeton University Press.

World Bank. 1975. *Land Reform*. Sectoral Policy Paper. Washington, D.C.

______________. 1981. *Manpower and Labor Migration in the Middle East and North Africa*. Report prepared by I. Serageldin, J. Socknat, S. Birks, B. Li and C. Sinclair. Washington, D.C.

York, E. T., et. al. 1982. *Egypt: Strategies for Accelerating Agricultural Development*. Ministry of Agriculture of Arab Republic of Egypt and the U.S. Agency for International Development in cooperation with the U.S. Department of Agriculture. Washington, D.C.

TABLE 1: NET EFFECT OF EGYPTIAN AGRICULTURAL PRICE TRANSFERS, 1973-76 (Millions of LE)

| *Item* | *1973* | *1974* | *1975* | *1976* |
|---|---|---|---|---|
| Transfers to Treasury of Cotton Organization | 64.8 | 136.8 | 54.0 | 92.4 |
| Exchange Rate Gains | 114.0 | 177.0 | 129.0 | 100.0 |
| *Total Transfers Out* | *178.8* | *313.8* | *183.0* | *192.4* |
| Direct Agricultural Subsidies | 15.8 | 12.7 | 101.5 | 56.8 |
| All Public Sector Investments in Agriculture | 51.0 | 54.0 | 84.0 | 49.0 |
| Current Expenditure of Ministry of Agriculture | 16.4 | 19.8 | 21.3 | 26.0 |
| Current Expenditure of Ministry of Irrigation | 18.4 | 19.9 | 26.0 | 28.8 |
| *Total Transfers In* | *101.6* | *106.4* | *232.8* | *160.6* |
| *Net Flow* | -77.2 | -207.4 | +49.8 | -31.8 |

Source: Ikram (1980: 212).

TABLE 2. AVERAGE ANNUAL GROWTH RATES[a] OF OUTPUT PER HECTARE

(a) Average Annual Growth Rates, 1948-52 to 1963-67 (Percent)

| | Cotton (*Lint*) | *Wheat* | Rice *Paddy* | *Maize* | *Sorghum* |
|---|---|---|---|---|---|
| 36 Developing Countries[c] | + 1.96 | + 1.59 | + 2.38 | + 1.10 | + 0.67 |
| Egypt | + 1.47 | + 2.44 | + 1.96 | + 2.98 | + 2.28 |

(b) Average Annual Growth Rate, 1963-67 to 1978-82 (Percent)

| | Cotton (*Lint*) | *Wheat* | Rice *Paddy* | *Maize* | *Sorghum* |
|---|---|---|---|---|---|
| 36 Developing Countries[c] | + 1.48 | + 2.34 | + 1.70 | + 1.52 | + 0.95 |
| Egypt | + 2.66 | + 1.52 | + 0.67 | + 1.09 | - 0.08 |

Notes:

a Average annual growth rates calculated here are simple and unweighted growth rates.

b In 1978-82 these five crops (cotton, wheat, rice, maize, and sorghum) accounted for about 70 percent of Egypt's total cropped area.

c The 36 developing countries include: Afghanistan, Argentina, Bangladesh, Brazil, Burma, Chile, China (People's Republic), Colombia, Ethiopia, Guatemala, Guinea, India, Indonesia, Iran, Ivory Coast, Kenya, Korea, (Republic), LIbia, Madagascar, Malaysia, Mexico, Morocco, Nigeria, Pakistan, Panama, Peru, Philippines, Senegal, Sri Lanka, Syria, Thailand, Tunisia, Turkey, Venezuela, Yemen (Dem.), and Zaire.

Sources: Cotton figures from *USDA* (1984).

All other data from *FAO Production Yearbooks* (various issues) and *FAO Production Yearbook Tape* (1980).

TABLE 3: NUMBER OF LANDLESS AND NEAR-LANDLESS MALES IN AGRICULTURAL WORK FORCE, *MARKAZ* EL-DIBLAH AND EGYPT, 1979 and 1980

| | *Markaz* (district) *El-Diblah, 1979* | *Egypt, 1980* |
|---|---|---|
| 1) Rural population | 155,000 | 23,526,000 |
| 2) Rural male population | 79,050 | 11,998,000 |
| 3) Rural male population older than 20 | 36,360 | 5,519,000 |
| 4) Rural male population in non-agricultural activities | 8,730 | 1,324,000 |
| 5) Rural male population in agriculture | 27,630 | 4,195,000 |
| 6) Number of landholdings | 17,890 | 3,474,000 |
| 7) Number of landholdings held by non-agricultural work force | 1,430 | 278,000 |
| 8) Number of landholdings held by agricultural work force | 16,460 | 3,196,000 |
| 9) Number of landless males in agriculture | 11,170 | 999,000 |
| 10) Number of males in agriculture with access to less than one feddan | 6,605 | 1,453,000 |
| 11) Landless males as percentage of male agricultural work force | 40 | 24 |
| 12) Landless and near-landless males as percentage of male agricultural work force | 64 | 58 |

(Table 3 continued next page)

Notes and Sources:

Row 1: *Markaz* El-Diblah figure obtained from district mayor in 1979. Egypt figure estimated at 56 percent of the 1980 Egyptian population as recorded by United Nations data.

Row 2: Figures estimated at 51 percent of the total rural population, which is the proportion observed in successive Egyptian population censuses.

Row 3: Figures estimated at 46 percent of the total male rural population, which is the proportion published in ILO (1979: 15). The age of 20 was selected as the age of "economic manhood" because most Egyptian peasants marry around this age.

Row 4: Figures estimated at 24 percent of the total rural population, with government service accounting for 16 percent and the private sector accounting for 8 percent of total rural non-agricultural employment. These estimates are similar to those made by Hansen and Radwan (1982: 144).

Row 5: Figures obtained as a residual; the difference between rows 3 and 4.

Row 6: *Markaz* El-Diblah figure includes the landholdings of members in all 29 agricultural cooperatives in the *markaz*. Egypt figure extrapolated from 1975 count conducted by Egyptian Ministry of Agriculture and cited in Harik (1979: 39).

Row 7: In Egypt from rural males employed in non-agricultural activities also own land. We want to arrive at the number of rural males who are landless, yet dependent on agriculture. It is therefore necessary to deduct the landholdings of all those who derive their primary livelihood from non-agricultural sources, e.g., a government salary or rural business. In both cases it was estimated that eight percent of the total landholdings were owned by rural residents who had a non-agricultural means of support.

Row 8: Figures obtained as a residual; the difference between rows 6 and 7.

Row 9: Figures obtained as a residual; the difference between rows 5 and 8.

Row 10: *Markaz* El-Diblah figure obtained from district agricultural headquarters. Egypt figure extrapolated from 1975 count conducted by Egyptian Ministry of Agriculture and cited in Harik (1979: 39). In both instances it was estimated that eight percent of the males in the near-landless category had a non-agricultural means of support.

TABLE 4: DISTRIBUTION OF LANDHOLDINGS IN MARKAZ EL-DIBLAH AND EGYPT, 1975 AND 1979

| Size of Holdings (Feddans) | Markaz, El-Diblah, 1979 | | | | Egypt, 1975 | | | |
|---|---|---|---|---|---|---|---|---|
| | Number of Holdings | % | Area of Holdings | % | Number of Holdings | % | Area of Holdings | % |
| Near-landless (under 1) | 7,334 | 41.0 | 2,922 | 9.7 | 1,124,300 | 39.4 | 739,000 | 12.4 |
| Small peasants (1 - < 3) | 7,353 | 41.1 | 9,489 | 31.5 | 1,160,100 | 40.7 | 2,023,400 | 33.8 |
| Middle peasants (3 - < 10) | 2,737 | 15.3 | 10,122 | 33.6 | 503,300 | 17.6 | 2,130,000 | 35.6 |
| Rich peasants (over 10) | 466 | 2.6 | 7,591 | 25.2 | 65,200 | 2.3 | 1,091,300 | 18.2 |
| T o t a l | 17,890 | 100.0 | 30,124 | 100.0 | 2,852,900 | 100.0 | 5,983,700 | 100.0 |

Sources: *Markaz* El-Diblah data obtained from the district agricultural headquarters in the *markaz* and include the landholdings of members of all 29 agricultural cooperatives in the *markaz*. Egypt figures from A.R.E. Ministry of Agriculture and cited in Harik (1979).

# 7

# Food Subsidies and State Policies in Egypt

*Harold Alderman*

## INTRODUCTION

Few developing countries allow food prices to be determined by unhindered market forces. More commonly, governments employ a variety of instruments -- consumer subsidies, quantity rations, import and export restrictions, parastatal marketing companies, forced procurements, and foreign exchange under-valuation -- which influence consumer and producer prices.[1] Egypt combines all of these instruments in a complex tapestry of policy interventions that is noteworthy both for its scale and its durability. Furthermore, like many complex weavings, it is difficult to isolate the various strands. Major and minor motifs form new meanings with alterations of the background while retaining their basic shapes. Some of these motifs can be traced to Pharaonic, Fatamid and Mamaluke times,[2] others to the contingencies of twentieth-century wartime crises. Yet the current meaning of these themes needs to be seen in the contemporary setting of a state neither fully committed to materials planning and quantity restrictions nor comfortable with a laissez-faire market.

Egyptian food policy includes both policies aimed primarily at raising and stabilizing consumption of basic food commodities and policies which are designed to manage and tax agriculture. The two themes are parallel during recent Egyptian history and frequently interact, but there is no strong causal relationship between them. They are related, rather, mainly through the macro economy. Food policies in Egypt are hardly interventions at the margin -- fiscal costs for consumer subsidies accounted for 10-15 percent of total public expenditures in the second half of the 1970s and early 1980s, while agricultural taxation was above 17 percent of sector output during that period. Consequently, food policies bear on the country's foreign exchange position, its ability to invest, and its domestic inflation. There is, then, a continual tension between the economic costs of the policies and their distributional benefits. This interplay will be presented first by describing the consumer benefits of the food subsidy and ration system in some detail and then by outlining the distributional consequences of implicit and explicit agricultural taxation. Detail is necessary, as any aggregation of benefits or costs masks the consequences of various instruments. The macro economic effects will be illustrated with the results of econometric studies which link such policies to foreign trade and domestic inflation.

The final section focuses on the main theme of this workshop -- how do food policies fit into the state's larger goals and what circumstances influence the formation and modifications of these policies? The Egyptian economy is not static; neither are subsidy policies. The evolution of these food subsidy policies, then, reflects the larger issue of the powers and limitations of the government.

## CONSUMER-ORIENTED PRICING POLICIES[3]

The principal government expenditure on food subsidies comes from the subsidy on coarse and refined flour and bread. As illustrated by Scobie,[4] Egyptians have always expected the government to stabilize wheat prices. In this century, export restrictions and imports on government account have both been employed to achieve such stabilization. During the 1970s, the stabilization evolved into a general subsidy policy as domestic prices were held constant in nominal terms in a period of inflation and currency devaluation. As there are no quantity restrictions on purchase, the government, in effect, makes the domestic supply curve horizontal, with imports and aid making up the difference between growing demand and stagnating production. By 1980 imports of wheat and flour were three times the quantity produced locally. Domestic consumption of wheat and wheat products exceeded 180 kilos per capita in 1981-82 in flour equivalents, with rural consumers *purchasing* 184 kilos (60 percent of that through directly subsidized government channels). While rural consumers purchase more subsidized flour, urban residents buy more bread.

Consumers also obtained subsidized commodities through a ration system. Virtually the entire population -- over ninety-two percent of all households -- have a ration card which guarantees a monthly quota of sugar, tea, oil and rice at low subsidized prices. In addition, beans and lentils are seasonally available in the ration shop. Rations are not new. They were distributed during World War II and were reintroduced during the acute foreign exchange crisis of 1966. However, originally they did not involve a general subsidy. Indeed, with the government having monopolies on the import of many foods, rations on various commodities earned profits for the government in the early 1970s. This reflects the initial goal of the system, which was to provide regular and equitable access to scarce commodities with quantity rather than price mechanisms determining distribution. While licensed private grocers are the ultimate link to consumers, the government, distrustful of private middlemen, serves as a wholesaler or principal staple commodities.

In addition to using the ration system, consumers can purchase goods from a network of cooperatives. Membership is not required for purchase, nor do fixed quotas exist. Supplies, however, are limited and willingness to queue serves as a principal distribution mechanism.

For most families, goods available through the ration system are inframarginal; the majority of families make additional purchases at the cooperatives or the higher-priced open market. The entire subsidy system can be viewed mainly as an income transfer system. The implicit income transfer can be calculated as the difference between a reference opportunity cost -- in this study the c.i.f. price of the commodity evaluated at the official exchange rate -- and the various rations and cooperative prices. These transfers are slightly skewed to the urban sector; relative to income, the transfers are highest for the rural poor (see Table 1). Table 1 also indicates a sizeable inherent transfer to consumers from open market sales of cereals. Over half of this is from purchase of flour sold at subsidized prices in rural areas and resold in another village without a flour shop. While there is a small -- and legal -- markup for transportation and for scale, the government incurs a fiscal cost from these sales which accrues to the final consumer. The remainder of the transfer in open market cereal sales is due to the difference between border prices and low domestic prices, which are opportunity costs to the producers but not costs to the exchequer. Similarly, negative transfer from other open market sales indicated in Table 1 represent losses to consumers -- particularly urban upper classes -- from the purchase of meat and other commodities which have protected domestic prices.

## IMPLICATIONS FOR THE AGRICULTURAL SECTOR[5]

The distributional implications of food policy cannot, however, be determined by looking at consumption figures alone. The net transfer effects of a subsidy program depends on the manner by which it is financed. Financing for subsidies is seldom distinguished from the overall budget. Even cross-subsidization policies, or agricultural taxation policies, do not inherently finance consumer subsidies, as the revenue could just as well be used to cover other government costs.

Often, discussions about the subsidy system include reference to Egypt's policy of taxing agriculture through forced procurement at prices well below international parity prices. While this taxation does allow the government to carry some subsidies as implicit costs rather than explicit outlays, there is no logical reason why these two policies are necessarily linked. Indeed, the total net tax burden on agriculture declined during the 1970s while the subsidy bill increased.[6] This reflects increased subsidies on agricultural inputs during the period as well as a tendency to shift from indirect taxation to direct financing of food subsidies. Agricultural taxation, nevertheless, remains a particular concern in this essay, not only because it indicates attitudes and goals of the state but also as the taxation may contribute to agricultural stagnation. In conjunction with the spur to consumption from the subsidies, this stagnation increases the import dependency of Egypt.

Frequently, agricultural economists view agricultural taxation as an unalloyed evil. The negative connotations of the phrases "agricultural burden" and "surplus extraction" conjur up images befitting political cartoons. The state, however, needs revenues for investment as well as current expenses, and there is no inherent difference between the concept of agricultural taxation and general taxation. In many developing countries, agriculture provides the largest share of GDP and, hence, is a logical source of state revenue. What is of concern is the level of taxation; is it so large as to impair seriously future productivity or even, as observed in various periods of history, the physical survival of the peasantry? These questions are frequently paired with the related question of how the government makes its investments, particularly whether agricultural taxation supports investment at all or only urban consumption. Also of concern is the distribution of the burden between sectors of the economy and between classes of producers. Finally, the manner of taxation is of interest. Clearly, land taxes have a different impact on output and crop mix than *ad valorem* taxes on some or all crops.[7]

Implicit agricultural taxation has a long pedigree in Egypt. Mohammed Ali financed his investments and adventures through his monopoly on cotton exports.[8] Conversely, during the century following his rule, land taxes were a more important source of revenue. Abdel Nasser, however, fixed land taxes at low levels which have changed little in nominal terms despite inflation. Abdel Nasser also eliminated private trade in cotton and virtually eliminated private trade in grains. With the agricultural cooperative as the government's agent in agricultural marketing and with a system of planting quotas, the state has been able to tax agriculture again by purchasing crops at prices substantially below those at which it is able to sell them[9] This has been particularly the case for crops like cotton and sugar cane. Virtually the total production of these crops is sold to the state. These crops have largely been introduced in modern times as the state's investment in water control increased cultivation in the months prior to the Nile's spate. Other crops which are part of the farmer's diet -- rice, wheat, beans, and lentils -- have also been taxed through forced procurement. With these crops, however, there have been per *feddan* (roughly one acre) quotas. The quotas are calculated to leave farm households a subsistence amount of the crop while the state markets much of the remainder.

Farmers sell production above the quotas on the open market. It is therefore of interest to determine whether quotas are determined by revenue requirements or are determined as a function of past productivity. In the former case, agricultural taxation is a fixed cost of production and procurement prices are not important at the margin. In the latter case, taxation will have a greater influence on the crop mix or on inputs devoted to the particular crop.[10] There may, in fact, be a taxation treadmill in Egypt in which increases in productivity lead to increase in quotas -- this is not proven. Yet, the incentive to which the profit maximizing farmer responds should still be his opportunity on the open market.

Wheat is no longer procured by quotas. In part, this is because potential domestic procurement is dwarfed by imports, and the government need not rely on such procurement to meet its marketing goals. This, then, is consistent with a quantity planning approach in which procurement is viewed more as a means to assure supplies in a country with under-developed markets than as a source of revenue.[11]

There is another unique aspect of wheat pricing. The ratio of procurement prices for crops like cotton and rice to international prices have fluctuated in the past decades. Nevertheless, the domestic prices have always been below the border price, frequently as much as eighty percent.[12] Not so for wheat. In eleven of the years between 1960 and 1973, domestic prices for wheat were above international prices.[13] Producers, then, received a subsidy, although consumers frequently did so as well. Since 1973, however, following two years of the above trend for international prices and the subsequent devaluation of the Egyptian pound, the domestic price has been below the international one. This pattern is also evident since 1973 with other crops. The implicit taxation of many crops increased subsequent to devaluation and then fell slowly as domestic procurement prices were raised annually.

The comparisons in the preceding paragraph were made using official exchange rates. While the picture is somewhat different using shadow exchange rates, the general pattern remains.[14] The total burden on agriculture peaked in 1974 (see Table 2). One of the interesting features of Table 2 is the gain to producers of meat and milk since 1976. This comes from policies which restrict imports and allow domestic prices to exceed the import parity prices. Producers of berseem, the price of which is determined by demand for meat, have also benefited from the protection of the livestock sector.

Similarly, as vegetables and fruit crops are not taxed as much as other crops, their prices have risen relative to grains and cotton. These distortions of relative prices have contributed to resource allocation in the agricultural sector. While the supply of a single crop may be substantially affected by pricing policies, it is less obvious that the sector as a whole -- with a relatively fixed land base -- is greatly depressed by price distortions. Von Braun and de Haen consider the cross-price effects on various crops along with constraints on inputs -- particularly water-cropping calendar and planting quotas. They estimate that price distortions lead to reductions in agricultural output equivalent to 1.5 percent of national income -- 7.5 percent of agricultural production in 1979/80.[15]

Pricing policies, then, are only a partial explanation for virtual agricultural stagnation in Egypt. Investments, or the lack of them, clearly affect the sector's performance. Much of agricultural investment is the role of the state. In part, this is because of the importance of distributing the flow of the Nile as well as preventing waterlogging. Investment in research and extension is also essential. The share of total government spending devoted to agriculture reached a low point in 1973 and 1974, years in which consumer subsidies were especially high. Since then, total spending on agriculture has grown faster than the total budget, mainly as input subsidies have increased. Agricultural investment has also grown in this period. There is a negative correlation of the shares to agricultural investment and food subsidies.[16] Causality, however, cannot be implied, and it is difficult to say what the level of investment would have been in the absence of a consumer food subsidy program. The relationship of agricultural investment to subsidies is, perhaps, better indicated by looking at total investment and how it is affected by policies which stabilize food consumption. However, before doing that it is useful to look at the distribution of agricultural taxation.

Since levels of implicit taxation are different for various crops, the distribution of the burden on agriculture will vary if cropping patterns differ by farm size. This is evident in Table 3. Small farms, with a relatively high component of family labor, concentrate on meat and dairy, as well as berseem[17] and benefit from the protection of these commodities. Table 3 also indicates that implicit taxation on cereals and pulses is only 25-33 percent as large as taxation on cotton and cane, for which there is virtually no home consumption. Note that this table does not report vegetables and fruits which are commonly grown on large farms. These crops are relatively profitable and to a modest degree contribute to dualism in Egyptian agriculture, but are not major components of the tax burden on agriculture.

## FOOD POLICY AND THE MACRO ECONOMY[18]

Studies of food policies generally deal with micro-level questions such as: how do pricing policies affect consumer budgets or cropping patterns? Clearly, however, interventions on the scale which occur in Egypt effect the entire economy. The issue of food security in Egypt is not so much a question for the agricultural sector -- farm incomes are far more stable in Egypt than in most developing countries due to the relatively reliable irrigation -- as it is an issue of trade stability. While current world market conditions make the likelihood of physical unavailability of imports low, Egypt's reliance on food imports means that its foreign exchange position is sensitive to fluctuation in world food prices. Furthermore, attempts to stabilize food imports transmit instability to other imports, particularly to investment goods, but also to industrial inputs. Scobie found that a ten percent rise in the cost of imported foods will result in a fall of one to two percent of industrial output due to such a crowding-out effect.

Policy interventions used to achieve this stabilization of food imports are not limited to food subsidies, though such price wedges clearly do not transmit fluctuation of international prices to domestic consumers. Subsidies also influence the macro economy through the deficit. Any decrease in government spending or increase in revenue can reduce the deficit. If such a change in the deficit is achieved by a ten percent decrease in the subsidy bill, the net impact on the free market exchange rate would be a three percent increase in the value of the Egyptian pound. Such a change in subsidies would also reduce the inflation rate by five percent of its original rate.

It is, however, a mistake to view food subsidies as either wholly responsible for the deficit or as a zero-sum proposition with government investment. The subsidy bill grew at a time when total resources available to the economy were expanding. Only one-seventh of the *growth* of such resources between 1970 and 1981 were devoted to increasing subsidies. Moreover, public investment -- including human capital investment, i.e., education -- grew faster than did subsidies in that period, while expenditures on defense were substantially reduced.

## PERSISTENCE OF SUBSIDIES

The benefits from the subsidies discussed above are well known in the aggregate and, indeed, are frequently mentioned in speeches as an indicator of the government's commitment to the general welfare. The costs, however, while not as widely known are nevertheless a topic of discussion within the government and in the newspapers. It is not, then, for unawareness of the heavy costs that the subsidies remain. The government continues to subsidize, in part because they want to and in part because they are able to. These two factors have interacted, and at times when ability to pay has eroded, the government has made attempts to moderate the programs. The results of such attempts illustrate further the widespread belief in the moral obligation of the government to provide food and indicates both the set of possibilities and limitations of the government.

### *Ideology and Intent*

Despite the role of external circumstances -- fluctuations of the price of food and oil as well as international politics -- price policies cannot be viewed merely as a passive response to external events. In the three decades since the overthrow of King Farouk, the successive governments have voiced, and acted upon to various degrees, an ideology of socialism and of redistribution. In the first of these decades, equity was largely promoted through confrontation -- appropriations of land and businesses. While the policy continued to the 1960s, partially as a tool to neutralize enemies, the main thrust towards equity was achieved through a more crusading approach; in this period free education and extended access to health and government services was promoted. Subsequently, Sadat recognized some of the economic limitations of the central planning approach to development and allowed for faltering steps towards a more market-oriented economy, using price policies as a means of maintaining some of the equity gains of the previous decade.

The *Infitah* (or "opening up") policy announced in 1974 represented a sharp break with the previous view of the economic role of the state and of the position of foreign investment. Despite the fact that Sadat's popularity was at its apex following the October War, it is unlikely that he could have risked a major break with equity policies at the same time. To allow *Infitah* to be linked in the public eye with massive price changes following the 1973/74 international grain shortage would have pre-judged the experiment in its formative stage. Yet, subsidies continued to grow in real terms after the world price of grain subsided. This is not likely an accident but rather a deliberate policy to compensate the portion of the population who failed to benefit from the general growth of the economy. During this period, subsidies were not merely continued on a constant quota or ration but were at an increased volume per capita -- in rural as well as urban areas -- as expectations and the understanding of the social contract changed.

The term "social contract" is not used just by political scientists for journal articles; it appears in speeches and in discussions on the future of policy in Egypt.[19] This contract is also mentioned in regards to the possibility of compensating government employees for their relative decline in wages during the *Infitah* period. This class of workers, including those in state-owned industry, is both large and concentrated, although not necessarily organized. They have seen their earnings stagnate while wages in the private sector, once below theirs, have risen.[20] Note that to the degree that the government finds it necessary to compensate this sector with higher wages if subsidies should be removed, changes in food pricing policy will merely shift fiscal costs from one item in the budget to another with possibly regressive distributional implications.[21]

*Pricing Policy and Legitimacy*

The theme of social contract can be viewed in terms of maintaining the state's legitimacy. States in transition face legitimacy crises as new coalitions form.[22] Waterbury argues that under Sadat, Egypt approached the limits inherent in the early phases of import substitution industrialization and was forced to make accommodations to technocrats and domestic as well as foreign entrepreneurs.[23] This, of course, risks alienating a broad but weak base of previous support.[24] In order to maintain sufficient room to maneuver, it was necessary for the state to guarantee cheap food, cloth, and energy.

Of course, other approaches are possible. Sri Lanka and Jamaica are examples of states which reversed popular policies of price supports at the same time as they reoriented the economy. Both nations did so, however, only after a clear electoral mandate in which the direction of the economy -- but not necessarily food policy -- was widely debated.[25] Other nations have done so following coups. Sadat, however, had no widely acknowledged mandate -- the referenda he called were neither widely debated nor were the results believed -- and exhibited an ambivalence towards authoritarianism. Discontent had few channels in which it could be heard, yet as events later proved, it was not crushed as completely as under Abdel Nasser. To a large degree, then, food pricing (along with religion) became a focal point for a variety of frustrations. Preempting discontent on food policy, therefore, could assist in preempting general criticism of economic policy.

Widespread riots in January 1977 challenged the entire legitimacy of the state. The riots followed the abrupt announcement of price increases for a number of foods as well as butagas, gasoline, and cigarettes (see Table 4). It is interesting to note that prices for *balady* (coarse) bread, as well as a number of basic food commodities, were not increased. It is a legitimate speculation then as to how much the riots were food riots as opposed to a more general protest galvanized by the proximate incident.[26] They may be considered social equity as much as food riots.

In a similar vein, the warning strikes in Helwan and Alexandria in late 1980 that persuaded the government to cancel a signed order to raise the price of a portion of rationed sugar may reflect the symbolic importance of food pricing rather than any particular hardship introduced by the move. The riots in Kafr el-Dawar in October, 1984 may again reflect a concern over the entire role of the government as much as food prices. In this case, the riots were localized and began as a protest over increases in wage withholdings, unfortunately timed following an announcement of price increases.

In these cases the government responded swiftly by rescinding all price increases. While the extent and bloodshed of the 1977 riots surely represented a threat to the survival of the government, it is less likely that the more recent protests reached that point. Unlike other governments faced with similar demonstrations, the Egyptian government did not choose to endure a round of violence while at the same time blaming international forces for the hardship. The risk that protests over food prices would be tinder to ignite other discontent was apparently too large. The experience has left a legacy. The state has reason to expect riots; the populace has reason to expect riots will achieve price rollbacks. It is likely, then, that the seeds of future protests have been planted.

The government has, however, achieved some reforms of pricing policy. In 1980 bread and flour prices were raised in a complicated minuet with changes of loaf size, extraction rates, baker's protests, and reversals of policies.[27] A similar process has been observed in the six-month period following the Kafr el-Dawar disturbances. During that period, the percentage of loaves available in the market which were made from coarse flour and available at one piaster has declined while more refined loaves at two piasters increased in availability. In this manner, the average subsidy on a loaf of bread has declined -- although with no obvious flash point. In the same period, flour prices have increased to the relative detriment of the rural population.[28] It should be noted that the bread and flour price increases introduced between 1980 and 1985 have more or less kept pace with inflation in that period. The 1984 price increase does not represent an increase in the real price of bread over that period.

Also in 1980, 300,000 families were removed from ration book roles (a reduction of 3.7 percent). These families, however, were still entitled to a quota of subsidized goods but at a higher price. A similar reduction was announced in 1983 and is in the prices of being implemented in autumn, 1984.

The difficulty the government has had in making more than slow incremental changes in consumer price policy has been explained in terms of negative power;[29] while there is no interest group sufficiently strong to regularly initiate policy, many coalitions are in a position to veto change. While this may be a partial explanation, it does not fully explain the willingness to use that veto. To be sure, the poorest members of the society received 15-20 percent of their real income through subsidies, but were they isolated they would not necessarily have the power to protect subsidies. However, on this issue they have similar interests with a broader spectrum of society. There is no obvious coalition that finds it in their interest to deny the benefits of the subsidies to other groups. Not only is the symbolic nature of the welfare commitment important across a number of interest groups, but also the benefits of the system accrue to virtually the entire population. The costs, however, are not obviously ascribed to any group. Taxes on income and capital gains are a relatively small part of general revenues, the majority of which come from profits on petroleum and the Suez Canal as well as from foreign aid.[30] Furthermore, Egypt has not been on the brink of financial crises in recent years and, therefore, has not needed to be tough through a food policy crisis which has a dubious outcome. Under such conditions the broad alliance that protects subsidies need not be deep.

As Waterbury has illustrated, contemporary Egypt has both benefitted from and been harmed by international politics.[31] War with Israel drained resources and derailed Abdel Nasser's development plans. Peace has both gained and lost friends, while geography has guaranteed that the superpowers will not lose interest in the country.

Sadat indicated that the economy was at a "zero point" prior to the 1973 war, after which Arab funds were available. Why, then, did Egypt risk modifying the subsidy system in 1977? Indeed, at that time a number of economic indicators seemed to point toward reduced pressures on the subsidy system. World prices of food had been declining and domestic production of oil had begun to approach exportable levels. The government deficit had declined from the previous year. Even the sizable trade imbalance had declined slightly. Tourism, workers' remittances, and canal receipts had increased, making for a substantial decline in the current accounts deficit.

Trends, however, do not pay bills. Because foreign reserves were limited, aid, investments or loans were needed to fill the gap. Egypt's foreign debt at the beginning of 1977 was LE 4,824 million (seventy-two percent of the GDP of 1976), and further lines of credit were restricted.[32] Some of this debt came from rolling over the short-term loans that were required to finance food imports prior to 1974, when food aid increased.[33] The debt outstanding in 1977 included LE 834 million of these short-term loans, repayable within a year at interest rates of fifteen to eighteen percent.

Though the Gulf Organization for the Development of Egypt, a consortium of leaders from Arab states, refused to grant a loan of U.S.$1 billion to fund the balance-of-payments deficit in late 1976, it granted a loan of $1.5 billion within a month following the riots. Similarly, International Monetary Fund credits, bilateral loans, and credits from commercial banks were obtained in the first quarter of 1978.

In the post-riot years, Egypt was able to pay most of its bills. Furthermore, creditors were not in position, nor were they inclined to demand price reforms. Egypt was able to increase subsidies as they experimented with the implementation of *Infitah*. With increasing aid as well as profits on oil and the Canal, they were able to moderate agricultural taxation. The subsidies were increasingly financed through explicit budgetary allocations rather than by implicit taxation of agriculture. With a broad base, the state no longer needed to rely as heavily on the agricultural taxation for its maintenance and investments. Also in this period, wheat procurement quotas were removed as the state chose to have imports rather than domestic production meet urban needs. Also, a number of producer prices inched upwards at rates somewhat faster than the inflation rate and the rate at which the pound was devalued.

Economic forecasts for Egypt are currently mixed. Furthermore, reliance on tourism, oil, the Suez, and remittances for foreign exchange exposes the economy to risks of a severe downturn due to international events. Nevertheless, debts are nowhere as large, relative to the economy, as in some Latin American countries, and world grain surpluses are sufficiently large to inspire price wars between the United States and France. Egypt, then, has some time to forestall future economic crises that would force it to move abruptly. It has room to seek consensus on the introduction of price reforms or of approaches to raising revenues. If the social contract needs to be renegotiated, it will require more than technocratic input in reaching a new consensus on the obligation of the state.

## FOOTNOTES

[1] Saleh, A. "Disincentives to Agricultural Production in developing Countries: A Policy Survey," *Foreign Agriculture* 13 (1975 supplement) pp. 1-10, lists the interventions affecting producers in 50 developing countries.

[2] Shoshan, Boaz, "Fatimid Grain Policy and the Post of the Muhtasib," *International Journal of Middle East Studies* 13 (1981) pp. 181-9, and "Grain Riots and the 'Moral Economy': Cairo 1350-1517," *Journal of Interdisciplinary History*, 10 (1980) pp. 459-78, report examples of price interventions in two regimes, including a familiar-sounding incident in which market inspectors fixed the price of coarse and fine breads.

[3] This section draws heavily upon Alderman, H.; J. von Braun, and A.S. Sakr, *Egypt's Food Subsidy and Rationing System: A Description*, Research Report 34 (Washington, D.C.: IFPRI, 1982); and Alderman, H. and J. von Braun, *The Effects of the Egyptian Food Ration and Subsidy System on Income Distribution and Consumption*, Research Report 45 (Washington, D.C.: IFPRI, 1984).

[4] Scobie, Grant M. *Government Policy and Food Imports: The Case of Wheat in Egypt*, Research Report 29 (Washington, D.C.: IFPRI, 1981).

[5] This section is based in part on von Braun, J. and H. de Haen, *The Effects of Food Price and Subsidy Policies on Egyptian Agriculture*, op. cit., and Alderman, H. and J. von Braun, *The Effects of the Egyptian Food Ration and Subsidy System on Income Distribution and Consumption*, op. cit.

[6] See von Braun, J. and H. de Haen, op. cit.

[7] See Hansen, B. and S. Radwan, *Employment Opportunities and Equity in Egypt*. (Geneva, Switzerland: ILO, 1982) which is daring enough to suggest a revival of land taxes in lieu of current pricing policies. Ironically, because of a statutory linkage of rent ceilings and tax rates, there has been some support for increased taxation by landowners. Such support, undoubtedly, differs from a base of support for a major overhaul of taxation policy.

[8] An original presentation is available in Landes, D. *Bankers and Pashas*, (Cambridge, MA: Harvard University Press, 1958). See also Rivlin, H. *The Agricultural Policy of Mohammed Ali in Egypt*, (Cambridge, MA: Harvard University Press, 1961).

[9] See Cuddihy, W. *Agricultural Price Management in Egypt*, Staff Working Paper 388 (Washington, D.C.: World Bank, 1980).

[10] See de Janvry, A.; G. Siam, and O. Gad, "The Impacts of Forced Deliveries on Egyptian Agriculture," *American Journal of Agricultural Economics*, 65 (1983) pp. 493-501.

[11] de Janvry, et al., op. cit., address this issue.

[12] Cuddihy, W., op. cit., indicates this using official exchange rates.

[13] See Scobie, G., op. cit.

[14] von Braun, J. and H. de Haen, op. cit.

[15] Similarly, Esfahani, H. "Agricultural Supply Response in Egypt: A System Wide Differential Approach," Working Paper No. 263, Department of Agricultural and Natural Resource Economics, University of California at Berkeley, 1983, also finds only moderate system-wide response to prices.

[16] See von Braun, J. and H. de Haen, op. cit. Shares to nonagricultural investment is positively correlated with shares to food subsidies.

[17] A similar pattern is observed by Soliman, I., J. Fitch and A. Aziz, "The Role of Livestock Production in the Egyptian Farm," Economic Working Paper No. 85, Agriculture Systems Project, (Cairo: Ministry of Agriculture, Cairo, and the University of California, 1982).

[18] This section relies heavily on G. Scobie, *Food Subsidies: Their Impact on Foreign Exchange and Trade in Egypt*, Research Report 40 (Washington, D.C.: IFPRI, 1983).

[19] One also hears the expression "social peace" -- al-salaam al-ijtima' -- mentioned in reference to the persistence of subsidies.

[20] Hansen and Radwan, op. cit.

[21] For an example of this in Sri Lanka, see Edirisinghe, N. "The Implications of the Change from Ration Shops to Food Stamps in Sri Lanka," Paper prepared for the IFPRI Workshop on Consumer-Oriented Food Subsidies (Washington, D.C.: May, 1984).

[22] de Janvry, A. "Why Do Governments Do What They Do?" in *Role of Markets in the World Food Economy*, (eds.) D.G. Johnson, and E. Schuh, (Boulder, Colo: Westview Press, 1983).

[23] Waterbury, J. *The Egypt of Nasser and Sadat* (Princeton, NJ: Princeton University, 1983).

[24] Similar difficulties in liberalizing from quantity restrictions on foreign trade are reported for a number of countries in A. Krueger, *Liberalization Attempts and Consequences*, (New York: National Bureau of Economic Research, 1975).

[25] Hopkins, R., compares Egypt with Sri Lanka in "Political Calculations in Subsidizing Food," Paper Prepared for IFPRI Conference on Consumer-Oriented Food Subsidies, Chiang Mai, Thailand, November 1984.

[26] Similarly, with the 1983 riots in Tunisia.

[27] See Alderman, H.; J. von Braun, and S.A. Sakr, op. cit.

[28] See Alderman, H. and von Braun, J. "Egypt: Implications of

Alternative Food Subsidy Policies in the 1980's." International Food Policy Research Institute, report to the Ford Foundation, Cairo, April 1985.

[29] See Richards, A. "Ten Years of *Infitah*: Class, Rent, and Policy Stasis in Egypt." *Journal of Development Studies*, pp. 323-338, 1984.

[30] Hansen and Radwan, op. cit., determine that taxes in Egypt are slightly progressive -- mainly from import duties.

[31] Op. cit.

[32] *Quarterly Economic Review of Egypt*, First Quarter, 1977.

[33] Goueli, Ahmed A. "Food Security in Africa: With Special Reference to Egypt," Paper presented to "Food Security in a Hungry World: An International Food Security Conference," San Francisco, CA, March, 1981.

**TABLE 1: INCOME TRANSFER DUE TO FOOD SUBSIDIES AND DISTORTED PRICES, 1981-82, IN LE PER CAPITA PER YEAR**

| | URBAN | | | RURAL | | |
|---|---|---|---|---|---|---|
| Transfer from: | Lowest Expenditure Quartile | 25-75% | Highest Expenditure Quartile | Lowest Expenditure Quartile | 25-75% | Highest Expenditure Quartile |
| Ration System | 8.85 | 8.83 | 8.48 | 6.37 | 6.59 | 7.11 |
| | (5.0) | (2.3) | (0.9) | (5.7) | (2.7) | (1.3) |
| Other Government Channels | 18.70 | 20.98 | 22.81 | 12.39 | 11.62 | 16.55 |
| | (10.6) | (5.5) | (2.4) | (11.1) | (4.8) | (3.0) |
| Subtotal | 27.55 | 29.81 | 31.22 | 18.76 | 18.21 | 23.66 |
| | (15.6) | (7.8) | (3.3) | (16.8) | (7.5) | (4.3) |
| Open Market Cereals | 0.71 | 2.62 | 1.34 | 6.58 | 11.62 | 19.30 |
| | (0.4) | (0.7) | (0.1) | (5.9) | (4.8) | (3.5) |
| Other Open Market | -5.91 | -14.85 | -36.57 | -5.26 | -8.65 | -17.59 |
| | (-3.3) | (-3.8) | (-3.8) | (-4.8) | (-3.5) | (-3.2) |
| Total | 22.34 | 17.58 | -4.01 | 20.08 | 21.18 | 25.37 |
| | (12.9) | (4.17) | (-0.4) | (17.9) | (8.8) | (4.6) |

Source: Calculated from Alderman, H. and von Braun, J. The Effects of the Egyptian Food Ration and Subsidy System on Income Distribution and Consumption. Research Report 45 (Washington, D.C.: IFPRI, 1984).

TABLE 2: AGGREGATE GAINS AND LOSSES OF PRODUCERS ON AGRICULTURAL COMMODITY MARKETS, 1965-80

| Year | Cereals, Pulses, and Sugar | Meat and Milk | Feed[a] | Cotton | Total Burden |
|---|---|---|---|---|---|
| 1965 | -432.20 | -152.17 | 163.83 | -528.79 | -949.34 |
| 1966 | -326.70 | -131.55 | 145.10 | -390.78 | -703.94 |
| 1967 | -278.16 | -72.38 | 125.32 | -311.79 | -537.01 |
| 1968 | -337.13 | -131.66 | 112.37 | -357.28 | -713.70 |
| 1969 | -414.40 | -175.56 | 149.16 | -608.81 | -1,041.62 |
| 1970 | -346.71 | -127.76 | 161.09 | -550.49 | -863.87 |
| 1971 | -184.97 | -142.66 | 122.55 | -473.76 | -678.84 |
| 1972 | -205.70 | -165.10 | 135.08 | -448.49 | -684.21 |
| 1973 | -609.26 | -217.37 | 186.10 | -505.04 | -1,145.56 |
| 1974 | -1,407.61 | -75.71 | 225.03 | -805.50 | -2,063.78 |
| 1975 | -1,082.17 | -13.03 | 172.95 | -606.46 | -1,528.72 |
| 1976 | -558.03 | 30.91 | 162.25 | -473.44 | -838.31 |
| 1977 | -190.88 | 54.98 | 104.19 | -605.01 | -636.72 |
| 1978 | -190.32 | 97.74 | 107.74 | -369.25 | -354.09 |
| 1979 | -286.62 | 46.56 | 147.79 | -266.15 | -358.62 |
| 1980 | -327.76 | 128.74 | 144.46 | -319.18 | -373.74 |

[a] This excludes berseem. It should be noted that the producer losses computed for the maize market are compensated for by the implicit producer gains from depressed feed maize prices to the extent that domestically produced maize is fed to animals.

Source: von Braun, J. and H. de Haen, The Effects of Food Price and Subsidy Policies on Egyptian Agriculture, Research Report 42 (Washington, D.C.: IFPRI, 1983).

TABLE 3: INCOME TRANSFERS DUE TO FOOD SUBSIDIES AND DISTORTED PRICES IN FARM HOUSEHOLDS IN 1981/82[a]

| | Farm Labor[a] | Farm Size Classes (*Feddan*)[b] 0-1 | 1-5 | Above 5 |
|---|---|---|---|---|
| | LE Per Capita Per Year | | | |
| Total Expenditure | 189.9 | 238.7 | 274.5 | 388.4 |
| Gains and (-) Losses in Production and Input Use: | | | | |
| Cereals and Pulses | - | -1.4 | -9.4 | -30.9 |
| Meat and Milk | .8 | 6.8 | 17.3 | 15.6 |
| Cotton and Sugar Cane | - | -6.0 | -29.7 | -95.9 |
| Inputs (Subsidies) | 1.6 | 6.7 | 12.9 | 30.6 |
| Subtotal | 2.4 | 6.1 | -8.9 | -80.6 |

[a] Classified by main occupation of the household.

[b] 1 *Feddan* = 1.038 Acres.

Source: Derived from 1981/82 IFPRI-INP survey reported in Alderman, H. and J. von Braun, *The Effects of the Egyptian Food Ration and Subsidy System on Income Distribution and Consumption*, Research Report 45 (Washington, D.C.: IFPRI, 1984).

TABLE 4: PRICE INCREASES ANNOUNCED AND RESCINDED AFTER RIOTS IN JANUARY, 1977

| Subsidized Items With No Price Increases | Items with Price Increase | Increase |
|---|---|---|
| | | (percent) |
| Balady Bread | Fino Bread | 50 |
| Beans | Refined Flour (72 percent extraction) | 67 |
| Lentils | Regulated Sugar | 4 |
| Rationed Sugar | Rationed Rice | 20 |
| Cooking Oil | Tea | Subsidy Cancelled |
| Fertilizer | Butagas | 46 |
| Insecticide | Gasoline | 26-31 |
| | Cigarettes | Various Amounts |

Source: *Al-Ahram*, Cairo, January 18-21, 1977.

# 8

# Politics and the Price of Bread in Tunisia

*David Seddon*

1984 began in bloody fashion in the Maghreb. Violent demonstrations, originating in the impoverished southwest and south of Tunisia at the very end of December and spreading throughout the country during the first week of January, followed the introduction of measures by the Tunisian government to remove food subsidies as part of their "economic stabilisation" programme approved by the International Monetary Fund and the World Bank. The sudden doubling of bread prices was a crucial factor in the outbreak of mass unrest, although official explanations identified a threat from "hostile elements" concerned to overthrow the government. Whatever the reality of this supposed threat to the regime of octogenarian President Habib Bourghiba, the state's response to the demonstrations was itself extremely violent. As the unrest spread, security forces opened fire on crowds in several towns, including the capital, Tunis; at least sixty people were killed -- as many as 120 according to some reports -- and many more injured. A state of emergency and a curfew were declared on January 3rd, public gatherings of more than three persons were forbidden, the prime minister Mohammed Mzali appeared on television to appeal for calm, and the state security forces -- police, national guard (*gendarmerie*) and army -- were visibly and massively poised for further developments. But the demonstrations and street violence continued; on January 4th there were numerous clashes, and on January 5th the army and police fired on "rioters" in Tunis, moving into the old *medina* to dislodge snipers. In the morning of January 6th, President Bourghiba appeared on television to rescind the price increases and promise the restoration of food subsidies -- an announcement evidently received with pleasure and relief by the crowds in the streets. Three weeks later, after a period of relative calm, the curfew was lifted; and by February it appeared that the immediate crisis was over.

As Tunisia returned, warily, to relative normality, further to the west Morocco was experiencing its own wave of mass demonstrations and street violence. Heavy news censorship prevented earlier publication of details, but over the weekend of January 22nd-23rd, the newspaper of the opposition party, *l'Opinion*, reported that the demonstrations had in fact begun two weeks earlier in the south, where drought conditions were particularly severe, notably in Marrakesh, and that troops from the western Sahara and Sidi Ifni had been brought in to quell the disturbances. In Morocco, as in Tunisia, the demonstrations (although in this case developing out of earlier protests at school and university fee increases) were closely connected to official proposals made at the end of December to raise the price of basic commodities, including food, only four months after major increases in August 1983. The proposals for further increases in price followed the recommendations of the International Monetary Fund, which in September had given its approval to a major programme of "economic stabilisation" involving, among other measures, the withdrawal of subsidies on basic goods. As social unrest spread through the towns of the barren and relatively impoverished north of the country, and broke out even in some of the larger cities of the Moroccan "heartlands," it was countered by heavy concentrations of state security forces. Press reports suggest that at least one hundred were killed (as many as four hundred according to some sources) and many more injured and arrested. As in Tunisia, official explanations for the troubles emphasised the role of "agitators" of various kinds. Nevertheless, King Hassan recognised the root cause of the disturbances and appeared on television in the evening of January 22nd to announce that there would be no further increase in the price of basic goods after all. This public statement by the monarch, together with the repressive measures taken against the demonstrators, ensured that "law and order" were restored within a few days; and by the need of January it could be said that Morocco, like Tunisia, had returned to "normal."

But if the immediate crisis for the Tunisian and Moroccan governments was over when the streets emptied of demonstrators and filled instead with crowds openly rejoicing over the decision -- announced by their "supreme leader" -- to halt food (and other) price increases, the underlying economic and political conditions that had given rise both to the upsurge of mass social unrest and to the brutal state actions of January 1984 had not changed. The explanations for "the January bread riots" and for the state's violent reaction lie deeper than in the immediate causes -- those factors which could be said to have triggered off the violence -- although these too require analysis; they lie in a detailed assessment of the distinctive economic policies and political structures of contemporary Tunisia and Morocco which have created such a potential for large-scale mass unrest and have failed to create suitable channels or mechanisms for the effective, but peaceful, expression of opposition to those policies and structures.

## ORGANIZED OPPOSITION OR 'SPONTANEOUS PROTEST'?

Governments commonly identify mass demonstrations of widespread popular anger and resentment as essentially the work of highly organised small groups of agitators -- preferably foreigners or at least foreign-inspired and supported; to accept that large numbers of ordinary citizens may be so moved, and so desperate, as to act openly and violently together would be to admit that deep-seated and intractable problems exist.

In the case of Tunisia, although foreign reports on the violent demonstrations that broke out first in the southwest between 29th December and 2nd January suggested that the doubling of the price of bread and other cereal-based products was largely responsible for the outbreak of social unrest among the poor and unemployed in a remote, arid and underprivileged region, official explanations laid emphasis on the role of small groups of organised agitators with political motives.[1] Thus, the governor of Kebili was reported as stating that foreign-inspired agitators were involved in the demonstrations in Kebili, Douz and Souk el Ahad -- all small southern towns to the east of the great salt depression of Chott el Djerid and to the south of Gafsa ("capital" of the south); while the governor of Gafsa itself identified Libyan -- and Lebanese -- trained Tunisians leading the demonstrations.[2] When, late on the evening of 3rd January, the Prime Minister Mohammed Mzali, appeared on television to appeal for calm, he blamed the troubles on the activities of agitators attempting to overthrow the regime. "There has been manipulation," he said; "the young people have been enticed and misled into demonstrations which appear spontaneous but behind which lies a plan for destabilisation and elements more or less inspired by certain influences whose declared objective is the overthrow of the regime."[3] Mzali said little in detail regarding the character or origin of these "influences," but appeared to allude to influences from abroad, probably from Libya. Meanwhile, in Paris, the Tunisian ambassador assured the French television audience that the price increase "has very little to do with the rioting,"[4] and blamed "uncontrolled elements." A few days later, after President Bourghiba had publicly cancelled the food price rises, Mzali reiterated his conviction that "we found ourselves faced with veritable insurrectionist commandos, well organised and co-ordinated,"[5] and that, but for this, the response to the increases in prices would have been far less dramatic. He argued that the economic imperatives behind the removal of subsidies had been explained to the people and proposals for compensation to the most disadvantaged already made public: "undoubtedly, it was necessary to attack bread; I did it. One must have the courage to tell the people the truth. We did it. But there was this political exploitation."[6]

But if the identification of such elements as scapegoats is not surprising, it must nevertheless be asked whether there was any basis for the conception of a threat to the regime from politically motivated and organised groups. For it could be argued that such a threat, if it existed in reality -- or even was genuinely perceived to exist -- might provide an explanation for the violent response by the state to the demonstrations even at the outset.

It is significant that the disturbance in Tunisia broke out in a region where political opposition to the regime is known to exist and has been openly manifested in the recent past. Only three years ago, Libyan-trained Tunisian dissidents attacked and held for over a week the southern town of Gafsa -- an action which provoked a crisis in relations between Tunisia and Libya. Since that time, economic cooperation between the two countries has increased significantly and relations are, in general, more cordial. But the fact that the majority of the sixty thousand Tunisians who work in Libya come from the south and southwest, together with the evidence of at least tacit support for the dissidents from the inhabitants of Gafsa, undoubtedly accounts to some extent for the government's fear of political subversion in this region. Furthermore, there is little doubt that Colonel Qaddafi's attitude towards the Tunisian regime under Bourghiba is equivocal to say the least; certainly, during the January troubles Qaddafi's public statements were generally critical of the Tunisian government's heavy use of state security forces to quell the disturbances. Also, it is known that Libya disapproved the haven provided by Tunisia for the PLO leader, Yasser Arafat, against whom it had sent brigades to fight in north Lebanon. Was it simply coincidence that the troubles began on the evening of the return to Tunis of the PLO leader? On the other hand, Qaddafi was at some pains to assure the Tunisian regime that he had no part in the organisation of the demonstrations in the south. After a telephone conversation with Mzali, it was announced by the Libyan press agency JANA, Colonel Qaddafi decided to send a delegation to Tunis to emphasise the point and to encourage "co-ordination and co-operation aimed at overcoming the present situation."[7] But concern about possible Libyan connections was reinforced when a pipeline carrying oil from Algeria to Tunisia was blown up on 7th January, apparently by a four-man commando group from Libya.

In both Tunisia and Morocco, observers -- both foreign and indigenous -- remarked on the evidence for agitation by Muslim fundamentalist groups. Some commentators have suggested that growing Islamic fundamentalism in Tunisia enabled groups of agitators to encourage violence against property representing "the symbols of luxury, corruption and foreign influence" and to adopt slogans such as "there is but one God and Bourghiba is the enemy of God."[8] It was observed that

> "the tactics used by the demonstrators in Tunis were reminiscent of those used in Teheran in 1978-79 before the overthrow of the Shah. The pressure of Islamic fundamentalist groups in Tunisia has been growing since then. Last year, for the first time, a group of junior army officers stood trial on charges of propagating religious ideas in the armed forces, while another

group of young fundamentalists were imprisoned for allegedly planning to blow up foreign cultural centres in Tunis.[9]

But this, albeit significant in general terms as regards the growth of Muslim fundamentalism in Tunisia, is circumstantial evidence as far as the January disturbances are concerned. The only direct indication of the involvement of Muslim fundamentalist groups, apart from the existence of some pamphlets and use of certain slogans, was the fact that the minarets of mosques were used, particularly in Tunis, to chant "Allah I Akbar" (God is Great) and other religious declarations during the course of the demonstrations. In neither Tunisia nor Morocco is there reliable evidence that Muslim fundamentalists were significant in orchestrating the demonstrations, although there is little doubt that they were involved and active. Certainly, in the south of Tunisia, where the earliest disturbance broke out, most local sources appear to agree that the role of Muslim fundamentalists -- and indeed, of pro-Libyan or other political groups -- was in fact extremely limited.[10]

Finally, there is little evidence that the parties or tendencies of the far left were behind the demonstrations. In Tunisia, the Mouvement d'Opposition Nationale Tunisien (MONT) claimed responsibility -- from Brussels -- for the demonstrations, and denounced "the repression by the Tunisian security forces of the "hunger rioters" (les insurges de la faim)";[11] but the recognised left-wing parties clearly intervened only after the early outbreak of mass protest, and then only to call on the government to resolve the crisis. The Tunisian Communist Party, for example, wrote to Prime Minister Mzali demanding that there should be "consultations" with all national forces to find a solution to the situation, and otherwise confined itself to condemning the violence.[12] The Mouvement des Democrates Socialistes (MDS) and the Communist Party both criticised the state's recourse to the army and laid the responsibility for the trouble at the feet of the government; both called for a postponement of the measures which had increased prices and referred to the lessons to be learned from other countries where subsidies on basic goods had been removed on the advice of the International Monetary Fund.[13]

There is little doubt that, despite the flimsy evidence, in both Tunisia and Morocco, the regime perceived a dangerous threat from small groups of organised militants. During and immediately after the street violence a systematic programme of arrest and interrogation of known activists was initiated in both countries. In Tunisia, known activists from both Muslim fundamentalist and left-wing groups were taken in for questioning; 30 or so militants of the Mouvement de Tendance Islamique -- which prior to the troubles was seeking to obtain recognition as a political party -- were interrogated, as were numerous Communist Party activists. Nevertheless, despite the fear of a threat from organised political groups, and the undoubted involvement of political activists in the demonstrations, there is little concrete support for the notion that these played a key role in orchestrating the social unrest and the mass demonstrations; it would seem rather, that they -- like so many others -- were taken by surprise by what was essentially a popular uprising and sought simply to join in.

Even the trade unions -- which in Tunisia had organised numerous strikes in 1977-78, culminating in the violence following the general strike of January 1978, when the army intervened and large numbers (estimates vary between forty-six and two hundred)[14] were killed -- were not evidently involved this time. Certainly, the UGTT foresaw the economic and social problems that might arise as a result of a dramatic and rapid price increase, and had sought to negotiate concessions for the poor, and a wage review, before prices were put up[15] -- but their discussions were with the government at top level and did not involve the union rank and file, let alone the organisation of rallies and strikes to back up their position. A meeting was in fact held on 5th January, after mass demonstrations had taken place throughout the country, between the president and secretary-general of the UGTT and government ministers, which produced what the president of UGTT described as "good and positive results."[16] The next day, President Bourghiba announced that the price increases would be rescinded; but it is not at all clear what influence, if any, the discussions with the union leadership had on the decision to reverse the decision on the removal of food subsidies. Mention of a possible general strike was made, but events had gone beyond this threat and it was not taken (possibly not even made) seriously.

One social category that was clearly and importantly involved in the demonstrations in both Tunisia and Morocco -- as it has been in the past during similar outbreaks of social unrest -- was that of the students, from high schools and from universities. In Morocco, school strikes helped to generate the open protest that gradually transformed the generally growing social unrest into overt opposition to the government's economic and social policies, and in particular against further price increases. In Tunisia, particularly in the north of the country students were actively involved in large numbers in the demonstrations. By 3rd January, students in Tunis were throwing stones at buses, shouting anti-government slogans and marching in the streets in solidarity with the demonstrators in the south;[17] during the next few days, as the students took to the streets, the authorities closed down the schools and university. It is interesting to note that those most vocal in their criticisms of the regime during the demonstrations were these children of the middle classes whose standard of living has generally improved substantially as a result of the economic policies of the past decade or so. But graduate unemployment, combined with the effective suppression of political opposition to the regime, ensure that significant numbers of the young, even from the relatively privileged social strata upon whom the regime so crucially depends, are disaffected and highly critical.[18]

Clearly, then, the social elements involved in the demonstrations of January 1984 in the Maghreb were various and diverse; equally clearly, no mass protest or social revolt that continues over a period of even a week can be sustained entirely through totally "spontaneous" action. It must be recognised, furthermore, that in all such essentially popular movements there is a "band-wagon effect." In the case of Tunisia, Godfrey Morrison argued in *The Times*: "as the unrest continued, other organised or semi-organised political forces, ranging from the far left, through Muslim fundamentalists to the well-organised trade unions, all tried to leap on the band-wagon." But, he continued, "the interesting thing about last week's disturbances, however, is that they were caused mainly by the young unemployed, a section of society who until now have been largely ignored by both President Bourghiba's government and political analysts." For Morrison, "right until the movement when President Bourghiba made his *volte face*, cancelling the increases, it was the rage of the unemployed which dominated the protest, and it was they who alarmed the government."[19]

In Tunisia, it may be suggested that the social unrest evolved in two relatively distinct phases: first, it broke out in the impoverished areas of the south and southwest, where the population depends heavily on food subsidies and consumes far more than the national average of around two hundred kilos of cereal products per person per year -- it started as a series of small local uprisings and gradually spread throughout the southern interior. In the second phase, when unrest developed in the north and coastal areas, political orchestration appears somewhat more credible as a factor; and certainly, new social elements were involved. Even there, however, the majority of those involved in the demonstrations were young unemployed people from the "popular" quarters and the shanty-towns. In both Tunisia and Morocco -- the specific immediate causes of the demonstrations -- increased school fees, dramatic price rises in basic commodities (particularly foodstuffs), and perhaps a degree of political agitation -- served to open up deep feelings of resentment and anger that stemmed from the underlying problems that are characteristic of contemporary Tunisia and Morocco: inequality, unemployment and poverty, and a sense of political and social marginalisation and impotence. The social unrest that broke out in January 1984 had its roots in disadvantage and deprivation and -- as far as any such process can be so identified -- was essentially "spontaneous"; as such it appears significantly different from the organised rallies and strikes of 1977-78 in Tunisia and 1979 and 1981 in Morocco, and indicates how wide spread and deep-seated are the fundamental contradictions of Tunisian and Moroccan economy and society today.

DETERMINANTS OF ECONOMIC POLICY

If we accept that the demonstrations and violence in both Tunisia and Morocco were largely triggered off by the increase (or prospect of further increases) in the prices of basic commodities, while the underlying factors were those of inequality, unemployment and poverty, it must be asked why the price of basic goods was to be raised, and why so dramatically. After all, the 1970s provide numerous examples of violent mass protest in response to such measures within the Middle East and North Africa, not to speak of elsewhere (eg., Brazil). In Egypt in 1977, the Sudan in 1979 and in Morocco itself in 1981, "bread riots" were a reaction to major increases in food prices.[20] In January 1977, on the advice of the International Monetary Fund and other financial backers to reduce a massive budget deficit, President Sadat cut or eliminated subsidies equivalent to $700 million annually on a wide range of consumer items; as a consequence, there were significant price rises in many basic goods, notably cooking gas. Street demonstrations, some spontaneous, some well organised, quickly assumed a violent, strong anti-regime character; when police were unable to halt the rioting of tens of thousands of young workers and student in Cairo, Alexandria and other cities, the army was brought in to contain the trouble. Over a two day period, some 80 people were killed, hundreds injured and 900 arrested. Only Sadat's early decision to rescind entirely the price increases averted a more serious test of his regime. In the summer of 1979, pressed by international creditors to cut a massive budget deficit, President Nimeiry ordered increases in the price of several basic commodities; a rise in the cost of food, fuel and transport brought mass demonstrations in the streets of Khartoum and other towns. The police finally gained control after ten days of disturbances, but not without the cancellation of the price increases by the government and direct state intervention to ensure adequate supplies of bread and meat. In Morocco, only three years ago, price increases in June 1981 for a range of basic commodities (notably sugar, flour, butter and cooking oil) provoked a warning strike by the Democratic Labour Federation (founded in 1978 to protest against price increases in staple goods) which in Casablanca turned into violent street demonstrations as workers in both the private and public sectors were joined first by small shopkeepers and then by students and the unemployed from the shantytowns. The social unrest brought special police units, the national guard and finally the army into action; in two days of clashes throughout the city an appalling number of demonstrators were killed: between 637 and one thousand depending upon the sources.[21]

In all three of the instances cited, it is fair to talk of mass movements of social protest. These are importantly different from the organised and carefully orchestrated strikes that were experienced in both Tunisia and Morocco during 1978-79, although those also received very substantial popular support and were subject to severe state repression. (In Tunisia, growing social discontent with economic conditions during the mid-1970s was expressed in a series of strikes; eventually, by autumn 1977 the strikes had reached such proportions that whole sectors of the national economy were effectively brought to a standstill, and the army was called in to deal with the striking workers. In response to this move by the government, the UGTT called a national strike for 26th January 1978, which was observed throughout the country. The hardliners in the cabinet voted for a massive repression of the strike movement with a view to destroying the power of the trade union movement, and when there were disturbances in Tunis during the general strike, the army was given a free hand. Estimates of the number killed in clashes vary between forty-six and two hundred; some eight hundred people were arrested at the time, and shortly afterwards thousands of trade unionists were sentenced by summary courts, while the leadership was arrested and jailed. These demonstrations and strikes did, however, obtain significant concessions in terms of wage increases for those who came within the protection of the law and the trade unions.

Despite the knowledge that raising the cost of living, and particularly the price of basic commodities as a specific policy measure, has in the recent past given rise to widespread relatively effective action in protest, both organised and "spontaneous," the governments of both Tunisia and Morocco decided towards the end of 1983 to adopt such measures. Why, given the evident risk?

First there can be little doubt that pressure from international creditors, and in particular from the powerful International Monetary Fund, to reduce large balance of payments deficits through specific "economic stabilisation" programmes encouraging the "liberalisation" of the economy and the removal of subsidies, has been important in the case of both Tunisia and Morocco, as it was in Egypt and the Sudan. In Morocco, King Hassan himself referred to pressure from the IMF and other creditors to implement austerity measures and further open the economy to the workings of "the free market." Liberalisation and the promotion of the "free market" are part of a package which the IMF has increasingly been making a condition of loans to Third World countries over the past few years. In the case of many countries, such a Tunisia and Morocco, which have adopted broadly "liberal" economic policies over the past decade (and longer in the case of Morocco), these supposedly "new" measures designed to solve critical economic difficulties in fact represent simply "more of the same." But the situation of both the Tunisian and Moroccan economies at the beginning of the 1980s looked grim, and it was clearly believed not only by external agencies but also by the national governments that even more stringent measures were required to improve the balance of payments situation and the medium term economic prospect.

In a period of increasing economic difficulties, given a commitment to the "liberal" approach to the national economy, the economic cost of maintaining subsidies on certain items of consumption may appear to governments too high to be borne, and the social costs of removing these subsidies simply the price to be paid for improved performance. If those upon whose support the government directly depends can be convinced of this need for austerity, and if the most obvious source of organised opposition to such policies can be either muzzled or co-opted by preferential treatment, it may well appear that the social and political repercussions of adopting a "hard line" on subsidies can be managed and controlled successfully.

The annual report of Tunisia's central bank warned last autumn of difficult years ahead. Clearly they believed that an economic crisis was a possibility. In the last few years, lower output and prices for oil and phosphate (the two major foreign exchange earners), a decline in the number of foreign tourists (put off in particular by the relatively high level of the *dinar* and more generally affected by the recession in Europe), and a slowing down of industrial growth, have all affected the balance of trade and balance of payments. In 1983, the trade deficit grew by twenty-four percent to 738 million *dinars* during the first ten months, which led to the restriction of imports of certain raw materials and semi-finished goods to eighty percent of 1982 volumes. Agriculture remained virtually stagnant in terms of output since 1976, and grain imports have become increasingly necessary. Inflation has also risen significantly in the last five yeers, to reach double figures in 1982. Under these circumstances, the burden of subsidies undoubtedly looked heavy to a regime strongly committed since 1970 to a "liberal" economic policy. In 1983, the bread subsidy alone cost around L112 million -- about two percent of GDP; in 1984 it was projected to climb to L140 million. Subsidies on all cereal-based products (bread, cous-cous, pasta) account for sixty percent of the total food subsidy of L255 million (259 million *dinars*).[22]

But, if the deterioration in the state of the Tunisian economy as a whole in the last five years is marked, it cannot be said to have reached a crisis yet. And, in the view of some commentators at least, "the financial need to remove subsidies was not so pressing. Food subsidies amount to two percent of GDP and the proportion of food imports is growing all the time. But Tunisia has not needed loans from the IMF to bail it out, like so many Third World countries. A foreign debt burden of $3.4 billion and a debt service ratio of sixteen percent, are modest."[23] *The Financial Times*, which adheres in general to an economic philosophy close to that of the IMF, observed that "the manner in which the Tunisian authorities set about reducing the growing budgetary burden of subsidies on basic food stuffs provides an object lesson in how not to do the right thing."[24] In its view, it was not the removal of subsidies that was at fault, but the suddenness and the size of the increase in the price of basic goods and the failure to consider seriously the social and political implications. It argued that "neither the IMF not the World Bank advocated, or would have advocated, the approach to subsidies adopted by the Tunisian government at the turn of the year."[25] While this is clearly *not* the case (given the evidence of IMF and World Bank pressure on numerous Third World countries, including Morocco, to adopt austerity measures without delay and with little heed for the social, and even political, implications), it is significant that this view -- that the measures adopted by the Tunisian government represented a tactical, but not a strategic error -- was held by some within Tunisia itself. Thus, the former Minister of Economic Affairs, Azouz Lasram, who had overseen the gradual and relatively trouble-free removal of subsidies on energy prices since 1980, resigned in October 1983 precisely because he was aware that a sudden withdrawal of the subsidy on cereal-based products would lead to unacceptably high price increases, which in turn might stimulate social unrest. Lasram argued that the poorer Tunisians should be protected; yet in the event the price of the *baguette* (mainly consumed by the middle classes) increased by less than that of the popular flat loaf that is the staple for the urban poor or of the cous-cous made from semolina so central to the diet of most in the far south. Also, it appears that the UGTT, although representing organised workers for the most part, also foresaw the economic and social problems that might arise as a result of rapid and inequitable price increases, and had sought to negotiate concessions for the poor and a wage review before prices were increased; certainly, they pressed for compensatory measures at their meeting with government ministers on 5th January in the aftermath of the violent demonstrations of protest, and in fact, the government did announce on television, on 2nd January, that measures would be taken to provide assistance through wage increases and benefit payments of 1.5 *dinars* a month per person (up to a maximum of six persons in a family -- that is, nine *dinars*) for hardship cases. But, as was heatedly pointed out by one Tunisian from the south, "compensation was to be directed only towards those in regular employment. It would not affect peasants, shopkeepers, seasonal and casual workers, or the unemployed -- that is to say, the majority of the people who live in the south. Nor would they affect old people, widows and orphans."[26]

In so far as the government was concerned about the effects of price increases on "the urban poor," it was primarily concerned about the political implications and the response from organised labour and trade unions who, in the past, had resisted such increases determinedly. In the event, however, it was not from organised labour that the protest came, but from the mass of the poor and disinherited, whose political marginalisation, combined with economic disadvantage and social deprivation assure their growing disaffection from the Bourghiba regime.

But the reference to the plight of the peasants is significant; for it is often taken for granted that, while a "cheap food policy" for the urban population results in lower prices obtained by farmers for their agricultural commodities and thus adversely affects both their incomes and output, a policy which reduces subsidies to the consumers of agricultural products tends to increase the price obtained by farmers, thereby stimulating production and raising farm incomes. It is certainly the case that higher prices for grain and other agricultural commodities tend to encourage capitalist farmers and even rich peasants to produce more for the market; but in the case of the majority of peasants, particularly those who depend heavily on the purchase of foodstuffs, including grain and cereal-based products, to maintain adequate levels of domestic consumption because of their inability to produce sufficient on their own small plots, an increase in the cost of cereals may well actually increase their hardship and poverty. In the past, the Tunisian government has guaranteed the price of cereals to the grower in order to increase farmers' confidence and to stimulate increased production, although such measures have tended to aid commercial farmers rather than the mass of peasant producers and to have been directed essentially towards the irrigated and more developed areas of production in the northern and coastal regions, rather than towards the central and southern regions where agriculture remains underdeveloped. Concern regarding Tunisia's poor performance in cereal production over the previous few years may well have been a factor behind the reduction in subsidies on foodstuffs, particularly on grain, for the "liberal economy" model would suggest that state intervention in the form of subsidies and guaranteed prices only serves to inhibit the effective dynamic of supply and demand relations and to suppress the price of grain below its "true" level, thereby discouraging farmers from increasing their production and their commitment to commercial activity. But, as noted above, such measures would tend to have an adverse effect on the livelihood of the poor for whom the cost of bread is a major burden, including the large numbers of rural producers unable to grow enough for their own needs and also obliged to buy food to survive.

When, on 6th January, President Bourghiba cancelled the price increases, he also stated that he had "asked the government to present in three months time a new budget which takes account of the poor and which reduces the effects for them."[27] The new draft budget presented to the national assembly in Tunis in March 1984 included proposals to raise revenues by increasing taxes on a variety of goods (such as cigarettes and petrol) and also to cut back on investment; together, these measures would generate approximately forty million *dinars*. Between March and July 1984 several small price increases were introduced for specific food stuffs and public services; and gave rise to no obvious social unrest. Equally, a slight increase -- up to ten *millimes* -- in the price of bread, semolina and the cereal-based products on 10th July 1984 occurred without any particular reaction from the mass of the Tunisian population.

Why, then, had the earlier decision to put up prices suddenly and dramatically been taken? One of the reasons was provided by Mzali, who is reported as stating, in the course of an interview, that the savings that would have been made through the removal of subsidies and doubling of the price of cereal-based products was around 140 million *dinars*, and he pointed out that "if the government had relied on taxes, all prices would have increased as in 1982 and the government would not have raised a fifth of that amount;"[28] he also observed that increased taxes would boost inflation -- which had been kept at 4.5 percent in 1983 compared with fourteen percent in 1982. Another is the confidence of the government, in general, that they had the strong support of the middle classes and the tacit acceptance of the unions and organised labour -- to whom they appealed through the promise of improved economic performance, wage increases and some concessions for the disadvantage -- for such "tough" measures. Finally, there was clearly a belief that the security forces could, if necessary, maintain control and prevent social unrest. In the event, the security forces were not able to control the social unrest that resulted from price increases effectively; instead the violence escalated and spread. The government had seriously miscalculated both the response of the Tunisian people and the capacity of the state to implement its "new" economic policies.

## THE UNDERLYING CAUSES OF SOCIAL UNREST

All of the evidence suggests that increased prices for basic goods, either actual or prospective, played a crucial part in triggering the violent upsurge of social unrest of January 1984, and that the majority of those involved were young unemployed or casually employed workers and students. It is no accident that, in both Tunisia and Morocco, the demonstrations appear to have been concentrated particularly in remote and under-privileged regions and that when they spread to other areas they mobilised the deprived and disadvantaged of the popular quarters and shanty-towns above all.

### *Regional deprivation and disadvantage*

In Tunisia, the social unrest began in the Nefzaoua, a semi-arid region south-east of the Chott el Djerid -- the salt depression that separates the Saharan south from the industrial north and northeast. The southwest is historically the poorest region in Tunisia; it has the highest unemployment rate, and many workers leave in search of jobs in the more prosperous towns of coastal Tunisia and in Libya where some sixty thousand are employed. It suffered severely from drought during the winter of 1983-84, and in the area south of the Chott el Djerid the date harvest, on which many rely, was disastrous. Poor households in the small towns of Douz, Kebili, el Hamma and Souk el Ahad, who live close to the bread line at the best of times, were particularly badly affected. Neglect of agriculture in the south, combined with the relatively rapid development of industry and tourism in the north and northeast over the past decade, has accentuated the historical regional division between north and south, between the coast and the interior. Even during the colonial period, the distinction between the well-watered and developed agricultural regions of semi-arid central steppes and pre-desert south on the other was marked. Attempts in the 1960s to bring cooperative agriculture to the central and southern regions experienced many problems when they were introduced after nearly a decade of neglect following the departure of the French, and despite ambitious plans for some cooperatives -- like M'Zara in the Sidi Bou Zid complex which was fully operational by 1967 -- social scientists pointed complex which was fully operational by 1967 -- social scientists pointed out at the time the potential for increasing economic and social inequality and the improbability of the official projections of employment and income for cooperative members.[29] These warnings appear in hindsight to have been entirely realistic. But if agricultural development in the central and southern regions has been feeble, industrial development has been virtually non-existent. The districts of the interior, such as Sidi Bou Zid, Kairouan, Gafsa and Kasserine, which have always been economically disadvantaged, received only 3.6 percent of the new factories established during the 1970s. And of the 86,000 or so jobs created between 1973 and 1978 in Tunisia as a whole, around 46,000 were in Tunis and the northeast; only just over four thousand in the south.[30]

*Unemployment*

The connection between economic disadvantage, large-scale unemployment and social unrest in the south of Tunisia was intimate; as one local member of the Communist Party remarked: "in Gafsa, out of 700,000 inhabitants, 12,000 are unemployed. Their role (in the demonstrations, DS) was crucial;"[31] another local observer in Kebili remarked that, if the price of bread was the spark which lit the fire and affected young and old alike, "it was not for bread that the young demonstrated, but because they were the victims of unemployment."[32] Even the minister of the interior, Driss Guiga, declared that the demonstrations in the south had been the work of "out-of-work, unemployed and hostile elements."[33]

In the impoverished regins of Tunisia and Morocco, the lack of investment in the rural areas has stimulated a massive rural exodus; unemployment in the countryside has contributed to the drift to he towns, even within the poorer regions; but in the absence of any real growth in employment possibilities within the urban areas, unemployment has grown there almost as rapidly as the population. In the rural and urban areas alike, unemployment and underemployment are the cause of low income and poverty; they are also the root cause of the frustration and resentment among the growing number of young people unable to find the means to help support their families and themselves.

Statistics on unemployment are notoriously unreliable but a figure for the total unemployed in Tunisia often cited is 300,000 (roughly five percent of the total population and about twenty percent of the active labour force); this is almost certainly an underestimate. With the rate of population increase well over two percent a year, some sixty per cent of Tunisia's 6.5 million inhabitants are under twenty; a high proportion of the unemployed and underemployed are therefore young. And with rapid urbanisation a large percentage of the young unemployed are located in the urban areas, largely in the popular quarter and shanty-towns which have mushroomed in the last ten years. Roughly twenty-one percent of the population of greater Tunis now lives in shanty-town areas; and twelve percent inhabit re-housing settlements. The "city' of 1975, had grown by 1979 to 28,000 and by 1983 had reached 65,000.[34] Morocco also has experience very rapid urbanisation, largely as a result of the massive rural exodus, particularly from the poorer underdeveloped regions; with a demographic growth rate of some 2.5 percent a year, a large majority of the population under twenty, a massive expansion of the size and population of the popular quarters and shanty-towns, and very considerable youth unemployment, the general features of the problem are similar to those of Tunisia, although arguably more serious. Even in 1971, the rate of unemployment and underemployment was estimated at around thirty-five percent of the labour force with half of those recorded as unemployed aged less than twenty-four years; and the situation has worsened, if anything, since that time.[35]

*The cost of living and the poor*

With such high levels of unemployment and underemployment, very large numbers of households rely on low incomes; among the mass of workers and small producers, even multiple activities (several household members in different occupations) often fail to maintain subsistence levels of income. In Morocco, where income distribution is very unequal, the past two decades have witnessed a steady decline in the purchasing power of the poor. In 1960, the poorest ten percent accounted for only 3.3 percent of the total value of consumption, but by 1971 this had declined to a mere 1.2 percent. The introduction to the 1973-77 national plan recognised that "the overall improvement in living standards far from diminishing differentials in standards of living has to a certain extent accentuated the differentials."[36] Between 1973 and 1977, food prices rose by an average of 11.1 percent a year,[37] substantially faster than wage increases, which in any case benefitted the lower-paid and irregularly employed only marginally. The rate of increase in the cost of living and in food prices slowed down somewhat in the period from 1977 to 1980 (with average annual increases in the cost of living between 8.3 and 9.8 percent), but then accelerated dramatically again in the early 1980s (with annual increases of 12.5 percent between 1980 and 1981, 10.5 percent between 1981 and 1982, and 8.1 percent in the first nine months of 1983). By the end of 1983, the cost of food index for Morocco, based on 1972-73 prices, had more than tripled; and in the five months between July and October 1983, largely as a consequence of the August price increases introduced as part of the IMF approved "economic stabilisation" programme, the food index rose 10.6 percent and the general cost of living index by eight percent.[38]

In Tunisia, despite a relatively high average per capita income, of about $1,500, the vast majority of households rely on substantially less than this; income distribution is not as unequal as in Morocco, but there are, nevertheless, substantial inequalities. The recent downturn in the Tunisian economy has seriously affected the situation of the lower paid and the unemployed, who now amount to between twenty and twenty-five percent of the labour force. Wage rises of around thirty percent to basic wage earners in industry in 1981 and 1982 had little impact on those with only seasonal jobs or without employment, or on those working in the now extensive "informal sector." Indeed, it could be argued that there is a significant divide between the organised workers in industry, who benefit from wage increases and from the protection of trade unions and legislation (health, safety, minimum wage, pensions, etc), and the mass of casually, seasonally, and unemployed. For those unable during the past twenty years to improve their incomes (certain sectors of organised labour, the better situated of the small businessmen and the middle classes as a whole) the rising cost of living has been associated with improved standards of living; for those unable to keep pace with the rising prices (the "unorganised" workers who account for the vast majority of the unemployed and underemployed, and some sections of the traditional petty bourgeoisie) the rise in the cost of living had meant declining welfare. As an official in Douz pointed out, with regard to the Tunisian government's proposal to compensate for the price increases by a raise of 1.9 *dinars* on the monthly wage of the most disadvantaged, "but what can Mabrouk, with his eight children, do when a kilo of meat costs four *dinars* and the price of flour is doubled? For the poor, it means despair."[39]

For the lower paid, who constitute the majority of workers in Tunisia and Morocco, and for the unemployed, the rising cost of living has had a devastating effect on their capacity to fulfill even their most basic needs. In a report completed only two and a half years ago, the World Bank suggested that well over forty percent of the Moroccan population was living below the absolute poverty level;[40] in Tunisia, a very large proportion of households in the southern interior live at or below the level of basic subsistence, while in some of the shanty-towns conditions are at least as bad. Infant mortality in the shanty-town areas of Tunis, for example, ranges from 112 per thousand to as high as 169 per thousand, while in the middle class residential area of El Menzah, for instance, it is only eight per thousand.[41]

When President Bourghiba appeared on television to cancel the price increases he nevertheless made some attempt to justify the original decision, remarking that he had been concerned that bread was so cheap that some were feeding their cats on it; such profligacy would be unthinkable for the majority of the population and reveals the yawning gap between the lived experience of rich and poor in Tunisia. According to *The Economist*, "the head of a household of five, earning the minimum legal monthly wage of L90 devotes five percent of his earnings to bread and other cereal products. This figure would have risen to eight percent if the prime minister Mr. Mohammed Mzali had had his way. The difference is not huge."[42] One can only speculate on the reliability of this "data" and stand amazed at the ignorance of the real situation displayed; the vast majority of households in Tunisia rely on incomes well below this "legal minimum wage," and for them, as Engel's law suggests, basic foodstuffs account for a very substantial proportion of total expenditure; furthermore, even a marginal increase in the cost of any one essential consumption item has an appreciable "knock-on" effect on the household's capacity to purchase its other basic requirements for minimum subsistence.

*Price increases and popular reaction*

When the price increase came in Tunisia at the end of December 1983, it was dramatic, and hit the poorest hardest. The price of the seven-hundred gramme flat loaf that is the basic staple for most poor people was raised from eighty *millemes* to 170 *millemes*; cheap bread by western standards, but when the average real income of the majority of urban households is low it represents a significant item of expenditure. In the far south of Tunisia, it was the increase in the price of semolina (used for cous-cous) that created the main impact; as one local explained, "the basic food is cous-cous. We also eat pasta and generally cook our own bread. But a sack of 50 kilos of semolina went from 7.2 *dinars* to 13.5, and a kilo of flour from 120 *millimes* to 295. Here, it was the revolt of cous-cous, not of bread, until Bourghiba stopped these intolerable increases."[43] In Morocco, the major increases came in August 1983, when the twenty percent reduction in subsidies on basic commodities had its first impact: tea (the national drink and much consumed by the poor) increased by seventy-seven percent and sugar by fourteen percent; butter went up by nearly half and cooking oil by eighteen percent; on top of these came increases in the price of soap and candles. On the 27th of December the King announced further increases, and at the beginning of January virtually all basic foodstuffs (flour, bread, tea, sugar and cooking oil) went up by at least twenty per cent, while cooking gas (much depended upon by poorer households) increased in price by five *dirhams* a bottle.[44] And the budget for 1984 proposed further increases still. The effect of these increases was not translated into open social unrest until January; it was reported at the beginning of December that "so far, the population has accepted the austerity measures and appears resigned to the lean years that lie ahead,"[45] but the second round of price rises, with the prospect of more to come, created an enormous sense of despair and anger which required only the trigger of the school strikes and demonstrations to burst out in open, violent protest.

Despite the emphasis in public announcements by the officials in Tunisia and Morocco on the role of politically motivated agitators, it is undoubtedly the case that the governments and heads of state in both countries recognised the massive threat represented by the upsurge of social protest to the stability of their regimes. In both countries, after a week or so of widespread violence and an attempt simply to suppress the unrest by the use of state security forces, both heads of state were obliged to recognise their inability to contain the problem in this way and to announce publicly the restoration of the status quo as far as basic commodity prices were concerned. When President Bourghiba cancelled the increases he stressed that he was concerned with its effects on the poor. "I do not want the poor to pay," he declared.[46] And even before this public statement of "concern," the government had asked the governors of some of the poorer provinces in the south to open public works sites for the unemployed; it was also reported that cash was sent to these provinces "to help the poorer members of the community and the unemployed."[47] In Morocco, King Hassan simply stated that, after having received the results of social investigation he had ordered carried out on 1st January throughout the country, he had decided that there would be no further increase in the price of basic necessities.[48]

If the government in Tunisia and Morocco recognised implicitly the crucial role of price increases in triggering widespread popular protest, the various opposition parties and movements were more explicit. In Tunisia, the Mouvement d'Opposition Nationale Tunisien denounced the repression of the "hunger rioters" by the security forces and argued that the *laissez faire* economic policies of Mzali had impoverished the deprived and enriched the privileged.[49] The Mouvement des Democrates Socialistes and the Communist Party both condemned state repression, and in particular the use of the army and assigned the responsibility for the disturbances to the government; the MDS provided a more elaborated critique of government policy which they argued was largely responsible for the "spontaneous popular revolt."[50]

## PROSPECTS FOR THE FUTURE

In both Tunisia and Morocco, the logic of the economic policies pursued over the previous decade -- economic "liberalism" -- led directly to the growth of inequality, unemployment and social deprivation which itself underlay the discontent and social unrest that erupted at the beginning of the year. Particularly in a period of world economic recession the "open door" strategy for economic development has proved a snare and a delusion. It has been observed, of Morocco, that it "seems to have become imprisoned within the logic of the economic policies pursued by the monarchy, which have resulted in increased food imports, a substantial and expanding trade deficit, and rising dependence on foreign capital and international financial institutions;"[51] while it has been remarked, of Tunisia, recently that "the government's decision to encourage the extroversion of the Tunisian economy has in many respects forfeited Tunisia's ability to determine its own economic future and many potential pitfalls lie ahead."[52] The pressures from the international agencies (particularly the IMF) and from the greater integration with the world economy that come from the increased "outward orientation" of both national economies, certainly provide their own constraints and impetus; but it must be said that the forces which determine economic and social policy are not only those that derive from "outside;" nor is it adequate to see economic policies as simply "pursued by the monarchy" or as a function of "the government's decision." Ultimately, both the economic policies pursued and the social consequences of these policies derive from the distinctive class structure and dynamic of contemporary Tunisia and Morocco and from the dominance of certain economic interests within the political sphere.

There is insufficient space here to attempt to develop a detailed analysis of the contemporary class structure and dynamic of Tunisia and Morocco, together with an assessment of the balance of forces which has enabled certain sections of the bourgeoisie to maintain their predominance in the political as well as the economic sphere, and thus generally to ensure that the governments pursue "liberal," export-oriented economic policies -- over the past decade in Tunisia and for roughly twenty years in the case of Morocco -- to their very considerable advantage ( but also undoubtedly to the general benefit of the middle classes as a whole) at the expense of the majority of workers and peasants. But if the struggle between the various sections of capital, and that between capital as a whole and organised labour, have resulted in the economic or social deprivation of a significant proportion of the population, and in the perpetuation of economic policies favouring big capital in general, it is also the case that these policies have created their own social and political contradictions, as well as deepening the crisis of the national economy. These contradictions are likely to increase rather than decrease in the coming years, particularly if, as seems likely, the world economy does not substantially recover from the recession until the late 1980s or 1990s and the economic problems associated with the pursuit of "liberal" policies in Tunisia and Morocco persist and grow.

As regards agricultural production and food grain availability, although both Tunisia and Morocco are included generally in the category of "major food producing countries" in the North African and Middle Eastern region, projections for cereal production, consumption and deficit indicate that both countries are likely to experience an increasing shortfall in cereals between 1980 and 2000 assuming the pursuit of economic policies encouraging an "open door" relationship with the rest of the region.[53] It is possible therefore to predict increasing pressure upwards on the price of food, particularly cereals and cereal-based products, in both countries.

For the time being however it would seem likely that the governments of Tunisia and Morocco will attempt to pursue broadly similar economic policies, albeit in a more "moderate" fashion given the social unrest created by the attempt to remove basic subsidies; at the same time there are many indications of an initial reaction to the troubles which stresses the need to strengthen the forces of "law and order." On 7th January, Prime Minister Mzali replaced former Minister of the Interior,

Driss Guiga, whose failure to cope with the early stages of social unrest in Tunisia led first to this dismissal and then to his indictment for treason; on taking up this additional office Mzali declared: "the first lesson to be drawn from the event of January is that it is necessary to re-organise the forces of "order" so that they can respond adequately to all situations."[54] It remains to be seen how long such a policy -- which amounts to "turning the heat down slightly and tightening the lid on the pressure cooker" -- will appear viable.

But even if the social unrest of January 1984 does not necessarily oblige an immediate re-assessment of the entire economic strategy (rather than a slight revision of the tactics adopted) on the part of government in Tunisia and Morocco, it may stimulate more serious consideration of an alternative economic strategy, particulary among those whose interests are not best served by the "liberal", "open-door" policies that have predominated in these two countries for so long, and with such disastrous results for the vast majority of the population. It should also require the opposition parties and trade unions to reconsider their own political strategies and to recognise the potential for a broad based working class movement to include the unorganised and unemployed as well as the "organised" workers and dis-affected members of the middle classes.

# FOOTNOTES

[1] In Morocco also, official statements tended to lay the blame for the troubles at the door of agitators of various kinds. For more detailed analysis of the Moroccan "bread riots," see David Seddon, "Winter of discontent: economic crisis in Tunisia and Morocco," *MERIP Reports*, no. 127, October 1984, pp. 9-16.

[2] *Le Monde*, 31st January 1984.

[3] *Le Monde*, 5th January 1984.

[4] Ibid.

[5] *Le Monde*, 7th January 1984.

[6] *Le Monde*, 7th January 1984.

[7] *Le Monde*, 6th January 1984.

[8] *Le Monde*, 6th January 1984.

[9] *The Financial Times*.

[10] *Le Monde*, 31st January 1984.

[11] *Le Monde*, 7th January 1984.

[12] *Le Monde*, 7th January 1984.

[13] *Le Monde*, 4th January 1984.

[14] W. Ruf, "Tunisia: contemporary politics," in (eds.) R. Lawless and A. Findlay, *North Africa*, Croom Helm & St. Martins Press, 1984, p. 109.

[15] The UGTT issued a statement as soon as the increases were announced calling on the government for an increase in wages to compensate, and warning against "the negative and dangerous effects on the purchasing power and living standards of the people of the measures adopted, which cannot but involve increasing tensions in the social climate," *Le Monde*, 4th January 1984.

[16] *The Financial Times*, 6th January 1984.

[17] *Le Monde*, 4th January 1984.

[18] cf. A. Zghal, "La Tunisie, derniere republique civile," *Jeune Afrique*, no. 1205, 8th February 1984.

[19] *The Times*, 7th January 1984.

[20] For a discussion of these, and the factors behind them, see M.G. Weinbaum, "Food and political stability in the Middle East," *Studies in Comparative International Development*, no. 15, Summer, 1980, pp. 3-26.

[21] *Le Monde* (English version) in *The Guardian Weekly*, 12th July 1981.

[22] *The Economist*, 14th January 1984.

[23] *The Financial Times*, 9th January 1984.

[24] *The Financial Times*, 9th January 1984.

[25] *The Financial Times*, 9th January 1984.

[26] *Le Monde*, 31st January 1984.

[27] *Le Monde*, 7th January 1984.

[28] *Le Monde*, 7th January 1984.

[29] M.P. Moore & M.S. Lewis, "Agrarian reform and the development of agricultural cooperation in Tunisia," in *Yearbook of Agricultural Cooperation*,, 1968, cited in R. Apthorpe, "Peasants and planistrators: rural cooperative in Tunisia," *The Maghreb Review*, vol. 2, no. 1, 1977, pp. 1-18.

[30] cf. A. Findlay, "Tunisia: the viscissitudes of economic development," in (eds.) R. Lawless & A. Findlay, *North Africa*, p. 225.

[31] *Le Monde*, 31st January 1984.

[32] *Le Monde*, 31st January 1984.

[33] *Le Monde*, 4th January 1984.

[34] A. Zghal (1984), p.35.

[35] A.M. Findlay (1984), p. 210.

[36] *Plan de Developpement Economique et Social 1973-1977*, Rabat, 1973, vol. 1, p. 14.

[37] A.M. Findlay (1984), p. 193.

[38] Banque Marocaine du Commerce Exterieur, *Monthly Information Review*, no. 46, November-December 1983, p. 26.

[39] *Le Monde*, 31st January 1984.

[40] *The Financial Times*, 24th January 1984.

[41] A. Zghal (1984), p. 35.

[42] *The Economist*, 14th January 1984.

[43] *Le Monde*, 31st January 1984.

[44] S. Bessis, "Mais qui peut-on reajuster dans ce pays?" *Jeune Afrique*, no. 1204, 1st February 1984.

[45] *The Financial Times*, 1st December 1983.

[46] *The Financial Times*, 7th January 1984.

[47] *The Financial Times*, 6th January 1984.

[48] *Le Monde*, 24th January 1984.

[49] *Le Monde*, 5th January 1984.

[50] *Le Monde*, 27th January 1984.

[51] P. Sluglett & M. Farouk-Sluglett, "Modern Morocco," in (eds.) R. Lawless & A. Findlay (1984), p. 89.

[52] A.M. Findlay, "Tunisia: the vicissitudes of economic development," in (eds.) R. Lawless & A. Findlay (1984), p. 236.

[53] N. Khaldi, "Evolving Food Gaps in the Middle East/North Africa: Prospects and Policy Implications," *Research Report* No. 47, International Food Policy Research Institute, Washington DC, December 1984, p. 70.

[54] *Jeune Afrique*, 8th February 1984.

# 9

# Migration and Labor Transformation in Rural Turkey

*Sunday Uner*

## INTRODUCTION

The objective of this paper is to examine aspects of the relationship between migration and rural economy in Turkey with some emphasis on rural employment. Since there are very limited data and available studies on the subject, we are forced to approach the subject matter at both macro and micro levels. Therefore, we begin by discussing rural-oriented policies in Turkey and their impacts on the rural economic structure. After discussing provincial migration flows, we use a macro approach to examine the population, labour force and employment situation in Turkey. Then we adopt a micro perspective to analyze the nature of interaction between agro-economic development and social changes of some selected fifteen villages of different regions in Turkey, focusing on the transformation of these rural communities such as subsistence, transitional and market-oriented villages. In this analysis, we have tried to discuss especially changes in land tenure and labour patterns. Finally, we turn to policy implications of our findings.

## RURAL-ORIENTED POLICIES IN TURKEY AND THEIR IMPACT ON THE RURAL STRUCTURE

In this section, the rural-oriented policies and their impacts on rural structure will be examined from 1950 onward. Agricultural development and structural change in Turkey accelerated in the 1950s. Change may be conceived as the interaction of two processes: the process of agricultural development and the process of change in the social structure. What is to be understood by a structural change in rural areas? This would generally mean a transformation from a traditional and primitive production technology to a new technology which employs modern agricultural inputs, such as mechanization, irrigation, fertilizer use, seeds of good quality, etc. With this perspective in mind, the slow change in rural structure which was observed until the 1940s accelerated during the 1950s.

In the early fifties, the Democratic Party Government used much of the Marshall Aid to import a large number of tractors and combines and to initiate credits for agricultural expansion. This rapid and unplanned mechanization, together with the "priority to agriculture" policy of the party in power, was in the interest of the large landowners and merchants who formed the backbone of the Democratic Party, and resulted in displacing large numbers of small farmers from their land as they could not compete.

The effects of this policy and the subsequent changes can be summarized as follows:

(1) A rapid increase in the number of tractors and combines, and the rapid displacement of the rural labour force.

(2) An increase in the volume of agricultural credits through the Agricultural Bank of Turkey (*Ziraat Bankasi*) and credit cooperatives.

(3) An increased tendency towards intensive cultivation in order to meet the demands of local and foreign markets, and an increase in production of industrial crops, vegetables, and fruits.

(4) An expansion of cultivated areas at the expense of pastures and woodland.

(5) As a result of intensive cultivation, an increased use of modern inputs (i.e. artificial fertilizers, pesticides and insecticides, seeds of good quality, irrigation) by large and middle-size land holdings, and an increase in extension services by the government.

(6) An increase in cash-cropping, integration of farm establishments of all sizes with wider economic units.

(7) An increased tendency to land polarization, i.e. a drop in middle-size land holdings, and an increase in very large and very small land holdings; the transformation of a proportion of sharecroppers to agricultural workers; increased pressure of the rural population on land and induced movement of rural population to urban areas.

The above mentioned developments did not occur simultaneously and in the same direction. Several distinct periods may be observed (Tekeli, 1977). The first period (1948-1956) was characterized by a sharp increase in the number of tractors, namely from 1,000 to 44,000. This increase was due to large imports through the Marshall aid. During this period, industry, construction and transport grew at a sizeable pace, though many people feel that these sectors could have grown faster due to the low baseline. Trade and banking also increased rapidly. Growth in agriculture however, was much slower, even given the major importation of farm machinery. At any rate, the expansion of cultivated land was prominent.

For the first four years of the Democratic Party period, agricultural crops were very good due to good weather conditions, but soon slowed down thereafter. Most of the imported technology was machinery, rather than chemicals and knowledge which could have produced an increase in productivity.

One of the distinct features of this period was an increase in cash-cropping. Farm establishments of almost all sizes began to produce for the market in order to meet local demand, and sought ways to integrate with wider economic units. The volume of agricultural credits increased and interest rates fell. Meanwhile, prices of agricultural products increased. The increase in wheat prices was sixteen percent between 1951-1955, price increases for sugar beet and cotton were twenty-three percent and forty-seven percent respectively for the same period. An extensive highway building programme was initiated. Correspondingly, transportation by tractors increased. Production increases were stimulated by the government's increased grain subsidies and enlargement of stocking capacity of the Government Office of Soil Products, together with the factors stated above.

Small farms which started to produce for the market found it difficult to compete under the circumstances. Since they could not pay their debts, they were forced to sell or leave their land in three or four crop seasons. On the other hand, rapid mechanization soon displaced those peasants who worked as sharecroppers in large establishments. Some of these sharecroppers became daily-paid agricultural workers and some were pushed to urban centers in order to seek jobs.

In this process, one should take into consideration the burden of the high growth rate of the rural population as one of the factors leading to the pressures on land. The so-called rural "push" had been dominant in this period, and the rate of urbanization reached 7.1 percent.

Development tendencies in Turkish agriculture after 1963 had been different in nature when compared to previous periods. Though the number of tractors doubled during this period, the expansion of cultivated areas was limited. This shows that area cultivated by tractors was realized at the expense of area cultivated by draft animals. Agricultural policies in the planned period, foresee the rapid development of the use of modern inputs as well as the increase of tractors and expansion of agricultural credits. As a matter of fact, the increase in the use of artificial fertilizers has been around nineteen fold between 1963 and 1970. The distribution of good quality wheat seeds reached 277,000 tons from 45,000 tons of the 1956-1962 period. Irrigated areas from 1.1 million ha increased to two million ha in 1971. The transformation to intensive cultivation had been prominent in this period. Hence, yields of industrial crops such as cotton and sugar beets have been quite high.

Labour demand in Turkish agriculture was affected by two tendencies (Tekeli, 1977). On the one hand, the area cultivated by draft animals has diminished, and subsequently, labourers were displaced. On the other hand, labour demand has increased because of utilization of modern inputs and production increases registered after the 1960s. However, the high growth rate of the rural population still induced a large flow of rural-urban migration, although the rate of urbanization which has been estimated as 5.5 percent per year for 1963-78, was somewhat lower than in previous years. (Yavuz, Keles and Geray, 1973).

*Changes in Land Tenure and Distribution*

The changes in land tenure and distribution in the last 25 years can be detected from different sources of information such as agricultural censuses and surveys, although these sources employ different coverage and techniques.

Small farm establishments are the major group in Turkish agriculture. The percent of farms in small land holdings below fifty decares[1] was 61.8 percent in 1950, 68.8 percent in 1963, and reached 72.9 percent in 1973. Areas cultivated by these small holdings covered 19.9 percent of the total areas in 1950, 29.0 percent in 1963, and 26.3 percent in 1973 and 20.1 in 1980. The average cultivated area per holding for small holdings below fifty decares was 25.2 decares in 1950, and dropped to 19.9 decares in 1973 indicating that decreasing size of small farms is an important problem.

On the other hand, the ratio of small and medium-sized land holdings between fifty to five hundred decares to total land holdings, which was 36.8 percent in 1950, showed a declining tendency and dropped to 30.7 percent in 1963, and 26.3 percent in 1973, then increased 39.8 percent in 1980. But areas cultivated by these holdings rose from 54.8 percent in 1950 to 58.3 percent in 1973, and further to 70 percent in 1980. Correspondingly, the average size of land holdings rose gradually from 124 decares to 133 decares.

The ratio of land holdings above five hundred decares was 1.6 percent of the total land holdings in 1950. This ratio dropped to 0.8 percent in 1973, to 0.4 in 1980. Areas cultivated by these holdings dropped from 26.3 percent in 1950 to 15.4 percent in 1973, and to 9.0 percent in 1980. The average size of holdings above five hundred decares was 1,357 decares in 1950 and 1,337 decares in 1973. (Table 1 shows some of these changes between 1963 and 1973).

It seems that land concentration in the form of extremely large farm establishments is not the case in Turkish agriculture. But such observations should not lead us to minimize the phenomenon of large landownership.

The Gini co-efficients as measures of inequality in land distribution, indicate also the above mentioned changes. The Gini co-efficient has been calculated as 0.591 in 1963, with a slight rise it became 0.605 in 1970, and has been calculated as 0.661 for the period 1970-1973 indicating increasing inequality in the distribution (Varlier 1978b).

Changes in land tenure and distribution by geographical regions seem more striking. In all regions, both the number of small land holdings (below fifty decares) and its share in the total land increased for the period 1950-1973. This increase is more pronounced in the Aegean and Marmara regions and in the Mediterranean region. The share of small land holdings in the Central Anatolian region remained the same. The shares of small holdings in Eastern Anatolia and especially in the Black Sea region, however, decreased (Varlier, 1978). A drop in the average cultivated area per holding below fifty decares may be observed specifically in the Black Sea and Mediterranean regions. Their average size dropped from twenty-five decares to fifteen decares during the same period indicating that the process leading to decreasing size of small farms is more rapid in the above-mentioned areas and in the Aegean and Marmara regions.

Meanwhile, the number and shares of land holdings above five hundred decares have been increasing in Central Anatolia and the Eastern Anatolia regions, and shares of holdings in the Black Sea, Aegean, and Marmara regions have decreased. In the Mediterranean region, although the number of large holdings has decreased, the total area of these holdings has increased. In this region, where modernization of agriculture and integration of farm establishments to national economy is taking place rapidly, a major tendency in land tenure becomes apparent: land control is increasingly concentrating into fewer hands. The average size of holdings above five hundred decares in this region was 514 decares in 1950 and rose to 859 decares in 1973.

As the average size of holdings above five hundred decares in the Aegean and Marmara regions remained the same for the same period, it increased from 1,206 decares to 1,381 decares in Central Anatolia, from 1,414 decares to 1,853 in Eastern Anatolia, and from six hundred decares to 788 decares in the Black Sea region.

Modernization of agricultural production in the sense of use of inputs such as fertilizers, pesticides, etc., but particularly in the sense of mechanized agriculture, is especially conspicuous in regions where the transition from subsistence to commercial agriculture is most advanced, notably the Aegean Valleys, coastal areas and the Cukurova area around Adana in Southern Turkey. Here high price support policy favoured all agricultural producers including also small and minimum-size farms.

On the Central Plateau where cereal production is largely practiced by extensive use of tractors, the share of large establishments on total holdings has increased, whereas in the Aegean, Marmara and Black Sea regions where industrial crops are cultivated, it has decreased. On the other hand, in the Mediterranean region where industries based on agricultural products are being developed, large land owning industrialists tend to cultivate larger areas in order to supply more raw materials to their industrial establishments.

Finally, and apart from regional diversities, the "modernization" process in agriculture and high population growth has led to an increase in the number of landless families. The proportion of landless families was 9.1 percent in 1963, rose to 17.5 percent in 1968, and reached 21.9 percent in 1973. Landless families and small landowners resort extensively to renting small-size land plots.

On the other hand, big landowners also rent small-size land plots, leading to a greater share of land under their effective control and to rapid land polarization. Table 2 contains a record of both types of renting and it is therefore not very easy to interpret since it includes both small-scale farmers operating plots which they do not own, and large-scale farmers, presumably renting and resorting to hired workers or other systems of indirect operations.

With this picture of landownership in mind, we now turn to a detailed picture of labor migration in Turkey.

## MIGRATION FLOWS IN TURKEY (1965-1970)

### *Types of Migration Flows in Turkey*

The statistics on population movements in Turkey are rather limited. Some of the sources, namely the 1968 and 1973 Surveys on "Family Structure and Population Problems of Turkey," conducted by the Hacettepe Institute of Population Studies, have limited coverage, being based on a small sample of "households."

The 1970 Population Census conducted by the Turkish State Institute of Statistics has, for the first time, probed the migration phenomenon between Turkish provinces over the period of 1965 to 1970. The 1970 Population Census reveals de-facto residence status of the population as on the date of census (25 October 1970), as well as their usual place of residence in 1965. This census accordingly offers good possibilities of study of the rather permanent rural-urban migration behaviour between 1965 and 1970 at the level of each of the sixty-seven provinces of Turkey.

A study by Uner (1977) investigates the general nature and characteristics of rural-urban population movements at the provincial level in Turkey between the intercensal period of 1965 and 1970. In order to understand the volume of rural-urban migration of each province in Turkey, the author observes other types of population movements at province levels. Therefore, three aspects of migration behaviour in each province have been considered.

(1) Rural-urban migration from one specific province to sixty-six other provinces.

(2) Rural-rural migration from one specific province to sixty-six other provinces.

(3) Urban in-migration to a specific province from the rural areas of sixty-six other provinces.

The analysis covered in this study focuses attention primarily on demographic, social and economic correlates of rural-urban migration behavior at the provincial level. Rural-urban migration behaviour does not reveal itself unless "push" and "pull" factors are isolated. "Push-factors" are termed as those which cause out-migration and "pull-factors" are those that are responsible for attracting in-migration. The "push-pull" theory has been enriched by many recent authors including Everett (1966), Bogue (1968), and Todaro (1969). In addition, many country studies on internal migration have shown that an individual decision to migrate depends not only on "push-factors," or "pull-factors," but very often on the counteracting effect of a number of push and pull factors.

The demographic factors include the age factor, growth rate of population (for both sexes), and child-woman ratio. The socio-economic factors include land/man ratio, index of landlessness, mechanization in agriculture, income factor, employment factor, occupational factor, accommodation potential, labour force participation rates, aggregate investments, and educational investments.

A detailed probe into the rural-urban migration behaviour of all provinces has also been made. Two separate regression models have been used for each province. First, a regression model has been attempted to ascertain how far rural-urban out-migration rates are influenced by the so-called "push factors" mentioned above. These have been applied for male and female rates separately. Second, another regression model has been attempted to ascertain how far urban in-migration rates (from rural areas only) are influenced by the so-called "pull-factors" stated above. The second model has also been applied for males and females separately.

*Migration Behaviour at Inter-Provincial Level*

a) *Rural-urban Migration Behavior:*

Broadly speaking, the major source area for rural-urban migration appears to be the north-northeastern belt of provinces. This belt runs from Artvin in the northeast to Bilecik in the northwest. Another belt starting from Kars and ending in Kirsehir and Nigde (at the central Anatolia) parallels the first one in the south. These two belts have some islands of stability: provinces such as Trabzon, Samsun and Zonguldak on the Black Sea coast and Amasya and Tokat on the inland. Provinces with the highest rural-urban migration rates are Gumushane, Sinop, Cankiri, Kastamonu, and Yozgat.

These two belts of out-migrating provinces are more pronounced for males than females. Rural-urban migration rates for males are higher than the rates for females. Hence the second belt includes more provinces for male migration: Malatya and Adiyaman in the south and Agri in the east, leaving Elazig and Kayseri as islands of stability. Afyon and

Kirklareli are the only provinces in the western part of Anatolia which show rather a mild rural-urban migration for both sexes. In the case of male migration, Burdur and Canakkale should also be included.

b) *Rural-rural Migration Behavior:*

Rural-rural migration behavior is stronger than rural-urban migration behavior for the majority of the provinces. The patterns which we have observed for rural-urban migration are more established for rural-rural migration. We can identify a more solid belt running from Artvin in the northeast to Adirne in the northwest, leaving only Zonguldak and Istanbul which are in-migrating provinces.

The second and rather lengthy belt running from Agri and Van in the east to Izmir in the west, has been surrounded in the north by provinces such as Tokat and Corum as islands of stability, and by provinces such as Ankara, Eskisehir and Bursa which are in-migrating provinces. The same belt is surrounded in the south by provinces stretching from Diyarbakir and Mardin to Antalya and Isparta. These provinces are also stable in terms of in- and out-migration. On these two belts, Hakkari, Van, Gumushane, Sinop and Nevsehir mark themselves as provinces with the highest rural-rural migration rates.

It is interesting to observe the directions of streams both for rural-urban and rural-rural migration from the same source (rural areas of a specific province). For most of the cases, the direction of rural-urban migration is towards the developed provinces. Istanbul, Ankara and Izmir provinces, seats of the three big urban centers, are the destinations of migrants. Then Bursa, Kocaeli, Sakarya, Zonguldak and Balikesir, are the provinces of destination for migrants of rural origin. These are all developed provinces. In addition to these provinces, neighboring provinces are also places of destination for rural-rural migration. The 'distance effect' is more valid for rural-rural migration in Turkey.

c) *Inter-Provincial Urban In-Migration Behavior*

Inter-provincial urban in-migration behavior shows rather a distinct pattern. Provinces with high urban in-migration form a rather high concentration belt running from Icel and Adana in the south, to Istanbul in the north via Kirsehir, Ankara, Eskisehir, Bilecik, Bursa, Kocaeli. This concentration belt is flanked both to the north and the south by provinces with high rural-urban migration rates.

Another pattern can be observed both in the west and the east as concentration pockets. One concentration pocket in the west is the province of Izmir, Manisa and Balikesir. Another pocket consists of the provinces of Burdur and Isparta. These are fed not only by surrounding and rather high out-migrating provinces, but also from two high rural-urban migration belts running from east to west as mentioned earlier. The concentration pockets in the east are provinces of Bingol, Diyarbakir, Bitlis, Siirt, Van and Hakkari in the southeast, and the provinces of Trabzon,

Rize, Erzurum, Erzincan in the northeast. Although these provinces are rather less developed, the construction of the Keban Dam (the biggest ever built in Turkey) between 1965 and 1970, is the main cause of the first concentration. For Hakkari, one of the least developed provinces in the country, the high urban in-migration rate can be explained by the construction of a new and modern prison during the same period. Hence, one could observe only the pseudo, compulsory type of migration (i.e. transfer of prisoners from other provinces) for that specific province.

*The Correlation Coefficients Involving Rural-Urban Migration*

The study reveals that urban in-migration rates show rather high correlations, more than those observed with rural-urban migration rates. This observation is especially valid for associations which are statistically significant.

In the push set, the growth rate of rural male population (GROPRUM) has shown the highest positive correlation with rural-urban out-migration rates indicating that out-migration rates increase in response to higher fertility rates. Similar observations can be made for rural females. There, the child-woman ratio (CHWORF) as a crude measure of rural fertility has also shown the highest positive correlation with out-migration.

The land-man ratio (LAMNR) has shown positive association with rural-out-migration rate somewhat contrary to expectations. Availability of more land per person could also mean the concentration of land, fewer people, together with the mechanization of agriculture and hence pushing people urbanward.

Mechanization in agriculture (MCAGR) has shown positive correlation with rural-urban migration rate as expected. Similarly, the index of disownment of land or landlessness (IDOLR) has shown positive correlation as expected. The occupational factors have shown correlations with mixed signs.

In the pull set, the industrial employment factor (INEMU) has shown the highest positive correlation with urban in-migration rate. This can be observed for both sexes.

The educational investments (EDINVT) have also shown high positive correlation with urban in-migration rate as expected. This can also be observed for both sexes.

The wage-income factor, (WAINU) has shown positive correlation with urban in-migration rate. On the other hand, occupational factors such as agricultural occupational factor for males (AGOCUM), has shown negative correlation with the in-migration rate. Industrial occupation factors for males (INOCUM) and service occupational factors for males (SVOCUM), as may be expected, have shown positive correlation.

Finally, the correlation between the in-migration rate and the female participation rate is also positive.

*The Regression Analysis*

The study emphasizes that at province level, the pull factors are having more pronounced effects than the push factors. This can be better observed from Appendix 2 which presents the coefficients of multiple determination ($R^2$) for each province's regression as pull and push model. The coefficient of multiple determination[2] is often interpreted as an indication of the extent to which a model succeeds as an explanatory framework. Push factors are dominant only in a few provinces like Adana, Icel and Maras, both for males and females, and in a few provinces like Afyon, Bitlis and Urfa, only for females.

*Rural 'Push'*

In order to analyze the determinants of the rural "push," we must understand and focus more on the mechanism of the changes in Turkey's rural structure outlined earlier. When agro-technical changes and innovations were introduced and relations with wider economic units began, changes in rural communities were different in areas where small or big landownership was dominant.

In areas where big landowners and share-croppers had prevailed, transition to a new agricultural production pattern, based on mechanization, irrigation and fertilizing, took place after the Second World War. As big landowners had the controlling power, they adopted modern technologies easily through agricultural credits and hence increased their production capacities three- to eightfold. This enabled them to pay their debts and to transform their farms into big modern agricultural enterprises. The peasants, previously working on these farms as share-croppers, were forced to leave the land as machines replaced them over a period of three or four crop seasons. Some became daily-paid agricultural labourers on jobs not yet fully mechanized, and the rest had to migrate to towns and cities in order to seek jobs. This transformation reveals that the old "feudal" relationships have disappeared, both for the peasants and the landlords, and a new form of relationship has emerged.

The old self-sufficient small landowners were also under the influence of this process of producing for the market with modern technology. The entire pattern of social relations of these types of peasants began to change also. In the process of modernization, these small landowners with very little surplus lost their land through the credit-interest mechanism and were transformed into landless agricultural labourers within a certain period of time. Observations have shown that when such a technological change from ox-drawn plough to tractor (involving also introduction of artificial fertilizer) occurs by borrowing money in land holdings approximately below two hundred decares, the payment of debts is very difficult. Thus, the peasants are forced to sell their land within a period of five years or so to pay their debts. This size of land does not seem large enough to repay the credit which is necessary for investment in order to transfer to a new operational unit. The land of those who undertake such a task is procured by one or two newly emerged rich peasants who expand their own land up to one thousand or more decares. The newly rich peasants are consequently able to hire wage labour and acquire the power of big landowners.[3]

Apart from this process of structural change in rural classes, there is another type of transition which is quite prevalent in Turkey and requires attention. This transformation reveals itself as a semi-developed social order in which self-sufficient small landowners who want to produce for the market without proper social and economic organization, find it difficult to establish the required production and marketing relations. It is most important for these peasants to establish market relations through a credit system. Some town merchants who are not directly involved in agriculture try to facilitate this relationship. It seems that not only the size of the land, but the type of crop, causes this sort of relationship. Usually crops can be produced with the labour force of a household without the aid of any machine. But transportation and the necessary steps for selling the crop in the market requires the aid of that merchant. As the peasant devotes all his land to marketed crops, he soon becomes dependent upon that merchant who lends the required cash money for consumption and other expenditures as well. Thus, the merchant plays a role in the social security of the peasant apart from being a mediator in his market and other relations. After establishing this sort of relationship between the peasant and the town-merchant, the latter is much more resistant to changes in the social structure than the former.

The peasant-merchant relation is a new one which did not exist in the previous order. But it also represents a structural change as clear as the transformation of big landowners to modern commercialized farmers, or the transformation of share-croppers to agricultural labourers. The peasant-merchant relations is a kind of buffer mechanism which has emerged under the pressure of social change in order to decrease the social tension, and maintains the integration of relations which will assist the adjustment to the new social order. But once it becomes a part of the structure, this state of semi-development obstructs the change from going further and reaching a certain stage of evolution.[4] Thus, in the areas where production of small landowners is transferred to the market through a merchant, social change is rather slow and lacks dynamism. This is particularly true of the areas where peasants transform to agricultural labourers.

Today, the "peasant" class of the old feudal structure has been differentiated into the following basic groups who control agricultural production:

(1) Big landowners: The agricultural production of this group is based on modern commercialized farming, as well as on traditional methods of farming still utilized by some families.

(2) Newly-emerged middle-size landowners: These are the farmers who have increased their lands from approximately two hundred decares to two thousand decares through the process of rapid polarization of land. They employ wage-paid agricultural labourers.

(3) a) Peasants who have lost all of their small land through the above mentioned mechanisms and who have transformed to agricultural labourers.

b) Small landowners at subsistence level who have to work partly as agricultural labourers.

c) Peasants who are still share-croppers.

(4) Small landowners who engage in cash-cropping but under the control of the town merchants.

(5) Town merchants who control agricultural production though they do not live in the villages.

Among these groups, the direction of change of the first and second groups is towards more control of production. These large and middle-size agricultural establishments seem to invest and/or transfer their agricultural profits partially to industry and mostly to import activities. All the sub-groups of Group 3 consist of the working class whose labour power obviously has been left to the control of the other classes. They preserve their dynamism (dynamism for social change) in order to increase their share in the benefits of production and participate in their distribution. The fourth group is composed of transitional strata with a very limited control of their production, although they own their land. On the one hand, they preserve the ownership of land, and on the other hand, they are very dependent upon town merchants. Hence they strive to keep the status quo in order not to lose their land. The town merchant (Group 5) who emerged under the new social order, benefitting from the lack of social security institutions in the rural areas for small landowners, struggles also against a change in the present system.

Among these groups, 3a, b, and c, seem to be the potential migrants. Regression results for the push model should be interpreted in the light of the above mentioned processes. The determining push factors do not differ much by sex. Usually, the joint effects of demographic and economic factors are the causes of rural push. Crude fertility increases such as growth rate of male population (GROPRM) and child-woman ratio (CHWOUF) are some of the main factors affecting migration behaviour in rural areas. In other words, rural-urban migration rates increase in response to higher fertility rates. The other push factors are the lack of service, industrial and even agricultural occupations (SVOCRM, SVOCRF, INOCRM, and AGOCRM, AGOCRF) for both males and females. In some Black Sea provinces, the high ratio of landless families (IDOLR) seems a major factor for rural push. Similar to occupational factors, migration rates are negatively associated with labour force participation rates.

In summary, the effects of push factors on rural-urban migration between 1965-1970 are rather limited. This is partially due to the fact that transformations from extensive to intensive agriculture after 1963, have increased the demand for labour. But, on the other hand, population pressure in rural areas still prevails and shows itself as the major factor of rural push.

*Urban 'Pull'*

In the majority of provinces, more than fifty-five percent of the variations of the urban in-migration rates is explained by the macro-measures of the socio-economic variables included in the "pull model." Particularly in some metropolitan areas like Istanbul, Kocaeli, a large part of the in-migration behaviour (more than seventy percent of the variation) is explained.

It is interesting to see that the industrial employment factor (INEMU) invariably becomes the dominant factor of the urban pull. Out of the sixty-seven provinces, in sixty-one provinces (for males) and in forty-six provinces (for females), (INEMU) is one of the major determining factors. The second major determinant of the urban in-migration behaviour is the availability of educational opportunities (EDINVT), defined as per capita educational investment. This factor appears in half of the regressions (both for males and females). Among other factors, the availability of service occupations (SVOCUM) in big metropolitan areas, and availability of accommodation (ACCOMP) for some urban centers, can be mentioned.

How are we to interpret these results? (EDINVT) can better be explained as educational attainment being one of the effective means of social mobility in Turkey. In explaining (INEMU), economic factors at this point have generally been emphasized as the primary motivation for internal migration, particularly for rural-urban migration.

Though the economy is shifting over to an industrial-based one, the balance of the labour force still resides in agriculture. For example, the distribution of the labour force by major economic sectors in 1965 was 71.4% in agriculture, 10.2% in industry, and 18.4% in services. The distribution has changed to 67.0% in agriculture, 12.1% in industry, and 20.9% in services in 1970. At the moment, although manufacturing output is expanding quite fast in Turkey, employment is growing less rapidly. Between 1965 and 1970, the value added of manufacturing increased ten percent per year (National Income and Expenditures of Turkey, 1948-1972, Table 9), while the number of workers in manufacturing only increased by 4.8 percent per year for the period (Census, 1965; Table 42; Census, 1970 -- sampling results, Table 7). Since much of the new investment in industry is on machinery of a fairly capital-intensive nature, manufacturing employment may grow even more slowly over the next few years.[5] Since the rate of urbanization is faster than the rate of growth of manufacturing employment, the major absorption of migrants has occurred in the service sectors: commerce, public services, and finance. For example, between 1965 and 1970, the value-added of commerce increased by 8.1% per annum while the increase in commercial employment was 15.6% per annum. Public services increased its value-added by 6.4% per year, and its share of employment by 13.8% per year. Finance also absorbed more labour than its increase in value-added would suggest, but this was from a low baseline (National Income and Expenditures of Turkey, 1948-1972; Table 9; Census 1965: Table 42; Census 1970 -- Sampling Results, Table 7).

Because of the slow increase in manufacturing employment (and the drop in agricultural employment), the majority have been pushed into jobs which show a very slow growth of productivity. Services are a residual employment category, and the concept in this case is slightly misleading for it involves all kinds of very unproductive and unofficial jobs: Part-time unskilled labourers, petty tradesmen and artisans, street sellers, petty services, as well as government employees and actually productive services. Tekeli has shown that the growth of a marginal sector has grown proportionally to the growth of urban areas.[6] Thus, one of the consequences of population growth is to shift the bulk of the population increases on to the urban areas, where the effects on the society and on the persons themselves become most evident.

Recent studies by Todaro and Harris, among others, have attempted to explain rural-urban migration flows in terms of economic behavioral models.[7] Formulating his model on the lines of permanent income theories (rather than wage differential theories), Todaro employs as the decision variable rural-urban expected income differential, that is, the income differential adjusted for the probability of finding an urban job. The crucial assumption in all these analytical migration models is that "rural-urban migration will continue so long as the expected urban real income at the margin exceeds real agricultural product." "Marginalization" of large urban centers, or the development of shanty towns and squatter settlements, can be explained by what Todaro calls a "two-stage migration phenomenon." Initially, the rural unskilled migrant workers can only be absorbed into the traditional urban sector; only after some time will he be able to obtain a more permanent job in the modern sector.

However, as suggested by others, rural-urban migration is motivated not only by the expected income differential between the rural sector and the modern urban sector, but also by the expected income differential between the rural sector and the traditional urban sector. Actually, real incomes of workers in the traditional urban sector are substantially higher if we include in their average earnings the subsidies that the urban community provides in terms of education, health and other public services, and cultural amenities, which persons in rural areas do not normally receive. Hence, paradoxically, although there may exist positive marginal productivity of labour in agriculture, continuing rural-urban migration in the face of substantial overt unemployment in urban areas probably does represent an economically rational decision on the part of the migrants.

A substantial flow of remittances from urban to rural areas also occurs as migrants send part of their earnings back to their families. This has the effect of reducing to some extent the apparent urban-rural income differential and is more efficient in some ways than moving more people. This transfer process also has the effect of raising the real utility or consumption value of the money so transferred: because prices are likely to be lower in the rural areas and because monetary income is more scarce, the marginal utility of monetary income is likely to be greater there than in the cities.

Income differentials and unemployment are actually only intermediate variables. The more fundamental factors are the rate of natural increase (supply factors) and the economic growth rate (demand factors), and hence the basic variable to consider is the population increase rate relative to the economic growth rate. Even if the rural natural increase rate is below or equal to the urban rate, the usual bias in the economic development in favour of the urban economy will generate net rural-urban migration. Unfortunately, many recent development plans, in their attempt to foster rapid economic growth, continue to give priority to development of urban infrastructure and public services while neglecting the need for these services in the rural areas. This fosters the flow of rural migrants to the cities.

## EFFECTS OF MIGRATION ON THE STRUCTURE OF THE RURAL ECONOMY

### *Population and Labour Force*

The level of fertility in Turkey, as a whole, has shown a considerable decline in recent years. The total fertility rate was 6.19 in the 1960s and was estimated to have dropped to 4.97 between 1970-75. However, regional differentiation retains the same old pattern. The fertility rates of the Western and Southern regions are lower than those of the Eastern and Black Sea regions. The fertility rate of rural areas dropped to 5.3 in 1973 from a rate of 6.1 in 1967-68. Similarly, the desired number of children dropped to 2.6 in 1973 from 3.2 in 1963.

The mortality rates also show regional variations. The infant mortality rates retain their high level although declining slowly over time. The infant mortality rate was 180 per thousand in 1962-1963, dropped to 158 in 1966-67, and to an estimated 130 for the period of 1970-1975. Although the adult mortality rate is low, life expectancy at birth is still well below the level of developed countries.

Urban centres are attracting people from rural areas through industrialization; thus, rural-urban migration continues. The volume of migration was around 880,000 for the period 1960-65; it is estimated that the volume of rural-urban migration reached 2.8 million between 1970 and 1975. Hence, the share of rural-urban migration in the process of urbanization increased from 42.6 percent in the 1960s to 63.0 percent in the 1970s. As migrants from rural areas are young, a negative effect on the age structure of rural areas is inevitable.

Another factor affecting the fertility and overall growth of the Turkish population is international migration as an extension of internal movement. By May 1977, 72.7 percent of the Turkish labourers abroad were located in the Federal Republic of Germany. At present, there are 1.1 million Turks in Germany of which 646,000 are males and 495,000 females. Out of this figure, 59.8 percent of the males and 29.5 percent of the females are reported to be labourers. 35.9 percent of the population abroad is below the age of 15, and the remaining are in the age group 15-55.

The above mentioned demographic factors also affect the age structure of Turkey's population. As fertility declines, the share of the 0-14 age group gradually decreases and the supply of active population (15-64) increases.

*Employment*

In 1972, 66.9 percent of the working population was engaged in agricultural activities. This percentage dropped to 61.8 percent in 1977, while the percentage engaged in manufacturing industries (construction included) rose from 14.0 percent to 16.2 percent for the same period. In the services, the ratio also rose from 19.1 percent to 22.0 percent between 1972 and 1977.

The employment problem in Turkey should be understood partly by taking into consideration the level of economic development and the demographic situation, and partly by the structural deficiencies caused by inadequate policies and measures.

The Fourth Five Year Plan (FFYP) estimates that the domestic surplus of labour supply increased from 2.0 million in 1972 to 2.2 million in 1977. Correspondingly, the ratio of domestic labour surplus to total labour supply rose from 13.3 percent to 13.5 percent for the same period. Agricultural labour surplus was estimated by the State Planning Organization (SPO) to be approximately 740,000 at the end of October 1977 (See Table 4).

The State Planning Organization states that the labour surplus in agriculture is in the form of disguised unemployment for the months of July and August when agricultural activities are at a peak.

A continuous decrease in the participation rates of both adult males and adult females (25-54 age group) in rural and urban areas for the period of 1950-1975, indicates that the number of unemployed who do not seek jobs shows a tendency to increase. The number of this group of unemployed is estimated to be 1.2 million out of the total of 2.2 million domestic labour surplus for the year 1977. The majority of this type of unemployed are members of rural households who are partly forced to leave villages due to technological changes in agriculture and partly due to demographic pressures. Also, a part of the open unemployed, especially those with less skills and education, transfers to "unemployed not seeking job" category in urban areas due to the economic cycle. The number of unemployed looking for jobs through the Employment Bureau, was 126,000 by October 1977. In addition, it is estimated that 115,000 people seek employment through other channels. Hence, 241,000 people are assumed to be unemployed and seeking jobs.[8]

International migration of labour to Europe, as an absorbing factor of domestic labour surplus, started around 1960 and has been continuing ever since. This flow is determined by the demands for labour in industrialized countries of Western Europe. The energy crisis of 1973 and the corresponding increase of unemployment in these countries, affected the volume of labour migration. Therefore, the number of Turkish labourers abroad began to decrease in 1973 and dropped to 707,900 in 1976 from 766,800 in 1973. As Arab countries started to receive Turkish labourers in 1977, this figure has now reached 711,000 (1979).

In order to assess the impacts of migration on the production structure and rural employment in Turkey, we wish to approach the problem by investigating the interdependency of agro-economic development and social change of rural communities through a few available studies. In the previous chapter, we attempted to describe the agro-economic development and its implications for the rural structure with a macro approach. A similar approach has been developed to investigate the migration behaviour among provinces. Here, in this section, we wish to investigate the problem by looking at certain villages of different development levels and attempting to observe economic and social differentiation among them.

In order to handle the two sides of the interdependency, namely analysis of the agro-economic development on the one hand, and certain relevant aspects of the social environment on the other, one should consider numerous variables and factors. As far as agro-economic development is concerned, one should focus upon technological modernization, changes in land tenure and farming patterns, changes in labour patterns and occupational structure, and income.

As regards the social environment, the following should also be investigated: consumption patterns and standards of living, since improvements in these are regarded as the anticipated and obvious results of development; changes in population characteristics and movements; family and kinship organization, since this is one of the main frames of reference for social interaction in less differentiated groups and has been extensively discussed in relation to development; selected values and attitudes toward actual life conditions and change; and social stratification as a power relationship, since, although not much is known about its place in development, it seems one of the most important social factors determining the degree and type of development.

According to this type of functional differentiation, villages may be defined within a broad typology as: (1) subsistence, (2) transitional, and (3) commercialized or market-oriented villages.

Communities can be defined as "subsistence villages" when economic self-sufficiency with traditional agricultural methods and a primitive level of technology prevail. Common features of "subsistence villages" are certain restraints on capital accumulation, lack of specialization, a general absence of wage labour opportunities, community solidarity and reciprocal labour arrangements, restricted degree of social and economic stratification, and few external relationships.

"Transitional villages" are an intermediate group, having some of the characteristics of commercialized villages before full integration with wider markets occurs. The introduction of new agricultural methods and partial mechanization begins with the penetration of wider markets and an increase of external demand. The number of landless families increases as a result of land polarization. New factors such as capital accumulation, crop rotation and timing, and other innovations which are required by the new technology, have been practiced first by a few "entrepreneurs" in the villages; in transitional villages, changes of structural and institutional nature also occur. The results of these changes finally reflect on the social stratification and control power of the villages.

"Market-oriented villages" are the most developed. Modern agricultural tools and machines largely replace primitive technology, and there is crop specialization. Share-cropping, which is prevalent in subsistence and transitional villages, changes in character and condition and is gradually replaced by agricultural wage labour. The small agricultural holdings become modern commercial enterprises. As a result of extreme concentration in land distribution, the small land owner is transformed into a landless wage labourer. The transition to market-oriented production proceeds in different patterns where small or big land ownership prevails. In some areas, where small land ownership is dominant, integration with external markets and utilization of modern technology is accomplished, not by buying machines, but by renting them. In some other villages, transformation to commercial enterprise without any technological change seems possible.

Such an analysis will be based primarily on the data of a village survey, conducted by the Hacettepe Institute of Population Studies. The village survey is a part of the "1968 Social Survey on Family Structure and Population Questions." The target population in the 1968 Village Survey was selected from the more than 40,000 villages in Turkey. Adopting the Turkish legal definition of a "village," the survey covered rural communities with less than 2,000 in population and governed according the the

Turkish Village Law. Five-person interviewing teams (each consisting of three male and two female university students) travelled to 148 different villages in all regions of Turkey during the summer of 1968. In each village visited, information on the village (village questionnaire) was collected from a group of people such as the headman, members of the Elders' Committee, the teacher, the religious leader, including official data from the government agencies at their respective province centers. Later, "Village Inventories" of the Ministry of Village Affairs were used for the reliability of data and some statistical adjustments.

A study by Uner[9] investigates the transformation of rural communities in fifteen selected villages of different regions, from subsistence to market-oriented villages using the above mentioned 1968 data of Hacettepe Institute of Population Studies.

*Land Tenure, Distribution and Degree of Polarization*

Land polarization seems to be one of the distinct features of the transformation of villages from subsistence to commercialization. Correspondingly, Gini coefficients were calculated as a measure of land concentration increases during the process. Land concentration and polarization is more pronounced in the Mediterranean, Eastern, and South Eastern Anatolian regions where big land ownership prevails (see Table 5).

Another indicator of land polarization is the increase in the number of landless families. In subsistence villages where small land holdings dominate, the percentage of landless families ranges from ten percent to twenty percent. The ratio increases to over thirty percent in transitional villages and reaches forty percent or more in commercialized villages. This ratio is sixty-seven percent in one of the commercialized villages of Eastern Anatolia (Gani Efenci Ciftligi of Erzincan province) (see Table 5).

In the observed subsistence villages of different regions, the maximum size of land holding does not exceed seventy decares. The average size of land holding in this type of village is around twenty-two decares. The distribution of land among families shows an even pattern. In other words, large land ownership is non-existent. Although pressure on land has caused fragmentation, resulting in farms with less than ten decares, small peasant ownership continues to be the dominant type of land tenure. Share-cropping in subsistence villages is still an affair among relatives and has not assumed the business-like character that may be observed in transitional and commercialized villages. The causes and effects of fragmentation are different for the various villages. In addition to heritage, another cause of fragmentation is the incipient subdivision of land following the breakdown of extended families as production units. This is one of the behavioural processes through which families pass to adjust themselves to socio-economic changes. There is reason to believe that, as the individualization process caused by growing contacts with the outside and increasing commercialization goes on, submarginal farms will rapidly multiply.

Land fragmentation increases in transitional and commercialized villages are parallel to land polarization and concentration. This phenomenon is more pronounced in the Mediterranean, Aegean, and Marmara regions.

Another phenomenon of land polarization is absentee landlordism. We have observed that in subsistence villages all landowners reside in the village, whereas in transitional and commercialized villages, large landowners reside outside the village. This situation creates important consequences in the process of agricultural development of these villages. When absentee landowners rent or lease their land to share-croppers, the major portion of surplus created in agriculture goes outside the village and a minor portion remains to be used as modern inputs in order to develop the production techniques.

*Labour Patterns*

Animal husbandry as one of the features of subsistence villages lost importance during the commercialization process. Introduction of new crops such as industrial crops, fruits and vegetables in transitional and commercialized villages, required a new arrangement of labour for all the seasons of the year in farm establishments of all sizes. Especially on the Mediterranean, Aegean, and Marmara coasts, the continuous care of fruits and plants limited the grazing land and feeds available for animals. The comparatively high income generated from new crops, pushed animal husbandry into second place as an income source. Consequently, the number of animals decreased in time.

Farming activities have been spread out more evenly throughout the year. Previously, labour-intensive activities such as harvesting in one month of the summer, tilling and plowing during spring and autumn, had left the labourers idle during winter and some months in summer. Now, activities to produce vegetables (also in green houses), fruits and industrial crops, are spread over the entire year. This development, together with the decrease in the number of cattle, also diminishes the importance of the "yayla" economy.[10]

On the one hand, rapid mechanization leads to the specialization of the labour force in occupations such as tractor-driving, operators of various farm equipment, and on the other hand, displaces the labourers, thus affecting directly the employment situation of these people inside and outside the village. As discussed in previous chapters, the introduction of new technology accelerates land polarization and transforms a considerable portion of small landowners to landless agricultural labourers within four or five crop seasons. Thus, new kinds of work relationships and conditions, based on work agreements, have emerged between large landowners and agricultural labourers.

The transformation from subsistence to commercialized villages also affects their demographic structure. The data in Table 6 suggest that family size may change in accordance with this transformation. If the effects of different levels of fertility and mortality among regions are eliminated, it is possible to observe that the family size decreases in transitional and commercialized villages. This effect is more pronounced in the Aegean, Marmara and Black Sea regions (Table 6).

The decrease in family size may be explained by the effects of out-migration. This phenomenon can also be traced from the last column of Table 6, as the percentage of families who migrated from the village in the last five years. This column clearly shows that percentages of out-migrating families are higher in subsistence villages than in transitional and commercialized villages.

Another demographic measure in Table 6 is the crude sex ratio expressed as number of males for one hundred females. Although we have no information on sex ratios in these villages by age groups, the crude sex ratio may be taken as an indicator of out-migration, for the majority of migrants are single males. Consequently, increased participation of women and children in agricultural work is observed following the migration of adult males. This is especially true in subsistence villages. The workload in this type of village primarily consists of farming activities carried out at a primitive level with the utilization of animal power.

Mutual aid and strong village solidarity are reflected in the unpaid help from relatives, friends, and neighbours, in preparing fields and harvesting crops of which only a small portion is marketed.

Another point observed in these villages is the high mobility of the labour force. A certain portion of the labour force temporarily leaves the village in order to work in agricultural and non-agricultural activities. As the labour requirements of market-oriented villages are higher than those of the transitional and subsistence villages, the percentage of seasonal migration is low (see Table 6).

The majority of seasonal migrants in the sampled villages are landless villagers and small landowners. Seasonal migrants usually work in construction and similar activities in urban centers for up to six months. For seasonal migrants working in other villages as agricultural workers, the duration of work changes between two to three weeks and one to two months (Table 6).

In the peak months of agricultural activities, additional workers are required for the market-oriented villages. The ratio of seasonal in-migrants to the villages' active population varies according to the nature of the agricultural practice and the kind of crops to be grown. For example in Dortyol, a village in the Amasya Province in the Black Sea Region, where tobacco and sugar beets are produced, the ratio of in-migrating workers reaches seventy-four percent in peak months (see Table 6). These seasonal migrants work on a contract basis like villagers and are paid weekly.

We have already noted the traditional and primitive level of technology in subsistence villages. The use of modern farm implements increases with the transformation of villages from subsistence to commercialized. We can clearly observe this from Table 7. The size of the farm holdings in the sampled villages appears as one of the factors affecting the number of tractors used. The Agricultural Bank of Turkey gives credit to villagers who own 250 decares or more land, for the purpose of buying tractors.

Correspondingly, modern vehicles of transportation are being used in transitional and commercialized villages. Instead of traditional two-wheeled animal-drawn carts of the subsistence villages, we observe more use of tractor-drawn carts in the market-oriented villages (Table 7).

EXTERNAL MIGRATION

In the early 1960s, Turkey began exporting workers to Western Europe; by 1971, combined official and unofficial migration had resulted in an estimated 750,000 to 790,000 Turkish workers residing abroad. In 1971 the demand for workers began to decrease, and by 1973 the recruitment of foreign workers[11] had virtually come to a halt. By 1978 it was estimated that 840,000 workers accompanied by a substantial number of dependents were residing abroad. In 1977, an estimated 72.4 percent of all Turkish nationals abroad were residing in West Germany: of these 1,141,000 individuals, 532,000 (46.7 percent) were workers (59.8 percent men, 29.5 percent women), and the rest were dependents, yielding an overall dependency ratio of 1.14 individuals per worker. In recent years the migration stream has been directed primarily to non-European countries, such as Libya, Saudi Arabia and Australia.

Estimates of returnees are extremely imprecise. Since 1973, an estimated 200,000 workers have returned to Turkey permanently. Assuming the same dependency ratio as among Turkish nationals in West Germany in 1977, the total number of returnees would be 428,000; but this can only be considered a very rough estimate. An estimated twenty-five to thirty thousand workers continue to return permanently every year.

International population movements of this magnitude inevitably have had far-reaching consequences for the Turkish economy and society. The remittances of workers provided the much-needed foreign exchange for the country's development effort. After 1970, these inflows of funds exceeded one billion dollars per year and provided foreign exchange revenues equalling approximately half those obtained from total exports every year. Turkey has become dependent on labour migration and its remittances, but the influx of money has caused inflation and speculation particularly in real estate and some production goods. Furthermore, the distribution of profits of the money from Europe has been very unequal. This has caused sharper differences between income groups within the regions of migration. The migrants' household received the direct profits from migration; the small group of old elite took the indirect profits, particularly in the trade and distributive sector. The losers are the non-migrants from the middle and lower income group.

Policies to stimulate better use of the remittances in Turkey have been confined to the initiatives of Village Development Cooperatives and Joint Stock Companies. Lack of consistent planning and help for these projects, however, have led, with very few exceptions, to the waste of millions of Turkish Liras.

Recently, the foundation of the State Industry and Workers Investment Bank (DESYAB) was approved by Parliament, but the bank is not yet in operation. Efforts by Turkish private and state banks to attract the workers' savings currently in European banks, have failed so far because the conditions offered are not sufficiently attractive for the workers.

The channelling of such large numbers of the active labour force abroad for more than a decade significantly eased the pressure of employment. In a country without reliable unemployment statistics and where unofficial estimates range from twelve percent to twenty percent of the labour force, immigration of workers in the face of rapid population increase has helped keep unemployment levels significantly lower than what they would have been otherwise. The recent closing of the Western European immigration outlets has eliminated this mechanism. In view of the fact that non-European outlets for Turkish workers cannot absorb manpower at levels comparable to those of the 1960s, Turkey will feel the burden of rapidly increasing numbers of unemployed in the years ahead. The current domestic crisis and the inability to allocate sufficient resources to investment for the continuation of the past growth rates mean less employment opportunities for the future and will further accentuate the problem.

Such movements of a large labour force, around four-fifths of which were men under forty and around one-third of which were characterized as qualified labour, had significant consequences for the domestic labour force during the last two decades. This issue of the adverse effects of migration on the domestic labour force and on the Turkish development effort needs to be explored. There do exist a few studies which indicate that the positive effects of international migration are negligible or non-existent and that migration in this form should be viewed as undesirable, because it leads to growing dependency and structural vulnerability. Therefore, policies should be directed towards adequate prevention of the necessity to migrate as in the case of internal migration; only by starting integrated regional development can employment be created and the negative consequences of migration neutralized, and possibly even converted into positive results.

## POLICY IMPLICATIONS

Turkey is a relatively large country with significant regional socio-economic and demographic disparities which increase along the east-west axis of the country. The region which is west of a line connecting the cities of Samsun in the north and Iskenderun in the south is the more developed part of the country with a greater concentration of people in urban areas.

The phenomenon of migration in Turkey can be characterized by the relatively large number of people moving across provincial and regional borders, the socio-economic disparities that exist between place of origin and destination, the westward direction of the migrant flow, the rural to urban movement patterns with relatively infrequent migration between urban places -- except in the later stages of a stepwise migration process -- and the domination of migration streams by the young.

During the period 1965-1970, twenty-two percent of all types of internal migration was directed to Istanbul, by far the largest metropolitan area. The Ankara metropolitan area received 11.3 percent of the total, and Izmir 7.1 percent. Cities with populations over 100,000 followed these three metropolitan areas.

A review of the literature on the determinants of internal migration in Turkey indicates that both push and pull factors are important. Among the push factors, high rate of population growth in rural areas, unequal distribution of land ownership, high levels of mechanization in agriculture in some regions, scarcity of cultivable land and low levels of average agricultural income can be singled out. With respect to pull factors, which are rather more dominant, a complex of factors related to urbanization and specific to major metropolitan centers are at work. In addition to employment opportunities in both industry and services, which is the major pull factor, access to better education opportunities and to other services is important.

Rapid urbanization and concentration of internal migration, particularly rural-urban migration, in several metropolitan centers during the 1950s started a series of political debates in the 1960s and 1970s on urbanization programmes, selected growth centers, the unproductive nature of a rural population distribution into small and scattered hamlets and the resettlement policies of the preceding two decades.

The First, Second and Third Five-year Development Plans have all contained policies on urbanization, regional development and employment. However, a number of inconsistencies regarding urbanization and the process of rural-urban migration have appeared in the national plans. For example, on migration and urban over-population the First FYP states:

> Inadequate employment opportunities in agriculture encouraged urbanization.... Special measures are suggested in order to solve employment problems.... The main principle underlying these

> measures is to keep migration to the cities on a level consistent with the new jobs to be created there and to prepare programmes that will encourage people to stay in the rural areas.
>
> Regional planning serves ... to find solutions to excessive urbanization and population problems....
>
> One of the country's social problems that needs special attention is over-population in the agricultural sector. The high rate of population growth makes the problem increasingly serious.

In the First FYP, community development, at the village level is seen as contributing towards the minimization of migration to urban areas. The 'problem' of urbanization is viewed from a limited rural perspective.

Although the First FYP acknowledged urbanization as an important factor for promoting social and economic development, it did not give whole-hearted support to the further growth of large metropolitan areas. Rather, it advocated preventing large cities from getting larger. It accepted a strategy of balanced urbanization which would permit cities to grow at a rate parallel to the creation of new jobs in those cities. It supported the creation of new urban centres having high social and economic growth potentials and a "system of dispersion" for urban development.

The Second FYP proposed that urbanization is a constructive part of economic and social development, and, therefore, that it should be used as a means of development in order to prevent regional disparities. The Plan encourages further urbanization, both in the small urban centers having high growth potential and in the large metropolitan areas. Therefore, the Second Plan advocates a mixed system of urbanization consisting of both "dispersion" and "selective concentration."

Both plans emphasized the necessity of overcoming regional disparity by giving priority to backward regions in the case of development. They also advocated giving priority to backward regions for the distribution of public services. It was expected that the provision of such services would generate a fairly equal distribution of income among the regions. The establishment of close relationships and cooperation among the regions, and between each region and the national centre, was indicated in both Plans. The encouragement of private investment in certain regions which had been designated by national planners as priority areas was another important policy decision shared by both Plans.

Yet, none of these discussions and recommendations have led to active programmes or to policies whose specific targets have been explicitly established.

One policy alternative which is still being debated is on the question of whether short-distance migration movements should be encouraged thereby concentrating these movements in regional growth centers. Despite the absence of regional growth policies to encourage short-distance migration movements, it is possible that the destination of such movements has begun to change from far-away metropolitan centers to urban centres within the same province.

The underlying basis of the current policy debate is the geographically scattered nature and sub-optimal size of the villages and hamlets which make provision for the basic social services very costly. Twenty-three million rural population live in 36,000 villages which are made up of 86,000 small and scattered hamlets. To date, two different approaches to the problem have been proposed. One is the "Central Village" approach of the Third FYP, on which no substantive action was taken, and the other is the approach of "Koy-Kent" (Rurban Center) being implemented in several pilot projects by the Government since 1978.

In 1978, Koy-Kent projects began to be implemented by two ministries, the Ministry of Village Affairs and Cooperatives and by the Ministry of Forestry. The latter initiated a pilot project in the province of Bolu in North-West Central Anatolia. The Ministry of Village Affairs' pilot project is located in the Ozalp district of Van province in Eastern Anatolia. There appears to be no close cooperation between the two ministries with regard to the implementation of the projects. In fact, they appear to be competing both for public funds and public attention.

Despite the fact that the concept of "Koy-Kent" has been part of the programmes of the Republican Party for years and the fact that its basic principles had been previously established, the lack of a system which would incorporate these basic principles into an integrated whole led to different designs and definitions of what is understood by the concept Koy-Kent. Sketched below is the current interpretation of the strategy by the Ministry of Village Affairs and Cooperatives.

The starting point for this Ministry is that the Koy-Kent project is basically a rural development proposal. The industrialization of agriculture and "urbanization" of rural areas constitute the framework for the desired transformation. The transformation will be brought about by increased use of technical inputs and more advanced technology in agricultural production. This effort will inevitably necessitate institutional changes such as a new land tenure system, agricultural production cooperatives, a new credit system, etc. Thus, in short, according to the view of the Ministry, Koy-Kent aims much beyond improvements in the physical characteristics of the villages.

What distinguishes the Koy-Kents from earlier projects, according to the same view, is the presence of a central residential area which provides the basic services such as health and education unavailable in the surrounding areas. Spatially speaking, this central residential area can however also be taken as the center of the "new production system" whose outlines have been described above. Thus, the aim of Koy-Kent "Rurban

Center" is to "urbanize the rural areas while industrializing agriculture." At this first stage, the project aims at establishing a hierarchy of population centers within each project area. At the top of the hierarchy will be the Koy-Kent from which the flow of goods and services will be coordinated. It remains to be seen how rural residential centers, spatial organization of the provision of basic services in the rural areas, and the transformation of the organization of rural production will be brought about.

For the other pilot project, Taskesti village in the Province of Bolu was chosen by the Ministry of Forestry to be the Koy-Kent rurban center for various activities. Its population and the surrounding twenty villages will not only come into possession of the modern services usually found only in large cities, but they will also be able to enter industrial activities in addition to forestry, agriculture and animal husbandry.

In order for villages properly to utilize forestry products, the government and villagers joined forces, and a sixty-seven million lira factory which will employ 455 workers will be built in this rurban area. Thus, people in Taskesti and the surrounding settlements will be able to work in their own factory without having to migrate to urban centers, leaving behind their families and homes. They will be able to sell wood products such as lumber parket, wall panels, etc., without a middleman, and in their own stores.

In addition, for more productive animal husbandry, poultry raising, and beekeeping, projects have been prepared for the cooperatives of the twenty villages by the Ministry of Village Affairs. For the realization of these projects, more than eighty million liras worth of credit will be extended. Also, in order for the villagers to build their own feed industry, milk collection center, and refrigerator depot, and to acquire the necessary vehicles and tools, the government will guarantee help, from credit and donations.

The scale of the projects and the scale of the necessary funds underlines the necessity of strong commitment at the highest political level. Potentially, Koy-Kent could turn into a huge project. Today, all Koy-Kent implementation is at a trial stage, having started in 1978.

With regard to its implication for internal migration, it might be argued that to the extent that urbanization and industrialization will spread in the rural areas, the rural areas' capacity to absorb the active population will increase. As stated earlier, the determinants of internal migration in Turkey constitute a complex and interrelated set; whether the actions and policies proposed by Koy-Kent will be able to create enough employment opportunities in rural areas and slow down the migration movements, remains to be seen.[12]

## FOOTNOTES

[1] 1 Decare = 0.1 hectare.

[2] Defined as the variation explained by the regression equation, divided by the total variation of the dependent variable.

[3] For a full analysis of such a transformation see: Hinderink, J. and Kiray, M.B., *Social Stratification as an Obstacle for Development*, New York: Praeger Special Studies, 1970.

[4] See M.B. Kiray, "Values, Social Stratification and Development." *The Journal of Social Issues*. Vol. XXIV, No. 2 (April 1968).

[5] Organization for Economic Cooperation and Development. *Turkey*. Paris, OECD: 1974.

[6] Tekeli, Ilhan. "Marginal Sector Within the Process of Economic Development: Its Occurrence and Effects," Paper presented to the Second Turkish Demography Conference, (October), Cesme, Izmir (1975).

[7] Michael P. Todaro, "A model of labor migration and urban unemployment in less developed countries." *American Economic Review* 59, No. 1 (March 1969), pp. 138,148.

John R. Harris and Michael P. Todaro, "Migration, unemployment and development: A two sector analysis," *American Economic Review*, 60, No. 1 (March 1970), pp. 126-142.

[8] The SPO believes that the exact number of unemployed is above this figure.

[9] S. Uner: *Kirsal Türkiye' de Bolgesel Farkliliklar* (Regional Variations in rural Turkey), unpublished PhD dissertation, Faculty of Political Sciences, Ankara University, 1972.

[10] Transhumance system in which lowland villages transfer to fixed summer pastures at higher elevations every year. This resulted in communities having a summer and a winter village.

[11] In 1973 Turkish workers and their dependents were estimated at 1.3 million.

[12] The Fourth Five-Year Plan foresees that the number of disguised unemployed which is estimated as 720,000 in 1978, will drop to 620,000 in 1983 through the implementation of Koy-Kent projects. Thus, total unemployment (agriculture and non-agricultural) is expected to decrease from a base of 2.3 million in 1978, to 1.7 million in 1983. (Fourth FYP, pp. 251).

TABLE 1: PERCENTAGE DISTRIBUTION OF AGRICULTURAL HOUSEHOLDS AND LAND AREA OWNED BY SIZE CLASSES, 1963, 1973 AND 1980

| Size of Unit | 1963 | | 1973 | | 1980 | |
|---|---|---|---|---|---|---|
| (decares) | % of Families | % of Area | % of Families | % of Area | % of Families | % of Area |
| 1-20 | 40.7 | 11.3 | 44.6 | 8.4 | 59.8 | 20.1 |
| 21-50 | 28.1 | 17.7 | 28.3 | 17.9 | | |
| 51-100 | 18.1 | 22.2 | 16.7 | 22.6 | 39.8 | 70.0 |
| 101-200 | 9.4 | 22.2 | 7.0 | 19.5 | | |
| 201-500 | 3.2 | 15.9 | 2.6 | 16.2 | 0.4 | 9.0 |
| 501+ | 0.5 | 10.7 | 0.8 | 15.4 | | |

Sources: State Planning Organization, Fourth Five-Year Plan, 1978-83, p.12, and Agricultural Census 1980.

TABLE 2: LAND RENTING AND SHARE-CROPPING: PERCENTAGE DISTRIBUTION BY LAND SIZE GROUPS OF NUMBER OF FAMILIES IN AREA, 1963 AND 1973

| Land Size | 1963 | | 1973 | |
|---|---|---|---|---|
| (decares) | % Family | % Land | % Family | % Land |
| 1-20 | 57.0 | 23.3 | 64.0 | 13.0 |
| 21-50 | 30.2 | 34.0 | 17.7 | 13.0 |
| 51-100 | 9.3 | 20.5 | 10.2 | 16.7 |
| 101-200 | 3.0 | 12.4 | 6.3 | 20.9 |
| 201-500 | 0.4 | 4.6 | 1.1 | 7.3 |
| 501-1000 | 0.1 | 2.2 | 0.2 | 2.3 |
| 1001+ | 0.0 | 3.0 | 0.5 | 26.8 |

Source: State Planning Organization, Fourth Five-Year Plan, 1978-83.

TABLE 3: PERCENTAGE DISTRIBUTION OF POPULATION BY MAJOR AGE GROUPS (1965, 1970, 1975)

| Age Groups | 1965 | 1970 | 1975 |
|---|---|---|---|
| 0-14 | 42.0 | 41.8 | 40.1 |
| 15-64 | 54.1 | 53.8 | 55.4 |
| 65 and over | 3.9 | 4.4 | 4.5 |

Source: State Institute of Statistics, 1975 Population Census.

TABLE 4: LABOUR SUPPLY AND UNEMPLOYMENT IN TURKEY, 1962-77

(15 years old and over, males and females)

| | 1962 | 1967 | 1972 | 1977 |
|---|---|---|---|---|
| | (thousand) | | | |
| 1. Total Labour Supply | 13,133 | 13,868 | 15,013 | 16,161 |
| 2. Non-agricultural Labour Surplus | 490 | 630 | 1,096 | 1,435 |
| a. Unemployed seeking job | 150 | 120 | 199 | 241 |
| b. Unemployed not seeking job or not expecting to find job | 340 | 510 | 897 | 1,194 |
| 3. Agricultural Labour Surplus | 950 | 1,050 | 900 | 740 |
| 4. Domestic Labour Surplus (1 plus 3) | 1,440 | 1,680 | 1,996 | 2,175 |
| 5. Domestic Labour Surplus as percent of Total Labour Supply | 11.0 | 12.1 | 13.3 | 13.5 |
| 6. Number of Labourers Abroad | 20 | 165 | 660 | 711 |

Source: State Planning Organization, Fourth Five-year Plan 1978-83, p. 26.

TABLE 5: PERCENTAGE OF LANDLESS FAMILIES AND GINI COEFFICIENTS FOR SELECTED VILLAGES

| Region | Village | Landless families (%) | Gini-Coefficients for land distrib. rate | Absentee landownership (exists+non-exist.) |
|---|---|---|---|---|
| | | **Subsistence Villages** | | |
| Central Anatolia | Basoren | 26 | .309 | - |
| Black Sea | Kadikoy | 10 | .328 | - |
| Aegean & Marmara | Mesruriye | 20 | .139 | - |
| Mediterranean | Babadirli | 30 | .286 | - |
| Eastern & South Eastern Anatolia | Yarusagi | 11 | .219 | + |
| | | **Transitional Villages** | | |
| Central Anatolia | Yukari Hamurlu | 32 | .363 | - |
| Black Sea | Hacibey | 34 | .405 | + |
| Aegean & Marmara | Davutlar | 15 | .318 | - |
| Mediterranean | Sofular | 33 | .372 | + |
| Eastern & South Eastern Anatolia | Avcilar | 39 | .479 | + |
| | | **Commercialized Villages** | | |
| Central Anatolia | Toklumen | 30 | .442 | + |
| Black Sea | Dortyol | 44 | .422 | + |
| Aegean & Marmara | Samli | 34 | .414 | + |
| Mediterranean | Hardallik | 45 | .710 | + |
| Eastern & South Eastern Anatolia | Gani Efendi Ciftligi | 67 | .549 | + |

Source: Sunday Uner, Kirsal Türkiye' de Bolgesel Farkliliklar (Regional Variations in Rural Turkey), Unpublished PhD Thesis, Faculty of Political Science, Ankara University, 1972.

TABLE 6: CHANGES IN LABOUR PATTERNS FOR SELECTED VILLAGES

| Regions | Village | Family size (1) | Crude sex ratio (2) | % Wage paid working families (3) | % Share cropping families (4) | % Seasonal in-migrant agr. workers (5) | Duration Seasonal in-migrant workers (6) | % Seasonal out-migrant agr. workers (7) | Duration Seasonal out-migrant agr. workers (8) | % Seasonal Out-migrant non-agr. workers (9) | Duration Seasonal out-migrant non-agr. workers (10) | % Families migrated in last 5 years (11) |
|---|---|---|---|---|---|---|---|---|---|---|---|---|
| **Subsistence Villages** | | | | | | | | | | | | |
| Central Anatolia | Bascren | 4.36 | 99 | 26 | 5 | - | - | 15 | 30 days | - | - | 23 |
| Black Sea | Kadikoy | 6.79 | 85 | 10 | - | - | - | - | - | 24 | 180 days | - |
| Aegean & Marmara | Mesruriye | 4.67 | 92 | 18 | - | - | - | - | - | 11 | 180 days | 20 |
| Mediterranean | Bahadirli | 5.56 | 104 | 30 | - | - | - | - | - | - | - | 9 |
| Eastern & S. Eastern Anatolia | Yarusagi | 4.22 | 100 | - | 11 | - | - | - | - | 42 | 180 days | 33 |
| **Transitional Villages** | | | | | | | | | | | | |
| Central Anatolia | Yukari Hamurlu | 4.57 | 89 | 32 | - | - | - | - | - | 30 | 180 days | 2 |
| Black Sea | Hacibey | 4.87 | 99 | 23 | 7 | - | - | 1 | 30 days | - | - | 5 |
| Aegean & Marmara | Davutlar | 4.11 | 107 | 15 | 1 | - | - | - | - | 19 | 180 days | 8 |
| Mediterranean | Sofular | 5.68 | 106 | 7 | 25 | - | - | 34 | 30 days | - | - | 4 |
| Eastern & S. Eastern Anatolia | Avcilar | 4.66 | 93 | 16 | 13 | 10 | 7 days | - | - | 3 | 180 days | 7 |
| **Commercialized Villages** | | | | | | | | | | | | |
| Central Anatolia | Toklumen | 4.39 | 106 | 24 | 1 | - | - | - | - | 15 | 180 days | 10 |
| Black Sea | Dortyol | 3.97 | 92 | 42 | 2 | 74 | 30 days | - | - | - | - | 5 |
| Aegean & Marmara | Samli | 3.81 | 96 | 31 | 2 | 51 | 30 days | 15 | 60 days | - | - | 2 |
| Mediterranean | Hardallik | 5.26 | 110 | 37 | 6 | 18 | 15 days | - | - | - | - | 2 |
| Eastern & S. Eastern Anatolia | Ganiefendi Ciftligi | 4.60 | 116 | 40 | 7 | 7 | 75 days | - | - | - | - | 1 |

Source: S. Uner, 1972.

TABLE 7: FARM IMPLEMENTS IN SELECTED VILLAGES

| | | Wooden Plow | Animal drawn iron plow | Tractor | Tractor-drawn plow | Combine | Planter | Motor pump | Ox-drawn cart | Horse-drawn cart | Romork | Truck | Jeep | Minibus |
|---|---|---|---|---|---|---|---|---|---|---|---|---|---|---|
| | | | | | | Subsistence Villages | | | | | | | | |
| Central Anatolia | Basoren | 15 | 5 | - | - | - | - | - | - | 13 | - | - | - | - |
| Black Sea | Kadikoy | 150 | 3 | - | - | - | - | 2 | 86 | - | - | 2 | - | - |
| Aegean & Marmara | Mesruriye | 35 | 20 | - | - | - | - | - | 32 | - | - | - | - | - |
| Mediterranean | Bahadirli | 100 | 55 | - | - | - | - | 8 | 17 | 1 | - | - | 1 | - |
| Eastern & S. Eastern Anatolia | Yarusagi | 15 | - | - | - | - | - | - | 14 | - | - | - | - | - |
| | | | | | | Transitional Villages | | | | | | | | |
| Central Anatolia | Yukari Hamurlu | - | 40 | 2 | 2 | - | - | - | 20 | 5 | 2 | 1 | - | - |
| Black Sea | Hacibey | 40 | - | 8 | 4 | - | - | - | 40 | 2 | 4 | - | - | - |
| Aegean & Marmara | Davutlar | 95 | 95 | 3 | 3 | - | - | - | 60 | - | 2 | - | - | - |
| Black Sea | Sofular | 67 | 32 | 2 | 2 | - | 2 | 5 | - | 15 | 2 | - | - | - |
| Eastern & S. Eastern Anatolia | Avcilar | 40 | - | 1 | 1 | | - | - | - | 10 | - | 1 | - | - |
| | | | | | | Commercialized Villages | | | | | | | | |
| Central Anatolia | Toklumen | - | 100 | 2 | 2 | - | - | - | 100 | 17 | 2 | - | - | 1 |
| Black Sea | Dortyol | 60 | 30 | 8 | 7 | - | - | 4 | 30 | 3 | 7 | - | - | - |
| Aegean & Marmara | Samli | 209 | 224 | 15 | 15 | 1 | - | 1 | 1 | 99 | 15 | - | - | - |
| Black Sea | Hardallik | - | 2 | 15 | 15 | - | 3 | 4 | - | 34 | 15 | - | - | - |
| Eastern & S. Eastern Anatolia | Ganiefendi Ciftligi | 25 | 35 | 10 | 10 | - | - | - | - | 30 | 10 | - | - | - |

Source: S. Uner, 1972.

## APPENDIX 1: LIST 1 - DEPENDENT AND INDEPENDENT VARIABLES FOR THE PUSH MODEL: MALE

| *Dependent Variable:* | *Abbreviation* | *Brief Description of Variable* |
|---|---|---|
| Rural-urban Migration Rate for Males | $MR_m (R_i—U)$ | Total number of male out-migrants from rural areas of a province (i) to urban areas of 66 provinces in 5 years (1965-1970) divided by rural population of province (i) (mid-period situation: 1967). |
| *Independent Variables:* | | |
| Land/man Ratio | LAMNR | Ratio of land under cultivation to total rural population (mid-period situation). |
| Index of Disownment of Land | IDOLR | Percent of Landless families to total rural families (mid-period situation). |
| Mechanization in Agriculture | MCAGR | Ratio of Area cultivated by tractors to total cultivated area (mid-period situation). |
| Age Factor for Rural Male | AGERM | Ratio of male 15-45 age group to total rural male population (mid-period situation). |
| Agricultural Occupation for Rural Male | AGOCRM | Percent of rural males engaged in agricultural occupations (mid-period situation). |
| Industrial Occupations for Rural Male | INOCRM | Percent of rural males engaged in industrial occupations (mid-period situation). |
| Service Occupation for Rural Male | SVOCRM | Percent of rural males engaged in service occupations (mid-period situation). |
| Growth Rate of Rural Male Pop. | GROPRM | Growth rate of rural male population of province (i) (mid-period situation). |
| Labour Force Participation Rate for Rural Male | LFPRM | Ratio of active male population 15 years and above to rural male population (mid-period situation). |

APPENDIX 1: (continued) LIST 2 - DEPENDENT AND INDEPENDENT VARIABLES FOR THE PUSH MODEL: FEMALE

| Dependent Variable: | Abbreviation | Brief Description of Variable |
|---|---|---|
| Rural-urban Migration Rate for Females | $MR_f$ $(R_i\text{-}U)$ | Total number of female out-migrants from rural areas of a province (i) to urban areas of 66 provinces in 5 years (1965-1970) divided by rural population of province (i) (mid-period situation: 1967). |
| **Independent Variables:** | | |
| Land/man Ratio | LAMNR | Ratio of land under cultivation to total rural population (mid-period situation). |
| Index of Disownment of Land | IDOLR | Percent of Landless families to total rural families (mid-period situation). |
| Mechanization in Agriculture | MCAGR | Ratio of Area cultivated by tractors to total cultivated area (mid-period situation). |
| Age Factor for Rural Female | AGERF | Ratio of female 15-45 age group to total rural female population (mid-period situation). |
| Agricultural Occupation for Rural Female | AGOCRF | Percent of rural females engaged in agricultural occupations (mid-period situation). |
| Industrial Occupations for Rural Female | INOCRF | Percent of rural females engaged in industrial occupations (mid-period situation). |
| Service Occupation for Rural Female | SVOCRF | Percent of rural females engaged in service occupations (mid-period situation). |
| Growth Rate of Rural Female Pop. | GROPRF | Growth rate of rural female population of province (mid-period situation). |
| Labour Force Participation Rate for Rural Female | LFPRF | Ratio of active female population 15 years and above to rural female population (mid-period situation). |
| Child-woman Ratio for Rural Areas | CHWORF | Ratio of (0-4) age group children to 15-44 age group rural female population (mid-period situation). |

APPENDIX 1: (Continued) LIST 3 - DEPENDENT AND INDEPENDENT VARIABLES FOR THE PULL MODEL: MALE

| Dependent Variable: | Abbreviation | Brief Description of Variable |
|---|---|---|
| Urban Immigration Rates for Males of Rural Origin | $MR_m (R-U_i)$ | Total number of male immigrants to urban areas of a province (i) from rural areas of 66 provinces in 5 years (1965-1970) divided by urban population of province (i) (mid-period situation: 1967). |
| **Independent Variables:** | | |
| Accommodation Potential | ACCOMP | Number of construction permits of new dwellings issued by municipalities per urban population of a province (i) (mid-period situation). |
| Educational Investment | IDINVT | Per capita educational investment of a province (i) (mid-period situation). |
| Age Factor for Urban Male | AGEUM | Ratio of male 15-44 age group to total urban male population (mid-period situation). |
| Agricultural Occupation for Urban Male | AGOCUM | Percent of urban males engaged in agricultural occupations (mid-period situation). |
| Industrial Occupations for Urban Male | INOCUM | Percent of urban males engaged in industrial occupations (mid-period situation). |
| Service Occupation for Urban Male | SVOCUM | Percent of urban males engaged in service occupations (mid-period situation). |
| Income Factor | WAINU | Annual average income per person in large-scale manufacturing industries of a province (i) (mid-period situation). |
| Industrial Employment Factor | INEMU | Percent of employed in large-scale manufacturing industries to total population of a province (i) (mid-period situation). |
| Growth Rate of Urban Male Pop. | GROPUM | Growth rate of urban male population of province (i) (mid-period situation). |
| Labour Force Participation Rate for Urban Male | LFPUM | Ratio of active male population 15 years and above to urban male population 15 years and above (mid-period situation). |
| Total Investments | TOTINVT | Per capita investment of a province (i) (mid-period situation). |

APPENDIX 1: (continued) LIST 4 - DEPENDENT AND INDEPENDENT VARIABLES FOR THE PULL MODEL: FEMALE

| Dependent Variable: | Abbreviation | Brief Description of Variable |
|---|---|---|
| Urban Immigration Rates for Females of Rural Origin | $MR_f (R\text{-}U_i)$ | Total number of female immigrants to urban areas of a province (i) from rural areas of 66 provinces in 5 years (1965-1970) divided by urban population of province (i) (mid-period situation: 1967). |
| **Independent Variables:** | | |
| Accommodation Potential | ACCOMP | Number of construction permits of new dwellings issued by municipalities per urban population of a province (i) (mid-period situation). |
| Educational Investment | IDINVT | Per capita educational investment of a province (i) (mid-period situation). |
| Age Factor for Urban Female | AGEUF | Ratio of male 15-44 age group to total urban male population (mid-period situation). |
| Agricultural Occupation for Urban Females | AGOCUF | Percent of urban females engaged in agricultural occupations (mid-period situation). |
| Industrial Occupations for Urban Females | INOCUF | Percent of urban females engaged in industrial occupations (mid-period situation). |
| Service Occupation for Urban Female | SVOCUF | Percent of urban females engaged in service occupations (mid-period situation). |
| Income Factor | WAINU | Annual average income per person in large-scale manufacturing industries of a province (i) (mid-period situation). |
| Industrial Employment Factor | INEMU | Percent of employed in large-scale manufacturing industries to total population of a province (i) (mid-period situation). |
| Growth Rate of Urban Female Pop. | GROPUF | Growth rate of urban female population of province (i) (mid-period situation). |
| Labour Force Participation Rate | LEPRUF | Ratio of active female population 15 years and above to urban female population 15 years and above (mid-period situation). |
| Total Investments | TOTINVT | Per capita investment of a province (i) (mid-period situation). |
| Child-Woman Ratio for Urban Areas | CHWOUF | Ratio of 0-4 age group children to 15-44 age group urban female population (mid-period situation). |

APPENDIX 2: THE COEFFICIENTS OF MULTIPLE DETERMINATION ($R^2$) FOR 67 PROVINCES.

| | *Push Model* | | *Pull Model* | |
|---|---|---|---|---|
| | *Male* | *Female* | *Male* | *Female* |
| *Province* | $R^2$ | $R^2$ | $R^2$ | $R^2$ |
| Adana | 0.349 | 0.428 | 0.237 | 0.150 |
| Adiyaman | 0.145 | 0.189 | 0.348 | 0.235 |
| Afyon | 0.282 | 0.364 | 0.403 | 0.283 |
| A˜gri | 0.202 | 0.187 | 0.519 | 0.508 |
| Amasya | 0.257 | 0.259 | 0.558 | 0.536 |
| Ankara | 0.267 | 0.140 | 0.552 | 0.453 |
| Antalya | 0.160 | 0.120 | 0.388 | 0.333 |
| Artvin | * | 0.105 | 0.547 | 0.479 |
| Aydin | 0.102 | 0.108 | 0.329 | 0.374 |
| Balikesir | 0.202 | 0.147 | 0.435 | 0.382 |
| Bilecik | 0.170 | 0.016 | 0.406 | 0.332 |
| Bingöl | 0.099 | 0.099 | 0.401 | 0.358 |
| Bitlis | 0.274 | 0.677 | 0.532 | 0.313 |
| Bolu | 0.276 | 0.179 | 0.622 | 0.613 |
| Burdur | 0.125 | 0.049 | 0.038 | 0.128 |
| Bursa | 0.136 | 0.235 | 0.510 | 0.486 |
| Çanakkale | 0.384 | 0.339 | 0.463 | 0.397 |
| Çankiri | 0.278 | 0.224 | 0.556 | 0.536 |
| Çorum | 0.113 | 0.167 | 0.524 | 0.541 |
| Denizli | 0.070 | 0.064 | 0.438 | 0.452 |
| Diyarbakir | 0.154 | 0.204 | 0.333 | 0.312 |
| Edirne | 0.230 | 0.225 | 0.468 | 0.444 |
| Elazi˜g | 0.157 | 0.156 | 0.510 | 0.534 |
| Erzincan | 0.153 | 0.011 | 0.473 | 0.470 |
| Erzurum | 0.232 | 0.152 | 0.688 | 0.692 |
| Eskişehir | 0.094 | 0.153 | 0.626 | 0.631 |
| Gaziantep | 0.238 | * | 0.373 | 0.320 |
| Giresun | 0.187 | 0.155 | 0.456 | 0.421 |
| Gümüşhane | 0.343 | 0.130 | 0.590 | 0.616 |
| Hakkari | 0.036 | 0.050 | 0.544 | 0.358 |
| Hatay | 0.097 | 0.273 | 0.329 | 0.330 |
| Isparta | 0.017 | * | 0.608 | 0.651 |

(continued next page)"

* not completed due to lack of data at province level.

(Appendix 2 continued)

| | *Push Model* | | *Pull Model* | |
|---|---|---|---|---|
| | *Male* | *Female* | *Male* | *Female* |
| *Province* | $R^2$ | $R^2$ | $R^2$ | $R^2$ |
| Adana | 0.349 | 0.428 | 0.237 | 0.150 |
| Adiyaman | 0.145 | 0.189 | 0.348 | 0.235 |
| Afyon | 0.282 | 0.364 | 0.403 | 0.283 |
| Ağri | 0.202 | 0.187 | 0.519 | 0.508 |
| Amasya | 0.257 | 0.259 | 0.558 | 0.536 |
| Ankara | 0.267 | 0.140 | 0.552 | 0.453 |
| Antalya | 0.160 | 0.120 | 0.388 | 0.333 |
| Artvin | * | 0.105 | 0.547 | 0.479 |
| Aydin | 0.102 | 0.108 | 0.329 | 0.374 |
| Balikesir | 0.202 | 0.147 | 0.435 | 0.382 |
| Bilecik | 0.170 | 0.016 | 0.406 | 0.332 |
| Bingöl | 0.099 | 0.099 | 0.401 | 0.358 |
| Bitlis | 0.274 | 0.677 | 0.532 | 0.313 |
| Bolu | 0.276 | 0.179 | 0.622 | 0.613 |
| Burdur | 0.125 | 0.049 | 0.038 | 0.128 |
| Bursa | 0.136 | 0.235 | 0.510 | 0.486 |
| Çanakkale | 0.384 | 0.339 | 0.463 | 0.397 |
| Çankiri | 0.278 | 0.224 | 0.556 | 0.536 |
| Çorum | 0.113 | 0.167 | 0.524 | 0.541 |
| Denizli | 0.070 | 0.064 | 0.438 | 0.452 |
| Diyarbakir | 0.154 | 0.204 | 0.333 | 0.312 |
| Edirne | 0.230 | 0.225 | 0.468 | 0.444 |
| Elaziğ | 0.157 | 0.156 | 0.510 | 0.534 |
| Erzincan | 0.153 | 0.011 | 0.473 | 0.470 |
| Erzurum | 0.232 | 0.152 | 0.688 | 0.692 |
| Eskişehir | 0.094 | 0.153 | 0.626 | 0.631 |
| Gaziantep | 0.238 | * | 0.373 | 0.320 |
| Giresun | 0.187 | 0.155 | 0.456 | 0.421 |
| Gümüşhane | 0.343 | 0.130 | 0.590 | 0.616 |
| Hakkari | 0.036 | 0.050 | 0.544 | 0.358 |
| Hatay | 0.097 | 0.273 | 0.329 | 0.330 |
| Isparta | 0.017 | * | 0.608 | 0.651 |

*not completed due to lack of data at province level.

(continued next page)

(Appendix 2 continued)

| | *Push Model* | | *Pull Model* | |
|---|---|---|---|---|
| | *Male* | *Female* | *Male* | *Female* |
| Province | $R^2$ | $R^2$ | $R^2$ | $R^2$ |
| Içel | 0.405 | 0.402 | 0.273 | 0.278 |
| Istanbul | 0.342 | 0.468 | 0.716 | 0.617 |
| Ismir | 0.119 | 0.031 | 0.461 | 0.375 |
| Kars | 0.237 | 0.223 | 0.671 | 0.682 |
| Kastamonu | 0.246 | 0.126 | 0.457 | 0.434 |
| Kayseri | 0.139 | 0.118 | 0.567 | 0.573 |
| Kirklareli | 0.270 | 0.182 | 0.460 | 0.434 |
| Kirşehir | 0.172 | 0.175 | 0.475 | 0.478 |
| Kocaeli | 0.135 | 0.126 | 0.598 | 0.564 |
| Konya | 0.196 | 0.142 | 0.649 | 0.505 |
| Kütahya | 0.163 | 0.199 | 0.320 | 0.268 |
| Malatya | 0.080 | * | 0.510 | 0.491 |
| Manisa | 0.041 | 0.270 | 0.324 | 0.298 |
| Maraş | 0.200 | 0.202 | 0.198 | 0.099 |
| Mardin | 0.049 | 0.314 | 0.323 | 0.419 |
| Muğla | 0.262 | * | 0.341 | 0.383 |
| Muş | 0.387 | 0.227 | 0.589 | 0.515 |
| Nevşehir | 0.174 | 0.139 | 0.501 | 0.507 |
| Niğde | 0.449 | 0.306 | 0.534 | 0.457 |
| Ordu | 0.159 | 0.271 | 0.487 | 0.446 |
| Rize | 0.193 | 0.167 | 0.668 | 0.566 |
| Sakarya | 0.348 | 0.300 | 0.675 | 0.663 |
| Samsun | 0.211 | 0.195 | 0.525 | 0.509 |
| Siirt | 0.056 | 0.219 | 0.483 | 0.444 |
| Sinop | 0.352 | 0.278 | 0.475 | * |
| Sivas | 0.197 | 0.216 | 0.536 | 0.532 |
| Tekirdağ | 0.255 | 0.190 | 0.452 | 0.415 |
| Tokat | 0.113 | 0.417 | 0.576 | 0.583 |
| Trabzon | 0.152 | 0.080 | 0.587 | 0.528 |
| Tunceli | 0.166 | 0.109 | 0.555 | 0.602 |
| Urfa | 0.145 | 0.261 | 0.171 | 0.167 |
| Uşak | 0.148 | 0.111 | 0.320 | 0.253 |
| Van | 0.373 | 0.303 | 0.489 | 0.366 |
| Yozgat | 0.192 | 0.116 | 0.504 | 0.504 |
| Zonguldak | 0.106 | 0.104 | 0.514 | 0.481 |

* not completed due to lack of data at province level.

# 10

# Rural Labor Markets in Egypt

*Samir Radwan*

## INTRODUCTION

Egypt used to be a favourite textbook example of a less developed surplus labour economy. With India and Jamaica, Egypt was singled out by W. Arthur Lewis[1] as a country definitely burdened with a large surplus of labour in the sense that labour could be absorbed in an industrialisation process without loss of production elsewhere in the economy. The surplus labour hypothesis went unchallenged, and, for Egypt, the figures of twenty to thirty per cent of the total labour force were officially adopted. Twenty-five years later, this situation was almost completely reversed. In stark contrast to the earlier situation with abundancy and possibly local surpluses, the labour market of the 1980s appeared to be characterised by widespread shortages. The principal cause for this change was the massive flow of emigration from Egypt to the neighbouring oil-rich economies. At present, and as a result of the recession in the international economy as well as the decline in oil revenues, the demand for Egyptian labour has decreased, and return migration became a phenomena since the mid-1980s. The purpose of this paper is to trace these developments, assess their impact especially on the standards of living of the rural population and end up by providing some policy perspectives for labour market management.

## LONG-TERM TRENDS IN POPULATION AND LABOUR FORCE

One of the major problems facing the Egyptian economy since the 1930s has been the absorption of the increase in population and the labour force. Traditionally, agriculture has been the major employer. However, labour was absorbed in Egyptian agriculture at low level of productivity per worker (but at very high levels of productivity per unit of land). Thus the 1960s were characterised by the problem of underemployment in agriculture, and as a result, real wages continued more or less without a change until the mid-1970s.[2] Up until then, the behaviour of agricultural wages followed the Ricardian theory of wage where monetary wages were guided by the movement in food prices, thus wages could consequently rise in spite of persistent un- and underemployment. Since the mid-1970s, however, the tightening of the labour market due to migration led to the observed increase in real wages. During this period, a number of factors have emerged which influenced both the supply and demand for labour. Among these factors are the increase in education which lowered the supply of labour, and the tremendous increase in demand due to rapid rural-urban migration and emigration to neighbouring countries. These changes are reflected in Tables 1 and 2. A number of observations emerge from these tables. First, the rate of growth of the labour force appears to be low between 1960 and 1976, but it should be recalled that females in the agricultural labour force seem to be increasingly under-enumerated and that, everything else being equal, the population might have been as much as 1.4 million and the labour force perhaps one million larger in 1976 had the large-scale emigration to OPEC countries not taken place. The hypothetical growth rate of population would then have been 2.4 per cent and that of the labour force 2.7 per cent. How employment and unemployment would have been affected in the absence of emigration is difficult to say. Although it should be obvious that a country with a labour force of some ten million cannot supply about a million emigrant workers and absorb another million into the Government and armed forces in less than a decade without straining the labour market, no matter what labour surplus may have existed at the beginning, these imbalances are not easy to pinpoint statistically.

Second, measured unemployment appears to be growing rapidly. A residual, non-specified group in the Population Censuses (PCs), usually identified with the unemployed, increased from about 1.5 per cent in 1966 to 7.8 per cent in 1976.[3] Detailed breakdowns, however, indicate that the rising measured unemployment rates should be seen as indicators of increasing labour market maladjustment rather than of a generally slackening labour demand, since the rising flood of young, inexperienced jobseekers, many of whom are graduates from secondary and higher education, has according to the PCs been accompanied by a tightening of the market for experienced workers.

Third, and perhaps the most important, is the decline in both absolute and relative terms of agricultural employment. The picture that emerges from Table 2 is a remarkable one by any standards, and it indicates profound structural change. Manufacturing, construction and the Government more than absorbed the full net increase in employment, agriculture lost a substantial part of its labour force (about one-tenth) while the "other" category, which includes most of the informal sector in villages, was practically speaking stagnant and relatively lost in importance as an employment outlet. The forces active in creating this development have been emigration and government employment policies.

During the early years of emigration to Arab OPEC countries, the flow consisted mainly of skilled and construction workers. Despite a loss that may even have exceeded the total construction labour force in 1971, the construction sector more than doubled its employment during the 1970s, absorbing and training large numbers of agricultural workers. This process was accompanied by the sharp increase of construction workers' wages, pulling agricultural wages along in its wake. The loss of labour in agriculture during recent years, to some extent have been made good through increased work by the family, including women and children; nevertheless, agriculture may be suffering production losses,[4] and this fact, combined with the strong relative and absolute increase of agricultural wages, may explain, at least partially, the structural changes in Egyptian agriculture in the direction of mechanisation and less labour-intensive cultivation patterns and methods.[5]

In absolute terms, government (administration proper and public services) absorbed more labour than any other sector; in relative terms it was second to construction only. The expansion of the Government is closely related to the guaranteed employment schemes for military conscripts and graduates from secondary education and upwards. The former, in force from 1973 to 1976, served to overstaff the Government with illiterate employees and drain the countryside of young, able-bodied males. The latter, which has been in force since 1966, had the pernicious effect of overstaffing government administration with formally educated by vocationally entirely unskilled employees in relatively high wage grades.

The Government's wage policies have been marked by restraint; public sector wages (including those in public enterprises) have lagged considerably behind both consumer prices and private-sector wages; in fact, medium grades (including new graduates) and higher echelons have suffered substantial real wages declines, although the lowest grades have experienced a substantial real wage increase. Second jobs (in principle illegal but in practice very common) have to some extent compensated for the decline in real wages, the ease with which they are obtained being indicative of the tight labour market situation outside the public sector.

The negligible increase of employment in the traditional private service sectors and the informal sector may partly reflect government employment policies. In the absence of the guaranteed employment scheme for graduates, many might have found their way into services and informal occupations, perhaps never caring about obtaining the educational certificate which now serves as the entrance ticket to government employment. The second jobs of government employees are mostly located in such occupations and do not appear in the statistics. To an unknown extent, employment increases in these sectors are therefore underestimated. Even so, the trends are probably the most striking indication of the generally high level of employment in Egypt.

Another noteworthy feature of Table 2 is the large share absorbed by mining, manufacturing, etc. Almost half the absolute increase in employment took place in this sector. This may be partly explained by overstaffing in public enterprises, to which the guaranteed employment scheme for graduates applied until 1978. Most of the increase, however, was in productive employment in the private sector, which leads one to the conclusion that small-scale manufacturing, which flourished during this period, must have been much more important in this regard.

## THE STRUCTURE AND FUNCTIONING OF THE LABOUR MARKETS

Figure 1 provides a schematic presentation of the different labour markets and the relative importance of each as expressed by its share in total employment. It is clear that agriculture remains by far the most important sector in terms of employment creation. Private agriculture provides employment for 42.5 per cent of the labour force while 7.5 per cent find employment in the non-agricultural rural sector. The Government and public sector rate second in terms of employment creation with the Government sector employing 20.8 per cent and public enterprises offering jobs to 10.4 per cent. The urban private sector accounts for some nineteen per cent of employment. Finally, the newly emerging market, that of emigration, accounts for five to ten per cent of the labour force.

An important phenomenon about the Egyptian labour markets is the intersection between these markets (the shaded areas in Figure 1). These intersections represent the multiplicity of activities for some members of the labour force. Thus, some agricultural workers supplement their income by non-farm activities or by commuting to work in the nearby urban areas. Similarly, Government and public sector employees try to increase their earnings through "multiple jobbing". It is common at present for such employees to work as taxi drivers or professionals in the service sector in particular. These articulations have become all the more widespread since the mid-1970s where a combination of inflation and rigidity of public sector salaries have pushed employees to seek an increase in their earnings through an intensification of their labour supply.

The forces that have generated the development of the labour market, as just described, are fairly well understood. Specific government policies in combination with fortuitous international developments are major responsible factors. We shall discuss these factors in this section. The possible role played by the Government's general fiscal and monetary policies will be discussed in the next section; suffice it to mention here that the strong inflationary policies of the 1970s undoubtedly contributed to the tightening of the labour market.

The Government's general development and investment policies can only to some extent be given credit for the relatively rapid long-term expansion of employment. Government investment projects appear mostly to have erred on the capital-intensive side and have not been particularly employment oriented. Industrialisation, in Egypt as in other developing countries, has not been the major source of employment, although its role has been far from negligible.

The most important employment-generating government policies have been the expansion of, and overstaffing in, the public sector, government as well as public enterprises, to which the schemes of guaranteed employment for university and other graduates and for military conscripts have greatly contributed. This trend continued even under the "open-door policy", or *Infitah*. From 1966-67 to 1973, government employment (excluding the armed forces) increased by 6.7 per cent annually. From 1973 to 1978 the rate of increase was 7.0 per cent annually.

Another source of demand for labour was emigration. After the 1973 War and the first oil price boom, Arab OPEC countries opened the gates wide for Egyptian immigration. There is much uncertainly about the number of emigrants. Estimates based on the 1976 Population Census, put the number of migrants at about 1.4 million, of which one million are assumed to be economically active.[6] According to the Central Agency for Public Mobilisation and Statistics (CAPMAS), migrants grew at the same rate as that of population since 1976. Therefore, they estimated that Egyptian migrants abroad amounted to 1.8 million by the beginning of 1985. On the other hand, estimates by the Ministry of Manpower, based on reports of Labour Attachés put the number of migrants in 1984 at 2 million. Fergany's pioneering study, based on a comprehensive survey, comes to the conclusion that all these estimates may have been exaggerated.[7] According to Fergany, the number of migrants at the beginning of 1985 could not have exceeded 900,000, with the experience of migration involving 2.5 million Egyptians between 1974 and 1984, of whom 2 million were active, 400,000 dependents and 60,000 visitors. These last figures are the closest to reality, and we can safely assume that ten to fifteen per cent of the labour force have emigrated. The question is what were the effects of such a labour move? If an emigrant were not in the labour force while in Egypt, his departure would have no direct effect on labour force, employment or measured open unemployment. Students might be a case in point, but these would presumably, after some time, have entered the labour force, either as employed or unemployed. We can take it, therefore, that emigrants, economically active abroad, have reduced the domestic labour force by their number. We can also assume that they have reduced unemployment by the same number. This is obvious if before emigration they were in fact unemployed. If employed privately before emigration, the employer would hire replacements and unemployment would fall;[8] on the other hand, this might not happen if the emigrant was underemployed in the public sector or if replacement was impossible. The latter case has been considered important. Highly skilled professionals, specialists and craftsmen have emigrated in large numbers. A replacement seems, however, typically to have been found, albeit, presumably, of lower quality, and very high wage increases for such labour have limited demand and expanded supply. The construction industry is a case in point.

Apart from public sector overstaffing, emigrants economically active abroad must have lowered both the domestic labour force and domestic unemployment by their numbers. Indirect domestic demand effects via changes in domestic spending should not be ruled out, although it is difficult to predict their direction. In any case, such effects are dwarfed by the demand effects from emigrant remittances (in 1980 amounting to some ten per cent of GNP). If not used to finance duty-free imports, partly placed on foreign exchange accounts, these remittances may be invested abroad, but large amounts have undoubtedly found their way to domestic, rural and urban real estate markets and helped to drive up prices of land and residential buildings, and have created huge capital gains and stimulated private investments as well as consumption. Emigrant families have benefited, with effects on both consumer demand and labour supply. While consumer demand may have led to an increase mainly in imports, building activity financed and stimulated by remittances must have led to increased domestic construction activity and employment. Finally, the improved balance-of-payments situation caused by the remittances has permitted a more expansionary (inflationary) fiscal and monetary policy than would otherwise have been feasible.

## EMPLOYMENT, POVERTY AND FOOD ENTITLEMENTS

Michal Kalecki, in his essay on *Unemployment in Underdeveloped Countries*, has provided an insightful characterisation of the relationship between employment and food production. He stated that:

> "any increase in employment implies generation of additional incomes and thus, if no adequate increase in agricultural output is forthcoming, and inflationary increase in the prices of necessities will be unavoidable
> . . . nothing is changed in this setup by the fact that a large part of the additionally employed is drawn from the ranks of underemployed peasants, who are anyway consuming at a level equal to average productivity on the farm . . . Thus, in order to tackle the problem of unemployment and underemployment in underdeveloped countries it is necessary to expand agricultural production rapidly . . . The high supply of food will make it possible to feed those who transfer to non-agricultural employment."[9]

This view by Kalecki provides an apt description of the situation in Egypt. As we observed earlier, one-tenth of the agricultural labour force were seeking employment either in the urban areas or by emigrating abroad. Moreover, the increase in rural incomes, resulting from remittances coming from outside the sector, and the increase in real wages within the sector, must have increased the demand for food. This coincided with another development in Egyptian agriculture viz. the drastic change in the cropping pattern which shifted resources from field and food crops consumed by the poor towards high value food crops (especially *berseem*, which is used as feed for animals) as well as export crops (rice, vegetables, fruits). As a result of all these changes, we note drastic shifts in the demand and supply for principal agricultural commodities (see Table 3). It is clear from the table that the demand-supply gap has increased during the 1970s. At present, seventy-five per cent of Egypt's consumption of cereals is imported. The imports of cereals have increased from 3.9 million tons in 1974 to 6.7 million tons in 1982. Moreover, there has been a parallel shift in the relative prices of various agricultural products. De Janvry and Subbarao[10] have summed up these shifts as follows: the increase in the demand for meat has led to a shift in land use from food to feed; the same shift in the relative price of meat has led to a shift in animal use from power to meat and dairy products; this, in turn, combined with the relatively cheap cost of capital equipment on one hand, and the increase in labour cost on the other hand, has led to a shift in farm energy from labour and animal power to mechanical power.

An important question that may be raised here is what were the implications of these changes for income distribution and poverty in the rural areas? Long-term trends in income distribution are difficult to establish, but evidence from household expenditure surveys suggests that, despite the persistence of a wide rural-urban income gap, income distribution in Egypt up to the mid-1970s may have been less unequal than in other developing countries at similar stages of development; that rural income was more equally distributed than urban income; and that, between the mid-1960s and the mid-1970s, the distribution of urban income improved slightly, while that of rural income perhaps showed some improvement during the period 1958/59 - 1964/65 and apparent deterioration in the following decade. Table 4 sums up these trends.

How has income distribution developed since the mid-1970s in the rural areas?

Two factors assume primary importance as determinants of changes in both distribution and poverty in the rural areas: access to productive assets, notably land, and employment entitlements. Recent developments in rural Egypt can be largely explained by changes in these two factors. Thus we find that the trend towards more unequal distribution of land ownership and size of landholding in recent years to a large extent explains similar trends in income disparities.[11] The Gini coefficient of concentration of landholdings increased from 0.46 to 0.55 between 1974/75 and 1979. This was accompanied by the emergence of very small farms at the bottom of the scale and the reappearance of large landholdings at the top. In 1965, smallholders (below five *feddans*) represented ninety per cent of owners and had fifty-seven per cent of the land, while large landowners (over fifty *feddans*) represented 0.3 per cent of owners and controlled 12.6 per cent of the land. By 1977, each group kept its relative position in terms of percentage of owners, but the share of land of smallholders decreased to fifty-two per cent while that of large landowners increased to 14.5 per cent. The average farm size for smallholders decreased from 1.2 *feddans* to 0.9 *feddans* during the same period.

This pattern of landholding has important implications for employment generation. Smallholdings may act as a "trap" for family labour, particularly adult males, who, although they are idle during the slack season, have to be available during the peak season and thus cannot look for stable employment elsewhere. The result is a higher incidence of underemployment in this category. Data generated by the Farm Management Survey carried out in 1977 show that, on average, "the head of the family is working around ninety days per year, which means that he is employed for one-third of his time."[12] A paradoxical situation thus exists in which underemployment coincides with rising agricultural wage rates. The high incidence of underemployment in smallholder households should not be confused, however, with the development of their standard of living. The household income may in fact, have improved during this period due to a shift in the cropping pattern on small farms towards the production of vegetables, especially in the green belts around Cairo and other large cities, or by specialising in livestock breeding and using their small plots to grow feed for animals. Moreover, small farms are less able to benefit from technological change or to shift to more profitable crops. The net result of all these characteristics (subdivision of landholdings, underemployment and lack of technical progress) is low incomes for the majority of small farmers. Finally, pressure on the land (which has long been constant in supply but is now actually diminishing by some 60,000 - 70,000 *feddans* a year, or one per cent of total cultivated area, as a result of the urban construction boom), together with labour shortages, has led to the emergence of some types of land tenure - such as share-cropping - which may reinforce the trend towards greater inequality. All these changes point to the need for a fresh look at agrarian reform.

Employment is another determinant of income distribution. The new features of the labour market have to be borne in mind when any agrarian policy is devised. Prominent among these are the effects of the tight labour market on rural wages. On the one hand, this must have led to an improvement in the lot of rural wage earners, who represent ten to fifteen per cent of the total rural labour force or twenty-five per cent of the agricultural labour force. On the other hand, the increase in wages may be partly responsible for the growing trend towards mechanisation, especially of ploughing and irrigation, as reported in a recent survey.[13] The effect of wage behaviour on future employment opportunities should therefore be borne in mind.

Another factor affecting rural income distribution is remittances from emigrant workers.[14] Although its net effect is unclear owing to the paucity of information, if the experience of other countries with substantial emigration (e.g. Turkey) is anything to go by, remittances affect income distribution in two ways. First, they may improve it if the migrants were landless peasants, as is often the case with Egyptian migrants to the Arab OPEC countries. On the other hand, remittances may worsen income distribution within the lower income groups, since those who do not receive remittances will be relatively worse off than those who do. Finally, recent changes may have affected the nature of the poverty groups. Certainly wage earners are no longer "the poorest of the rural poor", rather, poor households are those with little or no diversity of income sources, whereas even a very small farmer with a migrant member in the Gulf may be relatively well off. It appears therefore, that -- apart from the disabled and the old -- the poor are those with very small farms who cannot escape from them and those working in the low-productivity tertiary sector in the villages.

The above picture can best be understood in terms of the analysis of the survival strategies pursued by the Egyptian rural households vis-a-vis the external shocks that influence their behaviour. Thus, in the 1960s where employment opportunities in the urban economy were primarily limited to the government and the public sector, thanks to the employment guarantee scheme, we find that an important survival strategy by the households was to invest in the education of their children. Education in that situation was an important determinant of the mobility of rural labour, and ensured access to the urban labour markets. In the 1970s and 1980s, by contrast, survival strategies differed as a result of the changes in the external factors influencing the rural areas. Thus, the households reacted by ensuring that at least one member migrates abroad, and failing that, work in the construction or private trading sectors in the urban areas where wages increased tremendously during the last decade. The recent developments reflected in the decline in the demand for labour, both by the urban sector and for emigration, posed a real problem for the rural household to resolve.

## CONCLUSIONS

The case of Egypt provides a significant illustration of the impact of external factors on local labour markets. As we have seen, the labour markets in the 1960s conformed to a typical developing country situation where agriculture provided the major source of employment. With productivity more or less stagnant and real wages showing no trend, population increases had to be absorbed elsewhere. This situation lead to the increase in rural-urban migration and the pressure on the Government to accommodate the new entrants to the labour market in the government administration and the public sector. These last sectors have thus acted as the regulators of the labour market in the sense that they have absorbed the outflow of rural labour and set the pace for wage determination in the economy as a whole. Since the mid-1970s, and due to the increase in demand for Egyptian labour by oil-rich countries, and the construction boom in the urban areas of Egypt itself, the picture has changed. We have seen how the public sector has lost its role as a wage maker and how the new market, the international labour market, has assumed primary importance in this respect. The behaviour of the Egyptian worker of the 1980s can best be understood in terms of his perception of a hierarchy of labour markets: at the top there is the lucrative market in the oil-rich countries, followed by the newly emerging markets in the private construction and services sector at home, with the Government and agriculture at the bottom of the league.

The problems facing Egyptian employment planners are complex. To some extent they are shared by all developing countries. Their solution requires a mixture of investment policy, educational policy, land reform and, above all, labour market policy, taken in a wide sense so as to include wage policies. As a minimum, a solution to the employment problem should include the following range of policies, which should be pursued simultaneously:

(1) hedging against possible foreign exchange shortfalls;

(2) contingency plans to handle possible massive return of emigrant workers;

(3) retraining and relocation of unproductive and redundant government employees;

(4) co-ordination of investment and educational policies so as to match current and future demand and supply of labour by skills and occupations;

(5) agrarian reform to cope with underemployment on very small farms, which already exists and may take on serious proportions in an employment crisis.

External events, largely related to the oil price increases of 1973 and 1979, profoundly changed the Egyptian employment situation during the 1970s. Formerly a stagnant labour-surplus economy, Egypt developed with astonishing speed into a high employment economy with serious labour market imbalances where shortages of skilled and unskilled manual and technical labour now coexist with increasing surpluses of educated workers. A reversal of the external events responsible for this metamorphosis could easily and even more abruptly reverse the employment situation. Repercussions from the current oil glut, temporary though they may be, clearly indicate the vulnerability of Egypt's high growth, high employment economy. Therefore, determined efforts to rectify existing labour market maladjustments and the mismatch of labour force skills with productive requirements should be accompanied by contingency plans to hedge against possible external events that might seriously threaten the general foreign exchange and employment position.

The mismatch of available and required skills should be solved through reforms of the pay systems in the public sector (government and public enterprises) and the systems of general education and vocational training and the introduction of appropriate incentives. A shift of the resources of the general educational system so as to lay increased emphasis on elementary and technical secondary education should be undertaken, combined with a complete reorientation of university studies. Because no reliable methods for centralised planning of the detailed occupational and skill composition of the labour force exist and only industries and enterprises can predict occupational and skill requirements with any certainty, vocational training should be decentralised to industry and enterprise level.

A special problem is the massive overstaffing of the public sector as a consequence of guaranteed employment for graduates. Since overstaffing in some branches is accompanied by shortages in others, wage reforms in the public sector should be accompanied by special intra-governmental retraining and re-education programmes. The employment guarantees could be phased out over a five-year period, provided that the necessary educational and training reforms were undertaken.

Parallel with these measures, agriculture will need to be restructured to eliminate underemployment and increase productivity.

In order to hedge against adverse external foreign exchange and employment developments, the investment programme needs to be stepped up and reoriented. Industries earning foreign exchange over and above current needs should be established. Should the additional foreign exchange earnings not be needed to compensate for unexpected shortfalls they can always be used for expanding domestic consumption. If they are accompanied by a reversal of the emigration flow, contingency employment programmes, carefully planned in advance and the above policies would help to protect the working population against the uncertainties of external developments and should be an integral part of any basic needs strategy the Government may adopt.

# FOOTNOTES

* This paper draws on the earlier work by Bent Hansen and Samir Radwan, *Employment Opportunities and Equity in a Changing Economy: Egypt in the 1980s* (Geneva, ILO, 1982).

[1] W. Arthur Lewis, "Economic Development with Unlimited Supplies of Labour", *The Manchester School*, May 1954.

[2] See Samir Radwan, *Agrarian Reform and Rural Poverty: Egypt, 1952-75*, ILO, Geneva, 1977, pp. 31.

There are many problems in the data. For a detailed discussion see Bent Hansen and Samir Radwan: *Employment Opportunities and Equity in a Changing Economy: Egypt in the 1980s. A labour market approach. Report of an inter-agency team financed by the United Nations Development Programme and organised by the International Labour Office* (Geneva, ILO, 1982). See also I.H. El-Issawy: *Employment Inadequacy in Egypt* (technical paper No. 3 of the ILO/UNDP comprehensive employment strategy mission to Egypt, 1980) (Geneva, ILO, 1983).

[4] There is no conclusive evidence on this point, but sporadic examples exist. In Upper Egypt for instance, onion crop has suffered from scarcity of adult male labour.

[5] For an excellent discussion of mechanisation, see Alan Richards and Philip L. Martin (eds.), *Migration, Mechanisation and Agricultural Labour Markets in Egypt*, Westview Press, 1983, especially Chapters 2, 8 and 10.

[6] Estimates of emigrants vary widely. For a review of these estimates and their bases see Galal Amin and Elizabeth Awny, *International Migration of Egyptian Labour: A Review of the State of the Art*, IDRC-MR108e, May 1985.

[7] Nader Fergany, *Migration and Remittances by Egyptians between Myth and Reality*, mimeo, Cairo, March 1986.

[8] This is obvious if we think in terms of competitive firms; but the result would be the same in a disequilibrium setting because there is no reason why the employer should perceive a change in demand for his output just because one of his own workers gave notice.

Michal Kalecki, "Unemployment in Underdeveloped Countries", in *Essays on Developing Economies*, Humanities Press, Harvester Press, 1976, pp. 17-18.

[10] Alain de Janvry and K. Subbarao, "Wages, Prices, and Farm Mechanisation in Egypt: The Need for an Integrated Policy", in A. Richards and P.L. Martin (eds.), *Migration, Mechanisation and Agricultural Labour Markets in Egypt*, pp. 242-45.

[11] For details see, Samir Radwan and Eddy Lee, *Agrarian Change in Egypt: An Anatomy of Rural Poverty*, Croom Helm, 1986.

[12] A.A. Goueli: *Some Features of Agricultural Labour Employed in Egypt*, paper solicited by the ILO/UNDP comprehensive employment strategy mission to Egypt, 1980 (Cairo, 1980; mimeographed).

[13] M.M. El-Salhy, O.A. El-Kholei and M. Abbas: *Evaluation of the IBRD Agricultural Development Project of Menoufia and Sohag Governorates*. The situation before the project (Phase I) (Cairo, Ministry of Agriculture, 1980; mimeographed).

[14] The impact of remittances on income distribution has not been well documented. Various studies have looked at the pattern of expenditure by migrants, while others have looked at the pattern of use of savings. For a survey of the results of these studies see, Galal A. Amin and Elizabeth Awny, *International Migration of Egyptian Labour: A Review of the State of the Art*, IDRC-ME108e, May 1985, pp. 130-145.

TABLE 1: POPULATION, LABOUR FORCE, EMPLOYMENT AND UNEMPLOYMENT, 1960 AND 1976

| | Population census ('000) | | Growth rate |
|---|---|---|---|
| | 1960 | 1976 | Percent |
| <u>Population censuses</u> | | | |
| Population, total | 25,841 | 36,626 | 2.20 |
| Manpower basis, total[1] | 17,436 | 25,580 | 2.42 |
| Labour force[2] total of which: | 7,822 | 11,037 | 2.18 |
| employed | 7,647 | 10,090 | 1.81 |
| residual group[3] | 174 | 847 | 10.40 |
| <u>Labour force surveys</u> | | | |
| Labour force[2] total of which: | 6,034 | 9,983[4] | 3.20 |
| employed | 5,742 | 9,718[4] | 3.34 |
| unemployed | 288 | 265[4] | 0.52 |
| <u>Ministry of Planning, estimate</u> | | | |
| Employment, total | 6,360[5] | 9,646 | 2.64 |

<u>Notes</u>: 1 Population aged 6-64, including employed persons over 65 but excluding disabled persons.

2 Persons aged 6 and over actually employed or actually seeking work on the census or survey day, excluding foreigners.

3 Labour force minus employed figure.

4 Average of 1975 and 1977. No LFS was taken in 1976.

5 Average of 1959/60 and 1960/61.

<u>Sources</u>: Population censuses and labour force surveys; publications of the Central Agency for Public Mobilisation and Statistics (CAPMAS); Ministry of Planning, information supplied to the ILO/UNDP comprehensive employment strategy mission to Egypt, 1980.

TABLE 2: EMPLOYMENT OF THE RESIDENT LABOUR FORCE, 1971-79

| Sector | No. of persons ('000) | | Increase 1971-79 | | Annual compound rate of increase 1971-79 |
|---|---|---|---|---|---|
| | 1971 | 1979 | '000 | % | % |
| Total employed[1] | 8,252.5 | 9,565.3 | 1,312.8 | 15.9 | 1.8 |
| Agriculture, fisheries, etc. | 4,469.5 | 4,002.0 | -467.5 | -10.5 | -1.4 |
| Mining, manufacturing, etc.[2] | 1,063.2 | 1,620.4 | 557.2 | 52.4 | 5.4 |
| Construction | 193.2 | 448.5 | 255.3 | 132.1 | 11.1 |
| Govt. administration, etc.[3] | 1,270.5 | 2,200.0[4] | 929.5 | 73.2 | 7.0 |
| Other[5] | 1,265.1 | 1,294.4 | 38.3 | 3.1 | 0.4 |
| Total labour force[1] | 8,405.6 | 10,023.5 | 1,617.9 | 19.2 | 2.2 |

Notes: 1 Not including the armed forces, which increased from 378,000 in 1971 to 445,000 in 1979.

2 Mining, quarrying, manufacturing, electricity, gas, etc.

3 Not including authorities and public enterprises.

4 Approximate figure: 1978 = 2,065.3.

5 Trade, transportation, communications, finance, other services, unspecified.

Source: Central Agency for Public Mobilisation and Statistics: Labour force surveys, and Central Agency for Organisation and Administration: Development and Employment in Government Administration, 1965/66-1978, Data Services No. 11 (Cairo, Information Centre, 1979), p.15.

TABLE 3: DEMAND AND SUPPLY DEVELOPMENTS FOR PRINCIPAL AGRICULTURAL COMMODITIES (AVERAGE ANNUAL PER CENT CHANGE)

| | 1960-1974 | | | | 1974-81 | | | |
|---|---|---|---|---|---|---|---|---|
| | Per Capita Demand | Total Demand | Domestic Supply | Demand-Supply Gap | Per Capita Demand | Total Demand | Domestic Supply | Demand-Supply Gap |
| **Basic Food Commodities** | | | | | | | | |
| Wheat | 4.1 | 6.6 | 1.8 | 4.8 | 3.8 | 6.4 | 0.6 | 5.8 |
| Maize | 1.8 | 4.3 | 3.7 | 0.6 | 3.9 | 6.4 | 3.5 | 2.9 |
| Sugar | 2.6 | 4.8 | 3.5 | 1.3 | 8.9 | 11.6 | 2.6 | 9.0 |
| Beans | -3.2 | -0.9 | -1.5 | 0.6 | -0.2 | 2.3 | -1.6 | 3.9 |
| Lentils | -0.3 | 2.0 | 1.1 | 0.9 | 1.4 | 3.8 | -29.0 | 32.8 |
| Edible Oils | 3.6 | 6.1 | 1.3 | 4.8 | 4.6 | 7.2 | 0.6 | 6.6 |
| **Exportable Field Crops** | | | | | | | | |
| Cotton | 1.3 | 3.7 | -0.9 | 4.6 | 4.2 | 6.8 | 1.8 | 5.0 |
| Rice | 2.4 | 4.9 | 2.2 | 2.7 | 0.3 | 2.8 | 1.5 | 1.3 |
| Onions (winter) | 0.7 | 1.6 | 0.8 | 0.8 | 2.5 | 4.9 | 1.3 | 3.6 |
| Groundnuts | -3.4 | -1.9 | -0.3 | 1.6 | 2.9 | 6.1 | 3.9 | 2.2 |
| **Fruits and Vegetables** | | | | | | | | |
| Citrus | 5.1 | 7.3 | 8.3 | -1.0 | -0.5 | 2.0 | 1.4 | 0.6 |
| Potatoes | 3.7 | 6.2 | 5.2 | -1.0 | 5.9 | 8.5 | 7.9 | 0.6 |
| Tomatoes | 1.6 | 4.1 | 4.1 | 0.0 | 2.5 | 5.1 | 5.1 | 0.0 |
| **Livestock Products** | | | | | | | | |
| Red Meat | -1.0 | 1.2 | 1.6 | -0.4 | 3.8 | 6.4 | 1.8 | 4.6 |
| Poultry | 0.1 | 2.5 | 2.5 | 0.0 | 7.2 | 9.9 | 2.8 | 7.1 |
| Fish | -2.9 | -0.4 | -0.6 | 0.2 | 10.2 | 13.0 | 4.5 | 8.5 |
| Milk | -0.7 | 1.7 | 1.5 | 0.2 | 4.9 | 7.5 | 1.6 | 5.9 |

Source: World Bank, Arab Republic of Egypt: Issues of Trade Strategy and Investment Planning, World Bank, Washington, DC, January 1983, p. 101.

TABLE 4: INDICATORS OF INCOME DISTRIBUTION: GINI COEFFICIENT OF HOUSEHOLD EXPENDITURE, SELECTED YEARS

| Year | Rural | Urban | Nationwide |
|---|---|---|---|
| 1958/59 | 0.37 | 0.40 | 0.42 |
| 1964/65 | 0.35 | 0.40 | 0.40 |
| 1974/75 | 0.39 | 0.37 | 0.38 |
| 1981/82 | 0.35 | 0.39 | 0.38 |

Source: Derived from Family Budget Surveys.

FIGURE 1: THE EGYPTIAN LABOUR MARKET, 1976

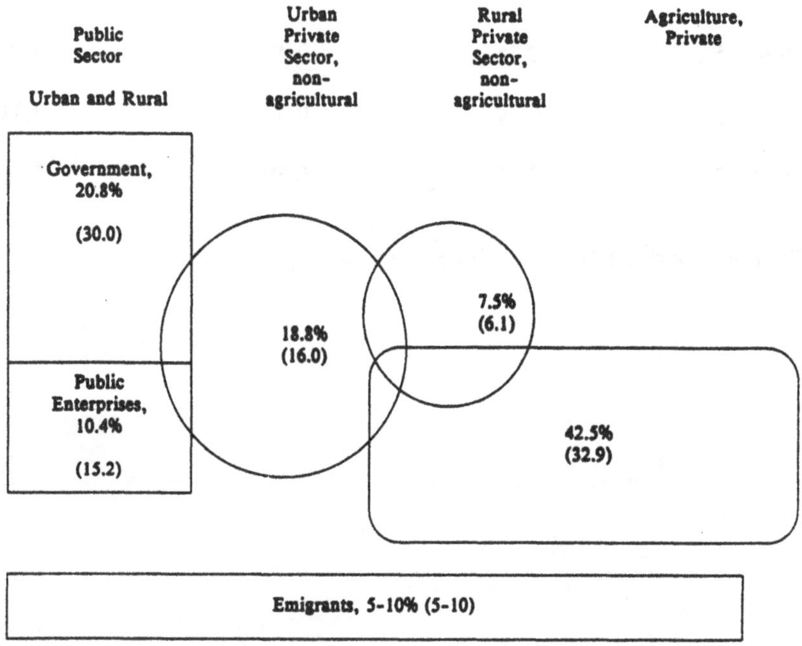


Note: Non-bracketed percentages refer to total civilian, resident, adequately described *labor force*, age 15 years and above, not including unpaid labor. Percentages in brackets refer to *employees* in labor force. Percentages add up to 100. Agriculture defined by occupation. Public sector includes publicly employed agricultural workers. Population census 1976. Source: CAPMAS, unpublished tabulations. Emigrants guesstimated. For details, see Section I.

# A Note on the Contributors

A. Tosun Aricanli is Assistant Professor of Economics, Harvard University, Cambridge, Mass., USA.

Richard H. Adams, Jr. is Research Associate, International Food Policy Research Institute, Washington, D.C., USA.

Harold Alderman is Research Associate, International Food Policy Research Institute, Washington, D.C., USA.

Haluk Kasnakoglu is Associate Professor of Economics, Middle East Technical University, Ankara, Turkey.

Roger Owen is Lecturer in Recent Economic History, St.Antony's College, Oxford University, Oxford, U.K.

Samir Radwan is Senior Researcher, Rural Employment Policies Branch, Employment and Development Division, International Labor Organization, Geneva, Switzerland.

Alan Richards is Associate Professor of Economics, University of California, Santa Cruz, USA.

David Seddon is Lecturer, School of Development Studies, University of East Anglia, Norwich, U.K.

Kutlu Somel is Economics Director, Farm Systems Research, International Center for Agricultural Research in Dry Areas, Aleppo, Syria.

Suday Uner is Deputy Director, Institute for Population Studies, Haceteppe University, Ankara, Turkey.

